CONTENTS

2	Introduction	
3-19	**Environment Agency**	

20	River Location Map	
24	How to use the guide	

25-47	**CORNWALL SECTION**	
28	River Fishing	
31	Stillwater Coarse	
39	Stillwater Trout	
42	Sea Fishing	
45	Where to Stay	

49	South West Lakes Trust	
52	Westcountry Rivers Trust	
54	The River Camel	
55, 56	Competitions	

57-109	**DEVON SECTION**	
62	River Fishing	
73	Stillwater Coarse	
94	Stillwater Trout	
103	Sea Fishing	
107	Where to Stay	

110	South West Rivers Association	
111	Anglers Conservation Association	
113	Carp on a Dry Fly	

115-128	**DORSET SECTION**	
117	River Fishing	
121	Stillwater Coarse	
125	Stillwater Trout	
126	Sea Fishing	
128	Where to Stay	

129	British Disabled A.A.	
131	The Match Fishing Scene	

133-138	**HAMPSHIRE SECTION**	
135	River Fishing	
136	Stillwater Coarse	
137	Stillwater Trout	
138	Sea Fishing	

139	Recreational Sea Angling Update	
142	Anglers Helping Flylife	

143-173	**SOMERSET SECTION**	
146	River Fishing	
155	Stillwater Coarse	
167	Stillwater Trout	

171	Sea Fishing	
173	Where to Stay	

	Contacts	
	oat Trust	
	Fisheries	

	Kids	
	ing from the Shore	

	WILTSHIRE/GLOUCS SECTION	
	River Fishing	
191	Stillwater Coarse	
194	Stillwater Trout	
196	Gloucs	

198	Sexy Trout!	
199	Salmon & Trout Association	

200-201	**SERVICES & SUPPLIERS SECTION**	

203-208	**ADVERTISERS INDEX**	

Published by Diamond Publications Ltd
PO Box 59, Bideford, Devon EX39 4YN.
Tel: 01271 860183 Fax: 01271 860064
Email: info@gethooked.co.uk
www.gethooked.co.uk

Editor: Graham Sleeman	01566 785754
Distribution: Jane Diamond	01271 860183
Advertising: Mandi and Jane	01271 860183
Printed by St Ives Web	01726 892400

Cover Picture: Courtesy Dave Roberts - 01643 703892

 Get Hooked is printed on environmentally friendly paper

ISBN 0-9527547-9-7

The title 'Get Hooked! Guide to Angling in South West England' and the contents of this publication are protected by copyright. No part of this publication may be copied or reproduced in any form without the prior written consent of the publisher.

© Copyright

THE GET HOOKED GUIDE

Welcome...

To the 12th annual edition of the Get Hooked Guide to Angling in South West England published in association with the Environment Agency.

To get the most from your copy please read the detailed 'how to use the guide' instructions on page 24.

The core of this publication is the concise and up to date details of over 800 fishing venues throught the region. This information re affirms our reputation as THE guide to angling in the South West of England.

If your club or fishery does not appear in these pages and you would like it to please contact us with details. Remember an entry in this guide and on the web site is absolutely FREE! for anyone offering day ticket fishing.

The Environment Agency seasons and byelaws are updated and published on the following pages for easy reference. The 'Fishing is Fun!' feature from the Environment Agency is an encouraging ongoing initiative that is actively recruiting new participants to the sport.

Pictures used throughout the guide have, as ever, been supplied by fisheries and anglers throughout the region, thanks to you all and annual apologies to those whose pictures did not make it, we always seem to have too many.

Our tuition feature offers professional guidance for beginners and experienced anglers alike. Remember you are never too young to start and never too old to learn! From venturing into angling for the first time to brushing up on your casting technique or perhaps trying your hand at fly fishing from the shore instead of the bank, however good you think you are everyone can learn more.

Last year I enthused over the improving facilities and promotion of angling and this year seems to be carrying the theme forward. The commercial value of angling is being realised across all branches. It would seem the hard work put in by people within the sport is bearing fruit. Within the south west, and Nationally, fishing is being supported and promoted at all levels.

The South West of England truly is a fabulous place to go fishing. From Salmon and Sea Trout on Cornish spate rivers to world class reservoir fishing. From superb coarse stillwaters to the world renowned rivers Avon and Stour and mile upon mile of coastline there is nowhere that offers the diversity and quality of sport that we do.

Fishing tackle has never been so good, so widely available and such good value for money. Tuition and events introducing new people to the sport has never been so prolific.

There has never been a better time to start, return to, or just continue fishing, and there has never been so much on offer.

Enjoy your fishing

Graham Sleeman - Editor
editor@gethooked.co.uk

Please note..

All of the information on fisheries, clubs and charters in this guide is published in a fully searchable format on our web site at

www.gethooked.co.uk

The web site includes additional information that does not appear in the guide. There is also a database of tackle shops and further information on accommodation.

The Environment Agency is the leading public body for protecting and enhancing the environment in England and Wales.

INCIDENT HOTLINE

If you see a pollution or an illegal fishing incident taking place, please immediately telephone the Environment Agency's 24 hour Communications Centre on

0800 80 70 60

Do not wait until the evening or the next day – report it NOW! If you tell us immediately of illegal fishing occurring in rivers, lakes, estuaries or sea, we can prevent damage to your fish stocks.

It is our job to look after your environment and make it a better place. We make sure that everyone in today's society looks after the air, land and water so that tomorrow's generations inherit a cleaner, healthier world.

Our work includes tackling flooding and pollution incidents, reducing industry's impacts on the environment, cleaning up rivers, coastal waters and contaminated land, and improving wildlife habitats.

Visit our website at www.environment-agency.gov.uk to find out more about our work and your local environment.

There are extensive fisheries pages on our website, including interesting news stories about our work.

In the South West we believe our fisheries are very important. Fish are one of the best indicators of the state of rivers and lakes. Healthy and abundant freshwater fish stocks and populations will demonstrate the Environment Agency's success in contributing towards sustainable development.

Our work helps fisheries in many ways. Some good examples are pollution-prevention, dealing with low river flows and habitat improvements.

In addition, fisheries staff carry out a number of vital tasks.

These include:
- Controlling the pressure on fisheries through issuing licences and making byelaws
- Preventing damage to fish and fish stocks by effective enforcement of fishery laws
- Ensuring the health and abundance of fish stocks through regular fisheries surveys
- Rescuing fish when pollution incidents occur and minimising damage to fish stocks
- Carrying out habitat improvements
- Constructing and maintaining fish passes
- Monitoring of fish stocks i.e. catch returns, juvenile surveys and fish counters
- Carrying out fisheries research to allow future improvements and developments
- Stocking fish to restore and improve fisheries

Fisheries operations in South West Region are organised by staff based in our four areas.
They can be contacted as follows:

Cornwall:

Environment Agency
Sir John Moore House
Victoria Square
BODMIN PL31 1EB
Tel: 08708 506506
Fax: 01208 78321

Devon:

Environment Agency
Exminster House
Miller Way
EXMINSTER EX6 8AS
Tel: 08708 506506
Fax: 01392 316016

North Wessex:
Environment Agency
Rivers House
East Quay
BRIDGWATER TA6 4YS
Tel: 08708 506506
Fax: 01278 452985

South Wessex:
Environment Agency
Rivers House
Sunrise Business Park
Higher Shaftesbury Road
BLANDFORD DT11 8ST
Tel: 08708 506506
Fax: 01258 455998

Regional policy and forward-planning issues are co-ordinated by the Strategic Environment Planning staff at Manley House, the Regional Office.

The Region is advised by the South West Regional Fisheries, Ecology and Recreation Advisory Committee. The Committee usually sits four times a year and its meetings are open to the public and the media. In each of the four areas local consultation takes place with interested parties.

National Rod Licences

Before fishing for salmon, sea trout, trout, freshwater fish or eels in any* water in England and Wales, it is necessary to have both a current Environment Agency rod fishing licence and permission to fish from the owner of the fishery.

Except in waters where a general licence is in force - please check with the owner of the fishery in advance.

The area where a rod licence is required for fishing for salmon, sea trout, trout, and freshwater fish includes estuaries and the sea out to six miles from the shore.

In most cases in tidal waters, a rod licence is not required to fish for freshwater eels, although there are exceptions. Before fishing for eels in tidal waters, please check with your local Area Environment Agency Office.

The Environment Agency has a national rod fishing licence. This means that fishing in all regions, including Wales, is covered by one licence. It does not cover you to fish in Scotland.

Licences are available for coarse fish and non-migratory trout or for all-inclusive fishing, including the above species in addition to salmon and sea trout.

- .... Area Administrative Boundaries
- —— Regional Boundary
- ● Area Office
- ▲ Regional Headquarters

The licence structure is aimed at raising approximately £17 million for essential fisheries work.

Coarse fish and non-migratory trout

The price of the full annual licence (2005/2006) for coarse fish and non-migratory trout is £23.50 (£11.75 concessions [disabled anglers in receipt of invalidity benefit or severe disability allowance, and anyone aged 65 years and over]).

A short-term coarse fish and non-migratory trout licence covers a period of eight consecutive days, giving anglers the benefit of being able to fish over two weekends. This costs £8.25 (no concessions). A one-day licence, aimed at beginners and casual anglers costs £3 (no concessions).

Junior Licence

Children under 12 years of age do not require a licence. A full annual junior licence is available for coarse fish and non-migratory trout priced £5. Junior licences are available to anyone less than 17 years old.

Salmon and sea trout

The price of the full annual licence (2005/2006) for salmon and sea trout (also including coarse fish, eels and non-migratory trout) is £63.50 (concessions £31.75 - including juniors). An 8-day licence costs £20.00 and a 1-day licence is £6.50. There are no concessions on the 8- or 1-day licence.

Licences are available from every Post Office in England and Wales or from a range of local distributors. A list of these local distributors is available from the Environment Agency offices. If necessary, you may obtain your licence by post. A form to do this is available from Environment Agency offices.

Alternatively a 'telesales' service operates from 8am to 8pm, 7 days a week, except bank holidays, for full, junior and concessionary licences. The number to ring is 0870 166 2662.

It is also now possible to obtain full licences, 8- and 1-day and the new full junior licence - through the Environment Agency's 'on-line licensing system'. Details are available on the fisheries web site: www.environment-agency.gov.uk/fish

Payment by credit/debit card for 'telesales' and 'online': the licence will be immediately valid as the purchaser will be provided with a reference number to quote if challenged when fishing. Proof of identity will also be needed until the full licence has been received.

The 2005/2006 licences will be valid until 31 March 2006. Licences are issued on a 12-month basis and are subject to price reviews.

The licence has the following benefits:

* You can use a rod and line anywhere in England and Wales.
* You can use up to two rods per licence, subject to the National Byelaws included in this Guide and subject to any local rules.
* Your rod licence will help the Environment Agency continue to improve the vital work it carries out, including:
* Management of fish stocks.
* Improvements in fisheries and the fish's environment.
* Protection of stocks through enforcement activities, including anti-poaching patrols.
* Rescue of fish which would otherwise be lost through drought, pollution or other causes.
* Surveys, essential for picking up changes and problems.
* Advice on fishing and management issues.
* Fish rearing and stocking of rivers.

Please note that:

1. The licence gives you the right to use a fishing rod and line but does not give you the right to fish. You must always check that you have the permission of the owner or tenant of the fishing rights before starting to fish.

2. Your licence is valuable - if it should be lost, a duplicate can be issued from PO Box 432, National Rod Licence Administration, Environment Agency, Richard Fairclough House, Knutsford Road, Warrington, WA4 1HH. A charge of £5 will be made.

Please make a note of the Licence Stamp Number before going fishing.

3. The licence is yours alone; it cannot be used by anyone else. Please make sure that you sign the licence before you go fishing.

4. Your licence must be produced on demand to an enforcement officer of the Environment Agency who produces his or her warrant, a

police officer or to any other licence holder who produces his or her licence. Failure to do so is an offence and may make you liable to prosecution (maximum fine £2,500).

5. The licence is only valid if the correct name, address and date of birth of the holder, and the date and time of issue are shown without amendments, a stamp of the correct duty is attached and the licence is signed by the holder and the issuing agent.

6. A national rod licence is not required where a General Licence is in force. Please check with the owner in advance.

7. The catch return form attached to the salmon and sea trout licence is very important. This information is required by law and you should send in the return form, even if you recorded a 'nil' catch. Please fill in and return the form in an envelope when your licence expires, using the FREEPOST address.

8. Details of local rod fishing byelaws and angling information can be obtained from Environment Agency offices. Fishery byelaws may vary between different Environment Agency regions - if in doubt, check first before going fishing.

Details of the main byelaws applying to the Environment Agency in the South West can be found in the following pages.

Salmon and sea trout kelts

Salmon and sea trout which are about to spawn, or have recently spawned but have not recovered, are known as unclean. The law says that fish in either condition, if caught, must be returned to the water with as little damage as possible. Fish about to spawn are identifiable by the ease with which eggs or milt can be extruded from the vent.

Those having recently spawned are called kelts and can be identified from clean fish by using the comparison given below.

Kelt:
1. Line of back and belly parallel
2. Gill maggots almost invariably present (salmon only)
3. Distinct 'corner' or change of direction in profile of body at back of skull
4. Fins invariably frayed
5. Vent suffused red and easily extruded by pressure
6. Belly normally blackened

Clean:
1. Back and belly convex in relation to each other
2. Gill maggots only present in previous spawners or fish which have been some time in the river
3. Head tapers into body without a break
4. Fins entire; rarely frayed
5. Vent firm and compact
6. Belly normally pale

Smolts and parr

Young salmon known as parr look very similar to brown trout and are often caught by trout anglers. These parr are destined to run the rivers in a few years as adult salmon after feeding at sea. It is an offence knowingly to take, kill or injure these parr, and any which are caught by mistake must be very carefully returned to the water.

Salmon parr can be identified from trout by using the comparison given below. In March, April and May, salmon and sea trout parr begin to migrate to the sea. The spots and finger marks disappear and the body becomes silvery in colour. They are then called smolts and must be returned to the water if caught.

Salmon Parr
1. Body slightly built and torpedo-shaped
2. Tail distinctly forked
3. A perpendicular line from the back of the eye will not touch the maxillary bone
4. Eight to twelve finger marks, even in width, well-defined and regularly placed along the sides
5. No white line on leading edge of fins
6. No red colour on adipose fin

Trout
1. Body thicker and clumsier looking
2. Tail with shallow fork
3. A perpendicular line from the back of the eye will pass through or touch the maxillary bone
4. Finger marks less numerous, uneven in width, less defined, irregularly placed along the sides
5. Normally white line on leading edge of fins
6. Adipose fin generally coloured with orange or red.

ROD FISHING SEASONS

The 'Open Seasons', i.e. the periods when it is permitted to fish, are set out in the table on this page.

There is no statutory close season for coarse fish and eels in stillwaters, but some clubs and fishery owners may impose their own close seasons.

There may also be a close season in place because of the status afforded to the area as a site of scientific interest. If in doubt check with your local office.

NATIONAL BYELAWS TO PROTECT SALMON STOCKS

A summary of the byelaws is as follows:

Mandatory catch and release of all salmon for all rivers before 16 June.

Fly and spinner only (where not already limited by existing byelaws) before June 16 for salmon fishing.

These measures replace some of the existing measures already in place.

Catch and release of salmon is mandatory to 16 June, removing the earlier bag limit of two salmon before 1 June on the Taw and Torridge. It also supersedes any early season voluntary bag limits.

Anglers are still encouraged to fish catch and release after 16 June and especially to return any large red fish late in the season which may be 'springers'. The 70 cm limit in August/September on the Taw and Torridge still applies.

Permitted baits are restricted to artificial fly and artificial lure until 16 June. Exceptions where other restrictions remain include the Taw and Torridge (fly only from April 1) and North and South Wessex (fly only before 15 May).

These national byelaws are designed as a baseline and are considered to be the lowest common denominator across the country addressing the national problem of a decline in early-run large salmon.

Measures to address other local stock problems will continue to follow a river-by-river approach based on the programme of individual Salmon Action Plans being developed by the Environment Agency with local fisheries interests.

FISHERY DISTRICT	MAJOR RIVERS WITHIN DISTRICT	ROD & LINE OPEN SEASON (dates inclusive) Starts	Ends
SALMON			
Avon (Devon)	Avon (Devon)	15 Apr	30 Nov
	Erme	15 Mar	31 Oct
Axe (Devon)	Axe, Otter, Sid	15 Mar	31 Oct
	Lim	1 Mar	30 Sept
Camel	Camel	1 Apr	15 Dec
Dart	Dart	1 Feb	30 Sept
Exe	Exe	14 Feb	30 Sept
Fowey	Fowey, Looe, Seaton	1 Apr	15 Dec
Tamar & Plym	Tamar, Tavy, Lynher,	1 Mar	14 Oct
	Plym, Yealm	1 Apr	15 Dec
Taw & Torridge	Taw, Torridge	1 Mar	30 Sept
	Lyn	1 Feb	31 Oct
Teign	Teign	1 Feb	30 Sept
Frome (Dorset) & Piddle		1 Mar	31 Aug
	All other rivers in North & South Wessex Areas	1 Feb	31 Aug
MIGRATORY TROUT			
Avon (Devon)	Avon (Devon)	15 Apr	30 Sept
	Erme	15 Mar	30 Sept
Axe (Devon)	Axe, Otter, Sid	15 Apr	31 Oct
	Lim	16 Apr	31 Oct
Camel	Camel, Gannel, Menalhyl Valency	1 Apr	30 Sept
Dart	Dart	15 Mar	30 Sept
Exe	Exe	15 Mar	30 Sept
Fowey	Fowey, Looe, Seaton, Tresillian	1 Apr	30 Sept
Tamar & Plym	Tamar, Lynher, Plym, Tavy, Yealm	3 Mar	30 Sept
Taw & Torridge	Taw, Torridge, Lyn	15 Mar	30 Sept
Teign	Teign	15 Mar	30 Sept
	All rivers in North & South Wessex Areas	15 Apr	31 Oct
BROWN TROUT			
	Camel	1 Apr	30 Sept
	Other rivers in Devon & Cornwall Areas	15 Mar	30 Sept
	All rivers in North & South Wessex Areas	1 Apr	15 Oct
	All other water in Devon & Cornwall Areas	15 Mar	12 Oct
	All other waters in North & South Wessex Areas	17 Mar	14 Oct
RAINBOW TROUT			
	Camel & Fowey	1 Apr	30 Sept
	Other rivers in Devon & Cornwall Areas	15 Mar	30 Sept
	All rivers in North & South Wessex Areas	1 Apr	15 Oct
	Reservoirs, Lakes & Ponds	★ No statutory close season	
GRAYLING, COARSE FISH & EELS			
	Rivers, Streams and Drains including the Glastonbury Canal	16 Jun	14 Mar
	Enclosed waters - Ponds, Lakes & Reservoirs		
	All other Canals	★ No statutory close season	

PERMITTED BAITS

The use of particular baits for fishing is regulated by byelaws and in some cases additional restrictions are imposed by the fishing association or riparian owner. The byelaw restrictions are shown in the table below:

*This restriction only applies to water where a statutory coarse fish close season is applicable. It does not apply to stillwaters. See also section on rod fishing seasons and the note on canal close seasons (page 12).

** All references to 'Trout' include migratory trout and non-migratory trout.

***This is a change introduced in 1998.

No spinning for trout in waters included within the Dartmoor National Park, the Exe above Exebridge, Otter above Langford Bridge, Torridge above Woodford Bridge, Bray above Newton Bridge, Mole above Alswear Bridge, Little Dart above Affeton Bridge, and the whole of the Okement, Lyn and Barnstaple Yeo.

Artificial baits which spin: When fishing for salmon or trout in the Avon (Devon), Axe (Devon), Exe, Dart, Taw and Torridge and Teign districts, use of any artificial bait which spins is restricted to those with only a single, double or treble hook. The width of the hook must not be greater than the spread of the vanes of the bait.

SIZE LIMITS

Length to be measured from tip of the snout to the fork or cleft of the tail.

The size limits, below which fish must be returned, imposed by byelaws are set out in the table below. Riparian owners and fishing associations may impose further restrictions with which anglers should familiarise themselves before fishing.

These size restrictions do not apply to:

(a) Any person who takes any undersized fish unintentionally if he/she at once returns it to the water with as little injury as possible.

(b) Non-migratory trout in any waters included within the Dartmoor National Park, the Exe above Exebridge, the Otter above Langford Bridge, the Torridge above Woodford

PERMITTED BAITS

FISHERY DISTRICT	SPECIES	BAITS (REAL OR IMITATION)
South West Region	Salmon	Artificial fly and artificial lure ONLY before 16 June
Avon (Devon)	Salmon & Trout **	No worm or maggot.
Axe (Devon)	Salmon & Trout	No shrimp, prawn, worm or maggot. Fly only after 31 July below Axbridge, Colyford.
Dart	Salmon	No worm or maggot. No shrimp or prawn except below Staverton Bridge.
	Trout	No spinning above Holne Bridge. Fly only.
Exe	Salmon & Trout	No worm or maggot.
Barnstaple Yeo (tidal)	All species (inc. sea fish)	No fishing
Taw & Torridge (except Lyn)	Salmon & Trout	No shrimp, prawn, worm or maggot. No spinning after 31 March. ***
Lyn	Trout	No worm or maggot before 1 June.
Teign	Salmon	Artificial fly and artificial lure ONLY after 31 August
	Trout	No worm or maggot before 1 June.
Camel & Fowey	Salmon	No byelaw restrictions on bait after 16 June
	Trout	No byelaw restrictions on bait
Tamar	Salmon & Migratory Trout	No worm, maggot, shrimp or prawn after 31 August.
North Wessex & South Wessex Areas	Salmon & Migratory Trout	Artificial fly only before 15 May.
North Wessex & South Wessex Areas	All species in rivers, drains and canals	No maggot (or pupae), processed product, cereal or other vegetable matter during the coarse fish close season. *

SIZE LIMITS

AREA, DISTRICT OR CATCHMENT	MIGRATORY TROUT	NON-MIGRATORY TROUT	GRAYLING
Camel, Fowey, Tamar and Plym	18 centimetres	18 centimetres	N/A
Avon (Devon), Axe (Devon), Dart, Exe, Taw & Torridge, Teign	25 centimetres	20 centimetres	N/A
River Lim	N/A	22 centimetres	N/A
North Wessex (except By Brook)	35 centimetres	25 centimetres	25 centimetres
By Brook & tributaries	35 centimetres	20 centimetres	25 centimetres
South Wessex	35 centimetres	25 centimetres	N/A

Bridge, the Mole above Alswear Bridge, the Little Dart above Affeton Bridge and the whole of the Rivers Okement, Lyn and Barnstaple Yeo.

MANDATORY BAG LIMITS

See section on National Byelaws to protect salmon stocks (page 7).

North Wessex Area. The bag limits set out in the table below are imposed by the byelaws, however, some riparian owners or angling associations obtain dispensation to increase their bag limits. Anglers should familiarise themselves with bag limits before fishing. Once a bag limit has been taken, the angler may continue fishing for the same species, provided that any fish caught are returned without injury. Freshwater fish other than grayling, pike and eels may not be permanently removed from the water.

MANDATORY BAG LIMITS

RIVER OR AREA	SPECIES	24 HOURS	7 DAYS	SEASON
North Wessex	Non-migratory Trout	2	N/A	N/A
	Grayling	2	N/A	N/A
Taw	Salmon	2	3	10
	Migratory Trout	5	15	40
Torridge	Salmon	2	2	7
	Migratory Trout	2	5	20

TAW AND TORRIDGE

The original size limit and bag limit byelaws, introduced following a public inquiry in 1997, expired in September 2001. The Department for Environment, Food and Rural Affairs (Defra) has renewed these byelaws which remain in place until 2008.

NOTE: Since 1 April 1999, with the introduction of national salmon byelaws, the bag limits apply after 16 June.

VOLUNTARY BAG LIMITS

See section on National Byelaws to protect salmon stocks (page 7).

Spring salmon - In addition to the national byelaws, the Environment Agency is encouraging salmon anglers to return any larger salmon, particularly red ones caught later in the season, as these are likely to be multi-sea-winter fish and valuable to the spawning stock. On many rivers a variety of voluntary measures have been adopted to protect fish stocks. All anglers should familiarise themselves with these rules before fishing. Details are provided below.

Rivers Camel/Fowey/Lynher (Cornish limit)

For the above combined Cornish rivers, a maximum of: Salmon – 2 per day, 4 per week and 10 per season. Sea trout – 4 per day. These numbers apply cumulatively to you as an individual and not as a limit from each river, i.e. on any particular day, you should not take more than 2 salmon in total, regardless of how many Cornish rivers you fish. Please check with your club or Association as more stringent rules apply on certain waters.

The Environment Agency is very worried about the poor state of salmon stocks on the Lynher. Estuary netting has already been suspended for 10 years, but anglers must also fish responsibly. We are hoping to ensure the catch and release rate is at least 2 out of every 3 fish returned alive during 2005.

River Fowey Bag Limits
Fowey River Association
Salmon - 1/day, 2/week, 5/season.
Sea trout - 4/day or night. All sea trout to be returned in September.

River Camel
Camel River Association
Same as Cornish limit above.
No fishing in April. All sea trout to be returned in September.
Bodmin Anglers Association have brought in a new rule for their club waters of only using Circle Hooks from the 31 August.

River Tamar
The Environment Agency is very worried about the poor state of salmon stocks on the Tamar. We are hoping to ensure the catch and release rate is at least 2 out of every 3 fish returned alive during 2005.
Tamar and Tributaries Fisheries Association
Salmon - 1 per day followed by catch/release.

All fish over 10 pounds returned from 1 September onwards. Return red/unseasonal fish.

River Tavy
The Environment Agency is very worried about the poor state of salmon stocks on the Tavy. We are hoping to ensure the catch and release rate is at least 2 out of every 3 fish returned alive during 2005.

Tavy Walkham and Plym Fishing Club
Salmon - 1 per day. Return of all hen fish, and alternate cockfish. Limited fishing methods.

Rivers Plym, Tavy
Plymouth and District Freshwater Angling Association
Salmon - 1 per day, 3/season;
Sea trout - 3 per day or night.

River Exe
River Exe and Tributaries Association
After 16 August, salmon of 27.5" or over (8 pounds) to be returned unless injured, in which event, the next salmon caught under size limit to be returned. Red or coloured fish to be returned, no fishing by prawn or shrimp in September.

River Teign
Lower Teign Fishing Association
Sea trout - 4 per 24 hours.
Upper Teign Fishing Association
Salmon - 2 per day, 5 per season. All salmon of 71cm (28in) or over to be released.
Brown trout - Catch and release except above Mill End Bridge, where there is a limit of 2 per day.
These are mandatory UTFA rules.

River Otter
Salmon - All salmon to be returned.
Sea trout - 1 mature and 2 school peal/season.

River Axe
Axe Fly Fishers
Salmon - Catch and release only for salmon. Fly only.

River Avon (Hants)
Avon and Stour Riparian Owners and Wessex Salmon Rivers Trust.
Salmon - Catch and release only for salmon. No worm fishing.

Some river associations will not have held their AGM prior to going to print. Please check with local club secretary for any voluntary measures that may have been agreed for other rivers before fishing.

CATCH AND RELEASE
With stocks of salmon under increasing pressure, the Environment Agency is seeking to do everything possible to protect the species for the future.

Catch and release is now becoming an established management technique for increasing spawning escapement, particularly where stocks are low. Salmon anglers are encouraged to consider this approach as a means of safeguarding salmon stocks in our rivers.

If you do decide to practice catch and release, the following guidelines may be useful to give your catch the best chance of surviving after you have returned it to the river:

Hooks - single hooks inflict less damage than doubles or trebles, barbless hooks are best. Flatten the barbs on your hooks with pliers.
Playing fish - fish are best landed before complete exhaustion and therefore all elements of tackle should be strong enough to allow them to be played firmly.
Landing fish - Fish should be netted and unhooked in the water, if possible. Use knotless nets - not a tailer or gaff.
Handling and unhooking - Make every effort to keep the fish in the water. Wet your hands. Carefully support the fish out of water. Do not hold the fish up by the tail, this may cause kidney damage. Remove the hook gently - if necessary, cut the line if deeply hooked. Take extra care with spring fish, as they are more susceptible to damage and fungal infection.

Do not under any circumstances keep out of the water for more than 30 seconds a fish which is to be returned. Changes in the fish's body affect survival within one minute.

Reviving the fish - Support an exhausted fish underwater in an upright position facing the current. Estimate weight and length in the water.

Avoid weighing. Handle the fish as little as possible. Be patient and give it time to recover and swim away on its own.

On the rivers Tamar, Tavy and Lynher, the Environment Agency is very worried about the poor state of salmon stocks. We are hoping to ensure the overall catch and release rate is at least 2 out of every 3 fish returned alive during 2005.

MANDATORY CATCH AND RELEASE OF SALMON

Byelaws have been introduced in 2005 to make catch and release of salmon mandatory in September on the Rivers Dart and Teign in Devon. Any salmon caught must be returned to the river with the least possible injury.

A ban on fishing for salmon with natural baits in September has also been introduced by byelaw on the River Teign to minimise damage to any salmon caught. Adequate method restrictions are already in place on the River Dart.

TESCO SWAP A SALMON SCHEME

An arrangement, originally negotiated with Tesco for the Hampshire Avon, by Wessex Salmon Rivers Trust, entitles an angler catching and returning a salmon after 16 June to a voucher to be exchanged for a farmed salmon. This scheme now applies to other rivers as follows: Frome, Piddle, Dart, Teign, Camel, Fowey, Tavy, Lynher, Plym, Otter and Fal. Contact your local fisheries office for further details.

WILD TROUT TRUST

Anglers are asked to return all brown trout caught on the East Dart above Postbridge, on the Cherry Brook and the Blackbrook; while on the West Dart between Blackbrook and Swincombe they are to return fish between 10" and 16" long, as part of a research project.

USE OF OTHER TACKLE

Use of float. The use of a float when fishing for salmon or trout in any waters within the Avon (Devon), Axe (Devon), Dart, Exe, Taw and Torridge, and Teign districts is prohibited.

Use of gaff is prohibited. See section on national byelaws Phase 1.

Limit on number of rods in use. See section on national byelaws Phase 1.

Prohibition of use of lead weights. No person shall use any instrument on which is attached directly or indirectly any lead weight (except a weight of 0.06 grams or less, or one of more than 28.35 grams) for the purpose of taking salmon, trout, freshwater fish or eels in any waters within the Agency's region.

Prohibited Fishing Area - Kilbury Weir. It is illegal to take, or attempt to take by any means, any fish in any waters within 50 yards below the crest of Kilbury Weir on the River Dart.

LANDING NETS, KEEPNETS AND KEEPSACKS

A national byelaw makes it illegal to use landing nets with knotted meshes or meshes of metallic material.

Similarly, keepnets should not be constructed of such materials or have holes in the mesh larger than 25mm internal circumference; or be less than 2.0 metres in length. Supporting rings or frames should not be greater than 40cm apart (excluding the distance from the top frame to the first supporting ring or frame) or less than 120cm in circumference.

Keepsacks should be constructed of a soft, dark coloured, non-abrasive, water permeable fabric and should not have dimensions less than 120cm by 90cm if rectangular, or 150cm by 30cm by 40cm if used with a frame or designed with the intention that a frame be used. It is an offence to retain more than one fish in a single keepsack at any time.

The retention of salmonids (adults or juveniles) in keepnets is illegal except when specially approved by the Environment Agency for collecting broodstock.

THEFT ACT

The Theft Act 1968, Schedule 1, makes it an offence for anyone to take or attempt to take fish in private waters or in a private fishery without the consent of the owner.

The Environment Agency may bring a prosecution under this Act on its own fisheries. It cannot do so on behalf of an individual, and any fishery owner who wishes such a prosecution to be brought should consult the police or a solicitor.

ATTENTION - SALMON AND SEA TROUT ANGLERS

Your catch return is needed by 1 January each year. Nil returns are also required. Send returns to:

Environment Agency, FREEPOST, P.O. Box 60, Patchway, Bristol, BS12 4YY.

Failure to submit a return is an offence.

NATIONAL BYELAWS

A number of national byelaws are now in place. These replace or modify regional byelaws that existed before.

A summary of the national byelaws is given below.

Phase I

1. The annual close season for fishing for rainbow trout by rod and line in all reservoirs, lakes and ponds has been dispensed with.
2. A close season for brown trout is to be retained on all waters.
3. Use of the gaff is prohibited at all times when fishing for salmon, trout and freshwater fish or freshwater eels.
4. The number of rods that may be used at any time is as follows:
a. One rod when fishing for salmonids in rivers, streams, drains and canals.
b. Two rods when fishing for salmonids in reservoirs, lakes and ponds (subject to local rules).
c. Up to four rods when fishing for coarse fish and eels (subject to local rules). When fishing with multiple rods and lines, rods shall not be left unattended and shall be placed such that the distance between the butts of the end rods does not exceed three metres.
5. Catch returns for salmon and migratory trout should be submitted no later than 1 January in the following year.
6. See separate section on landing nets, keepnets and keepsacks.

Phase II

1. Crayfish of any species whether alive or dead, or parts thereof may not be used as bait for salmon, trout, freshwater fish or eels.
2. Livebait may only be retained and used at the water they were taken from.
3. All salmon, migratory trout or trout, hooked other than in the mouth or throat, shall be returned immediately to any river, stream, drain or canal.
4. The byelaw limiting the length of a rod to not less than 1.5 metres (that may be used in North or South Wessex) has been revoked.
5. A rod and line with its bait or hook in the water must not be left unattended or so the licence holder is unable at any time to take or exercise sufficient control over the rod and line.

COARSE FISH CLOSE SEASON ON CANALS

There is no close season for coarse fish on canals within the region, with the exception of the Glastonbury Canal which is an open system with the South Drain.

FISH WITH ADIPOSE FINS REMOVED

As indicated on your rod licence, you may catch a fish from which the adipose fin has been completely removed. (These may carry a micro tag implanted within their nose - invisible to you.) If this occurs, you should follow the licence instructions.

Before 16 June, any salmon caught without an adipose fin should be returned to the water and reported to your local fisheries office.

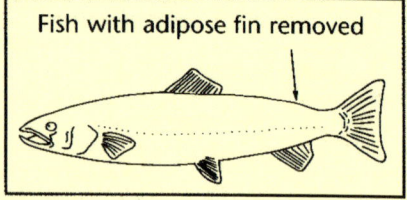
Fish with adipose fin removed

* Tell us your name, address and telephone number.
* Record details of your catch (where, when, size and species of fish).
* If the fish is caught after 16 June, keep the fish (or just the head) frozen if necessary and we will contact you to make arrangements for it to be inspected.

We will pay you a reward of £5 if it carries a micro tag and, of course, you keep the fish.

Details should be sent to the appropriate Area Fisheries Office.

PURCHASE AND RELEASE OF SALMON FROM LICENSED NETS

In recent years the Mudeford nets have voluntarily signed up to catch and release. In recognition of this agreement, the Avon and Stour Rivers Association recompense the Mudeford nets.

Similar schemes to reduce the numbers of salmon caught by legal netting have also operated on the rivers Tamar, Tavy, Lynher, Fowey, Camel and Taw/Torridge, funded by a variety of sponsors including South West Water, the Maristow Estate, fishery owners and European funding under the Habitats Directive.

STOCKING FISH - BUYER BEWARE

The Environment Agency has produced a free leaflet entitled 'Buyer Beware - Your guide to stocking fish'. The leaflet explains the Environment Agency rules on fish introduction (Section 30, Salmon and Freshwater Fisheries Act 1975) and the commonsense things which fishery owners can do to protect themselves and their fisheries when buying/stocking fish.

Before introducing (stocking) any fish (or fish spawn) into inland waters, you must obtain written consent of the Environment Agency. Failure to meet this obligation is a criminal offence and could lead to prosecution, with a fine of up to £2,500. In addition, the stocking of non-native species such as Wels Catfish or Grass Carp requires Defra approval under the Import of Live Fish Act - Prohibition of Keeping or Release of Live Fish Order 1998.

Mandatory health checks will be required where fish are to be moved into rivers, streams, drains or canals, or where the risk to other fisheries is high.

Health checks will not normally be required in waters where the risk of fish escape is minimal (e.g. enclosed waters). However, there may be occasions where the Environment Agency will still insist on a health examination.

Regardless of the Environment Agency's requirement for health checks, it should be stressed that establishing the health of fish before any stocking is essential. The Agency encourages everyone to follow the Environment Agency's 'Buyer Beware' code. Copies of the leaflet can be obtained from the customer enquiry line 08708 506506.

STOP THE SPREAD OF CRAYFISH PLAGUE

Crayfish plague now has an extensive hold in the south of the country although it is also spreading northwards. In the whole of the south west, native crayfish are now only known to occur in the catchments of the Bristol Avon, the Piddle and Allen in Dorset, the Fonthill Brook in Wiltshire and the Creedy in Devon. Meanwhile, signal crayfish are widespread on many other rivers in the south west region.

The plague can be accidentally spread on damp equipment such as fishing tackle, farm machinery etc.

Do not move between river catchments without either disinfecting or drying completely any equipment that has been in contact with river or lake water.

FISHERIES ACTION PLAN FOR NORTH DEVON

Fishing interests in north Devon, in partnership with the Environment Agency, are taking the initiative to increase access and availability of fishing and improve fisheries.

Starting with a small group of people, the aim is to gradually build on the momentum of this work. Following the river restoration project completed by the Westcountry Rivers Trust we hope to encourage riparian and fishery owners to make fishing more accessible by improved river and land management for both river and still water fisheries.

To get hooked on this initiative ring Alan Burrows, Environment Manager on 01392 316170 for further information.

LOOK OUT! - LOOK UP!
ADVICE ON SAFE FISHING NEAR OVERHEAD ELECTRIC POWER LINES

Several people have died and others have been seriously injured whilst using fishing rods and poles near overhead electric power lines. The following advice is designed to prevent these events recurring:

i Because rods and poles conduct electricity, they are particularly dangerous when used near overhead electric power lines. Remember that electricity can jump gaps and a rod does not even have to touch an electric line to cause a lethal current to flow.

ii Many overhead electric power lines are supported by wood poles which can be and are mistaken for telegraph poles. These overhead lines may carry electricity up to 132,000 volts, and have been involved in many of the accidents that have occurred.

iii The height of high voltage overhead electric power lines can be as low as 5.2 metres and they are therefore within easy reach of a rod or pole. Remember that overhead lines may not be readily visible from the ground. They may be concealed by hedges or by a dark background. Make sure you 'Look Out' and 'Look Up' to check for overhead lines before you tackle up and begin fishing.

iv In general, the minimum safe fishing distance from an overhead electric power line is 30 metres from the overhead line (measured along the ground).

v When pegging out for matches or competitions, organisers and competitors should, in general, ensure that no peg is nearer to an overhead electric power line than 30 metres (measured along the ground).

vi For further advice on safe fishing at specific locations, contact your local Electricity Company.

vii Finally, remember that it is dangerous for any object to get too close to overhead electric power lines, particularly if the object is an electrical conductor, e.g. lead cored fishing line, damp fishing line, rod or pole.

ENVIRONMENT AGENCY AREAS

Devon Area
Fishery Districts (Rivers in brackets):
Avon (Avon, Erme); Axe (Axe, Sid, Otter); Dart (Dart); Exe (Exe); Taw and Torridge (Taw, Torridge, Lyn); Teign (Teign). The River Lim is included in the Devon Area.

Cornwall Area
Fishery Districts (Rivers in brackets):
Camel (Camel, other streams flowing into the sea on the North coast between Marsland Mouth and Lands End); Fowey (Fowey, East and West Looe, Seaton, Tresillian, other streams flowing into the sea on the South coast between Lands End and Rame Head); Tamar and Plym (Tamar, Lynher, Plym, Tavy and Yealm).

North Wessex Area
River Catchments:
Bristol Avon (including all tributaries), Axe (Somerset), Brue, Parrett, Tone, Yeo and all other rivers, drains and streams flowing into the Bristol Channel between Avonmouth and Foreland Point.

South Wessex Area
River Catchments:
Hampshire Avon (including all tributaries), Stour (including all tributaries), Dorset Frome, Piddle, Wey, Brit and Char and all other streams flowing into the sea between Christchurch Harbour and Charmouth.

ROD LICENCE

In order to fish for salmon, trout (including migratory trout), freshwater fish and eels in any* waters in the South West Region, anglers will need an Environment Agency national rod licence and permission from the owner of the fishery.

ANGLERS MUST CARRY THEIR ROD LICENCES WITH THEM AT ALL TIMES WHILE FISHING.

* Except in waters where a General Licence is in force - please check with the owner of the fishery in advance.

* The Environment Agency does issue temporary rod licences to enable groups for specific events to have a go at fishing. For more information contact: Cheryl Kelly Tel. 01925 542266.

Environment Agency

FISHING IS FUN!
- have a go at angling in 2005

Sutton Bingham Reservoir

The Environment Agency in partnership with the National Federation of Anglers, Salmon and Trout Association, West Country Rivers Trust, South West Lakes Trust, fisheries owners and others is holding a wide number of 'have a go at angling' events across the South West this year.

This is a great opportunity to try fishing for the first time or to introduce a youngster or a friend to fishing – come and have a go!

Last year hundreds of people across the South West tried their hand at fishing for the first time through these special events. These events are for everyone, young and old alike.

Success at Bake Lakes

In Somerset at Sutton Bingham reservoir, near Yeovil, over 350 budding anglers had a go at fishing for the first time. The highlight at an event at Hunstrete Lakes near Bath was a four-year-old landing a 17 pound carp!

In Cornwall fun was had by all the family at a junior event at Bake Lakes near Saltash.

In Devon at Rackerhayes Pond, Newton Abbot over 230 people had a go at fishing - they ranged from 3 years up to 70 with whole families having a go.

In Hampshire at the Moors Valley Country Park many youngsters had a go at fishing through the school holidays.

A programme of angling participation events is planned for 2005 – over the page are some of the dates and venues confirmed as this guide went to press.

There are more events to come so visit our web site for an up to date list:
www.environment-agency.gov.uk/fish

Devon

6 August	'Learn to fish day'	Rackerhayes Ponds, Newton Abbot.
3 September	'Learn to fish day'	Kia Ora Ponds, Cullompton.

Both these events are primarily coarse angling, but there will also be sea and game angling casting sessions, pond dipping, face painting and quizzes.
For further information contact 01392 316032.

Cornwall

30 March	Treemeadow, Hayle (10-16 years)	trout
6 April	Tavistock (10-16 years)	trout
27 April	Stithians (ladies)	trout
2 May	Siblyback (family)	trout
25 May	Innis (over 50s)	trout
1 June	Siblyback (10-16 years)	trout
2 July	Tavistock (adults)	trout
13 August	Roadford (family)	trout
20 August	Siblyback (family) – with West Country Rivers Trust and South West Lakes Trust	trout
22 August	Treemeadow, Hayle (10-16years) - with West Country Rivers Trust	trout
23 August	Innis (10-16 years) – *with West Country Rivers Trust*	trout
24 August	Innis (10-16 years) – *with West Country Rivers Trust*	trout
25 August	Bake Lakes	coarse
26 August	Bake Lakes	coarse
27 August	Stithians (family) – with West Country Rivers Trust and South West Lakes Trust	trout
10 September	Stithians (family) – with West Country Rivers Trust and South West Lakes Trust	trout
5 October	Treemeadow, Hayle (adults)	trout
26 October	Bake Lakes (10-16 years)	coarse and trout

For more information ring 01208 265012.

Fishing is FUN!

Moors Valley Country Park

Century Pond, Keynsham

Rackerhayes Pond

Environment Agency

Dorset and Wiltshire

Throughout the summer holidays from July to beginning of September there are angling coaching sessions for young people at Moors Valley Country Park, Ringwood, Hampshire. Taster sessions for children of all ages who might like to try fishing. Fishing for parents and children for those with little or no previous knowledge. Sessions for children of eight years and over who have done some fishing and would like to learn more, and sessions for 10 year olds and over who want to improve their fishing skills. All delivered by fully qualified angling coaches and supported by the Environment Agency.

For more information ring 01425 470721, or visit www.moors-valley.co.uk

On 20 August an 'Angling Open Day' is being held at Somerley Lakes just north of Ringwood on the edge of the New Forest. Organised by Christchurch Angling Club, this is a great opportunity for all the family to have a go at fishing. Fly casting, beach casting, fly tying and the opportunity to identify aquatic 'creepy crawlies' is also on offer...in short...there is something for everybody. For further details visit the Christchurch Angling Club website nearer the day at www.christchurchac.org.uk.

Somerset

A wide variety of events are being organised for this year that range from projects with youth groups, such as the Pugwash Project on the Bridgwater and Taunton canal, to a have a go at fishing day at Sutton Bingham Reservoir in partnership with Wessex Water and the National Federation of Anglers.

On the 22 May why not have a go at fishing at the Bridgwater Centenary Celebrations as part of the River Parret Festival.

Improving the state of fisheries in the South West

Over the last year the Environment Agency has worked extensively with fishing clubs, fisheries owners, Local Authorities, Trusts and others across the South West to improve the state of the Region's fisheries.

Through investing rod licence money, Government Grant-in-Aid and working in partnership with others we are making a real difference on the ground. Projects have ranged from improving fish stocks through restoring and creating habitat for fish, fish stocking, developing and creating new opportunities to fish and improving access to fishing. Here are a few examples of what has been achieved. To find out more contact Lawrence Talks Environment Agency Fisheries Development Manager for the South West, Tel 01962 764822.

DEVON

CORNWALL

SOMERSET:
Improved access at Taunton Road Ponds, Bridgwater

The Environment Agency, Sedgemoor District Council and the Police have joined forces to breathe new life into a formerly derelict pond to create a safe place for local people to fish.

To find out more contact Dave Lloyd Tel. 01278 484665.

CORNWALL:
Disabled anglers given help to enjoy fishing at Wheal Rashleigh lake near St Austell

With a grant from the Environment Agency Roche Angling Club have built an all ability fishing platform that now allows wheel chair users to enjoy this popular fishery. To find out more contact Sally Mitchell Tel 01208 265012.

DORSET:
Creation of fish spawning habitat

The upper reaches of the Dorset Stour in the Blackmore Vale have very limited habitats for species which spawn on gravel, such as chub and dace. In collaboration with the Gillingham Angling Club a new spawning riffle has been created at West Stour which should considerably improve fish populations in this area. To find out more contact Allan Frake Tel. 01258 483328.

DEVON:
A new fishing lake at Ivybridge near Plymouth

The Environment Agency, Plymouth and District Coarse Angling Club and Ivybridge Town Council have created an exciting new coarse fishing lake. The project was funded by Environment Agency rod licence money, Plymouth and District AC and a Living Spaces grant from the Office of the Deputy Prime Minister, which is managed by Groundwork's Peoples Places scheme. To find out more contact Diane Holland Tel. 01392 316032.

THE GET HOOKED GUIDE

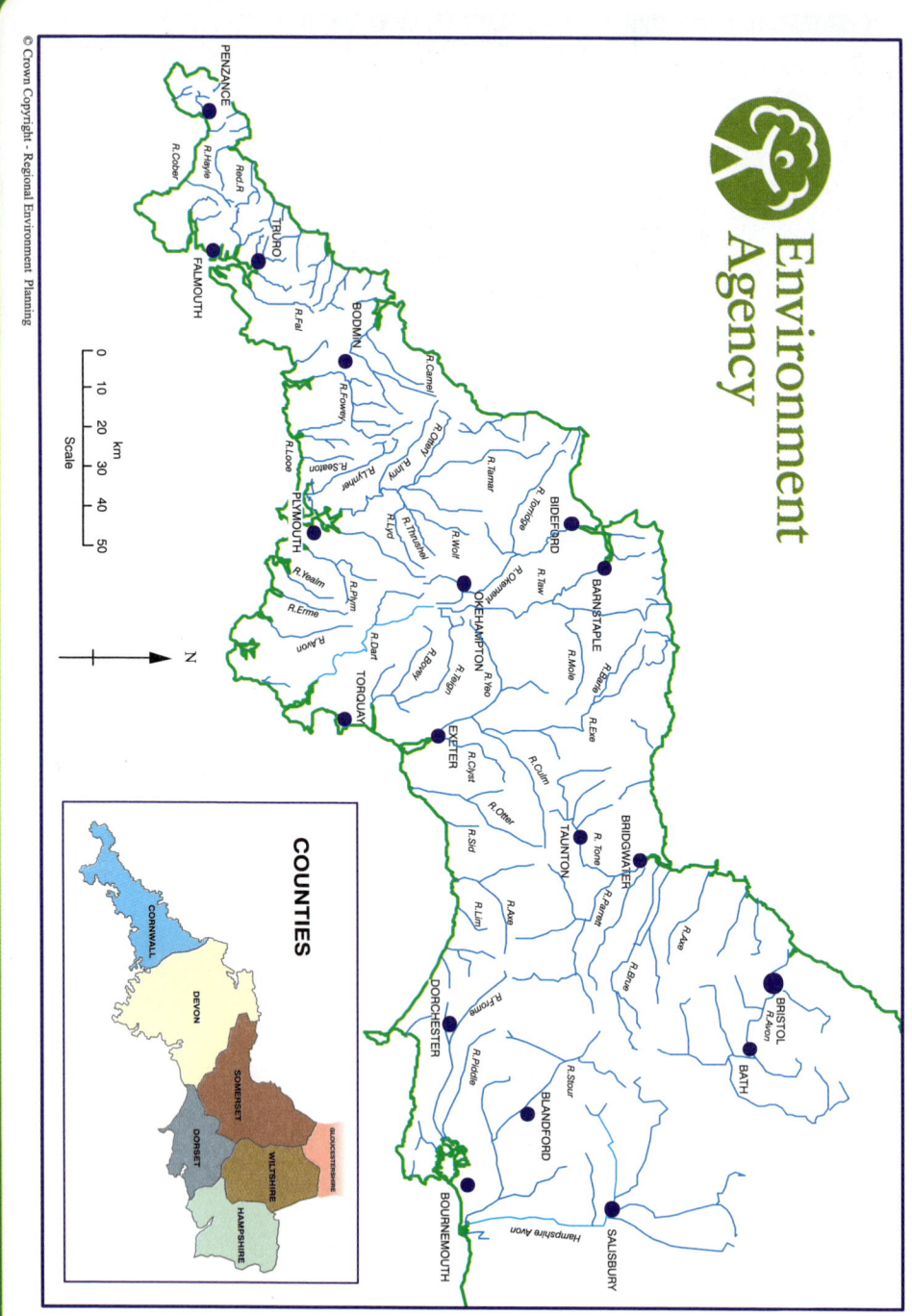

THE GET HOOKED GUIDE

Would you like a career in the environmental sector?

Foundation Degree in Sustainable River Basin Management

Westcountry Rivers Trust

A new Foundation degree in Sustainable River Basin Management - created by the Westcountry Rivers Trust and Duchy College, Stoke Climsland - is ready to run at the University of Plymouth in September 2005.

The two-year course delves into the biology, physics and geography of the river basin in relation to its management, including aspects of countryside maintenance, habitat management and river corridor monitoring (see the table below). The degree focuses heavily on generating the real life experiences and relationships necessary to gain employment within the environmental sector by maximising student-employer interactions and setting up work-based learning opportunities within environmental organisations.

Booking now!

We are already booking places for the September 2005 cohort, so if you are interested in pursuing a career in the environmental sector or would like to increase your knowledge, practical skills and experience of managing aspects of the river basin then this is the course for you. The Foundation degree is designed to stand alone but after completing successfully the two year course you could go on to complete a third year to gain a Bachelor of Science*.

If you would like more information please contact either the Trust on 0870 7740704 or Duchy College admissions (01579 372233 and stoke.enquiries@duchy.ac.uk).

* Subject to transferral routes and requirements

Year 1		Year 2	
SEMESTER 1	SEMESTER 2	SEMESTER 1	SEMESTER 2
Countryside maintenance		Business management	
Rural policy and farming systems		Research Project	
The physical environment and soil management		Environmental issues and education	
Ecology		Habitat Management	
River basin dynamics		Rural river basin management	
River corridor monitoring and management		Urban drainage and the political landscape	
Professional Development			
	Work-based learning		

Timetable for the Foundation Degree in Sustainable River Basin Management

THE GET HOOKED GUIDE

STOP!
THE SPREAD OF CRAYFISH PLAGUE

Until the 1980s, native white-clawed crayfish were widespread in most chalk rivers across the British Isles. Since then, their population has suffered a devastating decline due, in part, to a virulent fungal disease carried by American signal crayfish, which were introduced around this time. The disease called crayfish plague generally has no detrimental effect on the larger American species but wipes out the native British variety. Decline in numbers of native crayfish can also be attributed to direct competition with the larger signal crayfish.

Signal crayfish now have an extensive hold in the south east of England and are also spreading northwards. In the whole of the south west, native crayfish are now only known to occur in the catchments of the Bristol Avon, the Piddle, and Allen in Dorset, the Fonthill Brook in Wiltshire and the Creedy in Devon. Meanwhile, signal crayfish are widespread on many other rivers in the south west region.

Signal crayfish (non-native)

White-clawed crayfish (native to UK)

THE CRAYFISH CODE

CLEAN AND DRY EQUIPMENT
Plague can be accidentally spread on damp equipment such as fishing tackle, farm machinery etc. Do not move between river catchments without either disinfecting or thoroughly drying equipment that has been in contact with the river or lake water.

PROTECT CRAYFISH HABITAT
Native crayfish and the habitat in which they live are protected by law. Always seek advice from the Environment Agency before carrying out works in or near a watercourse which may disturb crayfish or their habitat.

NEVER USE CRAYFISH AS BAIT
It is illegal to take native crayfish from the wild, and is an offence under national fisheries byelaws to use any crayfish (dead or alive) or any crayfish part, as bait.

DO NOT INTRODUCE NON-NATIVE CRAYFISH
It is illegal to introduce non-native crayfish anywhere in England and Wales. To do so could accelerate the spread of disease and introduced populations are impossible to control.

REPORT ANY SIGHTINGS
If you see any crayfish, (in the wild or for sale alive), please contact the Environment Agency and ask for the Fisheries, Recreation and Biodiversity Team.

HELP US TO SAVE THE NATIVE CRAYFISH

The preventative measures will help to contain the further spread of crayfish plague and conserve the remaining native populations.
Call the Environment Agency on 08708 506506
Ask for the Fisheries, Recreation and Biodiversity Team
www.environment-agency.gov.uk

THE GET HOOKED GUIDE

time to buy your rod licence

Rod licences expire on 31 March.

All money raised helps provide better fishing.

Anyone aged 12 years or over who fishes for salmon, trout, freshwater fish or eels in England or Wales must have an Environment Agency rod licence. Children under 12 years of age do not require a licence.

Coarse and trout	2005/06
Full	£23.50
Concession	£11.75
Junior	£5.00
8 day	£8.25
1 day	£3.00

Salmon and sea trout	2005/06
Full	£63.50
Concession	£31.75
Junior	£31.75
8 day	£20.00
1 day	£6.50

You can buy your rod licence in four easy ways:
- At every Post Office in England and Wales
- By Direct Debit 01925 542 400
- Online at www.environment-agency.gov.uk/rodlicence
- Environment Agency Telephone Sales 0870 166 2662
  Lines open 8am-8pm, 7 days a week except Bank Holidays. Calls charged at standard rate. A small additional charge will be made.

Concessionary licences apply if:
- You are aged 16 or under
- You are aged 65 or over
- You have a Blue Badge parking concession. Please contact your local Social Services Department for more information on how to get a Blue Badge.

Failure to produce a valid Environment Agency rod licence could result in prosecution and a maximum fine of £2,500

THE GET HOOKED GUIDE

How to use the Guide

The guide is divided into the following County sections.

Cornwall
Devon
Dorset
Hampshire
Somerset
Wiltshire/Gloucs

Purely for ease of use Bristol has been incorporated into Somerset.

Please Note. *The guide covers the Environment Agency South West Region as depicted by the map on page 4. This area includes only part of Hampshire and a very small area of Gloucestershire.*

Within each county section the directory categories are:

River Fishing
Stillwater Coarse
Stillwater Trout
Sea Fishing
Where to Stay

There is a **Tuition Feature** on pages 178-180 providing details covering Game, Coarse and Sea angling across the region. There is also a **Services** section where advertisers provide services to fisheries throughout the region.

All entries **highlighted in blue** indicate an advertiser. The advert may contain additional information about the facilities on offer. If the advertisement is not adjacent to the directory entry it may be found by looking in the advertisers index at the back of the guide. Advertisers offering fishing are also located on maps (with road directions) at the beginning of each county section. There is a rivers map on page 20 which can be used in conjunction with the location maps.

Where clubs and organisations have fishing on rivers and stillwaters they will be listed or cross referenced under both sections.

An increasing number of fisheries offer both trout and coarse fishing. These entries will be cross referenced or have separate entries under the relevant sections. Where advertisers offer both coarse and game fishing their advert will appear in the most relevant section. They will be indexed under all relevant sections.

Tackle shops are located within the above sections. If you are, say, looking for tackle shops in Bristol then look within the Somerset section and under Stillwater Coarse - Bristol, Stillwater Trout - Bristol, Sea Fishing - Bristol or River Fishing - Bristol Avon.

Editorials are placed between the county sections and further advertisements may appear within these sections.

The contents page gives a clear indication of where the sections appear.

The **Advertisers Index** at the back of the guide also lists all advertisers cross referenced under all relevant headings.

Please note..

All of the information on fisheries, clubs and charters in this guide is published in a fully searchable format on our web site at

www.gethooked.co.uk

The web site includes additional information that does not appear in the guide. There is also a database of tackle shops and further information on accommodation.

The opinions expressed within the editorials in this guide are those of the contributors and not necessarily that of the publishers. Whilst every effort has been made to ensure that the information in this publication is correct at the time of going to press, the publishers cannot accept responsibility for any errors or omissions which may have occurred. Remember fisheries change hands and rules change.
Always phone if in doubt.

CORNWALL

- RIVER FISHING
- STILLWATER COARSE
- STILLWATER TROUT
- SEA FISHING
- WHERE TO STAY

CORNWALL

Cornwall Game Road Directions

1. Angling 2000 (Game & Coarse)
35 beats on the Tamar, Fal, Taw, Torridge & Camel catchments plus 3 coarse fishing lakes. Please telephone 0870 77 40686.

2. Bake Lakes (Game & Coarse)
A38 to Trerulefoot. At roundabout (half way between Plymouth & Liskeard) take minor road to Bake. Turn right at T-junction, then take first left. Fishery is 200 yards on right. Tel: 01752 849027 or 07798 583836.

3. Colliford
South West Lakes Trust fisheries are well signposted from major roads. Tel: 01409 211514.

4. Crowdy
South West Lakes Trust fisheries are well signposted from major roads. Tel: 01409 211514.

5. Drift Reservoir
Take A30 towards Lands End. In Drift village, turn right (signposted "Sancreed"). Reservoir car park is approx. 1/4 mile along this lane. Ticket sales enquiries please telephone 01736 363021 before travelling.

6. Fenwick Trout Fishery
From Bodmin take A389 toward Wadebridge, continue to village of Dunmere and turn immediate left off river Camel Bridge. Fishery is signposted. Tel: 01208 78296.

7. Siblyback
South West Lakes Trust fisheries are well signposted from major roads. Tel: 01579 346522.

8. Stithians
South West Lakes Trust fisheries are well signposted from major roads. Tel: 01209 860301.

9. Tree Meadow Trout Fishery
Off B3302 Hayle to Helston. Tel: 01736 850899 Mobile 07971 107156.

Cornwall Coarse Road Directions

10. Argal
South West Lakes Trust fisheries are well signposted from major roads. Tel: 01209 860301.

11. Avallon Lodges
From Launceston B3254 towards Bude town turn left at Langdon Cross (just before the Countryman Pub) then next right signed Clubworthy. Avallon is 1.5 miles along this road, up a short drive on the left. Tel: 01502 500500.

12. Badham Farm Holidays
A30 Liskeard turn off - Follow signs for St. Keyne. At St. Keyne take left hand turn just before church signed St Keyne Well & Badham. A38 at Dobwalls turn for Duloe & St. Keyne, then from St. Keyne as A30 route. Tel: 01579 343572.

13. Borlasevath Fishing Lakes
From Bodmin on A30 to Gossmore Bridge. Turn right on B3274 signposted Padstow. Continue 3.5 miles, turn right at Tremayne Farm by stone barn. You will find Borlasevath Manor Farm 1.25 miles on your left. Tel: 01637 880826 Mobile: 07973 767147.

14. Boscathnoe
South West Lakes Trust fisheries are well signposted from major roads. Tel: 01209 860301.

15. Bush Lakes
Over Tamar Bridge, at Saltash roundabout turn right (A388). Continue 3 miles to Hatt, turn left onto Pillaton road. Bush is signposted after one mile on the left. Tel: 01752 842148.

16. Bussow
South West Lakes Trust fisheries are well signposted from major roads. Tel: 01209 860301.

17. Crafthole
South West Lakes Trust fisheries are well signposted from major roads. Tel: 01822 855700.

18. Fentrigan Manor Farm
Please Telephone 01566 781264 for road directions.

19. Glenleigh Farm Fishery
From St. Austell take A390 towards Truro, after approx. 3 miles second hand car garage on left, turn left to Sticker, follow road to top of hill, immediately before bus shelter turn left, past mobile homes park, over bypass to bottom of hill, car park on right. Tel: 01726 73154.

20. Meadowside Fishery
Located on A39, just south of the roundabout junction with B3274 at Winnards Perch, within the Cornish Birds of Prey Centre at St. Columb Major. Tel:01637 880544.

21. Millbrook Fishery
Approach Millbrook on B3247, follow brown Tourist Signs from Tregantle Fort. Tel: 01752 823210.

22. Penpol Farm Coarse Fishery
From the A38 turn off at Tideford and head towards Blunts. At Blunts turn left, and left again to Quethiock. Penpol is the first farm on your left. Tel: 01752 851335.

23. Porth
South West Lakes Trust fisheries are well signposted from major roads. Tel: 01637 877959.

24. Retallack Waters
Just off the A39 between Newquay and Wadebridge at Winnards Perch, signposted 'American Theme Park'. Tel: 01637 881160.

25. Trencreek Farm Holiday Park
4 miles southwest of St. Austell. On the A390 fork left on to the B3287. Trencreek is one mile on, on the left. Tel: 01726 882540.

CORNWALL

26. Trevella Park
Proceed on the A30 as far as Indian Queens, turn right on to A392, follow signs to Newquay until you come to Quintrell Downs roundabout. Take signposted Crantock road which brings you to the Trevemper Bridge roundabout, turn left on to A3075, the Redruth road for 200 yards and you will see Crantock signposted. If you are in Newquay, take the A3075 to Redruth for one and a half miles until you see Crantock signposted. If you are approaching us from the west you will see Crantock signposted from A3075. Follow this road for one mile to T-junction sign to Newquay, where you turn right and then into Trevella Park entrance. Tel:01637 830308.

27. Upper Tamar
South West Lakes Trust fisheries are well signposted from major roads. Tel: 01288 321262.

28. White Acres Country Park
Follow the M4/M5 to Exeter, then the A30 past Okehampton and Bodmin. From the A30 turn onto the A392 to Newquay, travel over 1st roundabout. You will see entrance to White Acres shortly after the roundabout on the right hand side. Tel: 01726 862113.

29. Wooda Farm Park
From the A39 take the road signposted Poughill, Stampford Hill, continue 1 ml, through crossroad. Wooda Farm Park is 200yds on the right. Tel: 01288 352069.

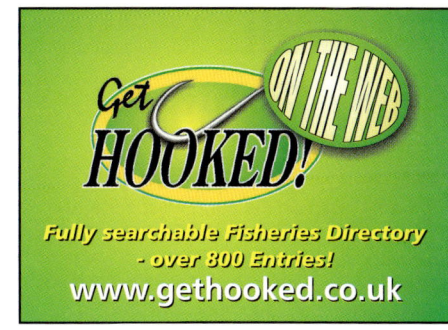

Only advertisers are located on this map.

Cornwall River Fishing

CAMEL
The Camel rises on the north west edge of Bodmin Moor and flows past Camelford to its estuary at Wadebridge. The run of Salmon tends to be late with some of the best fishing in November and December. Sea Trout in summer. Brown Trout in upper reaches and tributaries.

Angling 2000 (Camel)
Contact: Westcountry Rivers Trust, 10 Exeter Street, Launceston, PL15 9EQ, 0870 774 0686, *Water:* 1250m of single bank on the Camel. 1400m of single left hand bank on the De Lank and 1500m of single right hand bank on the Allen. Flexible permits fishing for Trout. *Species:* Salmon, Brown Trout & Sea Trout on Camel. Brown Trout - De Lank. Brown Trout & Sea Trout - Allen. *Permits:* From the above. *Charges:* from £5 per day. *Season:* Camel - 1st May to 31st August. Allen.1st April to 30th September - De Lank. 1st May to 30th September - Allen. *Methods:* See Angling 2000 day permit guide.

Bodmin Anglers Association (Camel)
Contact: Mr Burrows, 26 Meadow Place, Bodmin, 01208 75513, *Water:* 13 Miles on River Camel, 0.25 miles on River Fowey. *Species:* Salmon, Sea Trout. *Permits:* Roger Lashbrook at Stan Mays Store, Bodmin. D.Odgers, Gwendreath, Dunmere, Bodmin. Camel Valley Sportfishing, 5 Polmorla Road, Wadebridge. No visitors permits issued after 30 November. *Charges:* 1st May - end November £15 per day or £40 per week. Juniors half price. Membership details from Secretary. *Methods:* Fly, Worm, Spinner.

Butterwell
Contact: Tyson Jackson, Butterwell, Nr Nanstallon, Bodmin, PL30 5LQ, 01208 831515, *Water:* 1.5 miles River Camel, mainly double bank. *Species:* Sea Trout (to 10lb 2oz) & Salmon (to 18lb). 5 year average 50 Salmon and 200 Sea Trout. *Permits:* On site. *Charges:* £20/day, maximum 5 rods/day. Priority given to residents. *Season:* 1st May - 30th August, night fly fishing only for Sea trout. 1st September - 15th December for Salmon. *Methods:* Any method for Salmon after 1st September.

Fenwick Trout Fishery (River Camel)
Contact: David & Shirley Thomas, Old Coach Road, Dunmere, Bodmin, PL31 2RD, 01208 78296, *Water:* 570 yards on the river Camel. See also entry under Stillwater Trout. *Species:* Sea Trout and Salmon. *Permits:* On site. EA licence required. *Charges:* Please phone for details. *Season:* As current EA Byelaws. *Methods:* Fly fishing from bank only.

River Camel Fisheries Association
Contact: E.D.T. Jackson, Butterwell, Nr Nanstallon, Bodmin, PL30 5LQ, 01208 831515, *Water:* The association represents all major riparian owners and fishing clubs on the river Camel and agrees fish limits, conservation policy and enhancement projects in co-operation with the Environment Agency.

Tresarett Fishery
Contact: Mr Pope, Tresarrett Manor Farm, Blisland, Bodmin, PL30 4QQ, *Water:* 0.75 miles on the Camel. *Species:* Salmon, Seatrout and Brown Trout. *Permits:* You must have a valid EA licence. *Charges:* From £10-£20 depending on time of year. *Season:* May 1 to August 31 for Brown and Seatrout. Until December 15 for Salmon. *Methods:* Fly only to June 1. All legal methods after.

Wadebridge & Dist. Angling Association
Contact: Jon Evans, Polgeel, Polbrock, Washaway, PL30 3AN, 01208 812447, *Mobile:* 07732 921015, *Water:* 10 miles River Camel, 1 mile River Allen. *Species:* Salmon to 19lb, Sea Trout to 9lb in 2004. *Permits:* Day / Week permits, Camel Valley Sport Fishing, Polmorla Road, Wadebridge: 01208 816403. Padstow Angling Centre, The Drang, Padstow: 01841 532762. Rogers Tackle Shop, Stan Mays Store, Bodmin: 01208 78006. *Charges:* May to September - Day £15 / Week £60. October to November - Day £25 / Week £100. *Season:* Visitor permits limited to three per day in October and November. *Methods:* No maggots permitted. Fly and spinning, natural baits on some beats. Circle hooks only when worming for Salmon.

FAL
The Fal rises on the Goss Moor and flows down to join with the Truro and Tresillian Rivers entering the Carrick Roads estuary. Salmon have been making a few rare appearances back to the River due to an improvement in water quality, but the Fal is predominately a Brown Trout river which some Sea Trout present.

Angling 2000 (Fal & Tresillian)
Contact: Westcountry Rivers Trust, 10 Exeter Street, Launceston, PL15 9EQ, 0870 774 0686, *Water:* New beat added for 2005 on Tresillian. 1200m double bank and 1000m mixed double/single on fal and 1450m of single bank on Tresillian. Flexible day permits for Trout, Sea Trout and occasional Salmon. *Species:* Sea Trout, Trout and occasional Salmon. *Permits:* From the above. *Charges:* From £5 per day. *Season:* 1st April - 30th September. *Methods:* Please contact Angling 2000 for individual beat methods.

Fal River Association
Contact: Mr. Tom Mutton, 01872 273858, *Water:* Association protecting the interests of the River Fal. *Species:* Estuary - Pollock, Mackerel, Bass. River - Trout, occasional Sea Trout. *Permits:* Farmers permission.

FOWEY
Rises near the highest point of Bodmin Moor from which it flows south, then turns to the west, and finally south again through Lostwithiel to its long estuary. A late Salmon river. Also good Sea Trout fishing and some Trout fishing.

CORNWALL

Winter work on Fowey bankside access

RIVER FISHING

Bodmin Anglers Association (Fowey)
Contact: Mr Burrows, 26 Meadow Place, Bodmin, PL31 1JD, 01208 75513, *Water:* See entry under Camel. 0.25 miles River Fowey. *Permits:* Roger Lashbrook at Stan Mays Store, Bodmin. D.Odgers, Gwendreath, Dunmere, Bodmin. Camel Valley Sportfishing, 5 Polmorla Road, Wadebridge. No visitors permits issued after 30 November.

Fowey River Association
Contact: Chris Marwood (sec.), Withy Cottage, Huish Champflower, Taunton, TA2 2EN, 01398 371384, *Water:* An association of representatives of angling clubs and riparian owners on the Fowey whose aim is to secure and maintain the well being of the river and its ecology. It exists largely as a pressure group and negotiating body on behalf of its members. *Permits:* No fishing permits sold through the Association. For membership details please contact the secretary at the above address. *Methods:* E.A. Byelaws apply. Catch restrictions: Salmon 1/day, 2/week, 5/season; Sea Trout 4/day, all Sea Trout to be returned in September.

Lanhydrock Angling Association
Contact: Brian Muelaner, The National Trust, Regional Office, Lanhydrock, Bodmin, PL30 4DE, 01208 265211 or 01208 265235, *Water:* 2 miles on River Fowey. *Species:* Sea trout, Salmon. *Permits:* Available from the above telephone number. *Charges:* £15 Daily, £30 Weekly (maximum 6 tickets daily). *Season:* 1st April - 30th September, Sea Trout 31st August. *Methods:* Artificial bait only.

Liskeard & District Angling Club (Fowey)
Contact: Bill Eliot (Hon Sec), 64 Portbyhan Road, West Looe, Looe, PL13 2QN, 01503 264173, *Water:* 23 Miles of Rivers Fowey, Lynher, Inny, Seaton River, West Looe River; Map of waters with day/week tickets. *Species:* Salmon to 20lb (typically 5-12lb) & Sea Trout to 10lb (typically 2-4lb) *Permits:* Visitor tickets (available until 30 November for winter Salmon) from Tremar Tropicals Shop, Liskeard. Lashbrooks Tackle Shop, Bodmin. East Looe Chandlers, The Quay, East Looe. *Charges:* Adult: £20/day, £55/week, Membership £65. Joining fee £15. Membership limited to 250 adults. *Season:* River Fowey 1st April - 15th December; Sea Trout season closes end September. *Methods:* Spinning, fly fishing or bait. Artificials only on some beats. No groundbait, no maggots.

Newbridge Angling Association
Contact: Mr R Tetley, Trebyan Forge, Lanhydrock, Bodmin, PL30 5AE, 01208 75244, *Water:* One mile single bank on River Fowey. *Species:* Trout, Sea Trout & Salmon. *Permits:* Members only - no day tickets. For membership details please contact Mr. Tetley.

Wainsford Fishery (Fowey)
Contact: Paul Elliot, Wainsford Fishery, Twowatersfoot, Liskeard, PL14 6HT, 01208 821432, *Water:* Two miles on the Fowey. See also entry under Stillwater Trout, Liskeard. *Species:* Salmon to 16lb, Sea Trout to 10lb. *Permits:* On site. *Charges:* £15 per day. *Season:* Salmon: 1st April to 15th December. Trout: 1st April to 30th September. *Methods:* Fowey River Association limits apply.

LERRYN
Largest tributary of the Fowey.

Angling 2000 (Lerryn)
Contact: Westcountry Rivers Trust, 10 Exeter Street, Launceston, PL15 9EQ, 0870 774 0686, *Water:* 1400m of single bank. Flexible day permits for Trout, Sea Trout and occasional Salmon. *Species:* Sea Trout, Trout, Mullet and Salmon. *Permits:* From the above. *Charges:* £5 per day. *Season:* Salmon - 1st April to 15th December. Trout/Seatrout 1st April to 30th September. *Methods:* Any method. No more than 1 Salmon, 2 Trout or 2 Seatrout to be retained per day.

LYNHER
Rises on Bodmin Moor and joins the Tamar estuary opposite Plymouth. Brown Trout and runs of Salmon and Sea Trout.

Liskeard & District Angling Club (Lynher)
Contact: Bill Eliot, 64 Portbyhan Rd, West Looe, Looe, PL13 2QN, 01503 264173, *Water:* 23 miles of Rivers Fowey, Lynher, Inny, Seaton, West Looe; Map of waters with day/week tickets. *Species:* Salmon to 16lb & Sea Trout to 6lb (some very big ones April/May). *Permits:* Tremar Tropicals Shop, Liskeard. Lashbrooks Tackle Shop, Bodmin. East Looe Chandlers, The Quay, East Looe. *Charges:* Adult: £20/day, £55/week, Membership £65. Joining fee £15. Membership limited to 250 adults. *Season:* River Lynher & Inny; 1st March - 14th October; Sea Trout season closes end September. *Methods:* Spinning, fly fishing or bait. No groundbait, no maggots.

River Lynher Fisheries Association
Contact: Arthur White (hon.secretary), River Lynher Fisheries Association, 14 Wadham Road, Liskeard, PL14 3BD, 01579 345428, *Water:* Consultative body for the river Lynher. Membership comprises riparian owners, angling clubs, lessees of fishing rights, individual anglers and others interested in the Lynher valley environment. *Species:* Salmon, Sea Trout, Trout. *Permits:* Not applicable. *Charges:* £5 annual membership.

Woodcocks Club
Contact: Michael Charleston, The Gift House, Buckland Monachorum, Yelverton, PL20 7NA, 01822 853293, *Water:* Two miles of the lower and middle Lynher. *Species:* Salmon, Sea Trout and Brown Trout. *Permits:* Very limited number of annual permits for which there is a waiting list. No short term permits. *Season:* March 1st to October 14th. *Methods:* Fly only for Sea

CORNWALL

RIVER FISHING

Trout and Brown Trout except in spates. Return of Salmon (catch and release) is encouraged.

MENALHYL
Small stream starting near St. Columb Major and entering the sea north of Newquay. Brown Trout fishing.

St. Mawgan Angling Association
Contact: Mr. T. Trevenna, Lanvean House, St. Mawgan, Newquay, TR8 4EY, 01637 860316, *Water:* Stretch around Mawgan Porth. *Species:* Trout, Brown Trout. *Charges:* Limited day tickets from The Merrymoor, Mawgan Porth. Club membership restricted to those in parish of St. Mawgan. *Season:* April 1st - end September. *Methods:* See details on site.

SEATON
Small river to the east of Looe with good Sea Trout but very few Brown Trout.

Liskeard & District Angling Club (Seaton & West Looe)
Contact: Bill Eliot (Hon Sec), 64 Portbyhan Road, West Looe, PL13 2QN, 01503 264173, *Water:* Seaton River, West Looe River; Map of waters with day/week tickets. *Species:* Good small waters for Sea Trout (typically 2 to 4lbs). *Permits:* Visitor tickets available.Tremar Tropicals Shop, Liskeard. Lashbrooks Tackle Shop, Bodmin. East Looe Chandlers, The Quay, East Looe. *Charges:* Adult: £20/day, £55/week, Membership £65. Joining fee £15. Membership limited to 250 adults. *Season:* As for river Fowey 1st April - 15th December; Sea Trout season closes end September. *Methods:* Spinning, fly fishing or bait. No groundbait, no maggots.

TAMAR
The Tamar rises near the north coast, and for most of its course forms the boundary between Devon and Cornwall. It is always a lowland stream flowing through farmland and this fact is reflected in the size of its Trout which have a larger average size than the acid moorland streams. Around Launceston, the Tamar is joined by five tributaries - Ottery, Carey, Wolf, Thrushel and Lyd - which offer good Trout fishing, as does the Inny which enters a few miles downstream. There is a good run of Salmon and Sea Trout, the latter being particularly numerous on the Lyd. There are also Grayling in places.

Angling 2000 (Tamar)
Contact: Westcountry Rivers Trust, 10 Exeter Street, Launceston, PL15 9EQ, 0870 774 0686, *Water:* 11 beats on the Tamar, Inny, Lyd, Ottery, Carey and Kensey. Flexible permits fishing for Trout, Salmon, Sea Trout and Grayling. New beat for 2005. *Species:* Salmon, Roach, Dace, Sea Trout, Trout and Grayling. *Permits:* From the above. *Charges:* £5 to £10 per day depending on beat. *Season:* Trout - 15th March to 30th September. Salmon - 1st March to 14th October. Grayling - 16th June to 15th November. Please contact Angling 2000 for individual beat seasons. *Methods:* Please contact Angling 2000 for individual beat methods.

Arundell Arms
Contact: Mrs Anne Voss-Bark, The Arundell Arms, Lifton, PL16 0AA, 01566 784666, *Water:* 20 miles of private fishing on Rivers Tamar, Lyd, Carey, Thrushel, Wolf and Ottery. Also 3 acre private lake stocked with Rainbow and Brown Trout. *Species:* Rivers: Salmon, Sea Trout and Brown Trout. Lake: Rainbow & Brown Trout. *Permits:* Arundell Arms. *Charges:* Trout £23. Salmon & Sea Trout from £25. Lake £27. *Season:* Salmon March 1st to October 14th. Trout and Sea Trout March 15th to September 30th. Lake open all year. *Methods:* Fly and spinner for Salmon (1 in 3 fish after June 16 then catch and release). Fly only for Trout and Sea Trout.

Bude Angling Association
Contact: Mr L. Bannister, 2 Creathorn Road, Bude, EX23 8NT, 01288 353986, *Water:* 3 miles on the upper reaches of the River Tamar. *Species:* Brown Trout (wild) and occasional Grayling. *Permits:* Bude Angling Supplies, Queen Street, Bude. Webby's Tackle, 19 Fore Street, Holsworthy, Devon. Perdells Ltd, 5 Tower Street, Launceston. *Charges:* £4 day, week tickets available £15. *Season:* March 15th - Sept 30th. *Methods:* Fly only.

Dutson Tamar Fishery
Contact: Mr Broad, Lower Dutson Farm, Launceston, PL15 9SP, 01566 773147, *Mobile:* 01566 776456, *Water:* Half a mile on the river Tamar at Launceston. *Species:* Brown Trout, Salmon and occasional Sea Trout, Grayling. *Permits:* Homeleigh Angling and Garden Centre, Dutson, Launceston. Tel: 01566 773147. *Charges:* £5 per day. *Season:* 1st March - 14th October, Salmon as current EA Byelaws. *Methods:* See current EA Byelaws.

Launceston Anglers Association
Contact: Colin Hookway, 7 Grenville Park, Yelverton, PL20 6DQ, 01822 855053, *Water:* 6 miles on River Tamar and Carey, 7 miles River Inny. *Species:* Brown Trout, Sea Trout, Salmon, Grayling. *Permits:* Edwards Fishmonger, 19a Race Hill, Launceston PL15 8BB *Charges:* Salmon & Sea Trout; Day £15, Week £40. Brown Trout: Day £7.50, Week £25, Juniors £2 a day. Day tickets valid for 24 hours from time of purchase. Annual membership from £60. *Season:* From 1st March to 14th October. Winter Grayling on some beats. *Methods:* Brown Trout - fly only, Salmon & Sea Trout - any method subject to byelaws. Grayling - fly only.

CORNWALL

Stillwater Coarse

BODMIN
East Rose Farm
Contact: Veronica Stansfield, East Rose Farm, St. Breward, Bodmin Moor, PL30 4NL, 01208 850674, *Water:* Complex of five lakes with 22 permanent pegs (two specially constructed for disabled). 3 acres of water. *Species:* Mixed fishing in two largest lakes: Tench / Roach / Rudd and Crucian. Lower lake has Carp to 8lb. Deep Pool - Carp to 22lb & Tench to 4lb. Also specialist Tench only lake. *Permits:* Day tickets available from Farmhouse at East Rose. *Charges:* Day tickets: £4 adults, £2.75 OAP's, Disabled & under 16's. Reduced rate evening tickets. *Season:* No closed season, no night fishing. *Methods:* No keepnets unless by prior arrangement. Barbless hooks only.

Lakeview Coarse Fishery
Contact: Don, Old Coach Road, Lanivet, Bodmin, PL30 5JJ, 01726 810814, *Mobile:* 07733 345456, *Water:* 3 lakes, 4 acres in total. *Species:* 13 in total inc. Carp to 20lb, Tench to 6lb, Bream to 5lb, Roach to 5lb 3oz & Perch 4lb 9oz. *Permits:* On site Tackle Shop & Main Reception. *Charges:* £5/day/Adult, £3 Junior - O.A.P. - Disabled. Season ticket available. *Season:* Open all year 9am - 5pm. Closed Christmas Day. *Methods:* No boilies or night fishing

Prince Park Lake
Contact: John Brown, Prince Park Farm, St Wenn, Nr Bodmin, PL30 5SP, 01726 890095, *Water:* 1/2 acre pond. *Species:* Crucian Carp to 3lb, Common to 9lb, Tench, Roach, Bream to 4lb and Golden Rudd. *Permits:* Please telephone before travelling. *Charges:* £4 Adults, £3 Juniors/OAP. *Season:* Open all year, dawn to dusk. *Methods:* Nets must be dipped, barbless hooks only, no boilies.

BUDE
Bude Canal Angling Association
Contact: Mr Dick Turner, 2 Pathfields, Bude, EX23 8DW, 01288 353162, *Water:* Bude Canal (1.25 miles). *Species:* Mirror, Common, Crucian Carp, Bream, Tench, Roach, Rudd, Perch, Eels, Gudgeon, Dace. *Permits:* On the bank. *Charges:* Seniors day £4, Seniors week £18, Juniors & O.A.Ps day £2, Juniors & O.A.Ps week £10. *Season:* Closed season April 1st to May 31st inc. *Methods:* Micro barb or barbless hooks only, Strictly one rod only. No camping or any equipment deemed to be associated with camping.

Houndapitt Farm
Contact: Mr Heard, Houndapitt Farm, Sandymouth, Bude, EX23 9HW, 01288 355455, *Mobile:* 07968 171355, *Water:* Small pond. *Species:* Golden Tench, Rudd, various Carp. *Permits:* From Sandymouth Bay Holiday Park. *Charges:* £4 per day. *Methods:* Barbless hooks.

South West Lakes Angling Association
Contact: Roy Retallick, 21 Alstone Road, Tiverton, EX16 4LH, 01884 256721, *Water:* All 14 South West Lakes Trust fisheries plus 1 exclusive member only water at Lower Tamar. *Species:* All coarse fish - Carp 35lb, Pike 20lb plus, Bream 8lb plus, Tench 7lb plus, Roach 2lb, Perch 3lb 7oz, Eel 4lb. *Permits:* Please contact Roy Retallick. *Charges:* £10 per year membership, £7.50 junior, OAP and disabled. Entitles 10% discount on day and season tickets to fish any South West Lakes Trust coarse waters. *Season:* Open all year. *Methods:* As South West Lakes Trust rules displayed on site.

Upper Tamar Lake
Contact: South West Lakes Trust, 01566 771930, *Water:* Ranger Tel: 01288 321262. *Species:* Carp to 28lb. 50lb plus bags of Bream and 30lb plus bags of Rudd. Regular competitions. *Permits:* See South West Lakes Trust coarse advert. Self service permit hut on site. *Charges:* Full day £5, Concession £4, 24 Hour £9, Season Day £90, Season Concession £70, Season Child (under 16) £35, Season Day & Night £135, Additional Fisheries £20 each. This venue can be booked for competitions. *Season:* Open all year 24 hours a day. *Methods:* No child under 14 years may fish unless accompanied by an adult over 18 years. No child under 16 may fish overnight unless accompanied by an adult over 18 years, and then only with permission of parent or legal guardian (letter to this effect must be produced).

CALLINGTON
Angling 2000 (Penpoll Lake)
Contact: Westcountry Rivers Trust, 10 Exeter Street, Launceston, PL15 9EQ, 0870 774 0686, *Water:* 3.5 acre disused irrigation lake. *Species:* Carp to 20lb. *Permits:* From the above. *Charges:* £5 per day. *Season:* Open all year. *Methods:* Dogs under close control only. No keepnets. No boilies. Barbless hooks only, no cereal groundbait.

Angling 2000 (Polhilsa)
Contact: Westcountry Rivers Trust, 10 Exeter Street, Launceston, PL15 9EQ, 0870 774 0686, *Water:* 2 acre lake. *Species:* Carp, Rudd and Eels. *Permits:* From the above. *Charges:* £5. *Season:* Open all year. *Methods:* No Carp in keep nets, barbless hooks only.

DELABOLE
Ferndale
Contact: Steve Davey, Rockhead, Delabole, PL33 9BU, 01840 212091, *Mobile:* 07817 520417, *Water:* Three half acre lakes set in a sheltered valley 3 miles off the North Cornwall coast. *Species:* Roach to 1.5lb, Rudd to 1.5lb, Bream to 4.5lb and Carp to 14lb, Tench to 2lb & Crucian Carp. *Charges:* Adults £4 per day. OAP's and juniors £3 per day. After 5pm £3. Extra rod £1 per day. *Season:* Open all year from dawn to dusk.

FALMOUTH
Argal
Contact: South West Lakes Trust, 01566 771930, *Water:* Ranger Tel: 01209 860301. *Species:* Carp to 30lb plus, Bream, Tench, Pike to over 30lb, and Eels. *Permits:* Self service unit at Argal Car Park. See South West Lakes Trust coarse advert. *Charges:* Full day £5, Concession £4, 24 Hour £9, Season Day £90, Season Concession £70, Season Child (under 16) £35, Season Day & Night £135, Additional Fisheries £20 each. *Season:* Open all year 24 hours a day. *Methods:* No child under 14 years may fish unless accompanied by an adult over 18 years. No child under 16 may fish overnight unless accompanied by an adult over 18 years, and then only with permission of parent or legal guardian (letter to this effect must be produced).

STILLWATER COARSE

CORNWALL

STILLWATER COARSE

HAYLE
Marazion Angling Club
Contact: Mr Barry Little, 32 Trehayes Meadow, St Erth, Hayle, TR27 6JQ, 01736 756767 or 01736 756767, *Water:* St. Erth Fishery (3 acres), Bills Pool (2.5 acres), Wheal Grey (4 acres), River Hayle (600yd upstream from St. Erth Church). *Species:* Carp, Bream, Tench, Roach, Rudd, Perch, Golden Orfe, Golden Rudd, Gudgeon, Trout, Flounders & Eels; Wheal Grey reputed to hold Cornwall's biggest Carp (30lb plus). *Permits:* Available in local shops: Newtown Angling Centre, Praa Sands. West Cornwall Angling, Penzance. County Angler, Camborne. Post Office, St. Erth plus many more outlets (Please phone for more details) - Permits MUST be obtained prior to fishing. *Charges:* Full Senior £50, Ladies £35, Juniors (up to 16) £17.50, OAP & Disabled £35, Out of county £35. Family membership (2 adults & 2 children) £80. Day £5 - Ladies, Seniors, OAP, Disabled, Juniors £3. Night permit £75. *Season:* Open all year dawn till dusk, night fishing by appointment only, matches held regularly throughout the year. *Methods:* Barbless hooks, full rules & byelaws displayed at lake side (best baits: maggot, worm, pellet, sweetcorn, meat, boilies).

HELSTON
Middle Boswin Farm
Contact: Jonno, Middle Boswin Farm, Porkellis, Helston, TR13 0HR, 01209 860420, *Water:* 1 x Pleasure lake, 1 x Carp lake. *Species:* Roach 2lb, Rudd 1.5lb, Bream 4lb, Tench 3lb, Perch 2lb, Hybrid (Roach/Bream) 2.5lb plus single figure Mirror and Common Carp. Carp lake - Carp to 26lb. *Permits:* Day tickets available at farm. *Charges:* Adult £5, concessions/junior £4, Carp lake £6. *Season:* Winter; Dawn to Dusk, Summer 7am - 9 pm. (Night fishing only if pre-booked). *Methods:* Barbless hooks only, no fixed legers, no cereal groundbait, cat food, hemp or nuts, no trout pellets. No keepnets (except Matches) or Carp sacks.

LAUNCESTON
Dutson Water
Contact: Mr Broad, Lower Dutson Farm, Launceston, PL15 9SP, 01566 773147, *Mobile:* 01566 776456, *Water:* 0.75 acre lake. *Species:* Carp 19lb, Tench to 6lb 2oz, Bream to 5lb 2oz, Rudd, Perch to 3lb 4oz etc. *Permits:* Available at farm and Homeleigh Garden and Angling Centre, Dutson. Tel: 01566 773147. *Charges:* Day ticket £5. *Season:* Open all year. *Methods:* No Groundbait, Barbless hooks only.

Elmfield Farm Coarse Fishery
Contact: Mr J Elmer, Elmfield Farm, Canworthy Water, Launceston, PL15 8UD, 01566 781343, *Water:* 2 acre & 1.25 acre lake. *Species:* Carp to 24lb, Tench to 6lb, Roach to 3lb, Perch to 3.5lb, Bream, Orfe to 1lb, Chub to 3lb & Koi, also Barbel. *Charges:* £5 - 2 Rods, £4 Children/OAP's. *Season:* Open all year. *Methods:* No keepnets, ground bait in feeders only, barbless hooks, no boilies

Hidden Valley Coarse Fishing Lakes
Contact: Mr. P. Jones, Tredidon, Nr Kennards House, Launceston, PL15 8SJ, 01566 86463, *Water:* 2 acre & 0.75 acre lake. *Species:* Common, Mirror, Crucian & Ghost Carp to 23lb, Tench to 6lb, Roach, Bream & Rudd. *Permits:* Day tickets from Hidden Valley reception. *Charges:* Adults £5 for 2 rods, Child/OAP £4 for 2 rods *Season:* Open all year, 6am to dusk. *Methods:* Barbless hooks only. No groundbait.

St. Leonards Coarse Fishing Lake
Contact: Andy Reeve, St. Leonards Equitation Centre, Polson, Launceston, PL15 9QR, 01566 775543, *Mobile:* 07860 431225, *Water:* 0.75 acre lake. *Species:* Tench, Crucian, Leather, Mirror and Common Carp. *Permits:* From house. *Charges:* £4 per rod per day. *Season:* Open all year. *Methods:* Barbless hooks only.

LISKEARD
Badham Farm
Contact: Mr Jan Sroczynski, Badham Farm, St Keyne, Liskeard, PL14 4RW, 01579 343572, *Water:* 0.75 acre lake. *Species:* Carp 15lb, Roach 2.5lb, Tench 3lb and Rudd 2lb. *Permits:* On site. *Charges:* £4/rod/day. *Season:* Open all year dawn to dusk. *Methods:* Barbless hooks only; No boilies; No keepnets; Landing nets to be used at all times; No groundbait.

LOOE
Shillamill Lakes & Lodges
Contact: Shillamill Lakes, Lanreath, Looe, PL13 2PE, 01503 220886, *Water:* 3 Lakes totalling approx 5 acres. *Species:* Main specimen lake: Common, Mirror and Leather Carp. Second lake: Common, Mirror and Ghost, Roach, Perch. Third: Common and Mirror, Golden Rudd, Golden Orfe, Perch, Tench, Roach & Crucian. *Charges:* Private fishing for residents and season ticket holders only. *Methods:* Fishery requirements on application.

NEWQUAY

Goonhavern Fishery
Contact: S. Arthur, Oak Ridge Farm, Bodmin Road, Goonhavern, TR4 9QG, 01872 575052, *Water:* 2 acres. *Species:* Carp, Tench, Rudd, Roach, Perch. *Permits:* On the bank. *Charges:* £4 Adults. £3 children, OAP's. *Season:* Open all year. *Methods:* Barbless hooks, no Carp keepnets.

Gunnerbarn Syndicate Water
Contact: Karl or Roland, c/o Atlantic Angling Centre, 9b Cliff Road, Newquay, TR7 2NE, 01637 850777, *Mobile:* 07976 016845, *Water:* No day tickets, but limited syndicate vacancies at £250 per annum. New 70 peg match lake opening spring 2005, £6 per day ticket. *Species:* Mirror and Common Carp to 24lb, 3 acre lake stocked with 65 fish. *Permits:* 20 purpose built swims, totally private, please contact Karl or Roland at Atlantic Angling Centre. *Charges:* Tickets from Atlantic Angling Centre only. *Season:* Open all year.

Gwinear Pools
Contact: Simon & Jo Waterhouse, Gwinear Farm, Cubert, Newquay, TR8 5JX, 01637 830165, *Water:* 3 acre specimen lake, Carp to 30lb. 60 peg match lake, 5 hour match record 294lbs. *Species:* Carp, Roach, Bream, Perch, Rudd. *Charges:* Day tickets from farm and self service kiosk: £6 adult. £4 OAP's & Juniors. Evening £4 & £3. *Season:* No close season. *Methods:* Barbless hooks, no keepnets.

Legonna Farm Fishery
Contact: Mr Trebilcock, Legonna Farm, Lane, Newquay, TR8 4NJ, 01637 872272, *Mobile:* 07833 596120, *Water:* 1 acre lake. *Species:* Tench, Roach, Rudd, Perch, Carp to 16lbs. *Permits:* Permits/Day tickets available from Farmhouse. *Charges:* Adult £5 (2 rods), Junior/OAPs (2 rods) £3. *Season:* No close season.

Methods: Barbless hooks, no nuts of any type, no litter, no large fish in keepnets.

Mawgan Porth Pools & Lakes
Contact: Jeff & Janet Reynolds, Retorrick Mill, Mawgan Porth, TR8 4BH, 01637 860770, *Water:* 2 lakes - 1.5 acre 42 peg lake, plus specimen pool with 11 pegs. *Species:* Carp. *Permits:* On site. Disabled toilet on site, all paths and pegs disabled angler friendly. *Charges:* £5 (one rod). *Season:* Open all year, dawn to dusk or nights. *Methods:* No keep nets, all other nets must be dipped, no tiger nuts. 2 kilo groundbait max. Full list of rules at fishery. No keepnets, except for competition.

Oakside Fishery & Fish Farm
Contact: Brian & Sandra Hiscock, 89 Pydar Close, Newquay, TR7 3BT, 01637 871275, *Water:* 3 acre lake. *Species:* Carp to 24lb, Tench 6lb, Rudd, Bream 8lb, Perch, Roach 2lb, Crucians 2lb. *Permits:* Pay kiosk, checked by bailiff. *Charges:* Adult £4.50

CORNWALL

(Two rods), Junior, O.A.P's, Disabled £3.50 (Two Rods). *Season:* All year round. *Methods:* Barbless hooks, no tiger nuts or peanuts and no Carp in keepnets.

Penvose Farm Holidays
Contact: Jonathan Bennett, St. Mawgan, Nr. Newquay, TR8 4AE, 01637 860277 or 860432, *Mobile:* 07811 531881, *Water:* 3.5 acres of water set in a beautiful valley. *Species:* Carp (Common 15 - 16lb, Mirror 16-19lb, Ghost 19.5 - 22lb), Tench (Green 3 - 4lb, Golden 1lb) Bream 4 - 5lb, Crucians 1.5lb, Rudd 1.5lb, Roach 1lb. *Permits:* Post Offices nearby. *Charges:* Adults £5. under 14 £4. *Season:* No closed season, fishing dawn till dusk. *Methods:* Anglers must hold a valid licence. All nets to be dipped in solution tanks, no keepnets except for matches, landing nets must be used. Ground bait up to 2kg maximum. Barbless hooks only.

Porth
Contact: South West Lakes Trust, 01566 771930, *Water:* Ranger Tel: 01209 860301. *Species:* Bags of 130lb plus have been caught. Best Bream 9lb 2oz, Tench 9lb 12oz. Rudd to 3lb. Roach to 1lb 4oz plus. Mixed bags of Roach, Rudd, Skimmers to 60lb. Regular competitions. *Permits:* Self service at Porth car park. See South West Lakes Trust coarse advert. *Charges:* Full day £5, Concession £4, 24 Hour £9, Season Day £90, Season Concession £70, Season Child (under 16) £35, Season Day & Night £135, Additional Fisheries £20 each. This venue can be booked for competitions. *Season:* Open all year 24 hours a day. *Methods:* No child under 14 years may fish unless accompanied by an adult over 18 years. No child under 16 may fish overnight unless accompanied by an adult over 18 years, and then only with permission of parent or legal guardian (letter to this effect must be produced).

Trebellan Park & Fisheries
Contact: Mr Eastlake, Cubert, Nr. Newquay, TR8 5PY, 01637 830522, *Water:* 3 lakes ranging from 1 to 2.5 acres. *Species:* Carp 26lbs, Roach 3-4lbs, Rudd 3-4lbs, Tench 3-4lbs. *Permits:* Permits paid for on the bank. Bailiff collects. *Charges:* Day tickets - £3.50 for 1 rod, £5 for 2 rods. Season ticket (12 months) £60. *Season:* Lakes open all year. No night fishing. *Methods:* No keepnets, barbless hooks only, no ground baiting, no high protein baits, no night fishing.

White Acres Country Park
Contact: Tackle Shop, White Acres Country Park, Newquay, TR8 4LW, 01726 862113, *Water:* 15 lakes totalling approx 36 acres. *Species:* Wide range of almost all species (no Pike or Zander). *Permits:* Available from Fishing Lodge. *Charges:* Please call for info. *Season:* Fishery open all year round. *Methods:* 'The Method'

is banned, barbless hooks only, some keepnet restrictions, no peas, nuts, or beans.

PADSTOW
Borlasevath
Contact: Robert Hurford, Borlasevath Manor Farm, St. Wenn, Bodmin, PL30 5PW, 01637 880826, *Mobile:* 07973 767147, *Water:* 10 acres of water (5 lakes). *Species:* Carp, Bream, Tench, Rudd. *Methods:* Barbless hooks. All children under 14 years to be accompanied by an adult. No keepnets.

PENZANCE
Boscathnoe
Contact: South West Lakes Trust, 01566 771930, *Water:* Ranger Tel: 01209 860301 *Species:* Common Mirror and Crucian carp with fish into the 20lb range. Roach, Tench, Rudd and Bream also stocked. *Permits:* See South West Lakes Trust coarse advert. *Charges:* Full day £5, Concession £4, 24 Hour £9, Season Day £90, Season Concession £70, Season Child (under 16) £35, Season Day & Night £135, Additional Fisheries £20 each. *Season:* Open all year 24 hours a day. *Methods:* No child under 14 years may fish unless accompanied by an adult over 18 years. No child under 16 may fish overnight unless accompanied by an adult over 18 years, and then only with permission of parent or legal guardian (letter to this effect must be produced).

Choone Farm Fishery
Contact: Mr E.V. Care, Downs Barn, St. Buryan, Penzance, TR19 6DG, 01736 810658, *Water:* 2 lakes. *Species:* Carp, Tench, Perch, Rudd. *Charges:* 1 rod - £4/person, 2 rods - £5.50. *Season:* Please telephone before travelling. *Methods:* Barbless

CORNWALL

hooks only, no carp in keepnets, no ground bait.
Tindeen Fishery
Contact: J. Laity, Bostrase, Millpool, Goldsithney, Penzance, TR20 9JG, 01736 763486, *Water:* 3 lakes approx 1 acre each. *Species:* Carp, Roach, Rudd, Gudgeon, Perch, Tench, Trout. *Permits:* From above address. *Charges:* Adults £3, Juniors under 14 £2, Extra rod £1 each. *Season:* All year, night fishing by arrangement. *Methods:* Barbless hooks to be used.

SALTASH
Bake Fishing Lakes (Coarse)
Contact: Tony Lister, Bake, Trerule Foot, Saltash, 01752 849027, *Mobile:* 07798 585836, *Water:* 7 lakes adding up to over 15 acres, Coarse and Trout. *Species:* Mirror 28lb, Common 24lb 9oz, Ghost 24lb, Crucian Carp, Tench 6lb, Bream 8lb 4oz, Roach,

Ben with a 6lb Ghost Carp from the match lake 'Flamingo' at Bake Lakes.

Rudd. *Permits:* At Bake Lakes. *Charges:* £7 per day Specimen Lake. £6 per day small fish lakes. 2 rods per person, reduced rates for pensioners and juniors subject to change. *Season:* 8am - Dusk. Earlier by appointment, open all year. *Methods:* Barbless hooks, No nuts. No keepnets specimen fish. Landing mats. All nets to be dipped before fishing.
Bush Lakes
Contact: J Renfree, Bush Farm, Saltash, PL12 6QY, 01752 842148, *Water:* 3 Lakes from half to 1 acre. *Species:* Carp to 30lb plus, Tench to 3.5lb, Rudd to 1.5lb, Roach to 1.5lb, Bream, Perch to 4.5lb. *Charges:* Day ticket £6 - 2 rods) / £9 - 3 rods. *Season:* Open all year. *Methods:* Barbless hooks, landing mat, no nets for big carp.
Penpol Lakes
Holwood Farm, Blunts, Saltash, PL12 5AL, 01752 851250, *Mobile:* 07970 593423, *Water:* 3 acre disused irrigation lake. *Species:* Carp to 20lb. *Permits:* Through Angling 2000 scheme or at farmhouse. *Charges:* 2 x Angling 2000 tokens (£2.50 each), which can be purchased at farmhouse. Concessions for juniors. *Season:* Open all year, dawn to dusk. *Methods:* No night fishing, barbless hooks only, no keepnets.
Trewandra Lake
Contact: Mr & Mrs S.F. Delbridge, Trewandra Farm, Saltash, PL12 5JA, 01752 851258, *Mobile:* 07833 666899, *Water:* One acre lake. *Species:* Carp to 17lb. Tench to 6lbs. Roach to 2.5lbs and Bream to 3lb. *Permits:* Local Post Office. *Charges:* £5

CORNWALL

day, children £3. Evening Ticket £3, £2 children. Children under 13 years MUST be supervised by an adult at all times. *Season:* Open all year (dawn to dusk only). *Methods:* No dogs allowed, barbless hooks, no keepnets for Carp.

ST AUSTELL
Court Farm Holidays
Contact: Simon / Bill Truscott, Court Farm Holidays, St Stephen, St Austell, PL26 7LE, 01726 823684, *Water:* Natural Spring fed lake. *Species:* Roach, Rudd, Tench. Grass, Common and Mirror Carp. *Permits:* You must have a valid EA Rod Licence. *Charges:* Day tickets £5. *Season:* Open all year. *Methods:* Barbless hooks only. No keepnets.

Glenleigh Farm Fishery
Contact: Mr & Mrs A Tregunna, Glenleigh Farm, Sticker, St Austell, PL26 7JB, 01726 73154, *Mobile:* 07816 953362, *Water:* One acre lake. Access to enable parking adjacent to lake, allowing easy access for disabled persons and fully disabled friendly fishing platforms. *Species:* Carp (Common, Ghost, Mirror, Leather), Tench, Rudd, Roach, Eels, Gudgeon, Perch. *Permits:* Tickets from lakeside, permits from Sticker post office. *Charges:* £5 day, £4 child /OAP. £3 evening, £2 child /OAP. 12 month membership available. *Season:* Open all year dawn to dusk. *Methods:* Barbless hooks. No nuts, peas or beans. Max 2 rods per person. Mats to be used. No groundbait. No keepnets.

Roche (St Austell) Angling Club
Contact: Mr Ian Holland (Membership Secretary), No 6 Stanways Road, St Columb Minor, Newquay, TR7 3HF, 01637 879521, *Water:* 6 fresh water lakes in St Austell area. *Species:* Roach, Perch, Rudd, Tench, Eels, Carp, Pike & Bream. *Permits:* Fishing restricted to Members and their guests only. Membership applications available from membership secretary direct. *Charges:* Full Annual membership £35, concessionary £15 plus initial joining fee. Membership to Game and Sea sections only at reduced rates. *Season:* Open all year. *Methods:* As specified in club byelaws.

Sunnyview Lake
Contact: Philip Gale, PL26 8QX, 01726 890715, *Water:* Half acre lake. *Species:* Roach, Rudd, Tench, Perch & Carp. *Permits:* Limited day tickets available by prior booking only - please phone number above. *Charges:* £4 /day /person (maximum 4) Sole hire £16 per day. *Season:* All year, dawn to dusk.

ST COLUMB MAJOR
Meadowside Fishery
Contact: M Early, Meadowside Farm, Winnards Perch, St. Columb, TR9 6DH, 01637 880544, *Mobile:* 07787 135431, *Water:* 2 lakes mixed coarse fishery. *Species:* Carp 21lb, Roach 2lb, Perch 3lb, Rudd 1lb, Tench 5lb, Bream 6lb. *Permits:* Personal licence required. *Charges:* £4.50/1rod, concessions & juniors £3.50/1 rod, £1/extra rod, max. 2 rods. *Season:* No close season, 7.30am to dusk daily all year round. *Methods:* Barbless hooks, no keepnets, unhooking mats preferred.

Retallack Waters
Contact: Retallack Waters, Winnards Perch, St Columb Major, TR9 6DE, 01637 881160, *Mobile:* 01637 880057, *Water:* 6.5 acre main lake, separate match canal. *Species:* Common, Mirror and Ghost Carp, Pike, Bream, Tench, Perch, Roach and Rudd. *Permits:* Night fishing only available to season ticket holders. Please enquire for details. *Charges:* Canal: £6 adults, £5

CORNWALL

RETALLACK WATERS COARSE FISHERY
and 'Spirit of the West' American Theme Park

6.5 Acre Main Lake with
Carp to over 25lbs,
Pike to 30lbs, Bream to 9lbs
Tench to 7lbs
Rudd and Roach to over 3lb
SEPARATE FULLY PEGGED MATCH CANAL!

FACILITIES INCLUDE:
Fully Stocked Tackle Shop
OPEN 7 DAYS
All Bait Sales

TREAT THE FAMILY -
American Theme Park,
Horse Rides, Mining Camp,
Live Shows, Museums,
Cafe Toilets, Miles
of Trail Walks etc.

Tel: 01637 881160   Eves: 01637 880909
Winnards Perch, Nr St Columb, Cornwall
www.retallackwaters.co.uk

Mike Bolt with a fine Cornish Carp

STILLWATER COARSE

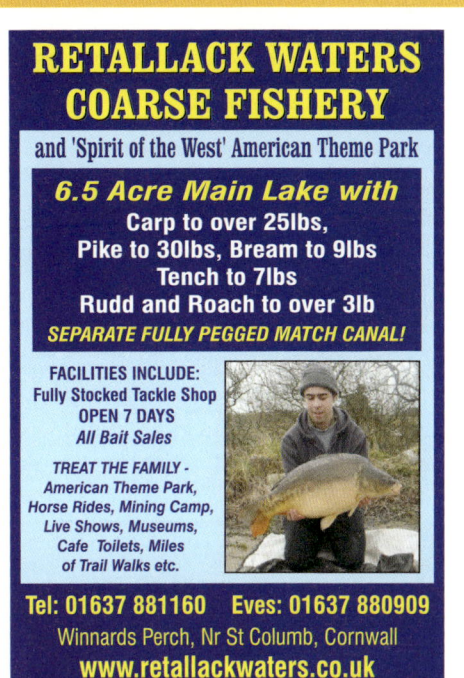

children/OAPs. Main specimen lake: £7 adult, £6 children/OAP's. *Season:* Open all year. *Methods:* Barbless hooks only. Unhooking mats and specimen landing net required on specimen lake. Dogs allowed by prior arrangement, please phone first.

ST IVES
Amalwhidden Farm Coarse Fishery
Contact: Neil Hodder, Towednack, St. Ives, TR26 3AR, 01736 796961, *Water:* 3 ponds & 1 acre lake. *Species:* Mirror Carp 14lb, Common Carp 20lb, Ghost Carp 12lb, Tench 4lb, Perch 3.5lb, Bream, Rudd, Roach and Gudgeon. *Charges:* Day tickets £5. *Season:* No closed season. *Methods:* No Carp sacks, barbless hooks only, no night fishing.

Bussow
Contact: South West Lakes Trust, 01566 771930, *Water:* Ranger: 01209 860301 *Species:* Rudd to 1.5lb. Roach, Bream and Carp. *Permits:* See South West Lakes Trust coarse advert. *Charges:* Full day £5, Concession £4, 24 Hour £9, Season Day £90, Season Concession £70, Season Child (under 16) £35, Season Day & Night £125, Additional Fisheries £20 each. *Season:* Open all year 24 hours a day. *Methods:* No child under 14 years may fish unless accompanied by an adult over 18 years. No child under 16 may fish overnight unless accompanied by an adult over 18 years, and then only with permission of parent or legal guardian (letter to this effect must be produced).

Nance Lakes
Contact: Mr or Mrs Ellis, Nance Lakes, Trevarrack, Lelant, St Ives, TR26 3EZ, 01736 740348, *Water:* Three lakes, various sizes. *Species:* Carp, Roach, Bream and Tench. *Charges:* £5 per day. Evening tickets - £3 after 5pm. *Season:* Open all year

8am to 5pm. *Methods:* Barbless hooks, no keepnets unless competition.

St. Ives Freshwater Angling Society
Contact: Jim Elgar, 52 Trelawney Avenue, St. Ives, TR26 1AS, 01736 796696, *Water:* 1.5 acre spring-fed lake with depths from 6 to 24 feet, situated in farmland, 5 miles from St.Ives. *Species:* Bream, Carp, Tench, Roach, Rudd, Perch, Gudgeon, and Eels. *Permits:* 1) Symons Fishing Tackle, Market Place, St Ives. 2) Mr. K. Roberts, Woonsmith Farm, Nancledra, Nr. Penzance. 3) Newtown Angling Centre, Newtown, Germoe, Penzance. Location maps available with permits. *Charges:* Adults: Day £5, Weekly £15. Juniors (under 16): Day £3, Weekly £9. *Season:* Open all year. No night Fishing. *Methods:* Barbless hooks only. No fish over 3 lb to be retained in a keepnet. All nets to be dipped in disinfectant tank before use. Good baits are maggots, casters, sweetcorn and trout pellets.

TORPOINT
Crafthole
Contact: South West Lakes Trust, 01566 771930, *Water:* Ranger Tel: 01822 855700. *Species:* Carp and Tench. Quality Carp up to 30lb. *Permits:* See South West Lakes Trust coarse advert. *Charges:* Full day £6 (limited availability from agent), Season Day £175, Concession £150. Family £250 (Husband, wife and up to 2 children under 16). Additional Fisheries £20 each. *Season:* Open all year 1hr before sunrise to 1hr after sunset (day ticket). *Methods:* No child under 14 years may fish unless accompanied by an adult over 18 years. No child under 16 may fish overnight unless accompanied by an adult over 18 years, and then only with permission of parent or legal guardian (letter to this effect must be produced).

CORNWALL

Millbrook
Contact: Mark or Rebecca Blake, Tregonhawke Farm, Millbrook, Torpoint, PL10 1JH, 01752 823210, *Water:* 1 acre water in sheltered, wooded valley. 150 year old reservoir. *Species:* Perch, Tench, Ghost Carp, Crucians, Common Carp, Mirror Carp, Roach, Rudd, Bream. *Permits:* Not applicable. *Charges:* £5 per day, evening ticket £3 after 5 p.m. £10 night fishing ticket. Annual permits £120. *Season:* Dawn until dusk, no closed season. *Methods:* Barbless hooks only. Keepnets are permitted, landing nets and disgorgers to be used.

South East Cornwall Taught Angling Society
Contact: Tony Savage, 79 Peacock Avenue, Torpoint, PL11 2EZ, 01752 812637, *Water:* The aim of SECTAS is not only to promote angling as a pastime amongst the youth of South East Cornwall, but also to promote social inclusion. SECTAS offers youngsters a way to meet new people, make new friends and become part of a group of like minded people. SECTAS is a not for profit group and funds are put back into the group to improve it, it's resources and to increase membership. *Charges:* There is a joining fee of £10 to show commitment and thereafter a £5 per year membership fee. The club caters for all aged 8 upwards.

TRURO

Mellonwatts Mill Coarse Fishery
Pensagillas Farm, Grampound, Truro, TR2 4SR, 01872 530808, *Water:* 2 acre lake. *Species:* Carp to 25lb, Common & Mirror, Roach, Tench, Golden Rudd. *Charges:* Day ticket £5, Evening £3. *Season:* Open all year. Night fishing by arrangement only.

Nanteague Farm Fishing
Maraznvose, Zelah, Truro, TR4 9DH, 01872 540351, *Water:* 1.5 acre lake *Species:* Carp to 22lb, Roach, Rudd, Bream and Perch. *Permits:* Limited season tickets by prior arrangement. Please telephone/e-mail. No day tickets.

Threemilestone Angling Club (Coarse Lakes)
Contact: Mrs T. Bailey, 9 Sampson Way, Threemilestone, Truro, TR3 6DR, 01872 272578, *Mobile:* 07734 445133, *Water:* Langarth Pools (2 Pools). *Species:* Carp, Tench, Roach, Rudd, Bream, Perch, Goldfish. *Permits:* At lakeside. *Charges:* Seniors £4, Juniors £3. *Season:* All season, no night fishing. *Methods:* Barbless hooks only, no Peanuts etc.

Tory Farm Angling
Contact: Mrs Betty Ayres, Tory Farm, Ponsanooth, Truro, TR3 7HN, 01209 861272, *Water:* 2.5 acre lake. *Species:* Mirror, Common, Wild and Ghost Carp to 28lb. Crucian to 2.5lb. Tench to 5.5lb. Rudd to 2.25lb. *Charges:* £6 per day, daylight hours only. Club membership available £70 per season (or part of). Ticket commences 1st June. *Season:* Open all year. *Methods:* Barbless hooks only, no keepnets, unhooking mats to be used. No nut baits. Hemp-specialist prepared only.

---

www.gethooked.co.uk
Check out our Web Site!
Get Hooked! ON THE WEB

Enjoy peace, tranquillity and a great day's fishing at ....

Millbrook Coarse Fishery
www.millbrookfishery.co.uk

Carp - Commons to 25lbs, Crucians 1.5lbs, Ghosts 20lbs, Perch 3lbs, Tench 8lbs, Roach 2lbs, Rudd 1lb, Bream 5lbs.

This 100 Year old Reservoir is home to a wealth of wildlife
KEEPNETS PERMITTED
Parking and Toilet on site
Access: dawn to dusk - night fishing by arrangement
Contact: Mark & Rebecca Blake, Tregonhawke Farm, Millbrook, Torpoint, Cornwall PL10 1JH
Email: rebeccaharris@millbrookfishery.fsnet.co.uk

Accommodation:
Fully equipped cottage sleeping 8
Self contained Apartment sleeping 2

Tel: 01752 823210

Stillwater Trout

BODMIN
Colliford Lake
Contact: South West Lakes Trust, 01566 771930, *Water:* Ranger Tel: 01409 211514. *Species:* Brown Trout. *Permits:* Colliford Tavern. *Charges:* Full day £10, Season £130, Reduced day £8, Season £95, Child/Wheelchair £2, Season £30. *Season:* Opens 15 March - 12th October. *Methods:* Catch & release option. Barbless hooks only. Fly fishing only.

Fenwick Trout Fishery
Contact: David & Shirley Thomas, Old Coach Road, Dunmere, Bodmin, PL31 2RD, 01208 78296, *Water:* 2 acre lake plus river fishing. See also entry under Camel. *Species:* Rainbow 1.5lb - 12lb, Browns to 10lb plus. *Charges:* £22 - 4 fish, £14 - 2 fish. *Season:* All year. *Methods:* Fly fishing only.

Temple Trout Fishery
Contact: Mr Julian Jones, Temple Trout Fishery, Temple Road, Temple, Bodmin, PL30 4HW, 01208 821730, *Mobile:* 07787 704966, *Water:* 2.7 acre lake. Plus 4.5 acre 'any method' lake. *Species:* Rainbows (18lb 9oz) & Brown trout (16lb 6oz). *Permits:* Available at fishery Tel: 01208 821730. *Charges:* 2004 Club membership £8, entitles members to 10% discount on tickets, to fish club events and to purchase a season ticket at £127.50 for 25 Trout. Full day £24, 5 fish - 3/4 day £21, 4 fish - half day £17, 3 fish - evening £12.50, 2 fish. Child under 16 & disabled £12.50, 2 fish all day, extra fish £6.50. Single fish on any method lake £6.50. *Season:* Open all year round from 9 a.m to dusk, in winter open 4 days a week Wednesday, Thursday, Saturday and Sundays or by appointment. *Methods:* Fly fishing on 2.7 acre lake. Any legal method on one bank of 4.5 acre lake and a sporting ticket available on 4.5 acre lake.

CAMELFORD
Crowdy
Contact: South West Lakes Trust, 01566 771930, *Water:* Ranger Tel: 01409 211514 *Species:* Brown Trout. *Charges:* Free to holders of a valid Environment Agency Licence. *Season:* 15th March - 12th October. *Methods:* Angling by spinning, fly or bait.

HAYLE
Tree Meadow Trout Fishery
Contact: John Hodge, Tree Meadow, Deveral Road, Fraddam, Hayle, TR27 5EP, 01736 850899, *Mobile:* 07971 107156, *Water:* Two lakes. 4 acres in total. Sedge lake to 14lb, Willow lake to 25lb plus. *Species:* Rainbow and Brown Trout & Blues. *Permits:* At Lodge Shop. *Charges:* Contact for details. *Season:* Open all year 9am to 1 hour after dusk. *Methods:* Catch and release after fish limit. Max hook size 10.

LAUNCESTON
Braggs Wood Fishery
Contact: Nigel Stephens Braggs Hill, Boyton, Launceston PL15 9RG, 01566 776886, *Water:* Half acre lake. *Species:* Brown and Rainbow Trout 1.5 to 10lbs and maybe more! *Charges:* 2 fish (half day) £12.00. 3 fish (half day) £16.00. 4 fish (full day) £19.00. 5 fish (full day) £22.00. *Season:* Dawn til dusk all year round.

Rose Park Fishery
Contact: Rose Park Fishery, Trezibbett, Altarnun, Launceston, PL15 7RF, 01566 86278, *Water:* Two lakes. *Species:* Rainbow 13lb, Wild Browns 2.5lb. Stocked Brown Trout 9lb 5oz. *Permits:* From the fishery. *Charges:* No catch, no charge. Rainbows £1.70

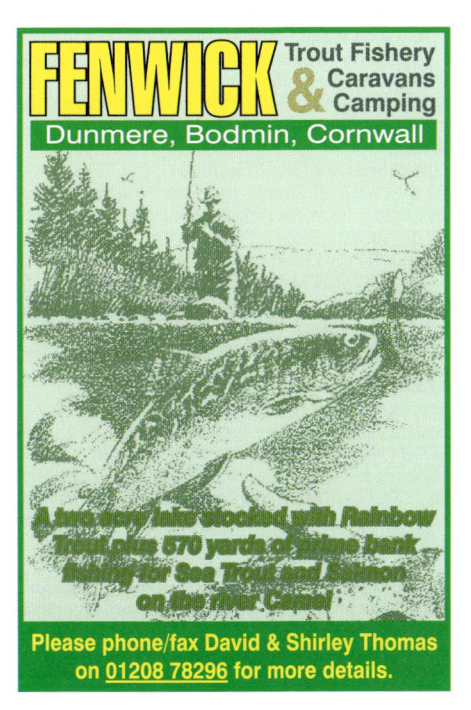

Rob Todd and Bob Eccles winners of Vranch House Charity competition heat at Bake lakes

CORNWALL

DRIFT Reservoir
Near Penzance, Cornwall

65 Acre Reservoir offering quality fishing for stocked Rainbow and Wild Brown Trout

Season, Week, Day and Evening permits available.

Telephone: 01736 363021

Email: mail@bolithoestates.co.uk

Bake Fishing Lakes

Open 365 Days a Year — 8am to Dusk

TACKLE • ROD HIRE • FLIES

TWO FLY LAKES

E.A. ROD LICENCES AVAILABLE

Catch and release for Rainbows & Browns to 15lb

Contact Tony Lister
Trerulefoot, Saltash, Cornwall.
Tel 01752 849027 & 07798 585836
Email: tony.lister@bakelakes.co.uk
www.bakelakes.co.uk

---

per lb, Browns £2.25 per lb. Fishing charge £2.50 on 1st & 2nd fish only. *Season:* Open all year from 8am till Dusk. *Methods:* Fly fishing. No catch and release.

LISKEARD
Siblyback
Contact: South West Lakes Trust, 01566 771930, *Water:* Angling and watersports centre: 01579 396522. *Species:* Premier Rainbow Fishery - Boat & Bank (boats may be booked in advance: 01579 342366). Rod average 2004: 3.2 fish per rod day. *Permits:* Self Service Kiosk at Watersports Centre. *Charges:* Full day £18, Season £400. Concession day £14.50, Season £295, Child/Wheelchair £3, Season £90. Evening £14.50. Season Permits can be used on any Premier Fishery only. Boats £11 per day inc. 2 fish extra to bag limits. *Season:* Opens 25th March 2005 - 31st October. *Methods:* Fly fishing only. No child under 14 years may fish unless accompanied by an adult over 18 years.

Wainsford Fishery (Trout Lake)
Contact: Paul Elliot, Wainsford Fishery, Twowatersfoot, Liskeard, PL14 6HT, 01208 821432, *Water:* Three Trout lakes. See also entry under River fishing - Fowey. *Species:* Brown Trout to 5.5lb. Rainbows to 12.5lb. *Permits:* On site. *Charges:* £15 per day. *Season:* Open all year.

PENZANCE
Drift Reservoir
Contact: Estate Office, Penzance, 01736 363021, *Water:* 65 acre reservoir. *Species:* Stock Rainbows (3 per day, 9 weekly) Wild Browns. Browns (3 per day, 9 weekly). *Permits:* Enquiries to Estate Office: 01736 363021 re. tickets and permits. *Charges:* Permit Charge - Rainbow/Brown. Season £120 - 9 Rainbows per week, 3 Brownies per day. Week £30 - 9 Rainbows per week, 3 Brownies per day. Day £10 - 3 Rainbows per day, 3 Brownies per day. Evening £7 - 2 Rainbows per evening, 2 Brownies per evening (after 4pm) (Sept-Oct after 2pm). *Season:* 27th March - 12th October Brown trout, 27th March - 31st October Rainbows. *Methods:* No static with boobies, any other traditional fly or lures.

REDRUTH
Cast Fly Fishing Club
Contact: Mark Randall, 1 Goonown Lane, St Agnes, TR5 0UU, 01872 553603, *Water:* Membership of 80, fishing Stithians and other waters. Monthly competitions. Juniors and ladies welcome. Tuition can be arranged. Members entitled to discounted tickets to fish Stithians. Club boat available at £2 per day. *Species:* Rainbows and Browns. Browns are wild fish, some Blues are occasionally stocked. *Charges:* £10 p/a Adult. Juniors first year free. *Season:* Please telephone Mark for info pack.

Stithians
Contact: South West Lakes Trust, 01566 771930, *Water:* Ranger Tel: 01209 860301 *Species:* Intermediate Rainbow & Brown Trout Fishery. Trout to 6lb. *Permits:* Stithians Watersports Centre (01209 860301), Sandy's Tackle, Redruth (01209 214877). *Charges:* Full day £12.50, Season £200, Concession day £11, Season £175, Child/Wheelchair £2, Season £40. Boats £11/day. *Season:* Opens 15th March - 31st October. *Methods:* Fly fishing only. Catch and release available - barbless hooks.

SALTASH
Bake Fishing Lakes (Trout)
Contact: Tony Lister, Bake, Trerule Foot, Saltash, PL12 5BU, 01752 849027, *Mobile:* 07798 585836, *Water:* 7 Lakes adding up to 14 plus acres, Coarse and Trout. Troutmaster Water. *Species:* Rainbow 16lb 7oz, Brown Trout 10lb. *Permits:* At Bake lakes. *Charges:* Sporting ticket £11 per day. Catch only £6.50 plus £5 - 1 fish, £14 - 2 fish, £18.50 - 3 fish, £23 - 4 fish, £26 - 5 fish, specimen to 15lb. £12 - 2 fish to £20 - 5 fish, Dunes. *Season:* 8am - Dusk, earlier by appointment. *Methods:* Catch and release on 1 lake. Barbless or debarbed hooks when releasing.

STILLWATER TROUT

CORNWALL

ST AUSTELL
Innis Fly Fishery
Contact: Mrs Pam Winch, Innis Fly Fishery & Innis Inn, Innis Moor, Penwithick, St. Austell, PL26 8YH, 01726 851162, *Water:* 15 acres (3 lakes), stream fed enclosed water. *Species:* Rainbow Trout. *Permits:* As above. *Charges:* Full day £21 (5 Fish), half day £11 (2 Fish), Catch and release £12.50. *Season:* All year, 8.00 a.m. to dusk. *Methods:* Barbless hooks when catch & release, no static fishing.

TRURO
Gwarnick Mill Fishery
Contact: Sue Dawkins, Gwarnick Mill, St. Allen, Truro, TR4 9QU, 01872 540487, *Water:* 1.5 Acre spring and river fed lake. *Species:* Rainbow Trout to 10lb. *Charges:* 4 Fish £23, 3 Fish £18, 2 Fish £13. *Season:* Open all year. *Methods:* Barbless hooks preferred.

Ventontrissick Trout Farm
Contact: Gerald Wright, St. Allen, Truro, TR4 9DG, 01872 540497, *Mobile:* 07762 781200, *Water:* Half acre. *Species:* Rainbow Trout 1.25lb - 10lb. *Charges:* £5.50 per day rod ticket, £1.60 per lb fish killed, first two fish to be killed, thereafter release optional. £10 sporting ticket. *Season:* 8.00am till 1hr after sunset 10 p.m. *Methods:* Fly only, barbless if releasing.

Camel Valley Sportfishing

Saltwater & Game Fishing Tackle and Accessories

Charter Boat Information

Permits available in season for Angling 2000 - Wadebridge A.A. Bodmin A.A.

Bass Flies & Lures - Salmon, Trout & Sea Trout Flies

Live & Frozen Sea Baits Lobworms and Dendrabaena
(subject to seasons and availability)

AIR GUNS AND AMMUNITION

5 Polmorla Road - Wadebridge - Cornwall PL27 7NB
Tel/Fax 01208 816403

DISCARDED TACKLE KILLS

Please do not leave litter, hooks, nylon or other items dangerous to wildlife

---

Tracey Bettison with her personal best 7lb 4oz Rainbow from Bake Lakes.

STILLWATER TROUT

Sea Fishing

BOSCASTLE
Boscastle Peganina
Contact: Ken Cave, 01288 353565,

CAMBORNE
Choughs S.A.C.
Contact: Sue, *Water:* Club fishing around the coast of Cornwall, membership open to all, meetings every 4th Sunday at the Choughs Inn, Camborne at 6pm. Regular matches every other weekend. Ladies, junior and boat section. Please contact Sue for more details.

CORNWALL REGION
Camborne Angling Association
Contact: Mr Ralph Elcox (Hon Sec), 44 Town Farm, Falmouth Road, Redruth, TR15 2XG, 01209 314389, *Mobile:* 07814 989707, *Water:* Sea Fishing Association. Shore and boat. Affiliated to the Cornish Federation of Sea Anglers and the Bass Anglers Sporting Society. *Species:* All sea fish apart from protected species. Minimum weight for all species. *Permits:* None required, other than possible harbour/pier charges. *Charges:* Family membership - £11, Couple - £9, Senior £8 and £3 Junior. *Season:* None *Methods:* Two rods, three hooks maximum, no netting.

Cornish Federation of Sea Anglers
Contact: Mr Ralph Elcox (Hon Sec), 44 Town Farm, Falmouth Road, Redruth, TR15 2XG, 01209 314389, *Mobile:* 07814 989707, *Water:* Sea Fishing Federation. Shore and boat. Affiliated to The Conger Club of Great Britain and The Bass Anglers Sporting Society. *Species:* All sea fish apart from protected species. Minimum weight for all species. *Permits:* None required, other than possible harbour/pier charges. *Charges:* C.F.S.A. affiliation £34 per annum per club. Personal members £7.50. Family membership (ie husband, wife and children under 16) £10. Optional third party insurance an extra £30 per club per annum. *Season:* None *Methods:* Two rods three hooks maximum. No netting.

FALMOUTH
Falmouth Duchy A.C.
Contact: Mrs L Crichton, 15 Trewarton Road, Penryn, TR10 8JB, 01326 372832, *Water:* Shore fishing. *Season:* April - September.

Gemini Breeze
Contact: Rob Searle, 01326 312116, *Mobile:* 07774 226046,

Leo I
Contact: Ken Dodgson, 10 Stratton Terrace, Falmouth, TR11 2SY, 01326 312409, *Mobile:* 07779 376641, *Water:* Normally up to 20 miles to sea from Falmouth. Longer trips by arrangement. *Species:* Conger Eel - 80lb 8oz (C.F.S.A. record). Ling 44lb 8oz (C.F.S.A. record). Coalfish to 27lb. Pollack to 25lb. Cod to 38lb. Whiting to 4lb 4oz. Plus all other usual species. *Charges:* Individuals £35. 8 hour boat charter £275. *Season:* Fishing all year round. *Methods:* Wreck, Reef and Shark. Anchored and drifting.

Mawnan Angling Club
Contact: Steve Rees, *Mobile:* 01326 377029, *Water:* Sea fishing club with boat and shore sections. *Species:* Sea fish. *Charges:* £15 family, £10 senior, £3 junior. Club meet on 1st Wednesday of month at Dipper Way, Falmouth. New members welcome. Enquiries to Tackle Box, Falmouth or Telephone Tim on number above.

Patrice II
Contact: Michael Tuffery, 01326 313265, *Mobile:* 07979 335181,

St Mawes S.A.C.
Contact: Mr P.A. Miller, 18 Percuil View, St Mawes, Truro, TR2 5AU, 01326 270953, *Water:* Shore angling, wreck trips. *Season:* Boat - from May onwards.

Versatile
Contact: Lyn or Spike, 07813 043538, *Mobile:* 07749 860581, *Water:* Modern, clean Offshore 105 charter boat. Licensed for up to 12 passengers up to 60 miles offshore.

HAYLE
Carnhell Green S.A.C.
Contact: Mrs J Williams, 55 Cathebron Road, Carnhell Green, TR14 0NB, 01209 831720, *Water:* Wreck, reef and rock fishing. *Species:* Pollack, Mullet, Conger, Mackerel, Bass, Flounder, Wrasse, 3 Bearded Rockling, Shore Rockling, Plaice. *Charges:* £6 Seniors / OAP's. £3 Junior. £10 Family (2 Adults / 1 Child). *Season:* All year - annual open competition 17th & 18th Sept 2005.

CORNWALL

MEVAGISSEY SHARK & ANGLING CENTRE
West Quay
Mevagissey

We offer a full charter service for individual and group bookings. Wreck and Shark fishing catered for. Rods for hire at extremely good prices.

RODS-REELS-TACKLE...
for all types of fishing. All Shakespeare and Abu rods and reels with at least 10% and up to 25% DISCOUNT - GREAT VALUE! Call in or phone BEFORE YOU BUY

We also sell all weather clothing (hats, waterproofs, smocks) knives (inc. Victorinox) and much, much more

Frozen bait available all year,
FRESH WORM - Easter to October
Open daily all year round
Call in or phone/fax (01726) 843430
Email: MevaSharkAng@fsbdial.co.uk

Padstow Angling Centre
Stockists of Live and Frozen Baits and Tackle

SHORE FISHING TRIPS
with "the rockhopper" Ed Schliffke

"ROCKHOPPER" VIDEOS AND BAITS

The Drang, Strand House, Padstow
Tel: 01841 532762
Mobile: 07929 233902

San Pablo III
Contact: Dougie Wright, 01209 716970, *Mobile:* 07974 409567, *Water:* Alternative mobile - 07714 514808

HELSTON
Helston & District Sea Angling Club
Contact: Stuart Athay, Atlantic Tackle, 36 Wendron Close, Helston, TR13 8PS, *Water:* Wreck fishing. *Charges:* 10% discount for club members in shops. *Season:* All year.

ISLES OF SCILLY
Falcon Faldork & Firethorn
Contact: David Stedeford, 01720 422886,

LISKEARD
Liskeard & District Sea Angling Club
Contact: Mr White, 14 Wadham Road, Liskeard, PL14 3BD, 01579 345428, *Water:* Mixture of sea fishing with club based in Liskeard. *Charges:* Annual subscription £10. *Season:* Shore fishing - all year. Boat - April to October (Newquay, Cornwall).

LOOE
Looe Angling Club
Contact: Billy Martin, Quay Street, East Looe, PL13 1DX, 01503 263337, *Water:* Clubhouse with club prices on all drinks. Open all day everyday. Membership full, but holiday membership available. Please contact clubhouse.

Mystique
Contact: David Bond, 11 Springfield Road, East Looe, PL13 1HB, 01503 264530, *Mobile:* 07900 472252,
Shark Angling Club of Great Britain
Contact: Linda Reynolds, The Quay, East Looe, PL13 1DX, 01503 262642, *Water:* Established 50 years. Boat booking agent for 8 boats in Looe for Shark, Reef fishing and Mackerel trips. Club open to new members - required to catch a qualifying length shark prior to joining. For more details please contact above.

MEVAGISSEY
Mevagissey S.A.C.
Contact: Mike Barker, 30 Lavorrick Orchard, Mevagissey, 01726 843357, *Water:* Wreck fishing, charter boat, lock and dingy. *Season:* All year.
Venus
Contact: Mevagissey Shark & Angling Centre, Mevagissey, 01726 843430,

NEWQUAY
Treninnick Tavern Angling Club
Contact: NFSA Head Office: 01364 644643,

PADSTOW
Blue Fox
Contact: Phil Britts, Padstow, 01841 533293, *Water:* All day charter fishing trips.
Emma Kate II (Lockin 33)
Contact: John Wicks, 01841 533319, *Water:* All day trips, 4 hour trips and Mackerel trips.
Grenville Sea Angling Club
Contact: John Keast, 01726 822954, *Water:* Meetings 1st Wednesday of each month, at St Dennis football club, St Dennis, St Austell at 8pm. New members welcome (Adult & Junior). *Species:* Sea angling from rocks or boat, covering cornish coast. *Permits:* Please telephone Marie for further information, or come to one of our meetings.
Padstow Angling Centre
Contact: Ed Schliffke, 01841 532762. Shore fishing trips.

PENZANCE
Goldsithney S.A.C.
Contact: NFSA Head Office: 01364 644643,

SEA FISHING

43

CORNWALL

M.B.A.S.
Contact: Mr G Wallen, 6 Alexandra Gardens, Penzance, TR18 4SY, 01736 351414, *Water:* Shore/boat fishing - wreck/reef.

Mounts Bay Angling Society
Contact: David Cains, Shangri-La, 9A Arundel Park, Connor Downs, Hayle, TR27 5EL, 01736 752037, *Mobile:* 07919 253065, *Water:* Regular monthly meetings open to all in area, regular matches fishing on Cornish waters. *Charges:* Seniors £12 per year, Juniors £6 per year, Family membership £20 (2 adults & 2 children).

Southwest Angling
Contact: Danny Mayers, 15b Gwavas Rd, Newlyn, Penzance, TR18 5NA, 07816 345471, *Water:* Guided shore fishing in south west Cornwall. *Charges:* £28 per person per 5 hour trip up to four people. 5th one is free. All tackle & bait is supplied. *Methods:* To teach tourists the art of sea fishing for sport & pleasure, and to keep safety in mind at all times.

Westward Casting Association
Contact: NFSA Head Office: 01364 644643,

PORTHLEVEN
The Starfish & The Danda
Contact: Porthleven Angling Centre, 01326 561885,

REDRUTH
Kenwyn SAC
Contact: Tim El-Balawi, 01637 872826, *Water:* Shore and boat fishing. Monthly shore competitions held around the Cornish coastline. Affiliated to CFSA. New members welcome. *Species:* All sea species apart from protected species. Minimum weight for all species. *Charges:* Gents £5, Ladies & OAPs £2.50, Juniors - no subscription fee. *Season:* All year. *Methods:* Sea and shore fishing. Two rods, three hooks maximum, no netting.

Redruth Sea Angling Association
Contact: Treve Opie (Hon Sec), 3 Colborne Avenue, Illogan, Redruth, TR16 4EB, 01209 842622, *Water:* Founded in 1962 by a group of anglers who regularly fished Porthowan beach which is not far from Redruth. HQ is the Redruth Albany Rugby Football Club at the bottom of Station Hill, Redruth. Meetings are held at 8pm on the first Monday of each month or the first Monday following a Bank Holiday. The club runs it's own competitions, social events, and takes part in team inter club competition. *Charges:* Subscriptions £7 for Seniors over 16 years and £2 for under 16 years.

ST AUSTELL
E.C.C. Ports S.A.C.
Contact: NFSA Head Office: 01364 644643,

Roche Angling Club
Contact: NFSA Head Office: 01364 644643,

ST IVES
Dolly Pentreath & The James Stevens (No.10)
Contact: Mike Laity, 01736 797269, *Mobile:* 07712 386162, *Season:* Easter - October.

St. Ives S.A.C.
Contact: NFSA Head Office: 01364 644643,

TORPOINT
Pot Black Sea Angling Club
Contact: NFSA Head Office: 01364 644643,

Raleigh S.A.C.
Contact: Mr S Marriott, 40 York Road, Torpoint, PL11 2LG, 01752 814582, *Water:* Established 25 years. New members welcome, youngsters encouraged. Fun club, with two competitions per month. Fishing from Saltash to Looe (shore and boat).

TRURO
Threemilestone Angling Club (Sea Fishing)
Contact: NFSA Head Office: 01364 644643,

A fine Cod for Kevin Legge. Picture by Wayne Thomas

CORNWALL

Where to Stay in Cornwall

Learning to fish with The South East Cornwall Taught Angling Society (SECTAS).

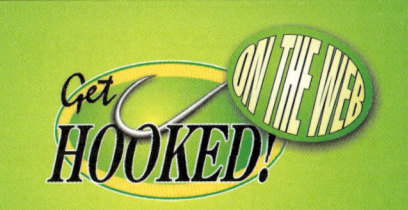

Get HOOKED! ON THE WEB

More accommodation available online at

www.gethooked.co.uk

Search online with the most comprehensive guide to fishing in the South West of England

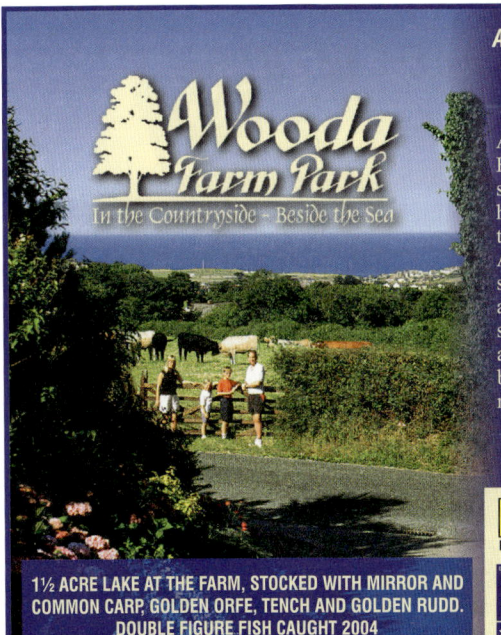

Wooda Farm Park
In the Countryside - Beside the Sea

1½ ACRE LAKE AT THE FARM, STOCKED WITH MIRROR AND COMMON CARP, GOLDEN ORFE, TENCH AND GOLDEN RUDD. DOUBLE FIGURE FISH CAUGHT 2004

Amidst some of the finest coastal scenery and sandy beaches on Devon and Cornwall's borders

A real Cornish welcome awaits you at Wooda Farm from the Colwill family. Enjoy a farm and seaside holiday with us. We offer luxury holiday homes and excellent facilities for touring and camping. Shop and laundry room. Activities include playground, coarse fishing, short golf course. In main season - indoor archery, tractor and trailer rides and clay pigeon shooting. Down at the farm there is a restaurant and beer garden. Also farmyard friends. Sandy beaches 1 1/4 miles. "Splash" indoor pool is nearby. Local village inn 5 mins walk

Upper Tamar Reservoir - South West's largest coarse fishery - within 5 miles

AA Premier Park

Write, telephone, fax or email for brochure and tariff to:
Mr. G.H. Colwill - Wooda Farm Park, Poughill, Bude, Cornwall. EX23 9HJ
Tel: 01288 352069 Fax: 01288 355258
Email: enquiries@wooda.co.uk
Website: www.wooda.co.uk

WHERE TO STAY

CORNWALL

"Trencreek Farm"
HEWASWATER, St AUSTELL, CORNWALL

Caravans, Bungalows and Camping

4 Small Coarse Fishing Lakes

Carp, Tench, Roach & Bream

One of Cornwall's Favourite Family Holiday Parks

BROCHURE 01726 882540
www.trencreek.co.uk

Avallon Lodges
Near Launceston, Cornwall

6 superb Norwegian Pine Lodges in idyllic surroundings within a working Dairy Farm

Well stocked lake with Carp to 25lb plus Roach, Bream and Tench

Booking - Hoseasons 01502 500 500

Haycorn Cottage

Comfortable cottage with original features and modern facilities, sleeping 3 - 5 people.
Conveniently situated for Angling 2000 venues, SW Lakes Trust waters and local game rivers.
Only 3/4 mile from Bake Lakes. Rural views. Use of games room and BBQ. Tuition and guided days available. Open all year for weekly lets or short breaks.

Trerulefoot, South East Cornwall
for further information
Tel: (01752) 851358 *or* E-mail: haycornholidays@yahoo.co.uk

WHITE ACRES
The No.1 Fishing Holiday

Set in over 160 acres of glorious Cornish Countryside and close to Newquay's eleven stunning beaches.
Short Breaks Available.

Call 0870 4585592
www.parkdeanholidays.co.uk

WHERE TO STAY

CORNWALL

Alasdare Lambert with a big River Exe Grayling.
Nick Hart Flyfishing.

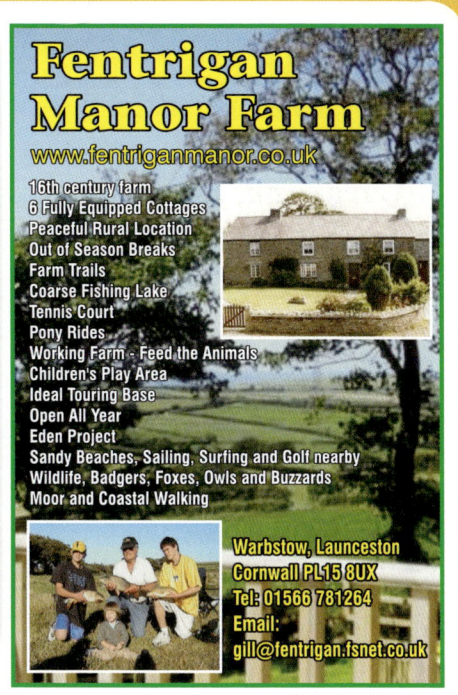

Fentrigan Manor Farm
www.fentriganmanor.co.uk

- 16th century farm
- 6 Fully Equipped Cottages
- Peaceful Rural Location
- Out of Season Breaks
- Farm Trails
- Coarse Fishing Lake
- Tennis Court
- Pony Rides
- Working Farm - Feed the Animals
- Children's Play Area
- Ideal Touring Base
- Open All Year
- Eden Project
- Sandy Beaches, Sailing, Surfing and Golf nearby
- Wildlife, Badgers, Foxes, Owls and Buzzards
- Moor and Coastal Walking

Warbstow, Launceston
Cornwall PL15 8UX
Tel: 01566 781264
Email:
gill@fentrigan.fsnet.co.uk

Trevella Park
CARAVAN & CAMPING PARK

LUXURY ROSE AWARD CARAVANS, SPACIOUSLY SITUATED

Family run with families in mind, located in beautiful parkland surroundings with modern spotless facilities and friendly service. Our park is renowned for its cleanliness and hygiene and we spare no effort to maintain this reputation.

There's plenty to do...
- Heated swimming & paddling pools
- Large adventure playground • Crazy Golf
- Television room showing FREE childrens videos
- Swings, see-saw, slide and roundabout • Pets corner
- Nature reserve and two FREE fishing lakes

Ideally situated to visit the **'EDEN PROJECT'**

CRANTOCK • NEWQUAY
• CORNWALL TR8 5EW
TEL: 01637 830308 **(24 HRS)** FAX: 01637 830155
EMAIL: trevellapark@aol.com
WEB: www.trevella.co.uk

WHERE TO STAY

THE GET HOOKED GUIDE

sw lakes trust
www.swlakestrust.org.uk

COARSE FISHING PERMIT AGENTS:
A: The Liscawn Inn, Crafthole, Nr Torpoint, Cornwall PL11 3BD Tel: (01503) 230863
B: Variety Sports, 23 Broad Street, Ilfracombe, Devon. Tel: (01271) 862039
C: Summerlands Tackle, 16-20 Nelson Road, Westward Ho!, Devon, EX39 1LF. Tel: (01237) 471291
D: The Kingfisher, 22 Castle St, Barnstaple, Devon, EX1 1DR. Tel: (01271) 344919
E: Bude Angling Supplies, 6 Queen Street, Bude, Cornwall. Tel: (01288) 353396
F: Bideford Tourist Information Centre, The Quay, Bideford, Devon Tel: (01237) 477676
G: Whiskers Pet Centre, 9 High Street, Torrington, Devon. Tel: (01805) 622859
H: Exeter Angling Centre, Smythen St, Exeter, Devon EX1 1BN Tel: (01392) 436404
I: Exmouth Tackle & Sports, 20 The Strand, Exmouth, Devon EX8 1AF. Tel: (01395) 274918
J: Budleigh News & Post Office, 23 High St, Budleigh Salterton, Devon EX9 6LD
K: Newtown Angling Centre, Newtown, Germoe, Penzance, Cornwall TR20 9AF. Tel: (01736) 763721
L: Sandy's Tackle, 7 Penryn St., Redruth, Cornwall TR15 2SP. Tel: (01209) 214877
M: Symons Ironmonger, Market Place, St Ives, Cornwall. TR26 1RZ. Tel: (01736) 796200
N: Heamoor Post Office, Heamoor, Gulval, Nr Penzance. TR18 3EJ. Tel: (01736) 65265
O: Parc-an-Creet Garage, Parc-an-Creet, St. Ives, Cornwall TR26 2ET . Tel: (01736) 795902

LOWER SLADE - Ilfracombe, Devon
Stocked with mirror and common carp to 20lb plus bream to 5lb plus, perch to 2.25lb, roach, rudd, gudgeon and pike.
Fishing Times: Open all year, 24 hours per day
Permits: From agents: B,C,D. Tel: (01288) 321262

JENNETTS - Bideford, Devon
Best fish: Common 22lb, Mirror 23lb. Produces quality bags of smaller carp, roach, and tench to float & pole.
Fishing Times: Open all year, 6.30am to 10pm.
Permits: From agents: C,D,E,F. Tel: (01288) 321262

DARRACOTT - Torrington, Devon
Roach up to 1lb. Mixed bags to 20lb plus of roach, rudd, bream, tench, perch to 2.25lb, carp to 15lb.
Fishing Times: Open all year, 24 hours per day.
Permits: From agents: C,D,E,F,G.
Tel: (01288) 321262
Seasons Permits - (01566) 771930

MELBURY - Bideford, Devon
Best mirror 27.75lb. Good mixed bags of roach, rudd, bream to pole, float and feeder.
Fishing Times: Open all year. 6.30am - 10pm.
Permits: From agents: C,D,E,F.
Limited season permits from our office.
Tel: (01288) 321262

Coarse Fishing

TRENCHFORD - Nr Christow, Devon
Pike weighing up to 30lbs.
Fishing Times: Open all year -
1 hour before sunrise to 1 hour after sunset.
Permits: Self service kiosk at Kennick Reservoir
Tel: (01647) 277587

UPPER TAMAR LAKE - Bude, Cornwall
Carp to 28lbs. 50lb plus bags of bream and 30lb bags of rudd. Regular competitions.
Fishing Times: Open all year, 24 hours a day.
Permits: From agents: C,D,E Tel: (01288) 321262

SQUABMOOR - Exmouth, Devon
Good head of carp to 25lb, roach to 3lb 2oz, Tench.
Fishing Times Open all year, 24 hours a day.
Permits: From agents: H,I,J
Season Permits from our office Tel: (01566) 771930

OLD MILL - Dartmouth, Devon
Carp to over 20lbs, roach to 2lb, tench and bream.
Fishing Times: Open all year, 24 hours a day.
Permits: Season permits from our office
Tel: (01566) 771930

PORTH - Newquay, Cornwall
Bags of 130lb plus have been caught. Best bream 9lb 2oz, tench 9lb 12oz. rudd to 3lb, roach to 1.25lb plus. Mixed bags of roach, rudd/skimmers to 60lb.
Fishing Times: Open all year, 24 hours a day
Permits: Agent L. Self service at Porth car park.
Season permits from our office. Great competition water. Tel: (01637) 877959

BOSCATHNOE - Penzance, Cornwall
Common, mirror and crucian carp with fish into the low 20lb range. Roach and bream also stocked.
Fishing Times: Open all year, 1 hour before sunrise to 1 hour after sunset. Season permits from our office.
Permits: From agents: K,L,M,N. Tel: (01579) 342366

ARGAL - Nr Falmouth, Cornwall
Carp to 20lb plus. Best fish: carp 26lb, bream 8lb 6oz, tench 8lb 8oz and eel 7lb, Pike over 30lb.
Fishing Times: Open all year, 24 hours per day.
Permits: From agents: K,L and self service unit at Argal Reservoir car park. Tel (01579) 342366
Season permits from our office (01566) 771930

BUSSOW - St Ives, Cornwall
Rudd to 1.5lb, roach bream and carp.
Fishing Times: Open all year, 24 hours a day.
Permits: From agents: K,L,M,O. Season permits from our office. Tel (01579) 342366

CRAFTHOLE - Nr. Torpoint, Devon.
Stocked with carp and tench.
Quality Carp up to 30lb.
Fishing Times: Open all year
1hr before sunrise to 1hr
after sunset.
Limited permits from agent A.
Season permits from our
office (01566) 7719305

sw lakes trust

South West Lakes Trust Fisheries

The South West Lakes Trust is an independent charity formed to promote and enhance sustainable recreation, access and nature conservation on and around inland waters in the South West of England for the benefit of the general public.

The Trust continues with its drive to introduce the sport to all newcomers, from children to pensioners. We intend to follow up on last year's successful introductory and training days in various aspects of coarse angling, (including our specialist pike and carp days), with the help of the E.A., N.F.A. accredited instructors, and local specialists. Juniors under the age of 12 years will again be able to fish for free (providing they are accompanied by an authorised adult angler). Fly fishing tuition and introductory days for both adults and juniors will be available at Wimbleball, Kennick, and sites in Cornwall, all run by qualified professional instructors, throughout the season. All aspects of the sport will be covered, as will the promotion of a responsible and healthy interest in the environment. We will also be building on the success of last year's series of Introductory Fly Fishing Days run in conjunction with the Environment Agency. These were held at Kennick and proved to be very popular, so this year we intend to introduce a 'follow-on' intermediate day. Juniors again will be encouraged to fish for trout – the parent/child ticket allows the youngster to fish for free and share the parent's bag limit. In conjunction with professionals throughout the region, there will again be a series of summer schools for youngsters at different fisheries.

The Trust is keen to encourage club members and other keen anglers to put something back into their sport, and to this end will again be offering the opportunity to gain the Joint Angling Governing Bodies recognised coaching qualification scheme to various levels in both coarse and game angling.

The 'Peninsula Classic' fly fishing bank competition will be held at Kennick on the 22nd May, in which there will be a special junior prizes category. The 'Wimbleball 2000' open pairs boat competition will be held on 25th September. The Snowbee / South West Lakes Trust bank team competition (club teams of four) has now become established as a firm favourite in the region, and will again be held at Siblyback - it will be on 2nd July, and this year will be an afternoon / evening competition.

The Trust will be joining forces with the West Country Rivers Trust and The Environment Agency to promote the sport during National Angling Week – there will be a family angling day at Siblyback to start the week on 20th August – everybody is welcome to come along and find out how to get started, how to improve techniques, or just meet other anglers (more information can be obtained from the Environment Agency). The week will end with an adult's fly fishing event at the brand new angling and watersports centre at Stithians (the centre will be holding a grand opening on 8th May).

A group of keen volunteers have been helping the Trust to make various improvements to the fishery at Argal over the winter, starting with a blitz on litter, and helping with access and swim improvements. Fish continue to thrive at Argal, with a number of pike (in excess of 30lb) and carp (to 40lb) being landed last season, as well as some excellent double figure bream. Porth and Upper Tamar continue to enjoy the reputation as first class large competition venues, and may be booked throughout the season. 2005 will see the launch of a new 'Wheely Boat' at Roadford, which will make the water accessible to a number of different users including anglers.

The Trust remains committed to angling and customer care, and welcomes all comments to help us provide what the angler really wants.

For further information, including instruction and competition information, please contact:
**Chris Hall, Head of Fisheries
on 01566 771930
Or E-mail: chall@swlakestrust.org.uk
Or visit our website:
www.swlakestrust.org.uk**

THE GET HOOKED GUIDE

swlakestrust
Trout Fishing

www.swlakestrust.org.uk

PREMIER RAINBOW FISHERIES
KENNICK - Nr Christow, Devon.
Permits: Self Service Kiosk
Season: 25 March - 31 October
Best Flies: Black Gnat/Montana/Damsel Nymph
Biggest Fish 1997: 10lb 14oz Rainbow.
Information: (01647) 277587
WIMBLEBALL LAKE - Nr Dulverton, Somerset.
Permits: Self Service at Hill Farm Barn
Season: 25 March - 31 October
Best Flies: Montana/Soldier Palmer/Buzzer.
Biggest Fish: 10lb 12oz Rainbow.
Information: Office hours (01398) 371372
SIBLYBACK LAKE - Nr Liskeard, Cornwall.
Permits: Self Service Kiosk at Watersports Centre
Season: 25 March - 31 October
Best Flies: Viva/Black & Peacock/Montana
Information: Ranger (01579) 342366

PREMIER BROWN TROUT FISHERY
ROADFORD - Nr Okehampton, Devon.
Permits: Angling and Watersports Centre at Lower Goodacre.
Season: 25 March - 12 October
Biggest Fish: 8lb 4oz Brown.
Information: (01409) 211514

INTERMEDIATE RAINBOW TROUT
STITHIANS - Nr Redruth, Cornwall.
Permits:
Stithians Watersports Centre (01209) 860301.
Sandy's Store, 7 Penryn St, Redruth (01209) 214877
Season: 15 March - 12 October
Information: Ranger (01579) 342366
WISTLANDPOUND - Nr Sth Molton, Devon.
Permits:
Post Office in Challacombe (01598) 763229.
The Kingfisher, Barnstaple (01271) 344919.
Calvert Trust, Wistlandpound (01598) 763221
Lyndale News, Combe Martin (01271) 883283.
Variety Sports, Ilfracombe (01271) 862039.
Season: 15 March - 12 October
Information: Ranger (01288) 321262

LOW COST RAINBOW & BROWN
BURRATOR - Nr Yelverton, Devon.
Permits: Esso Garage, Yelverton.
Season: 15 March - 12 October
Information: (01566) 771930
COLLIFORD LAKE - Nr Bodmin, Cornwall.
Permits: Colliford Tavern.
Season: 15 March - 12 October
Information: Ranger (01579) 342366
FERNWORTHY LAKE - Nr Chagford, Devon.
Permits: Self Service Kiosk
Season: 1 April - 12 October
Best Flies: Black Gnat/Invicta/G&H Sedge
Information: (01566) 771930

FREE TROUT FISHING
MELDON - Nr Okehampton, Devon.
Free to holders of a valid E.A. Rod Licence and is zoned into spinning, bait and fly.
Season: 15 March - 12 October
AVON DAM - South Brent, Devon.
Angling by spinning, fly or bait and is free to valid E.A. licence holders.
Season: 15 March - 12 October
VENFORD - Nr Ashburton, Devon.
Free to holders of valid E.A. Rod Licence and can be fished by spinning, bubble float and bait.
Season: 15 March - 12 October.
CROWDY RESERVOIR - Nr Camelford, Cornwall.
Free to holders of valid E.A. Rod Licence.
Season: 15 March - 12 October.

swlakestrust

THE GET HOOKED GUIDE

Angling 2000

Flexible day permits for quality fishing on Westcountry Rivers and Pools

New for 2005

- **New and extended beats on the Fal, Camel, Tamar and Torridge catchments**
- **Revised token charges - even better value!**

Fish for wild salmon, seatrout, trout and grayling in unrivalled surroundings

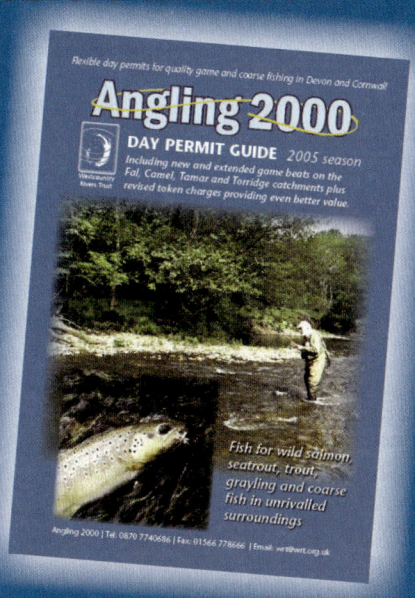

A total of 35 beats from Truro to Tiverton

Vouchers purchased from Angling 2000 are also valid on all Wye & Usk Foundation 'Passport' beats.

www.angling2000.org.uk

One — The Objective One Partnership for Cornwall and Scilly

Objective One is part-funded by the European Union

For further details and your FREE copy of the Angling 2000 booklet for this season please contact

Westcountry Rivers Trust, 10 Exeter Street, Launceston, Cornwall PL15 9EQ

Telephone: 0870 7740686   Email: martin@wrt.org.uk

The Trust promotes Game Angling in Cornwall...

David Haines
Director - Westcountry Rivers Trust

The rivers of Cornwall are renowned for their spectacular scenery, captivating energy and abundant flora and fauna. Rivers such as the Tamar, Camel and Fowey offer a variety of excellent game angling opportunities with fishing for wild brown trout, salmon, sea trout, and grayling. Indeed, as the increase in both visiting anglers and press coverage shows, Cornwall is gaining a reputation as a leading UK angling destination.

By taking an active role in these fisheries, anglers contribute to the protection of our streams, rivers and the wider environment. It is also apparent that, as a sport, angling provides significant socio-economic benefits. The Environment Agency's report 'Our Nations Fisheries' notes that more people go fishing than any other sport with 4 million anglers contributing over £3 billion to the UK economy every year. Recreational angling is increasingly important to many rural communities in the Westcountry. Anglers who fish for salmonids bring sustainable employment and provide income to hotels, B & B's, restaurants, tackle shops and a host of other local businesses. Importantly, angling helps to extend the tourist season and in Cornwall you can fish from March through to December.

The Westcountry Rivers Trust is the UK partner in an exciting new project called SALAR which is broadly aimed at promoting sustainable angling tourism. This two-year project is funded through the EU Interreg IIIB programme and includes partners from the regions of Asturias and Cantabria in Spain, Brittany in France and South West Ireland. Through the sharing of knowledge and experiences the partnership aims to identify common techniques for the sustainable management of salmonid rivers. In addition, the project provides a good opportunity to develop long-term angling tourism links between these regions.

Promoting Cornwall

The project generally aims to raise awareness of the excellent game fishing available in Cornwall whilst ensuring that the infrastructure is in place to make the fishing experience (and hence holiday) truly memorable. To this end, the Trust is developing a comprehensive map-based website which will include information on individual fishing beats, local angling clubs, tackle shops and links to accommodation providers. The project also aims to train guides who can assist visiting anglers and their families when 'out on the river'. In this way we hope to provide a complete game angling resource for both UK and overseas visitors coming to the region.

Increasing Participation

Introducing new people to angling is essential for the long-term development of this fantastic sport. The Trust is running a series of 'angling starter days' for both children and adults which aim to teach basic fly-fishing skills including aspects such as entomology and fly-tying. Increasing local interest and participation in angling will provide knock-on benefits to fisheries, angling clubs and the region as a whole.

Opportunities

The SALAR project presents a good opportunity to help businesses create new (and enhance existing) links to angling. WRT will be working with accommodation providers (B & B's etc) to help tailor their marketing and promotional activities in order to attract anglers. In addition, WRT is well placed to offer advice and support for farmers and landowners wishing to diversify. This may include identifying opportunities to increase fishing potential along rivers, installing new fishing ponds or developing accommodation based around angling. The success of schemes such as Angling 2000 highlights how, with effective marketing, stretches of river that were once un-fished can now be accessed by local and visiting anglers alike.

Management

It is fundamental that game angling is promoted in a fashion that is environmentally, so-

THE GET HOOKED GUIDE

cially and economically sustainable. Therefore, the project will encompass several desk based studies; the first, aims to evaluate the economic importance of game angling in the region and the second will compare the different fishery management techniques used across the partner regions.

Genetics

Other areas that the Trust is currently working include the ASAP project, an EU-wide programme focusing on developing a genetic database to allow salmon which are caught in the high sea fishery to be identified and linked to a natal river. This in turn allows collapsing stocks to be protected by perhaps levying a tax on at risk stocks. In addition, it will also provide valuable data pertaining to the eternal question, where do all the salmon go on their migratory route…

Partners of the ASAP project combined with other scientists from Europe, the US and Canada to form a consortium which met at a meeting convened in West Virginia and kindly hosted by the US Geological Service in September They discussed a range of issues including standardisation of techniques, and the commissioning of fundraising efforts to further develop this work.

The ultimate aim is to establish a network of scientists around the world who can share and benefit from each others work in this field, thus reducing duplication and enhancing data sets. It was agreed that Dr Bright of the Westcountry Rivers Trust and lead partner of ASAP would lead this initiative, closely supported by others from both Europe and the US.

Plans

Over the next 2 to 3 years, the network will collect samples from the majority of salmon rivers on the Western Atlantic coast of Europe and the Eastern seaboard of the US and Canada to generate a database of genetic identities. This database will form the basis of studies on:

- mixed stock fishers;
- the impact of past stocking;
- economic inequalities of fishing methods;
- the migration routes and timing of populations;

The reason for the scale of the study is that we must ensure that when salmon are sampled at sea, we stand a good chance of getting a fish from a genetically typed population. The more genetically typed populations there are, the higher the probability of successful assignment and the more information we have for management. Therefore this project and this consortium are most probably the most significant advance in fisheries per se for the last 50 years. The Trust is delighted to be involved in this work and we look forward to really impacting on salmon stocks not just in terms of scientific advance, but also by linking the science with policy via the politicians of the various countries. For once we really do have the opportunity to deal with this exploitation, and attach some sort of reward or penalty to the fish that are taken. We should seize this opportunity with both hands and give these scientists our full support.

Westcountry Rivers Trust

THE GET HOOKED GUIDE

The River Camel

Jon Evans
Secretary: Camel Fisheries Association

The River Camel rises on Bodmin Moor and reaches the sea about thirty miles later at Padstow on the North Cornwall coast. The Camel has been fished for salmon and sea trout for centuries and the first royal charter was granted in 1199. Records show that in 1750 rights were available on payment of a fee to the Duke of Cornwall to take salmon by use of barbed spears. Needless to say, these rights have now been revoked.

There are four main tributaries, the Allen, the Ruthern, the de Lank and the Stannon and these provide wonderful nursery and spawning water. There are also countless small streams offering safe havens for sea trout and occasionally salmon. The Bodmin Anglers Association has worked extremely hard over the years to ensure that the upper reaches of this beautiful river are largely designated as sanctuary areas which should not be fished.

The Camel has a reputation for good runs of both species but things are not what they were. Even so, during the 2003 season, there were more than twice as many salmon caught on the Camel as any other river in the South West. There was also an excellent run of sea trout. In 2002, a salmon of 25lb was taken at Boscarne and this year, a 19lb hen fish was donated to the hatchery. There are about twelve miles of fishable water and most is in the hands of the two main clubs, the Bodmin Anglers Association and the Wadebridge and District Angling Association. There are also a number of private riparians and a few private fisheries. The whole river and many of the tributaries are designated as SSSI and cSAC with the Atlantic Salmon and the Otter the two principal species; and the anglers welcome both.

The Camel Fisheries Association has been formed by the clubs and the private riparians to try to ensure, with the Environment Agency and English Nature, that the river stays in good heart, and provides a self sustaining environment, with a range of habitats, as well as excellent sport for the anglers. Most of the Camel runs through wooded valleys and farmland and this conditions the ways in which the river can be fished. Below Polbrock, the river is tidal and can be fished as far downstream as Wadebridge. Below this, you need a boat or an interest in fly fishing for Bass.

Most people fish the river with a spinner or worm, although both clubs have beats which are suitable for fly fishing and many sea trout are taken at night. There are also a number of salmon taken on fly on one of the private fisheries and on the tidal water where the trees have thinned out.

The season opens on May 1. This began many years ago so that kelts were not caught during the early weeks. A few spring fish are taken in May and June but the real sport at this time of year is with the early sea trout. Most seasons, one or two fish of eight or nine pounds, as well as a number in the 4lb class, will be caught in late May or June either on a worm or fly at night.

The main run of sea trout, school peal, will come in early July, but there will always be a number of good peal mixed in with the smaller fish of three quarters to a pound. There is a voluntary agreement that all peal will be returned after the end of August for conservation reasons.

The salmon run tends to get under way in late August or September. Grilse around the five pound mark start to come off the tidal water and if there is rain, they push on up through the lower stretches to Tresarrett and beyond. The best of the season, and the bigger fish, comes in October and the season ends on December 15. Throughout the winter months, fish of any size from a 4lb grilse to a 25lb. multi sea winter fish can be taken.

The Camel Fisheries Association runs a salmon restocking programme. This was started five years ago by the Secretary and another member of the Bodmin club who built a hatchery on the Clerkenwater Stream. Since 2003, the Wainsford hatchery on the River Fowey has provided the support for the Camel as well as the Fowey. In 2004, we returned 45,000 fry to the river. We are limited to 50,000 fry by the agreement with the Environment Agency and English Nature and expect to reach this during the 2004/5 season. The catch and release rates for both salmon and sea trout are rising each year, and although the river is currently reaching its spawning target there is a lot of local effort to ensure that we do not endanger the future of our sport. We have concentrated on habitat improvement and the restocking programme and hope to use genetic markers to allow us to demonstrate the success of our work.

We have also used the evidence from the broodstock programme to try to change some angling practices. Everyone will be aware of the danger of using treble hooks on spinning lures and each year we have a few fish damaged by these very large hooks. Of more significance is the work we have done on worming hooks. We have found that the traditional way of simply cutting the line when the fish is gut hooked in the belief that the fish will come to no harm and go on and spawn naturally is not the case. In 2003, all our deep hooked fish in the hatchery died before they could be stripped. We no longer take gut hooked fish for the hatchery and are trying to persuade anglers that the circle hooks which have been used by long line fishermen for years are effective for salmon. So far this year, the anglers using circle hooks have not lost a fish and the fish usually hook themselves in the scissors or the lip. Additionally, the eye of the hook is outside the mouth and this makes unhooking very easy.

These exciting programmes have re-energised our clubs and changed attitudes to conservation. Our efforts have added to the enjoyment of fishing this lovely river.

Vranch House School
FLY FISHING CHARITY CHALLENGE 2005
for children with cerebral palsy & all children with physical difficulties

Pairs of anglers are invited to enter the 14th Fly Fishing Charity Challenge to raise funds for children with cerebral palsy at Vranch House School & Centre, Exeter.

Heats and semi finals will take place from March to September at Bellbrook Valley, Kennick, Roadford, Stithians, Tavistock, Temple, Tree Meadow and Watercress. The semi-finals are at Bellbrook, Tree Meadow & Watercress and and the finals are at Tavistock.

The prize bag is £3,000. Prizes including lines, day tickets, garden statues and hooks. Entry is free provided the minimum sponsorship of £20 per person is raised. (Tavistock is £100 minimum)

Anglers who wish to enter please contact the fisheries or Sue Gould, Marketing Manager of Vranch House: Tel/fax Exeter 01392 873543 email gould@vranchhouse.org

Heat dates

Stithians , Redruth
  01209 821431   Sun 10 April
Kennick Reservoir, Bovey Tracey
  01626 332504   Sun 1 May
Bellbrook Valley, Tiverton
  01398 351292   Sun 8 May
Watercress, Chudleigh
  01626 852168   Sun 15 May
Tree Meadow, Hayle
  01736 850899   Sun 3 July
Temple, Bodmin
  01208 821730   Sun 26 June
Tavistock Trout, Tavistock
  01822 615441   Sun 4 Sept
Roadford Lake, Okehampton
  01392 873543   Sun TBA

The South West Federation of Fly Fishers

The South West Federation of Fly Fishers belongs to the Confederation of English Fly Fishers. The Confederation is, amongst other things, responsible for running National and International Fly Fishing Teams and Competitions. The grassroots of all the National and International Competitions are the Regional Eliminators run by Federations all over the Country.

The South West Federation runs Eliminators at Chew Valley Lake. This years dates are as follows:

FIRST ELIMINATOR: SUN 24 APRIL
SECOND ELIMINATOR: SUN 29 MAY
FINAL ELIMINATOR: SUN 19 JUNE

Competitors can ONLY enter ONE of the first two eliminators and if successful would qualify for the Final Eliminator. Thirty competitors compete in the Final Eliminator. We expect there to be approximately 12 places available in 2005 for the Loch Style National which will take place at Rutland Water on Saturday Sept 24th.

ELIGIBILITY

Anyone can enter provided that they are over 18 years of age, and have been domiciled in ENGLAND for 3 years.

Competitors can ONLY enter eliminators in ONE Region in any one year. Anyone who has previously fished at International Level for another Country is NOT eligible to fish.

If you are interested in competitive Fly Fishing, with the chance to fish for England, write to me at the address below or give me a ring.
J.A. Loud,
153/155 East Street,
Bedminster,
BRISTOL BS3 4EJ
Tel (Daytime) 0117 9872050
Tel (Evenings) 0117 9232166

West Country Federation of Fly Fishers

Fish for England by Lake and River

The WCFFF provides eligible adults with a yearly chance to fly fish for England. Qualifiers from Devon and Cornwall compete in the National Championships aiming to be in England's international squad for the following year. The competitions are against Ireland, Scotland and Wales in events called the Home Internationals. This is fishing to International Rules on either rivers or by boat on stillwaters.

2005 Rivers eliminator:
River Teign
Sunday 24 April.

2005 Loch Style eliminator:
Wimbleball Lake
Sunday 15 May.

Both eliminators are routes into England's European and World Teams.

Put your name on the mailing lists for the eliminators!

Contact:
Keith Gollop (Chairman WCFFF),
2 Upcott Mead Road,
Bakers Hill,
Tiverton,
Devon
EX16 5HX.
Tel: 01884 256544

DEVON

RIVER FISHING

STILLWATER COARSE

STILLWATER TROUT

SEA FISHING

WHERE TO STAY

Devon Game Road Directions

30. Angling 2000 (Game & Coarse)
35 beats on the Tamar, Fal, Taw, Torridge & Camel catchments plus 3 coarse fishing lakes. Please telephone 0870 77 40686.

31. Arundell Arms Hotel
Leave the A30 Dual Carriageway east of Launceston and follow signs for Lifton. The Arundell Arms is in the centre of the Village. Tel: 01566 784666.

32. Avon Dam
South West Lakes Trust fisheries are well signposted from major roads. Tel: 01822 855700.

33. Bellbrook Valley Trout Fishery
From Tiverton roundabout on A361 head towards Barnstaple. Take 3rd right (6 miles) signposted Bellbrook & Spurway. Continue down lane for 2 miles then sharp right signed "To the fishery" then 200yds on the right. From Oakford leave uphill, bear left at Pinkworthy Post (signposted Rackenford). Follow lane down hill, cross stream then fork left. Fishery 200yds on right. Tel: 01398 351292.

34. Blakewell Fishery
Take A39 from Barnstaple towards Lynton. 1.5 miles from Barnstaple turn left on to B3230 and follow signs to the fishery. Tel: 01271 344533.

35. Bridge House Hotel
The fishing is located just upstream of Oakford Bridge on the A396 approx. 15 miles from junction 27 on the M5. The Bridge House Hotel is in Bampton on the B3227 (A361 to Tiverton - A396 to Bampton). Please phone 01398 331298.

36. Buckfastleigh
South West Lakes Trust fisheries are well signposted from major roads. Tel: 01566 771930.

37. Burrator
South West Lakes Trust fisheries are well signposted from major roads. Tel: 01822 855700.

38. Clinton Arms
Take the Bideford to Torrington road (A386) and approx. 5.5 miles from Bideford there is a sign to Tarka Trail. Turn left and park outside the Puffing Billy. (Car park is council owned and free.) Fishing is to the right, (with Puffing Billy behind you.) Maps available at the Clinton Arms. Tel: 01805 623379.

39. Devon, Wiltshire & UK Fly Fishing School
Please telephone 01626 866532

40. Environment Agency Fisheries
Watersmeet & Glenthorne Fisheries. Directions are supplied with permits.

41. Fernworthy
South West Lakes Trust fisheries are well signposted from major roads. Tel: 01647 277587.

42. Fox & Hounds Country Hotel
At Eggesford on the A377 midway between Exeter and Barnstaple. Tel: 01769 580345.

43. Half Moon Hotel
Sheepwash lies 1 mile North of Highampton (A3072) between Hatherleigh & Holsworthy. Tel: 01409 231376.

44. Hayrish Farm
Please call Gill or David on 020 7256 9013 or 07736 628971.

45. Helemoor Fishery & Camping (Coarse & Game)
From centre of Moretonhampstead turn left opposite Co-op signed North Bovey. Take next left past playing field where you will see our sign. Tel 01647 440338

46. Highampton Lakes (Coarse & Game)
We are approx 1.5 miles south of the village of Highampton heading for Northlew. Tel: 01409 231216.

47. Hollies Trout Farm (Coarse & Game)
Situated near Dunkeswell halfway between Honiton and Cullompton. From Cullompton (M5 junction 28) take the A373 towards Honiton. After passing The Keepers Cottage (pub) on the right hand side, take the next turning on the left. Follow this road past Forest Glade (caravan park) on the left. At the staggered crossroads turn right then left past Westcott Farm (christian holiday centre) into Sheldon. From the top end of Honiton follow signs for Dunkeswell and Wolford Chapel. Pass Wolford Chapel on the left and take next turning on the left, signposted to Sheldon. Continue following signs for Sheldon and enter the village. Hollies Trout Farm is signposted from the main road - drive down the concrete road for a quarter of a mile to the bottom of the hill. Please note that some of the roads are narrow so do not assume you have gone the wrong way. Please telephone 0845 2267714 if you get lost.

48. Kennick
South West Lakes Trust fisheries are well signposted from major roads. Tel: 01647 277587.

49. Lower Bruckland Trout Fishery
Turn left at brown sign into Bruckland Lane off A3052. 3/4 mile east of Colyford and 70 yards after Bosshill. Tel: 01297 552861 Mobile 07721 429077.

50. Meldon
South West Lakes Trust fisheries are well signposted from major roads. Tel: 01822 855700.

51. Nick Hart Fly Fishing
J27 from M5. A361 on to A396 Tel: 01398 331660 or 07971 198559.

52. Rising Sun Inn
The Rising Sun Inn is on the A377 opposite T-junction with B3227 to South Molton. Tel: 01769 560447.

53. Roadford
South West Lakes Trust fisheries are well signposted from major roads. Tel: 01409 211514.

54. Robert Jones Fly Fishing
Please telephone 07020 902 090.

55. Southwood Fishery
From Barnstaple head for Bratton Fleming. Turn right at Bratton Cross, continue for approx 1/2 mile, turn left into fishery when you see our sign and continue down lane. Tel 01271 343608 or 01271 344919.

56. Tavistock Trout Fishery
Entrance on A386 one mile from Tavistock. Tel: 01822 615441.

Devon Coarse Road Directions

57. Valley Springs (Coarse & Game)
Half a mile from Cider Press, follow official tourist signs from Frogmore or Totnes Road. Tel: 01548 531574.

58. Venford
South West Lakes Trust fisheries are well signposted from major roads. Tel: 01566 771930.

59. Wiscombe Park Fishery (Game & Coarse)
Leave A30 at Honiton, take A375 towards Sidmouth, turn left at the Hare and Hounds cross roads towards Seaton, after 3 miles turn left towards Blackbury Camp, fishery signposted on the left. Tel: 01404 871474.

60. Wistlandpound
South West Lakes Trust fisheries are well signposted from major roads. Tel: 01398 371372.

61. Bickerton Farm Fishery
Please telephone 01548 511220 for road directions.

62. Clawford Vineyard
Take A388 from Holsworthy to Launceston. Turn left at crossroads in Clawton. After 2.5 miles turn left at T junction. Clawford is a further 0.6 miles on left. Tel: 01409 254177 or 07786 332332.

63. Cofton Country Holiday Park
From Junction 30, M5 Exeter, take A379 signed Dawlish. Park is on the left half mile after small harbour village of Cockwood. Tel: 01626 890111.

Only advertisers are located on this map.

DEVON ROAD DIRECTIONS

64. Coombe Water Fisheries
Half a mile from Kingsbridge on the B3210 road to Loddiswell. Tel: 01548 852038.

65. Coombelands Coarse Fishery
Only 15 mins from junction 28 M5. Approx. 3.5 mls from Tiverton, 0.75 mls from Butterleigh on the Silverton Rd, 3.5 mls from Cullompton, 1ml from Bunniford Cross on the Silverton Rd and 3 mls from Silverton on the Butterleigh Rd. Tel: 01884 32320.

66. Cranford Inn & Holiday Cottages
Please telephone 01805 624697 for directions.

67. Creedy Lakes
Travelling south down the M5 exit at junction 27. From Tiverton take the A3072 Exeter/Crediton road. At Bickleigh bear right towards Crediton. At Crediton town sign turn right. Follow blue and white fishery signs. Tel: 01363 772684.

68. Darracott
South West Lakes Trust fisheries are well signposted from major roads. Tel: 01409 211514.

69. Darts Farm
Leave M5 at junction 30. Follow signs to Exmouth (A376). After 2 miles follow brown tourist signs to Darts Farm Shopping Village.Tel: 01392 875587.

70. East Moore Farm Fishery
Please Tel: 01364 73276 or mobile 07976 559090.

71. Exeter & District Angling Association
Please Tel: 07970 483913 or enquire in local Tackle Shops.

72. Goodiford Mill Fishery (Coarse & Game)
From Cullompton take the Honiton road, continue for over a mile past Horns cross. Turn left at signpost for Wressing, Goodiford, Dead lane. Right at end of lane, fishery on left. Tel: 01884 266233.

73. Jennetts
South West Lakes Trust fisheries are well signposted from major roads. Tel: 01409 211514.

74. Kingslake Fishing Holidays
From Exeter at end of M5 take A30 to Okehampton, in the centre of Okehampton at the lights, turn right onto A386 to Hatherleigh. At Hatherleigh (7 miles) take left onto A3072 Holsworthy/Bude. Travel 7 miles then turn left at sign 'Chilla 2 miles' Kingslake is 0.75 miles along this road on left. Tel: 01409 231401.

75. Little Allers
From Exeter: Take Wrangaton Cross exit off A38, take 2nd road on left. From Plymouth: Take Ivybridge exit off A38. Go through Ivybridge to Wrangaton. Turn right and take 2nd road on left. Tel: 01364 72563.

76. Little Comfort Farm
From Junction 27 of M5 take A361 to Barnstaple. Leave Barnstaple on A361 to Braunton, pass through Braunton still on A361 towards Ilfracombe. Pass through Knowle village on A361. After 2/3 mile turn right towards Halsinger at Heddon Mills Cross. Proceed 1.8 miles turning left at the 2nd crossroads, then left again after a short distance. Continue for one mile down winding lane over small bridge and take 2nd entrance into Little Comfort Farm. Tel: 01271 812214.

77. Lower Hollacombe Fishery
Please telephone 01363 84331 for directions.

78. Lower Slade
South West Lakes Trust fisheries are well signposted from major roads. Tel: 01398 371272.

79. Luccombes Coarse Fishery
From Exminster, enter Exminster from Exeter on A379, pass the shops on right and Victory Hall on left, take first right into Days Pottels Lane, then next left into Towsington Lane, the fishery is situated approx. 0.5 mile on the left. Look out for our Brown Tourist sign. Tel: 01392 832858.

80. Malston Mill Farm
Follow A38 towards Plymouth. On passing Ashburton take next exit marked Totnes and Kingsbridge. Follow River Dart along A384. On reaching Totnes turn right at traffic lights onto A381 signed Kingsbridge. Continue approx 12 miles. On entering Kingsbridge exit on the Dartmouth road onto the A379. Follow this road for approx 1 mile along the estuary. At the bridge over the estuary turn left (Do not go over the bridge) Continue for exactly 2 miles. You will go through the hamlet of Bearscombe. After 2 miles you reach top of a hill. At crossroads see signpost Malston Mill, turn left. Proceed to bottom of this no through road approx 0.25 miles. Malston Mill Farm is last property on the right. Tel: 01548 852518.

81. Melbury
South West Lakes Trust fisheries are well signposted from major roads. Tel: 01409 211514.

82. Millhayes Fishery
2 miles from junction 28 (M5) on the A373 towards Honiton turn left at Post Cross to Kentisbeare. 1 mile to village centre, turn right at Post Office and go down hill for 300yds, turn right at sign for Millhayes. Tel: 01884 266412.

83. Minnows Touring Caravan Park
From the North or South exit M5 at junction 27 onto A361 signposted Tiverton. After about 600 yards take first exit signposted Sampford Peverell. Turn right at next roundabout, cross bridge over A361. Straight across at next roundabout signposted Holcombe Rogus. Site is on left. From N. Devon on the A361 - go to end of A361 to junction 27 of the M5. Go all the way round and return back onto the A361. Then follow the above directions. Tel: 01884 821770.

84. Newberry Farm
On A399 western edge of Combe Martin village. Tel: 01271 882334.

85. Oaktree Carp Farm & Fishery
From Barnstaple take the A361 to Newtown. Left onto B3227 Bampton Road for 2.5 miles and left at fishery signpost. Down hill and entrance signposted on right. From M5 junction 27 take A361 to Newtown, then as above. Tel: 01398 341568.

86. Old Mill
South West Lakes Trust fisheries are well signposted from major roads. Tel: 01566 771930.

87. Salmonhutch Fishery
A377 to Crediton, turn left after Shell Garage, follow road signed Tedburn St Mary for 1.5 miles, right at junction marked Uton, follow fishery signs. Tel: 01363 772749.

88. South View Farm Fishery
From Bristol follow M5 onto A38. After 1.5 miles turn off into Kennford. Continue through village following Dunchideock signs until Shillingford signs are seen. Follow Shillingford signs. Entrance to fishery on left at sharp bend before village. From Plymouth turn left off A38 following Dunchideock until sign for Clapham is seen on right heading down the hill. At Clapham follow signs for Shillingford. From Exeter follow signs

DEVON ROAD DIRECTIONS

Dave Pilkington fishing Arundell Arms water on the Tamar below Polson Bridge.

THE Wild Trout TRUST
Protecting and Enhancing the Stocks of Wild Trout in the rivers of the South West.
If you wish to find out more about the Wild Trout Trust, send for details to:
The Wild Trout Trust, PO Box 120, Waterlooville PO8 0DG
Tel: 023 9257 0985   Email: office@wildtrout.org
www.wildtrout.org

Get HOOKED! ON THE WEB
Fully searchable Fisheries Directory - over 800 Entries!
www.gethooked.co.uk

to Alphington then Shillingford St. George. Fishery on right after village. Tel: 01392 833694.

89. South West Lakes Angling Association
Please telephone 01884 256721.

90. Spires Lakes
On the A3072 Holiday Route (HR) from Crediton. Turn right at Newlands Cross towards Sampford Courtney. Spires Lakes are on the left after approx. 0.5 mile. Tel: 01837 82499.

91. Squabmoor
South West Lakes Trust fisheries are well signposted from major roads. Tel: 01566 771930.

92. Stafford Moor Country Park
Clearly signposted on the A3124, 3 miles North of Winkleigh, 9 miles South of Torrington. Tel: 01805 804360.

93. Sunridge Fishing Lodge
Travelling west on A38, just after South Brent take slip road for Ugborough & Ermington, turn left, travel 2 miles to crossroads, turn right onto B3210, continue 3 miles to T junction, turn right onto A379 towards Plymouth, continue 2 miles to second cross roads (just before garage) and turn right. Travel 1 mile and you will find Sunridge Nurseries on left. Lodge and lake situated within grounds. Tel: 01752 880438.

94. Tottiford
South West Lakes Trust fisheries are well signposted from major roads. Tel: 01647 277587.

95. Town Parks Coarse Fishing Centre
From Paignton take the A385 towards Totnes. Look for signs to Town Parks, approx 2.5 miles on the right. Tel: 01803 523133 or 07800 600535.

96. Trenchford
South West Lakes Trust fisheries are well signposted from major roads. Tel: 01647 277587.

97. Upham Farm Carp Ponds
From J30 on M5, take A3052 signposted Sidmouth. After approx 4 miles, after passing White Horse Inn on right, sign to fishery will be seen on left. Turn left and after 700 yds fishery will be found on left hand side. Tel: 01395 232247.

98. Upton Lakes Fishing Holidays
From Junction 28 of the M5 head towards Cullompton, then turn left towards Broadclyst, follow the main street, through the town and take left turning (Meadow lane) signposted Sports centre. Next T-junction turn right and cross over the motorway bridge. Take next left signposted Upton lakes, take first left along lane. Tel: 07830 199690.

99. Week Farm
From Exeter bypass Okehampton, leave A30 dual carriageway at Sourton junction. At end of sliproad cross A386 at staggered crossroad (signposted Bridestowe). Week signpost on right after 1.5 miles (bottom of hill left 0.5 mile). Or, from Bridestowe village turn right towards Okehampton, pass garage on left & take next left, Week is 0.75 mile. Tel: 01837 861221.

100. West Pitt Farm Fishery
Junction 27 off M5, take Barnstaple signed dual way, almost immediately exit signed to Sampford Peverell. Right at mini roundabout, straight over second roundabout. Turn left signed to Whitnage, next right, then at Pitt Crossroads turn left - Fishery is a few 100 yds on left. Tel: 01884 820296.

Devon River Fishing

AVON
South Devon stream not to be confused with Hampshire Avon or Bristol Avon. Rises on Dartmoor and enters the sea at Bigbury. Brown Trout, Sea Trout and Salmon.

Avon Fishing Association
Contact: Mr M Pickup, Grey Wethers, Vineyard, Dartington, Totnes, TQ9 6HW, 01803 867460, *Water:* River Avon *Species:* Salmon 11lb, Sea Trout 7lb 12oz and Brown Trout to 13 inches. *Permits:* Weekly, fortnightly and monthly tickets from Avonwick and Loddiswell Post Offices. *Charges:* £55 weekly, £70 fortnightly, £85 monthly. *Season:* Brown and Sea Trout 15th March to 30th September. Salmon and Seatrout 15th April to 30th September. *Methods:* Fly only.

Newhouse Fishery (River Avon)
Contact: Adrian or Paul Cook, Newhouse Farm, Moreleigh, Totnes, TQ9 7JS, 01548 821426 or 01626 852168, *Water:* 0.25 mile on the river Avon (also see entry under Stillwater Trout, Totnes, Devon). *Species:* Brown Trout, Sea Trout and Salmon. *Permits:* On site. *Charges:* Various tickets available. *Season:* As current E.A. Byelaws. *Methods:* As current E.A. Byelaws.

South West Rivers Association
Contact: Roger Furniss (secretary), Springfield, Higher Huxham, Exeter, EX5 4EW, 01392 841235, *Water:* South West Rivers Association is the regional organisation of the river associations of Devon, Cornwall and West Dorset, and is a consultative and campaigning body for the protection and improvement of south west rivers, their fish stocks and ecology.

AXE AND TRIBUTARIES
This quiet meandering stream rises in the hills of west Dorset, runs along the boundary with Somerset before flowing past Axminster to the sea at Seaton. The Axe is a fertile river with good Trout fishing and a run of Salmon and Sea Trout. The two main tributaries, the Coly and Yarty, are also Trout streams and the Yarty has a good run of Sea Trout.

Axmouth Fishing
Contact: Seaton Chandlery, The Harbour, Axmouth, 01297 24774, *Water:* Axmouth from lower end Pool below Coly-Axe confluence to Axmouth Bridge. *Species:* Mullet, Bass, Sea Trout. *Permits:* Seaton Chandlery. *Charges:* £5 Day Adult, £2.50 Child. £25 week Adult, £12.50 Child. *Methods:* Fishing from East Bank of Estuary Only.

Stillwaters (River Axe)
Contact: Michael Ford, Lower Moorhayne Farm, Yarcombe, Nr Honiton, EX14 9BE, 01404 861344, *Water:* One Sea Trout rod on River Axe also 1 acre lake see entry under Stillwater Trout Honiton.

Willows
Contact: Mark & Aneita Regan, Weycroft Mill, Axminster, EX13 7LN, 01297 34565, *Mobile:* 07929 577 842, *Water:* 100 yards on the river Axe (max 2 people per day). *Species:* Sea Trout and Salmon. *Permits:* Only from above address. *Charges:* £25 per day per person. (free to residents of holiday cottage). *Season:* 15 March to 31 October. *Methods:* Fly and spinner.

BRAY
One of the larger tributaries of the river Taw rising on Exmoor, the Bray offers good wild Trout fishing along with Salmon and Sea Trout fishing.

Nick Hart Fly Fishing (Bray)
Contact: Nick Hart, The Cottage, Benshayes Farm, Bampton, Tiverton, EX16 9LA, 01398 331660, *Mobile:* 0797 1198559, *Water:* 1.3 miles on river Bray. Many new bankside improvements creating new pools. (see also entries under Devon River Fishing - Torridge and Exe). *Species:* Brown Trout to 1lb, Sea Trout to 5lb. *Permits:* From Nick Hart Fly Fishing. *Charges:* £15 per day Brown Trout and Sea Trout (night fishing allowed). *Season:* 15 March - 30 September. *Methods:* Fly only. Catch & release of Wild Brown Trout compulsory. E.A. byelaws apply.

CLAW
This is a small tributary of the Upper Tamar River and has good Brown Trout fishing.

Perdells (Claw)
Contact: Fred Cogdell / Charlie Hart, 5 Tower Street, Launceston, PL15 8BQ, 01566 777621, *Mobile:* 07802 730695, *Water:* Half a mile on the Claw. See also entries under Tamar and Teign. *Species:* Trout. Sea Trout and Grayling. *Charges:* From £10 per day per rod. *Season:* 1 April to 31 October *Methods:* Fly only.

Tetcott Angling Club (Claw)
Contact: Mrs Nicola Mitchell, 2 Harkaway Cottage, Tetcott, Holsworthy, EX22 6Q?U, 01409 271381, *Mobile:* 07787 335566, *Water:* Approx half a mile of the river Claw. *Species:* Brown Trout. *Permits:* No day tickets - private club. *Season:* 16th March to 30th September. Daylight hours only. *Methods:* Artificial lures, fly, spinning, worm.

COLY
A tributary of the river Axe, the Coly offers good Brown Trout and Sea Trout fishing set in the unspoilt rolling countryside of East Devon.

Higher Cownhayne Farm
Contact: Mrs Pady, Higher Cownhayne Farm, Cownhayne Lane, Colyton, EX24 6HD, 01297 552267, *Water:* Fishing on River Coly. *Species:* Brown & Sea Trout. *Charges:* On application. *Methods:* Fly fishing, no netting.

CULM
The Culm is a tributary of the river Exe and issues from the Blackdown Hills. In its upper

reaches it is a typical dry fly Trout stream, with good hatches of fly and free-rising fish. From Cullompton until it joins the Exe, the Culm becomes a coarse fishery, with the Dace in particular of good average size.

Angling 2000 (Culm)
Contact: Westcountry Rivers Trust, 10 Exeter Street, Launceston, PL15 9EQ, 0870 774 0686, *Water:* 1900m double bank. *Species:* Trout, Chub, Dace, Roach and Pike. *Permits:* From the above. *Charges:* £5 to £7.50 per day. *Season:* Trout - 1st April to 30th September. Coarse - 16th June to 31st December. *Methods:* No dogs. Any method. No more than 2 Trout to be retained per day. All Salmon to be returned.

DART AND TRIBUTARIES
Deep in the heart of lonely Dartmoor rise the East and West Dart. Between their separate sources and Dartmeet, where they join, these two streams and their tributaries are mainly owned by the Duchy of Cornwall and provide many miles of Salmon, Sea Trout and Trout fishing for visitors. The scenery is on the grand scale and the sense of freedom enjoyed when you know that you can fish away over miles and miles of river is seldom realised on this crowded island. This is a moorland fishery - swift flowing, boulder strewn, usually crystal clear.
Below Dartmeet the river rushes through a spectacular wooded valley before breaking out of the moor near Buckfastleigh and flowing on to its estuary at Totnes. Although there are Brown Trout throughout the river, these middle and lower reaches are primarily Salmon and Sea Trout waters.

Buckfastleigh
Contact: South West Lakes Trust, Higher Coombepark, Lewdown, Okehampton, EX20 4QT, 01566 771930, *Water:* 0.25 miles on River Dart. Austins Bridge to Nursery Pool. *Species:* Salmon & Sea Trout. *Permits:* From South West Lakes Trust at above address. *Charges:* Season - £85. Limit of 16 rods. *Season:* 1st February - 30th September.

Dart Angling Association
Contact: Philip Prowse, 2 School Cottages, Stoke-in-Teignhead, Newton Abbot, TQ10 9HU, 01626 872374, *Water:* 9 miles on river Dart. (3.9 miles of main river open to visitors plus the tidal Totnes weir pool). *Species:* Salmon, Sea Trout, Brown Trout. *Permits:* All permits - Sea Trout Inn, Staverton Tel: 01803 762274. *Charges:* Membership details from secretary. Totnes weir pool £20 per day (only 1 day Salmon, 1 night Sea Trout ticket available). Buckfast (Austin's Bridge) - Littlehempston (left bank) only 2 per day (unless resident at the Sea Trout Inn). *Season:* Salmon 1st February - 30th September. Sea/Brown Trout 15th March - 30th September. *Methods:* Fly (some stretches fly only), spinning, prawn (below Staverton) see club regulations i.e. conservation measures in force.

4lb River Barle Salmon caught in September 2004 by Tracy Stevens.

Duchy Of Cornwall
Contact: Duchy Of Cornwall Office, Duchy Hotel, Princetown, Yelverton, PL20 6QF, 01822 890205, *Water:* East & West Dart Rivers and its tributaries down to Dartmeet. *Species:* Salmon and Trout. *Permits:* Buckfast Post Office, Buckfast Road, Buckfast. Holne Chase Hotel, Ashburton. Two Bridges Hotel, Two Bridges, Princetown, Yelverton. The Post Office, Postbridge, Yelverton. Princetown Post Office, Princetown, Yelverton. Prince Hall Hotel, Two Bridges, Princetown, Yelverton. The Arundell Arms, Lifton. James Bowden & Sons, The Square, Chagford. Badger's Holt Ltd., Dartmeet, Princetown. Exeter Angling Centre, Smythen Street, Exeter. The Forest Inn Hexworthy, Poundsgate, Yelverton. Peter Collings, Huccaby's News, 33 Fore St., Buckfastleigh. *Charges:* Salmon Season: £140, Week £78, Day £23. Trout Season: £57, Week £18, Day £6.50. *Season:* Salmon: 1st February to 30th September. Trout: 15th March to 30th September. *Methods:* Fly only. Additional information on permit.

Hatchlands Trout Farm
Contact: Malcolm Davies, Greyshoot Lane, Rattery, South Brent, TQ10 9LN, 01364 73500, *Water:* 600 yards, both banks of the river Harbourne (tributary of the Dart). *Species:* Brown Trout. *Charges:* On application. *Season:* See current E.A. Byelaws. *Methods:* Barbless hooks only.

Nurston Farm Fishery (River)
Contact: Mabin Family, Nurston Farm, Dean Prior, Buckfastleigh, TQ11 0NA, 01364 642285, *Water:* 3 miles River Dart (see entry under Stillwater Coarse, Buckfastleigh, Devon). *Species:* Roach, Carp to over 20lb, Tench, Rudd, Bream. *Charges:* On application. *Season:* Closed November, December and January. *Methods:* No dogs.

DEVON

Bridge House Hotel
& LICENSED RESTAURANT

Salmon & Trout Fishing on the Exe
Close to Wimbleball & Clatworthy
Superb Cuisine - Sporting Breaks
All Year round trout fishing at local fisheries
From £25 per person, per night including Breakfast
Email: festivales@aol.com
Bampton, Devon. Tel/Fax: 01398 331298

RIVER FISHING

Prince Hall Hotel
Contact: John Grove, Nr. Two Bridges, Dartmoor, PL20 6SA, 01822 890403, *Water:* Access to all Duchy water. *Species:* Wild Brown Trout 1.5lb, Sea Trout 6lb, Salmon 11lb. *Permits:* Duchy. EA Licences on sale 7 days a week at the hotel. *Charges:* Trout day EA £3, Duchy £6.50. Trout week EA £8, Duchy £18. Salmon day EA £6.50, Duchy £23. Salmon week EA £19.50, Duchy £78. *Season:* March - September for Salmon. March - October for Trout. *Methods:* Fly only.

Two Bridges Hotel
Contact: Two Bridges Hotel, Two Bridges, Dartmoor, PL20 6SW, 01822 890581, *Water:* Stretch of 600yds double bank fishing. *Species:* Trout & Salmon. *Permits:* At hotel reception. *Charges:* See Duchy permit. *Season:* E.A. Byelaws apply.

DEER

This is a small tributary of the Upper Tamar River and has good Brown Trout fishing.

Tetcott Angling Club (Deer)
Contact: Mrs Nicola Mitchell, 2 Harkaway Cottage, Tetcott, Holsworthy, EX22 6QU, 01409 271341, *Mobile:* 07787 335566, *Water:* Approx one mile of the river Deer. *Species:* Brown Trout. *Permits:* No day tickets - private club. *Season:* 16th March to 30th September. Daylight hours only. *Methods:* Artificial lures, fly, spinning, worm.

ERME

A small Devon stream rising on Dartmoor and flowing south through Ivybridge to the sea. The Erme is probably best known for its Sea Trout, but there is also a run of Salmon and Brown Trout are present throughout its length.

EXE & TRIBUTARIES

The Exe rises high on Exmoor and flows through open moorland until it plunges into a steep wooded valley near Winsford. By the time Tiverton is reached the valley has widened and from here to the sea the Exe meanders through a broad pastoral vale until it flows into the estuary near Exeter and finally into the sea between Exmouth and Dawlish Warren. It is the longest river in the south west. Throughout most of its length the Exe is a good Trout stream, the fast flowing, rocky upper reaches abounding in fish of modest average size, which increases as the river becomes larger and slower in its middle and lower reaches, where fish approaching a pound feature regularly in the daily catch. The Exe has a good run of Salmon and can produce big catches when the grilse arrive in summer. In the deep slow waters around Exeter there is a variety of coarse fish, as there is in the Exeter Ship Canal which parallels the river from Exeter to the estuary at Topsham. The Exe only has a small run of Sea Trout, but Grayling are plentiful in the middle and lower reaches. The two main tributaries - the Barle and the Culm - could not be more different in character. The Barle is a swift upland stream which rises high on Exmoor not far from the source of the Exe, and runs a parallel course, first through open moor and then through a picturesque wooded valley, before joining the parent river near Dulverton. It has good Trout fishing throughout and Salmon fishing on the lower reaches.

The Culm issues from the Blackdown Hills and in its upper reaches is a typical dry fly Trout stream, with good hatches of fly and free-rising fish. From Cullompton until it joins the Exe, the Culm becomes a coarse fishery, with the Dace in particular of good average size.

Bridge House Hotel
Contact: Brian Smith, Bridge House Hotel, Bampton, EX16 9NF, 01398 331298, *Water:* 1 Mile on River Exe. *Species:* Salmon, Trout and Grayling; (2000 Season: 12lb Salmon, 3lb Brown Trout). *Permits:* As above. *Charges:* Salmon from £25 per day, Trout £15 per day. *Season:* March 15th - Sept 30th. *Methods:* Fly, occasional spinner.

Devon, Wilts & UK Fly Fishing School (Exe)
Contact: Tom Hill, 25 Little Week Close, Dawlish, EX7 0RA, 01626 866532, *Water:* 3.5 miles of prime fishing on the river Exe divided into 3 beats, 4 rods per beat per day. Also 1 mile of river Taw and access to rivers Yeo, Creedy, Mole and Torridge. *Species:* Salmon, Brown Trout & Grayling on the Exe. *Permits:* Daily weekly and occasional season lets. *Charges:* Exe - £35 day. *Season:* Exe: 14th February - 30th September for Salmon. Brown Trout 15th March - 30th September. *Methods:* Fly & Spinner on Exe. All other waters fly only.

Exe Duck's Marsh (River Exe)
Contact: Exeter City Council, River & Canal Manager, Civic Centre, Exeter, EX1 1RQ, 01392 274306, *Water:* River Exe, left bank 1 mile downstream Salmonpool weir. *Species:* Salmon (Trout). *Permits:* River & Canal Office, Canal Basin, Haven Rd, Exeter. Angling Centre, Smythen Street, Exeter. Civic Centre, Paris Street, Exeter. *Charges:* Day tickets only: £6.40. *Season:* 14th

DEVON

February - 30th September; no night fishing. *Methods:* Permit restrictions & E.A. byelaw controls; only artificial fly & lures and all fish returned before June 16th.

Exeter & District Angling Association (River Creedy)
Contact: Terry Reed (Hon. Sec.), PO Box 194, Exeter, EX2 7WG, *Mobile:* 07970 483913, *Water:* Cowley Bridge; just a short walk from the Exe. *Species:* Roach, Dace, Gudgeon. *Permits:* Exeter Angling Centre, Smythen Street (Off Market Street Exeter). Bridge Cafe, Bridge Road, Exeter. Exmouth Tackle & Sport, The Strand, Exmouth. Tackle Trader, Wharf Road, Newton Abbot. Exe Valley Angling, West Exe South, Tiverton. *Charges:* £29 Adults, £3 for Juniors (annual). £4 day and £6 for 24 hour ticket. *Season:* Different on each water. Details in association handbook or from agents. *Methods:* Different restrictions on each water. Details in association handbook.

Exeter & District Angling Association (River Culm)
Contact: Terry Reed (Hon. Sec.), PO Box 194, Exeter, EX2 7WG, *Mobile:* 07970 483913, *Water:* Stoke Canon, Paddleford Pool, Killerton and Beare Gate; Smaller faster flowing river. *Species:* Superb catches of Chub, Roach and Dace possible throughout. An excellent, yet relatively easy Pike water. *Permits:* Exeter Angling Centre, Smythen Street (Off Market Street Exeter). Bridge Cafe, Bridge Road, Exeter. Exmouth Tackle & Sport, The Strand, Exmouth. Tackle Trader, Wharf Road, Newton Abbot. Exe Valley Angling, West Exe South, Tiverton. *Charges:* £29 Adults, £3 for Juniors (annual). £4 day and £6 for 24 hour ticket. *Season:* Different on each water. Details in association handbook or from agents. *Methods:* Different restrictions on each water. Details in association handbook.

Exeter & District Angling Association (River Exe)
Contact: Terry Reed (Hon. Sec.), PO Box 194, Exeter, EX2 7WG, *Mobile:* 07970 483913, *Water:* Tidal stretch of Exe at Countess Wear; big catches of Mullet, Dace and Bream. Non tidal stretch at Weirfield; big bags of Bream and Carp from 15 to 20lb. Shillhay runs nearly through the City centre; can produce big bags of Bream and Roach. Exwick is a faster flowing section adjacent to St David's railway section; good nets of quality Roach and Dace, fishes well in the autumn. Cowley Bridge is a relatively under fished stretch; good nets of Roach and Dace along the whole length. Oakhay Barton; fewer fish but good size and high quality fish. *Species:* Roach, Dace, Bream, Chub, Perch, Carp, Mullet. *Permits:* Exeter Angling Centre, Smythen Street (Off Market Street Exeter). Bridge Cafe, Bridge Road, Exeter. Exmouth Tackle & Sport, The Strand, Exmouth. Tackle Trader, Wharf Road, Newton Abbot. Exe Valley Angling, West Exe South, Tiverton. *Charges:* £29 Adults, £3 for Juniors (annual). £4 day and £6 for 24 hour ticket. *Season:* Different on each water. Details in association handbook or from agents. *Methods:* Different restrictions on each water. Details in association handbook.

River Exe (Exeter)
Contact: Exeter City Council, River & Canal Manager, Civic Centre, Exeter, EX1 1RQ, 01392 274306, *Water:* River Exe, 12 beats between Head Weir & Countess Wear. *Species:* Salmon (Trout). *Permits:* Annual, available by post with payment and photograph to Exeter City Council, Civic Centre, Exeter. EX1 1RQ. *Charges:* £60.00, limited permits. *Season:* 14th Febuary - 30th September. *Methods:* Permit restrictions and E.A. Byelaws apply. Only artificial fly & lures. All fish returned before June 16th.

ORVIS
SPORTING TRADITIONS
Since 1856

4 Cathedral Close, Exeter, Devon EX1 1EZ   Tel: 01392 848 606
1-2 Pulteney Bridge, Bath BA2 4AX   Tel: 01225 331 471

Our teams will be delighted to advise and help on all aspects of your new season's tackle requirements. Or simply just browse our exclusive range of fly fishing products including rods, reels, vests, waders and accessories.

www.orvis.co.uk

DEVON

Robert Jones Fly Fishing (Exe)
Contact: South Lodge, Courtlands Lane, Exmouth, EX8 3NZ, 07020 902090, *Mobile:* 07970 797370, *Water:* River Exe. Private and Hotel water. *Species:* Brown Trout and Salmon. *Permits:* Day permits. E.A. Beginners Licence agent. *Charges:* From £25 per day. *Season:* 15th March - 30th September. *Methods:* Fly and spinner.

Tiverton & District Angling Club (River Culm)
Contact: Exe Valley Angling, 19 Westexe South, Tiverton, EX16 5DQ, 01884 242275, *Water:* 0.75 miles river Culm at Stoke Cannon. Various stretches on several rivers in Somerset. See also entry under stillwater coarse, Tiverton. *Species:* Roach, Dace, Chub, Perch, Pike and Eels. Salmon and Trout in season. *Permits:* Please ring Exe Valley for details. Also available from: Exeter Angling Centre, Enterprise Angling Taunton, Topp Tackle Taunton & Minnows Caravan Park - beside Grand Western Canal. *Charges:* Senior: Day £4, Annual £20. Conc: Junior & OAP Day £2.50, Annual £8. *Season:* Coarse: closed 15th March to 16th June. Trout: open from 15th March to 30th September. Salmon: open 14th February to 30th September. *Methods:* Canal Methods: Any. Restrictions: Fish from permanent pegs, no night fishing, no cars on bank, no digging of banks or excessive clearance of vegatation. Lakeside Methods: Any. Restrictions: No night fishing, no boilies, Trout pellets or nuts, one rod only, fishing from permanent pegs, no dogs, nets to be dipped. Ring Exe Valley Angling for full details.

Tiverton Fly Fishing Association
Contact: Exe Valley Angling, 19 Westexe South, Tiverton, EX16 5DQ, 01884 242275, *Water:* 3.5 Miles on River Exe. *Species:* Trout & Grayling. *Permits:* Exe Valley Angling: 01884 242275. Fishing available to members and guests. Members must be in EX16 postcode area. *Charges:* Senior £15, Conc. £5, Guests £5, OAP £5. *Season:* 15th March - 30th September. *Methods:* Fly only.

LYN
Chalk Water, Weir Water, Oare Water, Badgeworthy Water - these are the streams that tumble down from the romantic Doone Country of Exmoor and join to form the East Lyn, which cascades through the spectacular wooded ravine of the National Trust's Watersmeet Estate. The main river has good runs of Salmon and Sea Trout, and wild Brown Trout teem on the Lyn and the tributary streams.

Cloud Farm Fishing
Contact: John, Cloud Farm, Oare, Lynton, EX35 6NU, 01598 741278, *Mobile:* 07814 011380, *Water:* Badgeworthy Water, tributary of the Lyn - 0.75 miles single bank fishing. *Species:* Salmon and Brown Trout. *Charges:* From £5 per day.

Environment Agency - Watersmeet and Glenthorne
08708 506506, *Water:* The fishery is in two parts: The Watersmeet Fishery, leased by the Agency from the National Trust - Tors Road, Lynmouth to Woodside Bridge, right bank only; Woodside Bridge to Watersmeet both banks; upstream of Watersmeet right bank only to Rockford. The Glenthorne Fishery - right bank only upstream of Rockford to 300 yards downstream of Brendon Road Bridge. Half a mile of Trout fishing is available on the Hoaroak Water between Hillsford Bridge and Watersmeet; this

---

Salmon, Sea Trout & Trout Fishing
On the River Lyn, North Devon
- Watersmeet & Glenthorne Fisheries -
A separate Environment Agency national rod licence is required on this fishery

3 miles with named pools
Season: Salmon - 1 March to 30 September. Trout - 15 March to 30 September

DAY PERMITS - Salmon & Sea Trout £13.50, Brown Trout £3
Week permits also available

Permits from: Tourist Information Centre, Town Hall, Lynton.
Mr & Mrs Rigby, Brendon House Hotel, Brendon.
Mrs Topp, Topp Tackle, 63 Station Rd, Taunton.
Mrs Fennell, Variety Sports, 23 Broad Street, Ilfracombe.
Environment Agency, Manley House, Kestrel Way, Exeter.
Porlock Visitor Centre, West End High Street, Porlock.
Rockford Inn, Brendon, Lynton.

Environment Agency

DEVON

is specifically for children, who only require a Trout rod licence when fishing this particular stretch if they are aged 12 years or over. WARNING: Anglers are advised that parts of the river are exceptionally steep and rocky and can be dangerous. River Lyn information line - 01398 371119. *Species:* Salmon, Sea Trout, Brown Trout. *Permits:* Mr & Mrs Rigby, Brendon House Hotel, Brendon. Tourist Information Centre, Town Hall, Lynton; Mrs J. Fennell, Variety Sports, 23 Broad Street, Ilfracombe; Mrs Topp, Topp Tackle, 63 Station Road, Taunton. Porlock Visitor Centre, West End, High Street, Porlock. Rockford Inn, Brendon, Lynton, N.Devon. *Charges:* Salmon & Sea Trout, season withdrawn for conservation reasons, week £35, day £13.50, evening (8 pm to 2 am) £4; Brown Trout, season £27.50, week £10, day £3. Bag Limits: 2 Salmon, 4 Sea Trout, 8 Brown Trout per day. 2 Salmon week, 6 Salmon per season. *Season:* Salmon 1st March - 30th September; Sea Trout & Trout 15th March - 30th September. Fishing permitted 8 am to sunset, except from 1st June - 30th September when fishing by traditional fly fishing methods is permitted until 2 am between Tors Road & Rockford. *Methods:* Brown Trout, fly only. Salmon, no shrimp or prawn. Artificial fly or lure only before 16th June. Catch and release of all salmon prior to 16th June. No weight may be used whilst fly fishing. The weight used for worm fishing and spinning must be lead free and not weigh more than 0.5 ounce and must be attached at least 18 inches from the hook.

MOLE
Main tributary of the river Taw.

Nick Hart Fly Fishing (Mole)
Contact: Nick Hart, The Cottage, Benshayes Farm, Bampton, Tiverton, EX16 9LA, 01398 331660, *Mobile:* 0797 1198559, *Water:* 1 1/2 miles mainly double bank. (see also entries under Devon River Fishing - Torridge and Exe). *Species:* Salmon, Sea Trout and Brown Trout. *Permits:* From Nick Hart Fly Fishing - pre booking advisable. *Charges:* Trout £20 per day. Seatrout and Salmon £30 per day. *Season:* Salmon - 1st March to 30th September. Sea Trout/Brown Trout - 15th March to 30th September. *Methods:* Fly only. E.A. rod licence and byelaws apply. Strictly no dogs. All wild Trout to be released unharmed.

OTTER
The Otter springs to life in the Blackdown Hills and flows through a broad fertile valley to join the sea near the little resort of Budleigh Salterton. This is primarily a Brown Trout stream noted for its dry fly fishing for Trout of good average weight. There is also an improving run of Sea Trout.

Clinton Devon Estates
Contact: John Wilding, Rolle Estate, East Budleigh, Budleigh Salterton, EX9 7DP, 01395 443881, *Water:* 0.75 mile single bank fishing on the River Otter from Clamour Bridge (footpath below Otterton) to White Bridge near Budleigh Salterton. *Species:* Brown Trout. *Charges:* Free to EA rod licence holders. *Season:* 1st April to 30th September.

Deer Park Hotel
Contact: Reception, Deer Park Hotel, Weston, Nr Honiton, EX14 3PG, 01404 41266, *Water:* 6 miles on River Otter. *Species:* Brown Trout. *Permits:* From reception desk at hotel. *Charges:* £30 per day. Season permits available. Prices on application. *Season:* 15th March - 30th September. *Methods:* Dry Fly only.

Otter Falls (River)
Contact: John or Carol, New Road, Upottery, Nr Honiton, EX14 9QD, 01404 861634, *Water:* 400 metre section of River Otter (see entry Stillwater Trout, Honiton). *Species:* Brown Trout. *Charges:* £15 per day 3 fish. £60 per week. *Season:* Booking only, 8am to 1 hour after sunset. *Methods:* On application.

River Otter Association
Contact: Alan Knights (Secretary), Cottarson Farm, Awliscombe, Honiton, EX14 3NR, 01404 42318, *Water:* Comprises riparian owners, anglers and conservationists concerned with the preservation of the total ecology of the river Otter. *Species:* Brown Trout, Sea Trout.

Robert Jones Fly Fishing (Otter)
Contact: South Lodge, Courtlands Lane, Exmouth, EX8 3NZ, 07020 902090, *Mobile:* 07970 797770, *Water:* River Otter. Private and Hotel water. *Species:* Brown Trout and Sea Trout. *Permits:* Day permits. E.A. Beginners Licence agent. *Charges:* £25 per day. *Season:* 15th March - 30th September. *Methods:* Fly only.

PLYM
A short stream rising on Dartmoor and running into Plymouth Sound. Trout fishing on the Plym and its tributary the Meavy, some good Sea Trout fishing on the lower reaches and a late run of Salmon.

12lb 8oz Tavy Salmon caught by John Shaw in October 2004.

DEVON

RIVER FISHING

Plymouth & Dist Freshwater Angling Assoc. (Plym)
Contact: David L. Bickell 2 Boundary Road, Dousland, Yelverton, Devon PL20 6NQ, 01822 854241 *Water:* 1 mile on River Plym, 1.5 miles on River Tavy. *Species:* Salmon, Sea Trout, Brown Trout. *Permits:* Snowbee, Drakes Court, Langage Business Park, Plymouth. *Charges:* £10 a day Monday to Friday up to 30th September incl.; £15 a day Monday to Friday from 1st October to 30th November for fishing the National Trust water on the river Plym. To join the association, contact secretary. Annual subscription is about £105. *Season:* Plym: April - 15th December; Tavy: March - 14th October. *Methods:* Artificial baits only.

Plymouth Command Angling Association (River)
Contact: Mr Vic Barnett Hon.Sec., 5 Weir Close, Mainstone, Plymouth, PL6 8SD, 01752 708206, *Water:* Fishing rights on the Plym, Tavy and Walkham plus a small private pond near Ivybridge. Access to rivers for serving members only. *Species:* Salmon, Sea Trout and Trout. *Permits:* Membership is open to all serving members of HM Forces. Associate membership is also open to ex-serving members of HM Forces, no matter when the time was served. *Charges:* Costs for full membership or associate membership are available on application or enquiry at the above contact. *Season:* Plym, Tavy and Walkham as per Environment Agency Byelaws.

Tavy, Walkham & Plym Fishing Club (Plym)
Contact: Roger Round, 7 Buenaviesta Close, Glenholt, Plymouth, PL6 7JH, 01752 701945, *Water:* River Plym. Also water on Tavy and Walkham. See entry under Tavy. Other water may be available, contact Roger Round. *Species:* Salmon, Sea Trout and Brown Trout. *Permits:* From: DK Sports, Barbican, Plymouth. Moorland Garage, Yelverton. Tavistock Trout Fishery, Mount Tavy,

Tavistock. *Charges:* Season Tickets for Salmon, Sea Trout and Brown Trout. Day Tickets available. Please ring for 2005 prices. *Season:* As E.A. byelaws. No day tickets after 30 September. *Methods:* No worm, prawn or shrimp fishing. Complete rules are issued with permit. Full returns must be made to the club secretary as a condition of purchase.

TAMAR

The Tamar rises near the north coast, and for most of its course forms the boundary between Devon and Cornwall. It is always a lowland stream flowing through farmland and this fact is reflected in the size of its Trout which have a larger average size than the acid moorland streams. Around Launceston, the Tamar is joined by five tributaries - Ottery, Carey, Wolf, Thrushel and Lyd - which offer good Trout fishing, as does the Inny which enters a few miles downstream. There is a good run of Salmon and Sea Trout, the latter being particularly numerous on the Lyd. There are also Grayling in places.

Angling 2000 (Tamar)
Contact: Westcountry Rivers Trust, 10 Exeter Street, Launceston, PL15 9EQ, 0870 774 0606, *Water:* 11 beats on the Tamar, Inny, Lyd, Ottery, Carey and Kensey. Flexible permits fishing for Trout, Salmon, Sea Trout and Grayling. New beat for 2005. *Species:*

The Arundell Arms
Lifton, Devon PL16 0AA.

England's premier sporting hotel offers the perfect fishing holiday

Twenty miles of exclusive Salmon, Sea Trout and Brown Trout fishing on the river Tamar and tributaries and a 3 acre stocked lake

Famous fly fishing school with casting champions.
Award Winning Restaurant with three AA Rosettes

For details ring the proprietor Anne Voss-Bark, herself a fisherman, on 01566 784666

Email: reservations@arundellarms.com   www.arundellarms.com

DEVON

Salmon, Roach, Dace, Sea Trout, Trout and Grayling. *Permits:* From the above. *Charges:* £5 to £10 per day depending on beat. *Season:* Trout - 15th March to 30th September. Salmon - 1st March to 14th October. Grayling - 16th June to 15th November. Please contact Angling 2000 for individual beat seasons. *Methods:* Please contact Angling 2000 for individual beat methods.

Arundell Arms
Contact: Mrs Anne Voss-Bark, The Arundell Arms, Lifton, PL16 0AA, 01566 784666, *Water:* 20 miles of private fishing on Rivers Tamar, Lyd, Carey, Thrushel, Wolf and Ottery. Also 3 acre private lake stocked with Rainbow and Brown Trout. *Species:* Rivers: Salmon, Sea Trout and Brown Trout. Lake: Rainbow & Brown Trout. *Permits:* Arundell Arms. *Charges:* Trout £23. Salmon & Sea Trout from £25. Lake £27. *Season:* Salmon March 1st to October 14th. Trout and Sea Trout March 15th to September 30th. Lake open all year. *Methods:* Fly and spinner for Salmon (1 in 3 fish after June 16 then catch and release). Fly only for Trout and Sea Trout.

Endsleigh Fishing Club
Contact: M.D.S. Healy, 52 Strode Road, SW6 6BN, 0207 6101982, *Water:* 12 miles double bank River Tamar. *Species:* Salmon maximum 23lb & Sea Trout maximum 9lb. *Charges:* £20 - 1st March to 15th June, £30 16th June to 31st August, £45 1st September to 14th October. Sea Trout £15 from 5pm. Trout £15 p/day. *Season:* March 1st - October 14th 2004 incl. *Methods:* Fly. Spinning only under certain conditions.

Perdells (Tamar)
Contact: Fred Cogdell / Charlie Hart, 5 Tower Street, Launceston, PL15 8BQ, 01566 777621, *Mobile:* 07802 730695, *Water:* 3 miles on Tamar. See also entries under Claw and Teign. *Species:* Trout. Sea Trout and Grayling. *Charges:* From £10 per day per rod. *Season:* 1 April to 31 October *Methods:* Fly only.

TAVY
A Salmon and Sea Trout river which rises high on Dartmoor and flows through Tavistock to its junction with the Tamar estuary north of Plymouth. There is moorland Brown Trout on the upper reaches and on the Walkham, its main tributary.

Plymouth & Dist Freshwater Angling Assoc (Tavy)
Contact: David L. Bickell 2 Boundary Road, Dousland, Yelverton, Devon PL20 6NQ, 01822 854241, *Water:* River Tavy above Tavistock. *Species:* Salmon, Sea Trout and Brown Trout. *Charges:* Tavy fishing is available to members of the association. Contact the secretary for membership details. See entry under River Plym. *Season:* 1st March to 14th October. *Methods:* Artificial baits only.

Tavy, Walkham & Plym Fishing Club (Tavy)
Contact: Roger Round, 7 Buenaviesta Close, Glenholt, Plymouth, PL6 7JH, 01752 701945, *Water:* Rivers Tavy, Walkham, Plym, Meavy. Other water may be available, contact Roger Round. *Species:* Brown Trout, Salmon, Sea Trout. *Permits:* Only through D.K.Sports, Barbican, Plymouth. Moorland Garage, Yelverton. Tavistock Trout Fishery, Tavistock. *Charges:* Season Tickets for Salmon, Sea Trout and Brown Trout. Day Tickets available. Please ring for 2005 prices. *Season:* See Environment Agency season dates. Please note, no day tickets after 30th September. *Methods:*

No worm, prawn, shrimp on club permit waters. Please note club rules on back of permit including the dates by which accurate returns must be made as a condition of taking a permit.

TAW
The Taw is a noted Salmon and Sea Trout river that rises high on Dartmoor and then flows through the rolling farmland of North Devon to its estuary at Barnstaple. Its main tributary, the Mole, also has good Salmon and Sea Trout fishing, and the Moles own tributary, the Bray, is a good little Trout stream.

Angling 2000 (Taw)
Contact: Westcountry Rivers Trust, 10 Exeter Street, Launceston, PL15 9EQ, 0870 774 0686, *Water:* 1600m of single right hand bank on the Little Dart. Flexible permits fishing for Trout. *Species:* Trout. *Permits:* From the above. *Charges:* £5 per day. *Season:* 15th March to 30th September. *Methods:* Fly only. No more than 2 Trout to be retained in a day. Dogs allowed under close control.

Barnstaple & District Angling Association (River)
Contact: S.R. Tomms (Secretary), Barnstaple & District Angling Association, Upcott Farm, Brayford, EX32 7QA, 01598 710857, *Water:* Approx 3 miles on the river Taw. See also under Stillwater coarse, Barnstaple. *Species:* Salmon, Sea Trout, Brown Trout, Rainbows. *Permits:* No day tickets. Fishing by membership only. Details from the Secretary above or Kingfisher Tackle Shop, Barnstaple Tel. 01271 344919. *Charges:* Membership £30, Juniors £10. *Season:* Current EA byelaws apply. *Methods:* Current EA byelaws apply.

Crediton Fly Fishing Club (Taw)
EX17 1EW, *Water:* See entry under Yeo. 1.5 miles River Taw. *Charges:* £15 surcharge. Membership £68. Joining fee £21. Over 65 £48.

Devon, Wilts & UK Fly Fishing School (Taw)
Contact: Tom Hill, 25 Little Week Close, Dawlish, EX7 0RA, 01626 866532, *Water:* 1 mile of river Taw also 3.5 miles of prime fishing on the river Exe divided into 3 beats, 4 rods per beat per day and access to rivers Yeo, Creedy, Mole and Torridge. *Species:* Salmon, Sea Trout & Brown Trout on River Taw. *Permits:* Daily weekly and occasional season lets. *Charges:* Taw - £30 per day. *Season:* Exe: 14th February - 30th September for Salmon. Brown Trout 15th March - 30th September. *Methods:* Fly & Spinner on Exe. All other waters fly only.

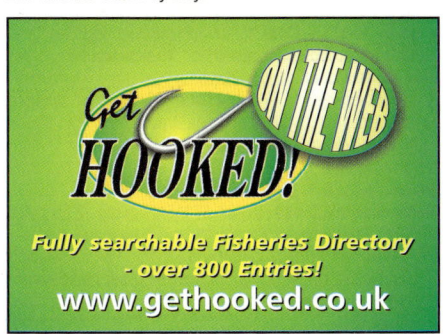

RIVER FISHING

Get HOOKED! ON THE WEB
Fully searchable Fisheries Directory - over 800 Entries!
www.gethooked.co.uk

DEVON

RIVER FISHING

SALMON, SEA TROUT & BROWN TROUT FISHING ON THE RIVER TAW
Tel: (01769) 580345
Friendly Country Hotel in Mid Devon
SPECIAL 3 DAY FISHING BREAKS
GHILLIE SERVICES AND TUITION AVAILABLE
EGGESFORD • CHUMLEIGH • DEVON • EX18 7JZ
relax@foxandhoundshotel.co.uk
www.foxandhoundshotel.co.uk

THE RISING SUN INN
Fine Food, Fishing and Ale

Dating back to the 13th Century, this old sporting inn overlooks the river in the beautiful Taw Valley.

It offers a warm, courteous atmosphere, and with Celesté and Liesel as your hosts, you can be assured of a wonderful stay.

For centuries, the Rising Sun Inn has enjoyed a premier position in North Devon for sporting and leisure pursuits. We can arrange access to some of the best fishing beats on the River Taw which is generally accepted as THE Sea Trout & Salmon river of the Southwest.

FULLING MILL TACKLE AVAILABLE
Tel: 01769 560447
E-mail: therisingsuninn@btopenworld.com
www.risingsuninn.com
The Rising Sun Inn, Umberleigh, North Devon, EX37 9DU

Fox & Hounds Country Hotel
Contact: Fox & Hounds Country Hotel, Eggesford, Chulmleigh, EX18 7JZ, 01769 580345, *Water:* Fishing on River Taw *Species:* Prime Salmon, Sea Trout & Brown Trout. *Charges:* Prime Salmon & Sea Trout £30/day (24 hrs) or £15 half day (12hrs). Brown Trout £15/day or £7.50 half day. 3 day fishing breaks £165 - to include 3 days fishing and 3 nights, including full english breakfast. *Season:* 1st March - 30th September. *Methods:* Spinning March only. Rest of season fly only.

Highbullen Hotel
Contact: Chris Taylor, Chittlehamholt, Umberleigh, EX37 9HD, 01769 540561, *Water:* 3/4 mile on Mole plus access to additional beats on Mole, Taw and the Bray. *Species:* Salmon 24.5lb (2000), Sea Trout 12lb (1998) & Brown Trout 2lb (2002). *Permits:* From Highbullen Hotel. *Charges:* Brown Trout £15 per rod day. Salmon and Sea Trout from £25 per rod to £40 per day. *Season:* Salmon 1st March - 30th September, Brown and Sea Trout 15th March - 30th September. *Methods:* Spinner March. Fly March - September. Local byelaw, August and September all Salmon over 70cm have to be returned.

Nick Hart Fly Fishing (Taw)
Contact: Nick Hart, The Cottage, Benshayes Farm, Bampton, Tiverton, EX16 9LA, 01398 331690, *Mobile:* 0797 1198559, *Water:* 1 mile on Taw available Fridays for 2 rods (see also entries under Torridge, Bray and Exe). *Species:* Salmon (to double figures), Sea Trout (excellent numbers). *Permits:* From Nick Hart Fly Fishing. *Charges:* £30 per day, 2 rods available. *Season:* 1st March - 30th September. *Methods:* Fly only. E.A. byelaws apply.

Rising Sun Inn
Contact: Liesel and Celeste Baower, Rising Sun Inn, Umberleigh, Nr Barnstaple, EX37 9DU, 01769 560347, *Water:* Day tickets available. Approx 6 miles of Taw fishing. *Species:* Sea Trout 11.5lb, Brown Trout, Salmon 23lb. A reasonable 2003 but 2004 shows a lot of promise! *Permits:* Post Office, Umberleigh for licence. *Charges:* £45 for 24 hours, 6am to 6am. *Season:* Salmon 1st March - 30th Sept, Sea/Brown Trout 15th March - 30th Sept. *Methods:* As per E.A. rules.

Taw Fishing Club
Contact: Mr J.D.V. Michie, Hillside Farm, Bratton Clovelly, Okehampton, EX20 4JD, 01837 871156, *Water:* 3.25 miles on River Taw between Brushford and Hawkridge bridges. *Species:* Brown Trout, Sea Trout and Salmon. *Permits:* Fishing by membership of club only. *Charges:* £60 season. *Season:* 15th March to 30th September. *Methods:* Fly only, barbless encouraged.

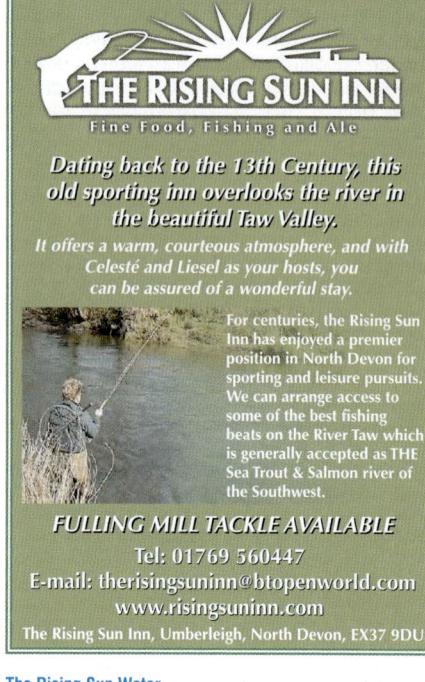

The Rising Sun Water
Contact: David Judge, No. 1 Telegraph Street, London, EC2R 7AR, 0207 2569013, *Mobile:* 07736 628971, *Water:* 1.75 miles (3 beats) on River Taw. Fishing from the favoured left bank. Please call for brochure. *Species:* Salmon (21lb in Sept 2004), Brown Trout & Sea Trout. *Charges:* £40 (24 hrs) per beat - ex vat. £625 for season rod (1 beat per week) - ex vat. *Season:* Salmon - 1st March to 30th September. Sea & Brown Trout - 15th March to 30th September. *Methods:* Spinning March only. Rest of season, fly only.

Tremayne Water
Contact: J.G. Smith, 01769 520652, *Water:* 1.5 miles single & double bank fishing on the upper Taw and Little Dart. *Species:* Salmon, Sea Trout. *Charges:* Limited season rods only. *Season:* E.A. Byelaws apply. *Methods:* E.A. Byelaws apply.

TEIGN

The Teign has two sources high up on Dartmoor which form the North and South Teign but the two branches of the Teign quickly leave the moor to join west of Chagford while still very small streams. Between Chagford and Steps Bridge the river runs through a dramatic wooded gorge which is at its most spectacular at Fingle Bridge, a popular beauty spot. All along the Teign the Spring fisherman is greeted by myriads of daffodils, which are at their most numerous around Clifford Bridge.

DEVON

The upper Teign offers good fishing for wild Trout and Sea Trout, with Salmon fishing in suitable conditions from April to the end of the season. Much of the upper river is controlled by the Upper Teign Fishing Association. From just south of the Moretonhampstead - Exeter road to the estuary at Newton Abbot. the Teign is mostly controlled by the Lower Teign Fishing Association. This water has plenty of Brown Trout but is essentially a Sea Trout and Salmon fishery.

Lower Teign Fishing Association
Contact: Mr R Waters (Secretary), 121 Topsham Road, Exeter, EX2 4RE, 01392 251928, *Water:* 14 miles River Teign. *Species:* Salmon, Sea Trout. *Permits:* 3 Beats with 3 tickets on each (beat 3 only available between 1st May and 31st August). One junior ticket per beat per day available. *Charges:* £20 per day (24 hour period - night-time Sea Trout fishing). Available from Tackle Trader, Newton Abbot. 01626 331613. 24hr bag limit (4 Sea Trout). *Season:* 1st Febuary - 30th September. *Methods:* Spinning, fly (fly only at night), no worming or maggots.

Mill End Hotel
Sandy Park, Chagford, TQ13 8JN, 0164 432282, *Water:* 3 miles plus access to a further 8 miles. *Species:* Brown Trout, Salmon and Sea Trout. *Permits:* At Hotel. *Charges:* £5 per day.

Perdells (Teign)
Contact: Fred Cogdell / Charlie Hart, 5 Tower Street, Launceston, PL15 8BQ, 01566 777621, *Mobile:* 07802 730695, *Water:* 400 yards on the Teign. See also entries under Tamar and Claw. *Species:* Trout. Sea Trout and Grayling. *Charges:* From £30 per day per rod. *Season:* 1 April to 31 October *Methods:* Fly only.

River Teign Riparian Owners Association
Contact: Mr Clive Tompkins, WBB Minerals, Lovering Lodge, East Gold Works, Kingsteignton Rd, Newton Abbot, TQ12 2PA, 01626 322331, *Water:* Riparian Owners Association representing interest of owners of fishing waters on River Teign. *Permits:* No day tickets available through the association.

Robert Jones Fly Fishing (Teign)
Contact: South Lodge, Courtlands Lane, Exmouth, EX8 3NZ, 07020 902090, *Mobile:* 07970 797770, *Water:* River Teign. Private and Hotel water. *Species:* Brown Trout, Sea Trout and Salmon. *Permits:* Day permits. E.A. Beginners Licence agent. *Charges:* From £25 per day. *Season:* 15th March - 30th September. *Methods:* Fly and spinner.

Upper Teign Fishing Association.
Contact: Richard Penrose or Chris Hall, 01647 433559 / 01837 840420, *Mobile:* 07782 375 551, *Water:* Approx 8 miles on upper Teign. *Species:* Brown Trout to 1lb 4oz, Sea Trout to 8lb & Salmon to 18lb. *Permits:* From: Fingle Bridge Inn, Drewsteignton (01647 281287). Drewsteignton Post Office. Bowdens, Chagford. Abbott Angling, Newton Abbot (01626 200198). Mill End Hotel, Sandy Park, Chagford (01647 432282). Clifford Bridge Caravan Park (01647 24216). Exeter Angling Centre (01392 436404). Orvis, Exeter (01392 272599). Post Office & General Stores, Cheriton Bishop. All anglers must be in possession of a current Environment Agency licence. *Charges:* 2004 prices (prices may change in 2005) - Ordinary Member - Annual Subscription £162 - full season for Salmon, Sea Trout & Brown Trout. Trout Member - Annual subscription £60 - full season for Brown Trout.

ROBERT JONES FLY FISHING
PERSONAL GUIDE & TUITION
BASS ON FLY
SEA TROUT BY NIGHT
RIVERS FOR TROUT & SALMON
EAST DEVON BASED
FISHING RIGHTS PURCHASE ADVICE
R.C. Jones B.Sc., F.R.I.C.S.
TEL: 070 20 90 20 90
Mobile: 0797 0797 770
Email: robertjones@eclipse.co.uk

Temporary Members' Tickets - Salmon & Sea Trout £15 per day (6 ticket limit per day from Anglers Rest plus 4 ticket limit - Salmon and Sea Trout from Drewsteignton Post Office). Sea Trout £7 per day (4 ticket limit per day from Bowdens, Chagford). Membership Enquiries to Secretary. Brown Trout Adult season £40, Juvenile (under 16) £15. Week £17.50. Juvenile £7. Day £5. Juvenile £2.50. *Season:* Brown Trout: March 15th - September 30th. Sea Trout: March 15th - September 30th. Salmon: February 1st - September 30th.

TORRIDGE
Throughout its length the Torridge flows through the rolling farmland of North Devon. It rises close to the coast near the Cornish border and swings in a great arc before flowing into the estuary that it shares with the Taw. The middle and lower reaches are best known for their Salmon and Sea Trout, but can offer surprisingly good Trout fishing.
The upper reaches and its tributaries, the Waldon and Lew, offer plenty of opportunities for Brown Trout fishing.

Angling 2000 (Torridge)
Contact: Westcountry Rivers Trust, 10 Exeter Street, Launceston, PL15 9EQ, 0870 774 0686, *Water:* Beats on the Waldon, Lew, Okement & Torridge. Flexible day permits. New beat for 2005. *Species:* Trout, Salmon and Sea Trout. *Permits:* From the above. *Charges:* £5 to £10 per day. *Season:* 1st March to 30th September. Please contact Angling 2000 for individual beat seasons. *Methods:* Please contact Angling 2000 for individual beat methods.

Clinton Arms
Contact: Wendy, Clinton Arms, Frithelstock, Torrington, EX38 8JH, 01805 623279, *Water:* Approx 1.5 mile of double bank on River Torridge (left hand bank only last 200yds). *Species:* Brown Trout, Sea Trout to 9.5lb, Salmon. *Permits:* The Clinton Arms on 01805 623279. *Charges:* £20/day/rod. *Season:* March to September. *Methods:* Fly fishing only.

Gortleigh Fishing
Gortleigh Farm, Sheepwash, Beaworthy, EX21 5HU, 01409 231291, *Water:* 1.5 miles double bank fishing. *Species:* Brown Trout, Sea Trout and occasional Salmon. *Permits:* From Farmhouse by prior arrangement - please phone first. You can

RIVER FISHING

DEVON

fish this beat with Angling 2000 tokens. *Season:* E.A. Byelaws apply. *Methods:* No dogs.

Half Moon Inn
Contact: Half Moon Inn, Sheepwash, Beaworthy, EX21 5NE, 01409 231376, *Water:* 12 miles river Torridge. *Species:* River: Sea, Brown & Wild Brown Trout, Salmon. *Permits:* Day tickets for residents & non-residents. *Charges:* Non-residents - Sea Trout & Salmon: £27, Brown Trout: 3 - fish £18. *Season:* Mid March - 30th September. *Methods:* Dry & Wet Fly only, Spinning in March.

Little Warham Fishery
Contact: Group Captain P. Norton-Smith, Little Warham House, Beaford, Winkleigh, EX19 8AB, 01805 603317, *Water:* 2 miles of River Torridge. *Species:* Salmon, Sea Trout, Brown Trout. *Permits:* As above. *Charges:* £20/day/rod, all species. *Season:* March 1st - September 30th. *Methods:* Fly only.

Mill Leat (River Fishing)
Contact: Mr Birkett, Thornbury, Holsworthy, EX22 7AY, 01409 261426, *Water:* Half mile of single bank on the Waldon (tributary of the Torridge). *Species:* Brown Trout & Coarse fish. *Charges:* £5 to fish the river. *Season:* E.A. Byelaws apply. *Methods:* E.A. Byelaws apply.

Nick Hart Fly Fishing (Torridge)
Contact: Nick Hart, The Cottage, Benshayes Farm, Bampton, Tiverton, EX16 9LA, 01398 331660, *Mobile:* 07971 198559, *Water:* Approx 0.5 mile single bank, superb tidal stretch of Sea Trout fishing. *Species:* Sea Trout & occasional Salmon. *Permits:* From Nick Hart Fly Fishing. *Charges:* £20 per day. Night fishing by arrangement. *Season:* 15th March - 30th September. *Methods:* Fly only, E.A. byelaws apply.

South Hay Fishery (Torridge)
Contact: Gill and Reg Stone, South Barn Farm, South Hay, Shebbear, Beaworthy, EX21 5SR, 01409 281857, *Water:* See entry under Stillwater Trout, Beaworthy. 2 miles on Torridge.

The Devil's Stone Inn
Contact: Paddy Gillies, The Devil's Stone Inn, Shebbear, Beaworthy, EX21 5RU, 01409 281210, *Water:* Access to 8 miles on the Torridge. *Species:* Salmon, Seatrout and Brown Trout. *Permits:* From the Devil's Stone Inn. *Charges:* From £20 per day. Night fishing available. *Season:* 1 March to 30 September. *Methods:* Fly only.

Torridge Fishery Association
Contact: Charles Inniss, Beeches, East Street, Sheepwash, Beaworthy, EX21 5NL, 01409 231237, *Water:* An association of riparian owners and Torridge fishermen, whose aim is to secure and maintain the well being of the river and its ecology. Several day permits available, please phone for details. *Species:* Salmon to 15lb. Sea Trout to 8lb. Brown Trout to 1lb. *Permits:* Half Moon Inn, Sheepwash, Beaworthy, Devon 01409 231376. Group P. Norton-Smith, Little Warham, Beaford, Winkleigh, Devon 01805 603317. *Charges:* Salmon and Sea Trout from £15 to £25 daily. Brown Trout from £7 to £15 daily. *Season:* March 1st to September 30th. *Methods:* Fly Only.

YEALM

The Yealm, (which is pronouced "Yam"), rises in the south of Dartmoor National Park, and runs into the picturesque Yealm Estuary. Brown Trout and Sea Trout fishing on the main River - a small late run of Salmon.

Upper Yealm Fishery
Contact: Snowbee U.K. Ltd., Drakes Court, Langage Business Park, Plymouth, PL7 5JY, 01752 334933, *Water:* 1 mile both banks River Yealm. *Species:* Sea Trout, Brown Trout, Salmon. *Permits:* Snowbee U.K. Ltd. *Charges:* Full membership £100, Half rod £50, day ticket (All species) £10. *Season:* Brown Trout & Sea Trout 15th March - 30th Sept, Salmon 1st April - 15th December. *Methods:* Fly fishing & spinning.

YEO

A tributary of the River Creedy which drains into the main Exe from the West close to Crediton. The Yeo has a good wild Brown Trout population.

Crediton Fly Fishing Club (Yeo)
Contact: David Pope, 21 Creedy Road, Crediton, EX17 1EW, 01363 773557, *Water:* 5 miles Rivers Yeo & Creedy, 1.5 miles River Taw. *Species:* Brown Trout, Sea Trout & Salmon. *Permits:* 01363-773557. *Charges:* Weekly (5 days) £20, Season £68, Juniors £10. Two day weekend (Sat-Sun) £20. Joining fee £21. Over 65 £48. *Season:* Environment Agency Season. *Methods:* Fly only.

HALF MOON HOTEL
SHEEPWASH, NORTH DEVON

One of Devon's Premier Game Fishing Hotels

- Salmon Trout and Sea Trout Fishing on 12 miles of the River Torridge.
- Tackle Shop, Fishing Licences, Tackle and Wader Hire, Expert Advice.
- Day Permits available for non-residents.
- 14 Rooms - all en-suite

Brochure on Request

Contact Estelle or Glen - 01409 231376
Half Moon Hotel, Sheepwash, Nr Hatherleigh, N. Devon
Email: lee@halfmoon.demon.co.uk
Web site: www.halfmoon.demon.co.uk

Devon
Stillwater Coarse

AXMINSTER
Summerleaze Pond
Contact: Summerleaze Farm, Kilmington, Axminster, EX13 7RA, 01297 32390, *Water:* 1 coarse fishing lake. *Species:* Carp, Roach, Perch. Best Carp 20lbs. *Charges:* On site, £3 adults, £1.50 children under 16. *Season:* Open all year, dawn to dusk. *Methods:* Please ask at fishery.

BAMPTON
Four Ponds Fishery
Contact: Phil & Geraldine Newton, Bowdens Lane, Shillingford, Nr Bampton, EX16 9BU, 01398 331169, *Water:* 1.25 acre lake + 0.75 acre match style lake. Proposed 3 acre specimen lake. *Species:* Carp 28.5lb, Tench 8lb, Perch 5lb (not verified), Roach 3lb, Koi 13lb, Bream 9lb, Rud and Golden Rudd to 1lb. *Charges:* Day tickets available on bankside, day ticket £7 for 2 rods and £8 for 3 rods. Night ticket £8 for 2 rods, £9 for 3 rods and spectators £3. *Season:* Open 1st March to 30th November. *Methods:* Strictly barbless hooks only, minimum 30" landing nets, no keepnets, landing mats to be used at all times, no sacking of fish, no homemade nut type baits to be used, no dogs, all nets and mats to be dipped in bin provided prior to fishing.

BARNSTAPLE
Barnstaple & District A. A. (Coarse Ponds)
Contact: S.R. Tomms (Secretary), Barnstaple & District Angling Association, Upcott Farm, Brayford, EX32 7QA, 01598 710857, *Water:* 4 mixed coarse fishing ponds in the Barnstaple area ranging from 0.5 acres to 2 acres. *Species:* Roach, Rudd, Carp, Perch, Bream, Tench and Eels. *Permits:* Members only. Details from the secretary or Kingfisher Tackle Shop, Barnstaple Tel. 01271 344919. *Charges:* £30 per year adult. Children (18 and under) £10 per year. *Season:* All year, dawn to dusk. *Methods:* Full rules in the membership book. Barbless hooks only.

Little Comfort Farm
Little Comfort Farm, Braunton, EX33 2NJ, 01271 812414, *Water:* 1.5 acre lake approx. *Species:* Carp - 15lbs, Rudd, Roach, Bream. *Permits:* Lakeside. *Charges:* £6 all day, £5 half day, £3 evening. Concessions £1 off all prices for OAPs and under 14. 2 rods each angler. *Season:* Open all year dawn to dusk. *Methods:* Barbless hooks, no keepnets.

Riverton House & Lakes
Contact: Anita & Paul, Riverton House & Lakes, Swimbridge, Barnstaple, EX32 0QX, 01271 830009, *Water:* Two 2 acre lakes. *Species:* Carp to 25lb, Bream, Tench, Roach, Perch, Chub, Rudd & Eels. *Permits:* Agent for Environment Agency rod licences. *Charges:* Adult day £5, Junior £3, Match bookings £4 (min 10 pegs). Specials: 'Dads and Lads' (one adult & one junior) £7. Family ticket (2 adults and 2 juniors) £12. Half day ticket available. Night fishing by appointment. *Season:* Open all year. *Methods:* Barbless hooks, care and consideration.

BEAWORTHY
Anglers Eldorado
Contact: Zyg, The Gables, Winsford, Halwill,, Beaworthy, EX21 5XT, 01409 221559, *Water:* Four lakes from 1 acre to 4 acres. *Species:* Carp to 25lb, Grass Carp to 18lb, Wels Catfish to 20lb, Golden Tench to 5lb, Golden Orfe to 6lb, Blue orfe to 5lb, Golden Rudd to 2lb, Koi to 10lb. *Permits:* Also from Halwill Newsagents. *Charges:* £4 per day per rod, £3 Juniors & O.A.Ps. £2 excess if fishing without permit. *Season:* All year, 8am-9pm or dusk (Which ever is earlier). *Methods:* Barbless hooks, No keepnets or sacks.

Anglers Shangrila
Contact: Mr Zyg Gregorek, The Gables, Winsford, Halwill, Beaworthy, EX21 5XT, 01409 221559, *Water:* Three match only lakes, 240 pegs. *Species:* Carp, Golden Tench, Golden Orfe. Top

21lb Common Carp from Salmonhutch

ANGLERS HEAVEN
FISHING TACKLE & BAIT SHOP
'QUALITY FOR LESS'

Call **COLIN** on (01237) 441725 Mob (07791) 215492
or **GRAHAM** on (01237) 475415 Mob (07977) 224942
13/14 BUTCHERS ROW, THE PANNIER MARKET, BIDEFORD

weights of 100lbs possible. *Permits:* From Zyg only. *Charges:* You can book the whole lake, charges depending on how many people. *Methods:* Barbless hooks.

BIDEFORD
Bideford & District Angling Club (Coarse)
Contact: Mr B. Ackland, Honestone Street, Bideford, EX39 3DA, 01237 478846, *Water:* Bideford based club with coarse, game, boat & sea sections; fishing throughout South West. Competition Friday 23rd May - Monday 26th. Please phone for further details. *Permits:* Membership form from club, open 7pm-11pm *Charges:* £5 per annum, £1 for juniors/OAP.

Fosfelle Country House Hotel (Coarse)
Hartland, Bideford, EX39 6EF, 01237 441273, *Water:* Approx half acre pond. *Species:* Carp, Tench, Roach, Rudd. *Charges:* £7 per day. *Season:* Open all year. *Methods:* Displayed on site.

Jennetts
Contact: South West Lakes Trust, 01566 771930, *Water:* Ranger Tel: 01409 211514. *Species:* Commons to 22lb, Mirrors to 23lb. Quality bags of smaller Carp, Roach and Tench to pole and float. *Permits:* See South West Lakes Trust coarse advert. *Charges:* Full day £5, Concession £4. *Season:* Open all year 6.30am to 10pm. Please note that there is no access to the car park outside these times. *Methods:* No child under 14 years may fish unless accompanied by an adult over 18 years. No child under 16 may fish overnight unless accompanied by an adult over 18 years, and then only with permission of parent or legal guardian (letter to this effect must be produced).

Little Weach Fishery
1 Weach Cottage, Westleigh, Bideford, EX39 4NG, 01237 479303, *Water:* 2 lakes totalling approx 1 acre. *Species:* Crucian, Common, Mirror and Koi Carp to 16lb, Tench 7lb, Roach 1.5lb, Rudd, Bream, Goldfish 1lb. *Charges:* £4 per day, £2 Children. Under 12's must be accompanied by an adult. *Season:* Open all year dawn to dusk. *Methods:* No keepnets or boilies.

Melbury
Contact: South West Lakes Trust, 01566 771930, *Water:* Ranger Tel: 01409 211514. *Species:* Best Mirror 27.5lb. Good mixed bags of Roach, Rudd and Bream to pole, float and feeder. *Permits:* See South West Lakes Trust coarse advert. Limited season permits from South West Lakes Trust. *Charges:* Full day £5, Concession £4, Season Child (u.16) £35, Season Day £85, Concession Season £65, Season Day and Night £125. Additional Fisheries £20 each. *Season:* Open all year from 6.30am to 10pm. *Methods:* No child under 14 years may fish unless accompanied by an adult over 18 years. No child under 16 may fish overnight unless accompanied by an adult over 18 years, and then only with permission of parent or legal guardian (letter to this effect must be produced).

Torridge Angling Club
Contact: A.J. Kelly (secretary), 4 Ridgeway Drive, Westward Ho!, EX39 1TW, 01237 476665, *Mobile:* 07779 193085, *Water:* Coarse match fishing at local waters. Quarterly meetings. New members welcome. Please contact the secretary. *Charges:* £5 per year. Concessions for juniors.

BOVEY TRACEY
Bradley Pond
Contact: Newton Abbot Fishing Association., Clive Smith (membership secretary), PO Box 1, Bovey Tracey, Newton Abbot, TQ13 9ZE, 01626 836661, *Water:* See entry under Newton Abbot Fishing Association. Full members only. 4 acre former clay pit. *Species:* Popular match and Carp venue with Roach to 2lb, Perch to 3lb 9oz, Tench, Skimmers, Carp to 28lb and large Trout.

BUCKFASTLEIGH
Castoffs Angling Club
Contact: Mr Pete Burgess, 01803 856990, *Water:* 3 acre 'Nurston Lake' near Buckfastleigh. *Species:* Roach, Rudd, Perch, Tench and Carp. *Permits:* Club open to membership from Brixham residents. *Charges:* £10 annual membership. No charge for children under 13 when accompanied by an adult. *Season:* Open all year. *Methods:* Barbless hooks only. No keepnets.

Nurston Farm Fishery (Coarse)
Contact: Mabin Family, Nurston Farm, Dean Prior, Buckfastleigh, TQ11 0NA, 01364 642285, *Water:* 2.5 acre lake (also see entry under River Fishing, Dart, Devon). *Species:* Roach to 2.5lb, Tench to 5lb, Rudd to 1lb, Bream to 4lb, Carp (different species) to 15lb. *Charges:* Dawn till dusk £5 / u14s £3 / 4pm till dusk £3. *Methods:* Barbless hooks, no keepnets, no boilies / match bookings.

CHUDLEIGH
Trenchford
Contact: South West Lakes Trust, 01566 771930, *Water:* Ranger Tel: 01647 277587. *Species:* Pike up to 30lb. *Permits:* Self service kiosk at Kennick Reservoir. *Charges:* Full day £5, Concession £4, 24 Hour £9, Season Day £90, Season Concession £70, Season Child (under 16) £35, Season Day & Night £135, Additional Fisheries £20 each. Full day boat + fishing

DEVON

Westsports Country Store

We stock everything for the fishing and shooting enthusiast

▶ **Fishing** — ABU, Shakespeare, Leeda, Fladen plus many other top names...

▶ **Shooting** — Browning, Berreta, Miroku, Sako, Tikka, Ruger, Steyr, Brono

▶ **Airguns** — Air arms, Theoben, Bsa, Webley, Falcon

▶ **Bait** — Live, Fresh and Frozen bait available

MIROKU · BROWNING WORLDWIDE · FLADEN Fishing · BERETTA · LE CHAMEAU

Opening times

Mon 9.30am - 5.00 pm	Thur 9.30am - 5.30 pm
Tue 9.30am - 5.30 pm	Fri 9.30am - 8.00 pm
Wed 9.30am - 5.00 pm	Sat 9.30am - 5.30 pm

20 Mill Street | Bideford | Devon | EX39 2JR
Phone 01237 425412 | Fax 01237 478475
Website www.west-sports.co.uk
E-mail borerp@aol.com

STILLWATER COARSE

DEVON

STILLWATER COARSE

NEWBERRY FARM
TOURING CARAVANS & CAMPING

COARSE FISHING

Two acre mixed Coarse Fishery well stocked with Carp, Tench, Roach, Rudd and Perch.

Excellent Touring Caravan and Camping Facilities just a few minutes walk from Combe Martin village, the beach and the North Devon coast

Further details and brochure from: 01271 882334
www.newberrycampsite.co.uk

Lower Hollacombe - FISHERY - CREDITON DEVON

One acre lake stocked with Common, Koi, Mirror and Crucian Carp, Rudd, Tench, Roach and Perch.

£5 PER DAY - £2.50 EVE - £3 UNDER 14
ACCOMMODATION AVAILABLE IN ON SITE CARAVAN.

Please telephone 01363 84331

£8.50 (boats must be booked 48 hrs in advance). *Season:* Open all year 24 hrs/day. *Methods:* No child under 14 years may fish unless accompanied by an adult over 18 years. No child under 16 may fish overnight unless accompanied by an adult over 18 years, and then only with permission of parent or legal guardian (letter to this effect must be produced).

COMBE MARTIN
Newberry Farm Coarse Fishing

Contact: Mr. & Mrs. Greenaway, Newberry Farm, Woodlands, Combe Martin, EX34 0AT, 01271 882334, *Water:* 2 acre lake. *Species:* Carp to 18lb & Green Tench to 8lb, Roach, Rudd & Perch. *Permits:* From above address. Environment Agency rod licence required. Available from local Post Office or by 'Telesales' service on 0870 1662662. *Charges:* £5/day, max 2 rods; half day tickets also available. *Season:* Open Easter till end October 8am - 8pm, or dusk if earlier (please book in advance to fish Nov - March). *Methods:* Barbless hooks only, No ground bait or keepnets. Children under 16 must be accompanied by an adult over 18 years. No dogs.

CREDITON
Creedy Lakes

Contact: Sandra Turner, Longbarn, Crediton, EX17 4AB, 01363 772684, *Water:* 4.5 acre & 1.75 acre spring fed lakes. *Species:* Common to 31lb 3oz, Mirror to 29lb 14oz. Koi Carp plus Tench. *Permits:* Self service on site, in car park. *Charges:* Day ticket £6 (up to 2 rods). £8 (3 rods), Evening ticket £3 (up to 2 rods). £4 (3 rods). *Season:* March through to end December. *Methods:*

CREEDY LAKES
ACCOMMODATION • CARP & TENCH FISHING

Phil Troake 28lbs 12oz

Central Devon location
 - just half a mile from Crediton
Two well stocked estate lakes
 - 4.5 and 1.75 acres
Day ticket waters
Predominantly Common Carp (to 31lb)
Good head of 20 pounders
Mirror & Koi plus Green and Golden Tench
On-site parking, level access and toilets

Four Quality Cottage Style Apartments at Manor House opposite the lakes

FREE BROCHURE ON REQUEST
Weekly or short stays

Stewart & Sandra Turner
01363 772684

www.creedylakes.com
info@creedylakes.com

www.creedymanor.com
info@creedymanor.com

76

DEVON

Barbless Hooks, minimum line 8lbs, no keepnets, no hemp or nut baits. No poles or beachcasters. Unhooking mats and 'Klinik' antiseptic compulsory. No night fishing. No unaccompanied children under 16.

Lower Hollacombe Fishery
Contact: Mr. C. Guppy, Lower Hollacombe, Crediton, EX17 5BW, 01363 84331, *Water:* Approximately 1 acre. *Species:* Common Carp, Koi Carp, Rudd, Tench, Mirror Carp, Crucian Carp, Roach, Perch. *Permits:* At bank side. *Charges:* £5 per day. £3 per day under 14. £2.50 evenings. under 16 must be accompanied by adult. *Season:* All year round. *Methods:* Barbless hooks, no boilies or nut baits.

Oldborough Fishing Retreat
Contact: Wendy Wilshaw, Oldborough Fishing Retreat, Morchard Bishop, Crediton, EX17 6SQ, 01363 877337, *Water:* 2 acres of lakes. *Species:* Mirror, Leather and Common Carp, Tench, Roach, Rudd, Perch and Eels. *Permits:* By prior arrangement. *Charges:* £5 per person per day. *Season:* Open all year. *Methods:* Barbless hooks only. No keepnets. No Boilies. No night fishing.

Salmonhutch Coarse Fishery
Contact: Mr Mortimer, Uton, Crediton, EX17 3QL, 01363 772749, *Water:* Three 1 acre spring fed lakes. *Species:* Mirror to 26lb 1oz and Common Carp to 20lb 12oz, Tench to 5lb, Rudd. *Permits:* The Post Office (fishing licence), Market Street, Crediton. Daily tickets to fish collected on site. *Charges:* Day fishing 7am to 10pm, from £5 for Adults. Night fishing 9pm to 7am, from £5 (prior booking required) Evening fishing from £3. *Season:* All Year. *Methods:* Barbless hooks, no long shank bent hooks, no permanently fixed lead rigs. Minimum 8lb line for carp, 4lb for general fishing. No carp in keepnets. Full rules from the fishery.

Franks Fishing & Pet Supplies
Specialists in Coarse Angling, with a small range of supplies for Game & Sea

Maggots, Boilies and Groundbait

Day tickets for local waters available

Open 9 - 5 Monday - Saturday

61 Fore St, Cullompton, Devon Tel: (01884) 32108

Shobrooke Lake
Contact: Clare Shelley, Shobrooke Park, Crediton, EX17 1DG, Tel: 01363 775153, *Water:* 9 acre lake in superb parkland setting. *Species:* Tench, Carp, Mirror, Rudd, Perch, Roach. *Permits:* Not from above address - Ladd's Sport Shop, Exeter Rd, Crediton 01363 772666 or Crediton Tourist Information Centre, Town hall, High Street, Crediton 01363 772006. *Charges:* Adult: £6/day, £12/week, £90/year; Under 16/Student & Pensioner: £4/day, £8/week, £60/year. *Methods:* Fishing by rod or line from bank only, no night fishing, no keepnets.

CULLOMPTON

Coombelands Coarse Fishery
Contact: Mr & Mrs Berry, Higher Coombelands, Bunneford Cross, Knowle, Cullompton, EX15 1PT, 01884 32320, *Water:* 4 Lakes

STILLWATER COARSE

SALMONHUTCH
COARSE FISHERY AND CARAVAN PARK

Mirror Carp over 26lb, Common Carp over 21lb, Rudd and Tench

17lb 10oz Common

All year fishing in three one acre spring fed lakes set in the most pleasant and beautiful countryside.

Caravan Park is sheltered and secluded with level pitches, toilets and a small shelter.
Caravans/tents from £3 per night.
Day or night fishing from £5.00.

www.caravancampingsites.co.uk/devon/salmonhutch.htm

UTON, CREDITON, DEVON TEL: 01363 772749 For a Brochure

DEVON

STILLWATER COARSE

Coombelands Coarse Fishery

Enjoy Peace and Tranquillity in a Secluded Valley Teeming with Wildlife

- Three Lakes
- Shelter Available
- Carp in excess of 20lb
- Tench, Roach, Rudd, Bream
- Night Fishing by permission
- Accommodation Arranged

Tickets available from
John Berry,
Higher Coombelands, Knowle,
Cullompton, Devon EX15 1PT

01884 32320

Email: jberry@billingsmoor.fsnet.co.uk

totalling approx 3 acres & 3 lakes in 1 acre. *Species:* 1 Carp lake, mixed coarse fishing ponds. *Permits:* Higher Coombelands. *Charges:* From £6 p/day, evening and season tickets available. Night fishing £6. *Season:* Open all year. *Methods:* Barbless hooks only, no keep nets, no boilies, night fishing with prior permission only, no dogs.

Exeter & District A.A. (Kia Ora)
Contact: Terry Reed (Hon. Sec.), PO Box 194, Exeter, EX2 7WG, *Mobile:* 07970 483913, *Water:* A recently built Association water. *Species:* Heavily stocked with mixed species coarse fish. *Permits:* Exeter Angling Centre, Smythen Street (Off Market Street Exeter). Bridge Cafe, Bridge Road, Exeter. Exmouth Tackle & Sport, The Strand, Exmouth. Tackle Trader, Wharf Road, Newton Abbot. Exe Valley Angling, West Exe South, Tiverton. *Charges:* £29 Adults, £3 for Juniors (annual). £4 day and £6 for 24 hour ticket. *Season:* Different on each water. Details in association handbook or from agents. *Methods:* Different restrictions on each water. Details in association handbook.

Goodiford Mill Fishery (Coarse Lakes)
Contact: David Wheeler, Goodiford Mill, Kentisbeare, Cullompton, EX15 2AS, 01884 266233, *Water:* 7 acre Coarse lake with over 100 doubles & twenties to 32lbs. *Species:* Carp: Common, Mirror, Crucian, Leather and Ghost. Tench, Roach and Bream. *Permits:* At Lodge. *Charges:* £6 day ticket (1 rod). £5 concession/Children under 14 must be accompanied by an adult (1 rod). Extra rod £1 each. *Season:* All year. *Methods:* Full rules on application, no keepnets, barbless hooks, nets must be dipped.

Knapp Farm Lakes
Contact: Mr B. Pretty, Knapp Farm Lakes, Clayhidon, Cullompton, EX15 3TH, 01823 680471, *Water:* Three lakes covering approx 3 acres. *Species:* Common and Ghost Carp to 12lb. Roach, Rudd and Tench to 3lb. *Permits:* Pay on site. Self service or pay Warden. *Charges:* £4 per day - all ages. *Season:* Open all year. *Methods:* No boilies. No keepnets for fish over 3lb. Barbless hooks only. Under 16s must be accompanied by an adult.

Millhayes Fishery
Contact: Mr Tony Howe, Millhayes, Kentisbeare, Cullompton, EX15 2AF, 01884 266412, *Water:* 2 acre spring fed lake, 0.5 acre Tench lake. *Species:* Carp 28lb, Tench 2lb, Roach, Rudd. *Charges:* £5 Adults, £3 Under 16, £3 Evenings. *Season:* 1st March - 31st December. *Methods:* Barbless hooks only, no boilies, no night fishing, no carp over 1lb in nets, nets to be dipped, no dogs.

Newcourt Ponds
Contact: Andy Hitt, Newcourt Barton, Langford, Cullompton, EX15 1SE, 01884 277326, *Water:* Four lakes totalling 1.5 acres.

GOODIFORD MILL FISHERY

7 acre Lake - over 100 doubles and twenties!

Tench 7lb 4oz
Perch 2lb 1oz
Bream 8lb 7oz
Roach 2lb 13oz
Rudd 1lb 11oz
Best Bag 151lb 13oz!

Quality Coarse & Trout Fishing

New luxury log cabins enquire for details

Six lakes in 32 acres stocked with Carp to over 32lb - plus Tench, Bream, Specimen Roach, Rudd and Perch

PLUS Fly Fishing for Quality Rainbows to 17lb and Browns to 20lb

Open all year - 8am to dusk. FREE Brochure   Just 2 miles from Junction 28 on the M5

Email: paul@goodifordmillleisure.co.uk   www.goodifordmillleisure.co.uk

Kentisbeare, Cullompton, Devon. EX15 2AS   Tel: 01884 266233

DEVON

STILLWATER COARSE

Millhayes Fishery
28lb plus CARP
TENCH, ROACH, RUDD
Day, 2 rods - £5/junior £3. Evening - £3
No Boilies, Barbless Hooks only, No Carp over 1lb in keepnets, all nets to be dipped, No night fishing, No dogs.
Self Catering Lodge - please phone for details
KENTISBEARE 01884 266412
Email: tonyh@chickplace.fsnet.co.uk

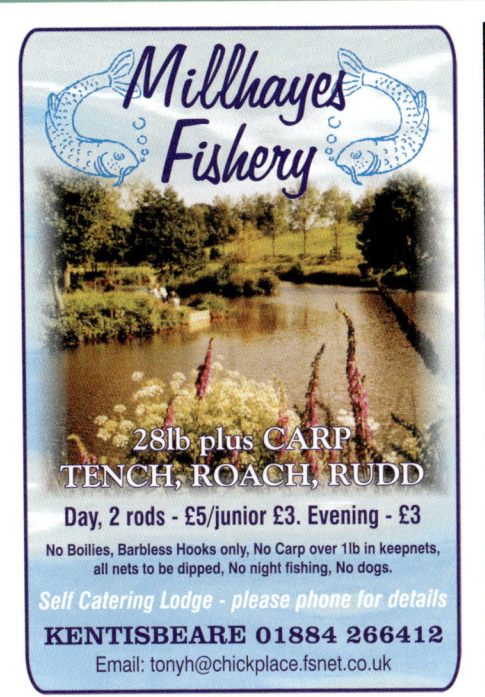

Cofton Country HOLIDAYS
Fishing Holidays in South Devon
Four private coarse fishing waters on award-winning park. Healthy carp up to 20lbs, roach, rudd, bream and tench. Touring caravans, camping, holiday homes, cottages and luxury apartments.
01626 890111
www.coftonholidays.co.uk
DAWLISH • SOUTH DEVON

Species: Carp, Tench, Bream, Golden Orfe, Rudd, Golden Tench. *Permits:* Collected on bank. *Charges:* Adults £4 two rods. Under 14 £3 one rod. Extra rods £1. *Season:* Open all year dawn to dusk. No night fishing. *Methods:* No Boilies. Barbless Hooks. No Carp over 2lb in nets. No dogs.

Padbrook Park
Contact: Garry Scargill, Padbrook Park, Cullompton, EX15 1RU, 01884 38286, *Water:* 3 acre lake. *Species:* Many Carp up to 20lb. *Charges:* £5 Day. *Methods:* No keepnets.

Pound Farm
Contact: Mrs A.M.Davey, Butterleigh, Cullompton, EX15 1PH, 01884 855208, *Water:* Small spring fed pond. *Species:* Mirror, Common Carp, Roach, Tench, Perch, Rudd. *Charges:* £3.50 per rod per day, £1.50 children. *Season:* All year. *Methods:* Barbless hooks only. No Boilies.

South Farm Holiday Cottages & Fishery
Contact: Mrs. Susan Chapman, South Farm, Blackborough, Cullompton, EX15 2JE, (01823)681078, *Water:* 4 lakes (1/3-2/3 acre each). *Species:* Carp, Roach, Chub, Perch. *Permits:* Environment Agency national rod licence required. *Charges:* £5/day. *Season:* All year. *Methods:* Barbless hooks, no keepnets, no boilies, net dip.

Upton Lakes
Contact: Richard Down, Upton Farm, Cullompton, EX15 1RA, *Mobile:* 07830 199690, *Water:* 1.5 acre and 1.25 acre match lake (day tickets available). *Species:* Carp 26lb 4oz, Bream 9lb 12oz, Tench 6lb, Perch 3lb, Crucian Carp, Roach & Rudd to 1lb plus. *Charges:* From April 2002 - £4 adults, £3 juniors, up to 3 rods; season tickets £70 adults, £40 juniors. Season tickets run on a 364 day basis. Pay as you arrive system, in place April 2003. Correct money therefore necessary. *Season:* Dawn until dusk, night fishing by prior arrangement only. *Methods:* Barbless hooks, no boilies, no peanuts.

DARTMOUTH
Old Mill
Contact: South West Lakes Trust, 01566 771930, *Species:* Carp to over 20lb, Roach to 2lb. Tench and Bream. *Permits:* See South West Lakes Trust coarse advert. *Charges:* Season Child (u.16) £35, Season Day & Night £175, Concession £150. Family (husband, wife & up to 2 children u.16) £250. Additional Fisheries £20 each. *Season:* Open all year 24 hours a day. *Methods:* No child under 14 years may fish unless accompanied by an adult over 18 years. No child under 16 may fish overnight unless accompanied by an adult over 18 years, and then only with permission of parent or legal guardian (letter to this effect must be produced).

DAWLISH
Ashcombe Fishery
Contact: Ashcombe Adventure Centre Ltd., Ashcombe, Dawlish, EX7 0QD, 01626 866766, *Water:* 3 Lakes approx 3 acres. *Species:* Carp 18lb, Tench 4lb, Roach 2lb. *Permits:* Day tickets/permits available from lakes (fishing inspector). No EA licence required, fishery covered by block licence. *Charges:* Adults £4.50, Juniors / OAP's £3.50. *Season:* Open all Year. *Methods:* Barbless Hooks, No large Carp to be kept in keepnets, No boilies.

DEVON

STILLWATER COARSE

Fishing Lakes
DARTS FARM
CARP - BREAM - TENCH
Situated in the beautiful Clyst Valley, Topsham, Exeter, Devon
Phone for details: 01392 875587

Exeter & District ANGLING ASSOCIATION
Offer 26 Miles of Fishing!
On Rivers, Ponds & Canal
Ideally situated in the heart of Devon
Visitors Welcome
PERMITS FROM LOCAL TACKLE SHOPS
PO Box 194, Exeter, EX2 7WG
Email: info@exeteranglingassociation.co.uk
www.exeteranglingassociation.co.uk

Michelle Vernalls 4lb pole caught Common Carp from South Reed

EXETER

Broadclyst Pond
Contact: Jarvis Hayes, Broadclyst, Exeter, EX5 3AD, 01392 461268, *Water:* One half acre lake. *Species:* Carp to 20lb plus. Tench 3.5lb, Perch 1.5lb, Rudd 12oz. *Permits:* On site - contact for details. *Charges:* £5 per day. *Season:* Open all year. No night fishing. *Methods:* No keepnets, barbless hooks only.

Bussells Farm
Contact: Lucy or Andy Hines, Bussells Farm, Huxham, Exeter, EX5 4EN, 01392 841238, *Mobile:* 07802 435934, *Water:* Three lakes covering 2.5 acres. *Species:* Carp to 24lb, Bream to 7lb, Tench to 7lb. Roach. *Charges:* £5 per day, £3 after 2pm. *Season:* Open all year. *Methods:* Barbless hooks only. No night fishing. No boilies.

Darts Farm Fishing Lakes
Darts Farm, Clyst St George, Topsham, Nr Exeter, EX3 0QH, 01392 878200, *Water:* 3 acres lakes. *Species:* Carp max 27lb, Bream max 8-10lb, Roach. *Permits:* Available from Darts farm shop. E.A. licence required. *Charges:* Adult: £5 p/day - max two rods. O.A.P/Child (under 16): £3.50 - max two rods. *Season:* All year round; Night Fishing by arrangement. *Methods:* Barbless hooks, disinfectant tanks for dipping tackle, no Carp in keep nets.

Exeter & District A.A. (Feneck Ponds)
Contact: Terry Reed (Hon. Sec.), PO Box 194, Exeter, EX2 7WG, *Mobile:* 07970 483913, *Water:* Two very prolific ponds. *Species:* Tench, Carp, Crucians, Roach and Rudd. *Permits:* Exeter Angling Centre, Smythen Street (Off Market Street Exeter). Bridge Cafe, Bridge Road, Exeter. Exmouth Tackle & Sport, The Strand, Exmouth. Tackle Trader, Wharf Road, Newton Abbot. Exe Valley Angling, West Exe South, Tiverton. *Charges:* £29 Adults, £3 for Juniors (annual). £4 day and £6 for 24 hour ticket. *Season:* Different on each water. Details in association handbook or from agents. *Methods:* Different restrictions on each water. Details in association handbook.

Exeter & District A.A. (Sampford Peverall Ponds)
Contact: Terry Reed (Hon. Sec.), PO Box 194, Exeter, EX2 7WG, *Mobile:* 07970 483913, *Water:* Two ponds. *Species:* All coarse fish present with Carp to 20lb. *Permits:* Exeter Angling Centre, Smythen Street (Off Market Street Exeter). Bridge Cafe, Bridge Road, Exeter. Exmouth Tackle & Sport, The Strand, Exmouth. Tackle Trader, Wharf Road, Newton Abbot. Exe Valley Angling, West Exe South, Tiverton. *Charges:* £29 Adults, £3 for Juniors (annual). £4 day and £6 for 24 hour ticket. *Season:* Different on each water. Details in association handbook or from agents. *Methods:* Different restrictions on each water. Details in association handbook.

Exeter & District Angling Association (Exeter Canal)
Contact: Terry Reed (Hon. Sec.), PO Box 194, Exeter, EX2 7WG, *Mobile:* 07970 483913, *Water:* This very old waterway is approximately 12ft deep, throughout its six mile length. *Species:* Carp to 40lb, Tench, Chub, Roach and specimen Pike to 30lb. *Permits:* Exeter Angling Centre, Smythen Street (Off Market Street Exeter). Bridge Cafe, Bridge Road, Exeter. Exmouth Tackle & Sport, The Strand, Exmouth. Tackle Trader, Wharf Road, Newton Abbot. Exe Valley Angling, West Exe South, Tiverton. *Charges:* £29 Adults, £3 for Juniors (annual). £4 day and £6 for 24 hour ticket, ask at agent. *Season:* Different on each water. Details in association handbook or from agents. *Methods:* Different restrictions on each water. Details in association handbook.

DEVON

Luccombe's Ponds

Five varied ponds set in the peaceful Devon countryside offering quality Coarse Fishing

Match Lake - Carp to 18lb, Tench & Bream

Level Car Park - Rod Hire - Toilets - Food & Drink

NEW TACKLE AND BAIT SHOP

Club and match bookings welcome

Towsington Lane, Exminster. Tel 01392 832858
Mobile 07748 568316

Upham Farm Ponds

Farringdon, Exeter, Devon.
Tel: 01395 232247
Mobile: 07971 827552

Six ponds offering superb Carp, Tench and Bream fishing for all types of angler

Carp to 27lb plus, Tench to 8.5lb

www.uphamfarm.com

South View Farm

Shillingford Saint George, Exeter

3 Spring Fed Ponds in a beautiful location provide Excellent Fishing all year round

Well stocked with Carp - many doubles, Green and Golden Tench, Bream, Roach, Rudd and Perch.

Tel/Fax: 01392 833694

Email: stamp-dexters@freeuk.com

STILLWATER COARSE

Exeter Ship Canal
Contact: Exeter City Council, River & Canal Manager, Civic Centre, Exeter, EX1 1RQ, 01392 274306, *Water:* 5.25 miles of canal, both banks; upper 2 miles free permits. *Species:* Roach, Bream, Tench, Carp, Pike & Eels. *Permits:* Free permits from - River & Canal Office, Canal Basin, Haven Rd, Exeter and Exeter City Council, Civic Centre, Phase II Reception, Paris Street. Angling Association permit from tackle shops. *Charges:* Free permits with proof of identity and E.A. licence. Lower level 3.25 miles on Exeter & District A.A. permit. *Season:* Open all year. *Methods:* No live or dead bait coarse fish.

Hogsbrook Lakes
Contact: Desmond & Maureen Pearson, Russett Cottage, Greendale Barton, Woodbury Salterton, Exeter, EX5 1EW, 01395 233340, *Water:* One 1.5 acre and one 2 acre lake. *Species:* Bream, Tench, Roach, Rudd, Golden Rudd, Carp. *Permits:* At lakeside from bailiff, Night fishing by prior arrangement. *Charges:* Day ticket £4 per day (One Rod) £1 extra per rod, Junior £2. Night £6 (One Rod) £1 extra per rod. *Season:* Open all year. *Methods:* Barbless hooks, keepnets by arrangement, no Carp in nets or sacks, all Carp anglers must have unhooking mats. No alcohol.

Home Farm Fishery
Contact: Mr F Williams, Red Cedars, Mamhead, Kenton, Exeter, EX6 8HP, 01626 866259, *Mobile:* 07779 811386, *Water:* 1 lake approx one acre. *Species:* Carp 20lb plus, Roach to 2lb, Tench to 4lb, Rudd to 12oz. *Permits:* From the cabin by the lake. *Charges:* 1 rod - £5, 2 rods - £5.50, weekly ticket £25 max two rods, concessions for children. Night fishing by arrangement. *Season:* Open all year. *Methods:* No groundbaiting with boilies, no tiger nuts.

Luccombes Coarse Fishery
Contact: Julian Harrod, Towsington Lane, Exminster, EX6 8AY, 01392 832858, *Mobile:* 07748 568316, *Water:* Five medium sized ponds set in 9 acres. Tench and Bream pond with Bream to 5lbs, Tench to 7lbs. New Match lake, Carp to 18lb, Tench to 2lb and Bream to 3lb. *Species:* Carp to 18lb. Tench to 6.5lb, Bream, Rudd, Koi and Roach. *Permits:* Season tickets available from the above. *Charges:* £6 day tickets on the bank. £4 after 4pm. £4 junior (under 16 accompanied). £120 season ticket (12 months). *Season:* Open all year from 6am to half hour before dark. *Methods:* No keepnets (except in matches) Barbless hooks ONLY, no nuts or seeds with the exception of hemp and sweetcorn.

Pengellies Carp Ponds
Contact: Mr Carr, Shillingsford Abbot, Exeter, EX2 9QH, 01392 832286, *Water:* Two small ponds totalling 1/4 acre. *Species:* Carp to 15lb, Roach. *Charges:* Tickets from office, £10 per day up to 3 rods; lake can be prebooked for exclusive fishing. *Season:* Open all year dawn to dusk, night fishing by arrangement only. *Methods:* Barbless hooks only, no boilies.

South View Farm
Contact: Mr B Stamp, Shilford, 11 The Williows, Shillingford St George, Exeter, EX2 9QS, 01392 833694, *Mobile:* 07970 439005, *Water:* 3 lakes totalling 3 acres. *Species:* Mirror, Common up to 28lb & Ghost Carp 15lb, Roach 2.5lb, Rudd 2.5lb, Perch 4lb, Bream, Green & Gold Tench to 3.5lb. *Permits:* Tickets on the bank. *Charges:* £6 for two rods, £5 Juniors (under 16, must be accompanied). Evening ticket after 5pm £3.50 adult, £3 junior. Weekly ticket £28 Adult, £23 Junior. *Season:* Open all year round. 6.30am or first light, whichever is latest, until dusk. *Methods:* Barbless hooks, no boilies, no keepnets.

Upham Farm Ponds
Contact: S.J.Willcocks, Upham Farm, Farringdon, Exeter, EX5 2HZ, 01395 232247, *Mobile:* 07971 827552, *Water:* 6 well stocked ponds. *Species:* Carp 27lb 1oz, Tench 8lb 8oz and Bream. *Permits:* Day tickets on bank. *Charges:* £6/day (concessions for O.A.P.'s, Junior). *Methods:* Barbless hooks, no keepnets, no groundbait.

EXMOUTH

Squabmoor
Contact: South West Lakes Trust, 01566 771930, *Water:* Ranger Tel: 01647 277587. *Species:* Good head of Carp to 25lb. Roach to 3lb 2oz, Tench. *Permits:* See South West Lakes Trust coarse advert. *Charges:* Full day £5, Concession £4, 24 Hour £9, Season

DEVON

STILLWATER COARSE

EXMOUTH
WE SELL SEA TACKLE
WE SELL COARSE TACKLE
WE SELL GAME TACKLE
WE SELL SECOND HAND TACKLE
WE ARE EXMOUTH TACKLE & SPORTS
20 THE STRAND, EXMOUTH. DEVON. EX8 1AF
TEL. 01395 274918
WE SPECIALISE IN READY TO FISH COMPLETE SETS

Day £90, Season Concession £70, Season Child (under 16) £35, Season Day & Night £135, Additional Fisheries £20 each. *Season:* Open all year 24 hours a day. *Methods:* No child under 14 years may fish unless accompanied by an adult over 18 years. No child under 16 may fish overnight unless accompanied by an adult over 18 years, and then only with permission of parent or legal guardian (letter to this effect must be produced).

HATHERLEIGH
Highampton Lakes (Coarse Lake)
Contact: Greenacre Farm, Highampton, Beaworthy, EX21 5LU, 01409 231216, *Water:* 1 acre Coarse Lake. Also 2 Trout lakes. *Species:* Mostly Carp to over 20lb. Tench. *Permits:* Day tickets available from lakes car park. *Charges:* Coarse fishing £5. *Season:* Open all Year. *Methods:* Barbless hooks only.

Legge Farm Coarse Fishery
Contact: Des Hudd, Church Road, Highampton, Beaworthy, EX21 5LF, 01409 231464, *Water:* 1.25 acre lake & two other ponds. *Species:* Carp (common to 20lb plus), Tench, Perch to 4.3lb, Roach, Rudd, Crucians, Grass Carp, Bream. *Permits:* E.A. licences sold on site. *Charges:* Adults £5, O.A.Ps & evenings after 4pm £3.50, juniors £3, disabled £3.50. *Season:* All year 7am - Dusk. *Methods:* Barbless hooks, landing nets, no radios or keepnets.

HOLSWORTHY
Clawford Vineyard
Clawton, EX22 6PN, 01409 254177, *Mobile:* 07786 332332, *Water:* 13 lakes totalling over 32 acres of water. *Species:* Common, Mirror, Crucian, Ghost & Grass Carp, Tench, Roach, Rudd, Orfe, Barbel, Golden Tench, Blue Tench, Golden/Pink Orfe, Green Rudd, Gold Carp, Goldfish, Catfish, Ide, Chub. *Charges:* On application. *Season:* Open all year. *Methods:* No live or deadbait. No particles or nuts except hemp or sweetcorn. Barbless hooks only. No carp whatsoever in keepnets. Full rules at the fishery.

Woodacott Arms
Contact: Stewart Le Comber, Woodacott Cross, Thornbury, Holsworthy, EX22 7BT, 01409 261162, *Water:* 2 lakes, 1.25 acre, 1 acre. *Species:* Carp 23lb, Tench 7lb, Bream 3lb, Rudd 1.5lb, Roach 1.5lb, Perch 4.5lb. *Charges:* Adults: Day Tickets 2 Rods £5, Juniors: 2 Rods £3. *Methods:* Barbless hooks, no keepnets, no boilies or peanuts.

HONITON
Fishponds House
Contact: Mr Michael Harley, Fishponds House, Dunkeswell, Honiton, EX14 4SH, 01404 891358, *Water:* 2 Lakes each over 1 acre. *Species:* Carp to 20lb, Rudd, Roach and Tench. *Charges:* £6.00 per day, Children under 11yrs £3.00 per day. *Season:* Open all year dawn to dusk. *Methods:* Barbless hooks, no boilies, no keepnets.

Hartsmoor Fisheries
Contact: John Griss, Bolham Water, Clayhidon, Cullompton, EX15 3QB, 01823 680460, *Water:* Two day ticket lakes - 2 acres and 1.25 acres, One syndicate lake - 3.5 acres, plus one 5 acre lake being developed. *Species:* Roach and Rudd to 2lb, Tench 6lb, Bream 7lb, Barbel 4.5lb, Perch 3lb, Crucians 3.5lb (not hybrids!), Blue Orfe 2.5lb, Chub 5lb, Carp 26.5lb (syndicate 35lb) Gudgeon 4oz. *Permits:* Day tickets on the bank, Syndicate - get your name on the waiting list. *Charges:* £6 per day. £6 per night by arrangement. *Season:* Day tickets dawn to dusk all year round. *Methods:* Barbless hooks. No nuts of any kind. No Carp over 2lb in keepnets. Loose feed and groundbait is permitted.

Hollies Fishery
Contact: Fiona Downer, Sheldon, Honiton, EX14 4QS, 01404 841428 / 0845 2267714, *Water:* Spring fed lake. *Species:* Carp and mixed coarse fish. *Charges:* £5 per day. £3.50 per half day (4 hours). *Season:* Open all year, dawn to dusk. Night fishing by prior arrangement.

Milton Farm Ponds
Contact: Brian Cook, Milton Farm, Payhembury, Honiton, EX14 3HE, 01404 850236, *Water:* 5 lakes approx 2 acres. *Species:* Carp to 27lb, Tench 8lb, Roach 2lb, Bream. *Permits:* Collected on bank. *Charges:* £4.50 per person per day - no charge for extra rods, £3 children 14 or under. Evening ticket £3 adults £2 children. Night fishing by arrangement. *Season:* Open all year round. *Methods:* No groundbaiting with boilies.

ILFRACOMBE
Ilfracombe & District Anglers Association (Coarse)
Contact: David Shorney, Victoria Cottage, 8B St Brannocks Road, Ilfracombe, EX34 8EG, 01271 865874, *Water:* No Club waters. Use Slade reservoir and Mill Park at Berrynarbor. *Species:* Carp, Bream, Perch, Roach, Rudd, Gudgeon and Pike. *Permits:* From Agents: Variety Sports, 23 Broad street, Ilfracombe and The Post Office, Slade, Ilfracombe, Devon, EX34 8LQ. *Charges:* Annual fee combines Sea & Coarse plus licence and permits. *Season:* January to December. Open charity competition in June. *Methods:* Barbless hooks. No Carp over 4lb in keepnets.

DEVON

Bickerton Farm Fishery
Hallsands, Kingsbridge, Devon
Two well stocked ponds with Carp, Roach, Rudd, Perch, Tench and Bream
Day Ticket - £5 per rod (£4 under 16)
NO NIGHT FISHING
MATCH BOOKINGS WELCOME
Tel: 01548 511220

Coombe Water Fishery
CARP - TENCH - BREAM - ROACH
3 secluded lakes in beautiful surroundings
Situated just half a mile from Kingsbridge.
IDEAL FOR MATCHES
Top Match Weight 149lb!
No EA Licence required
- Carp to 25lb
- Open dawn to dusk
- Self Catering plus Farmhouse B&B with full en-suite facilities

All enquiries please phone Jonathan & Beni Robinson
TEL: 01548 852038

10 year old James Thomas with a Golden Orfe

Lower Slade
Contact: South West Lakes Trust, 01566 771930, *Water:* Ranger Tel: 01398 371372 *Species:* Mirror & Common Carp to 20lb plus. Bream to 5lb plus. Perch to 2lb 4oz, Roach, Rudd, Gudgeon and Pike. *Permits:* See South West Lakes Trust coarse advert. *Charges:* Full day £5, Concession £4, 24 Hour £9, Season Day £90, Season Concession £70, Season Child (under 16) £35, Season Day & Night £125, Additional Fisheries £20 each. *Season:* Open all year, 24 hours a day. *Methods:* No child under 14 years may fish unless accompanied by an adult over 18 years. No child under 16 may fish overnight unless accompanied by an adult over 18 years, and then only with permission of parent or legal guardian. (letter to this effect must be produced).

Mill Park Coarse Fishing Lake
Contact: Brian & Mary Malin, Mill Park, Mill Lane, Berrynarbor, Ilfracombe, EX34 9SH, 01271 882647, *Water:* 1.5 acre lake between Ilfracombe and Combe Martin. *Species:* Bream, Carp, Perch, Roach, Rudd, Tench, Golden Orfe, Golden Tench, Crucian Carp. *Charges:* Adult £4.50, Junior £2.50, Adult & Junior £6.50. All juniors (under 16) must be accompanied by adult. Prices may change in 2005. *Season:* Lake open all year; day ticket 8am-9pm or dusk (whichever is earlier). *Methods:* Barbless hooks only, dip all nets, no night fishing.

KINGSBRIDGE
Bickerton Farm Fishery
Contact: Mr Graham Tolchard, Bickerton Farm, Hallsands, Kingsbridge, TQ7 2EU, 01548 511220, *Water:* 0.3 acre and 0.75 acre ponds. *Species:* Carp 15lb, Roach, Rudd, Perch, Tench, Bream. *Charges:* £4 Under 16's, £5 per rod Adults. *Methods:* Barbless hooks, No keepnets unless fishing match. No night fishing.

Coombe Water Fisheries
Contact: J.W. Robinson, Coombe Farm, Kingsbridge, TQ7 4AB, 01548 852038, *Water:* 3 Lakes. *Species:* Carp to 25lb, Bream to 4lb, Tench to 3lb, Roach to 2.5lb. *Permits:* No E.A. licence required. Lakes are covered by general E.A. licence. *Charges:* £6 day ticket, £3 Under 16. 1/2 day ticket £4. *Season:* All year dawn to dusk. Night fishing by arrangement only. *Methods:* Barbless hooks, no ground bait, no Carp over 1lb in keepnets.

Slapton Ley National Nature Reserve
Contact: Nick Binnie, Slapton Ley Field Centre, Slapton, Kingsbridge, TQ7 2QP, 01548 580685, *Water:* 180 acre

STILLWATER COARSE

DEVON

STILLWATER COARSE

Valley Springs
Lakeside Fishing Lodge

Fish from the verandah of your waterside lodge, in our beautiful South Devon valley...

One Lodge only, in the prettiest of settings. Comfortable, delightfully furnished and well equipped. Ideal for fishermen as well as non fishing guests. Heated Indoor Pool and Sauna - Pets Welcome - Open all year
SUPERB COARSE & FLY FISHING (Carp over 30lb)
See also our Directory entry in this guide

Tel: 01548 531574
www.valley-springs.com
Email: info@valley-springs.com

TACKLE TRADER
Coarse - Carp - Match Sea - Game....
- Top Quality Fresh Coarse & Sea Bait
- Match Carp & Sea Specialists
- All Local Coarse Licences
- Agent for Newton Abbot F.A.
- Sole Agents For Lower Teign F.A.
- Disabled Access

Expert Advice Always in stock!
FREE PARKING

SWITCH • EUROCARD/MasterCard • VISA • EUROCARD • DELTA

Tel: 01626 331613
2 Wharf House, Wharf Road, Newton Abbot (behind ATS Tyres)

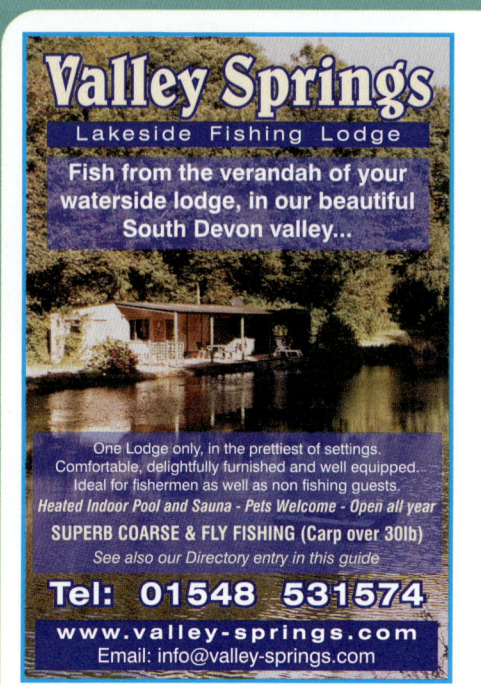

freshwater lagoon. *Species:* Pike, Perch, Roach, Rudd. *Permits:* Hired rowing boats only. *Charges:* Dependent on number in boat e.g. £18 for 2 anglers. *Season:* Close season 1st April - 31st July. *Methods:* No bank fishing, barbless hooks, no keepnets. Livebait is not to be used. All fish caught are to be returned.

Valley Springs Coarse and Trout Fishery (Coarse)
Contact: J. Bishop, Sherford, Kingsbridge, TQ7 2BG, 01548 531574, *Water:* 2 lakes totalling approx 3 acres, Trout & Coarse. *Species:* Coarse Fish - Carp to 32lb, Tench to 4.5lb, Roach/Rudd to 2lb. *Charges:* Seniors £10 per day, Juniors £5 per day. *Season:* Fishing by appointment only. Please ring. *Methods:* Barbless hooks.

LAUNCESTON

Angling 2000 (Wolf Valley Fishery)
Contact: Westcountry Rivers Trust, 10 Exeter Street, Launceston, PL15 9EQ, 0870 774 0266, *Water:* 1.25 acre lake. *Species:* Carp to 24lb, Tench to 4lb and Crucian to 1.8lb. *Permits:* From the above. *Charges:* £5. *Season:* Open all year. *Methods:* Dogs under close control. No Carp in keep nets, barbless hooks only.

LEWDOWN

Alder Lake
Contact: Mr Bob Westlake, Alder, Lewdown, Okehampton, EX20 4PJ, 01566 783444, *Water:* 4 acre Lake. *Species:* Perch, Carp to 25lb, Bream to 8.25lb, Specimen Roach and Tench. Plus natural stock of Trout. *Charges:* £5 per rod per day. *Season:* No closed season. *Methods:* No restrictions. Night fishing allowed.

LIFTON

Rexon Cross Farm
Contact: Mrs A. Worden, Broadwoodwidger, Lifton, PL16 0JJ, 01566 784295, *Mobile:* 07966 599134, *Water:* 1.5 acre lake. *Species:* Tench, Bream, Carp up to 21lb. *Charges:* £5 per day (1 rod per person). *Methods:* Barbless hooks, rules displayed at site, one rod per person.

NEWTON ABBOT

Exeter & District A.A. (Abrook Pond)
Contact: Terry Reed (Hon. Sec.), PO Box 194, Exeter, EX2 7WG, *Mobile:* 07970 483913, *Water:* Good looking pond with rustic bridges and plenty of lily pads. *Species:* Tench, Beam, Roach and Carp to mid twenties. *Permits:* Exeter Angling Centre, Smythen Street (Off Market Street Exeter). Bridge Cafe, Bridge Road, Exeter. Exmouth Tackle & Sport, The Strand, Exmouth. Tackle Trader, Wharf Road, Newton Abbot. Exe Valley Angling, West Exe South, Tiverton. *Charges:* £29 Adults, £3 for Juniors (annual). £4 day and £6 for 24 hour ticket. *Season:* Different on each water. Details in association handbook or from agents. *Methods:* Different restrictions on each water. Details in association handbook.

Finlake Holiday Park
Nr Chudleigh, TQ13 0EJ, 01626 853833, *Water:* 1 Acre - 30 Peg. *Species:* Crucians 1-4lb, Bream to 4lb, Tench 2-4lb, Skimmers, Roach to 2.5lb, Golden Orfe 12 inches, Rudd 1.5lb, Golden Rudd 8 inches, No Carp. *Permits:* On entry at security. *Charges:* £5 Adult, £2.50 to 14yrs. *Season:* All year round, Winter opening times: 8.30am - Dusk, Summer opening times: 8.30am - 6pm every day. *Methods:* Barbless hooks, no keep nets, no boilies, nuts, floating baits, pellets or paste. Strictly no ground bait, landing nets essential.

*Pete with a fly caught river Pike.
Pic - Nick Hart Flyfishing*

G. Thomas & Co. Ltd.
AIRGUNS & SHOOTING SUPPLIES

SWATKINS SILVERWARE • BSA • CROSSCUT
GERBER • WENGER • AIRARMS • WEIRACH
GAMMO • LOGAN • WHITBY • DAYSTATE
LUREFLASH • LEATHERMAN • WEBLEY
MAGLITE • VITRINOX • BUSHNELL

Precision Engraving - Sports Trophies
English Silver and Pewterware

Suppliers of Field & Country Sports Equipment
63 Queen Street, Newton Abbot, Devon, TQ12 2AU
Tel/Fax 01626 368530
E-mail: thomastrophies@aol.com

FLY FISHING EQUIPMENT
QUALITY OUTDOOR CLOTHING

STILLWATER COARSE

Learn To Fish In Newton Abbot
Contact: Paul Power, 103 Broadlands Ave., Newton Abbot, TQ12 1SH, 01626 205941, *Mobile:* 07814 060147, *Water:* Open to all who would like to learn to fish in Newton Abbot area. NFA & NFSA qualified Coach, coarse and sea angling covered. Tuition free of charge. *Species:* Carp - 33lb, Tench - 11lb, Bream - 9.5lb, Perch - 5lb, Roach - 2.5lb, Rudd - 2lb and Pike - 20lb. *Permits:* Tackle Trader, Newton Abbot - 01626 331613 *Charges:* £5 per day. *Methods:* Barbless hooks.

Newton Abbot Fishing Association (Coarse Ponds)
Contact: Clive Smith (membership secretary), PO Box 1, Bovey Tracey, Newton Abbot, TQ13 9ZE, 01626 836661, *Water:* 17 coarse ponds in the Newton Abbot Area. Also member of S.L.A.C. (Somerset Levels Association of Clubs) with stretches of the Parret, Brue and Isle. *Species:* Carp to 36lb, Tench to12lb, Bream to 8lb, Roach to 2lb, Perch to 3lb 9oz, Rudd to 1.5lb. *Permits:* From Tackle Trader, Newton Abbot. Abbot Angling, Newton Abbot. Oakford Filling Station, Kingsteignton. Sporting Lines, Torquay, Handy Baits, Paignton. Brixham Bait & Tackle. *Charges:* Day Tickets: £5 senior, £2 junior. Associate licence £41 senior (1 year fishing majority of waters). Full member £46 adult. £13 junior, £23 OAP/conc. (must live within 20 miles of Newton Abbot). *Season:* Ponds and lakes are open 24 hours a day, 365 days a year. Rivers are controlled by the national close season for coarse fish; Rocombe Ponds and Wapperwell Ponds open from dawn to dusk. *Methods:* Barbless or crushed barbs. 2 rods 1st April to 30th September. 3 rods 1st October to 31st March. No lead shot. No nut baits. No fires. No dogs. No keepnets at Rocombe.

Preston Ponds
Contact: Newton Abbot Fishing Association., *Water:* See entry under Newton Abbot Fishing Association. 4 ponds at Kingsteignton. Key Transport: Popular match water (full members only). Eddison Pond: small water. Sawmills: about 3 acres coloured by run off from local clay works but don't be put off! New Cross: Extremely deep former clay pit. *Species:* Key Transport: Skimmers, Bream, big Roach, Rudd, Perch, Tench and Crucians to over a pound. Eddison Pond: Most species with Tench, Crucians and mid-double Carp. Sawmills: Skimmers, Bream, Perch, Tench Carp and Roach to over 1lb with odd Perch to 3lb, Carp to 20lb a rumours of a single large Catfish!. New Cross: Some good Roach, Perch, the odd Tench.

Rackerhayes Complex
Contact: Newton Abbot Fishing Association, *Water:* See entry under Newton Abbot Fishing Association. 6 waters just outside Newton Abbot. Island Pond 5 acres (full members only), First Pond 2 acres, Dores Pond 9 acres, Linhay Pond 3 acres, Weedy Pond - 2000 small Carp introduced in 2003 (just under 1 acre) and Wheel Pond (juniors only). *Species:* Island Pond: most species, numerous Carp over 30lb.Tench over 10lb. Good sized Roach, Rudd, Pike, Bream and Eels. First Pond: Good head of Carp to 28lb, Tench, Roach, Bream etc. and a large number of jack Pike. Wheel Pond: Carp to 14lb, Roach, Rudd, Perch, Golden Orfe, Tench and occasional small Pike. Linhay Pond: Most coarse species with some excellent Bream. Dores Pond: Very large head of Carp to 30lb, superb Tench averaging 6lb and up to 11lb 15oz. Weedy Pond: most coarse fish including good Tench and some large Carp. *Permits:* See main entry.

Spring Ponds
Contact: Newton Abbot Fishing Association., *Water:* See entry under Newton Abbot Fishing Association. Three small farm ponds. *Species:* Middle pond has been heavily re-stocked.

DEVON

STILLWATER COARSE

RELAX! GO FISHING AT SPIRES LAKES
NORTH TAWTON, DEVON

TWO WELL STOCKED LAKES
2 acre higher lake - Carp, Tench & Orfe
30 peg match lake - Carp, Tench, Roach, Golden Rudd, Bream, Orfe, Ghost Carp, Crucian Carp and Perch.
IDEAL FOR MATCHES!
Level parking & Toilets close to the lakes
£5.50 day. £4.00 from 3pm
£4.00 Juniors and OAP's

For more information phone Barry on 01837 82499

Week Farm

Perfectly placed on the edge of Dartmoor for Walking, Cycling, Pony Trekking & Much More

DAY TICKETS AVAILABLE ON 3 WELL STOCKED COARSE LAKES
GENERAL LAKE
Common & Mirror Carp, Tench, Bream, Rudd, Roach, Crucians
TWO CARP LAKES
Stocked with quality hard fighting fish, many doubles plus specimens over 20lb
Environment Agency licence required
Rod Room with Toilets and Washing/Drying facilities

Good disabled access
www.weekfarmonline.com

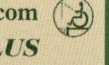

B&B AVAILABLE PLUS FOUR S/C BARN CONVERSIONS

Bridestowe, Okehampton, Devon EX20 4HZ
Phone/Fax: 01837 861 221

Top and bottom ponds well stocked with Carp averaging 2lb. Odd Carp to low double plus Tench, Roach and Bream. Almost guaranteed action.

West Golds
Contact: Newton Abbot Fishing Association., *Water:* A tidal water that is incorporated in the local flood defence system. Extreme care should be taken as flash tidal flooding is common. *Species:* Dace, Roach, Skimmers, Mullet and Carp to over 20lb. Stock changes with flow of higher tides.

NORTH TAWTON

North Tawton Angling Specimen Group
Contact: Mr. J.D. Mansfield, 4 Taw Vale Close, North Tawton, EX20 2EH, 01837 880048, *Mobile:* 07812 155035, *Water:* Fishing waters in Avon, Somerset, Devon & Cornwall. Lake, River & Sea fishing from shore only. *Species:* Any species listed in the British records. *Charges:* Membership: £8 per year adult. £4 under 14 and OAPs. *Season:* June 1st - May 31st. *Methods:* Abide by regulations laid out on lake or river that the group are fishing.

Spires Lakes
Contact: Barry Ware, Riverside, Fore Street, North Tawton, EX20 2ED, 01837 82499, *Water:* Two lakes, 30 peg match lake and 2 acre lake. *Species:* Carp 30lb, Tench 5lb, Roach 1lb 8oz, Rudd 1lb, Bream 3.5lb, Perch 1.5lb, Orfe 4lb, Ghost Carp 1lb, Crucian Carp 2lbs 8ozs. *Permits:* On site kiosk, self service. *Charges:* £5.50 Day ticket, £4.00 Evening, £4.00 Juniors & O.A.P.s. *Season:* Dawn to dusk. *Methods:* Barbless hooks, no boilies, no tiger or peanuts.

OKEHAMPTON

Millaton - Wrigley Fishing Syndicate
Contact: Mr Vic Barnett (Syndicate Sec.), 5 Weir Close, Mainstone, Plymouth, PL6 8SD, 01752 708206, *Water:* 3 small ponds, each cannot be seen from the other. A very private and secluded fishery. *Species:* Carp, Tench, Golden Tench, Bream, Perch, Gudgeon, Roach, Rudd, Large Brown Goldfish (2.5lb), Gold Carp. *Permits:* To join the syndicate, costs in the first year are: £10 joining fee, £50 for year. After the first year cost is £50 p.a. 5 day tickets - price on booking (around £5 per day). More details from the above contact or phone 01837 861100, allowing for a long ring please. *Charges:* As above. *Season:* No close season. *Methods:* Barbless hooks only. No Carp over 2lb to be retained in keepnets. Knotless nets only. No boilies. All spawning fish to be returned to the water immediately after photographing or weighing. Syndicate members may camp overnight and generally come and go as they wish.

Millaton Farm Coarse Fishery
Contact: Gareth or Jessica Charles-Jones, Millaton Farm, Bridestowe, Okehampton, EX20 4QG, 01837 861100, *Water:* 3 large lakes, 2 small (from 0.75 to 2 acres). *Species:* Carp - Koi 9lb, Ghost 10.5lb, Mirror 15lb, Common 14lb, Crucian 2.5lb, Leather. Tench, Bream 4lb, Perch 1lb, Roach, Rudd, American Sun Bass 2oz. *Permits:* Up to 5 day tickets allowed. You MUST RING day before to book space before setting out. *Charges:* £5 per day per rod. *Season:* Dawn to dusk all year round. *Methods:* Barbless hooks only. No boilies, hemp, peanuts. Groundbait in moderation. No keepnets, dogs, radios.

South Reed Fishery
Contact: Mr Vic Barnett, 5 Weir Close, Mainstone, Plymouth, PL6

DEVON

Town Parks Fishery

Best Carp caught 29lb 8oz

Fishing in the Heart of Devon!
Specimen Carp Lake with fish to 35lb
Match Lake With Carp to 12lb plus Tench, Roach, Rudd, Bream, Crucians, Chub and Perch.
Open all year round
Easy Parking
Disabled Access
Onsite Shop and Toilets
Tackle Hire
Regular Matches
Match Lake available for Club and Corporate Bookings
Fantastic Fishing for Novice or Expert
5 mins from Paignton on A385 Paignton-Totnes road.

For bookings and information phone 01803 523133 / 07966 589692
www.townparksfishery.co.uk
Totnes Road, Paignton, Devon TQ4 7PY
Email: townparks@btinternet.com

THE FISHING BOX

BAIT & TACKLE
Coarse, Carp, Sea and Match

The Old Fire Station, Silver Street, Ottery St Mary, Devon EX11 1DE
Contact Phil Penny on (01404) 814819

STILLWATER COARSE

8SD, 01752 708206, *Mobile:* 0771 0552 910, *Water:* Currently two lakes. The match lake at 4.5 acres and the specimen lake at 4 acres. *Species:* Carp, Koi and Tench. Carp from small to mid twenties. Tench from small to 7lb. Koi from small to 15lb. *Permits:* Bookings from the above ONLY. Valid EA licence required. To book the match lake takes a minimum of six anglers. No permits for 'individual' anglers. Specimen lake requires a minimum of four anglers and a maximum of six. *Charges:* Match lake £5 per person. Specimen lake £10 per person. Please note overnight bivvying can be arranged but there is NO night fishing. *Season:* No close season. *Methods:* Barbless hook's only. No nuts. Carp over 3lb may be photographed and returned immediately. Spawning fish to be returned immediately. Landing nets and unhooking mats to be used at all times. No open fires when bivvying overnight.

Stowford Grange Farm Fisheries
Contact: H Vigers & Sons, Stowford Grange Farm, Lewdown, Okehampton, EX20 4BZ, 01566 783298, *Mobile:* 07771 798363, *Water:* 2.5 acre, 1 acre and 1.25 acre lakes. *Species:* Roach, Rudd, Carp 20lb, Bream 10lb 2oz, Tench 6lb 4oz, Perch 4lb 14oz, Gudgeon, Golden Tench. *Permits:* At the farm. *Charges:* On application at the Farm. *Season:* Open all year. *Methods:* Barbless or whisker barbs, no boilies in bottom lake, no nuts, no large carp in nets.

Week Farm
Contact: John & Grenville Hockridge, Bridestowe, Okehampton, EX20 4HZ, 01837 861221, *Mobile:* 07866 854121, *Water:* Two 0.5 acre lakes & one 0.25 acre lake. *Species:* Mixed Carp (Common, Mirror, Crucian), Bream in 0.25 acre, Roach, Rudd & Green Tench. *Charges:* £4/day plus £1 extra rod, £2/evening, children & OAP half price. *Methods:* Barbless hooks only, all

nets to be dipped, night fishing by arrangement, no dogs. EA rod licence required.

OTTERY ST MARY
Escot Boat House Lake
Escot Aquatic Centre, Parklands Farm, Escot, Ottery St. Mary, EX11 1LU, 01404 822188, *Water:* 1 acre lake. *Species:* Mixed Coarse Fish, Bream, Crucian, Tench, Mirrors and Commons. *Permits:* On site at Aquatic Centre. *Charges:* £5 per day, £10 for 24 hour ticket. *Season:* Open 1st February - 1st October. *Methods:* No restrictions.

PAIGNTON
New Barn Angling Centre
Contact: Tony & Sharon Ryan, Newbarn Farm, Totnes Road, Paignton, TQ4 7PT, 01803 553602, *Mobile:* 07715 536718, *Water:* 6 ponds up to 1.25 acre suitable for juniors (parent supervision), beginners, pleasure and specimen anglers. *Species:* Carp to 28lb, Ghost Carp to 18lb, Tench to 7lb, Roach to 3lb, Bream to 6lb, Perch to 4lb, Rudd to 2lb 8oz, Eels (mirror lake only) 7lb 8oz. *Permits:* No EA rod licence required. Purchase day tickets on arrival. *Charges:* £6 for 1 rod, 2nd & 3rd rod £1 each - Junior £3.50. Adults (14+) 3 day ticket £16, 7 day ticket £32 (n.b. days taken anytime over a year). *Season:* Open all year 7am to dusk. Night fishing only available to holiday guests. 9 fishing shelters around main lake, first come first served. *Methods:* Barbless hooks only, no keepnets, no nuts. All baits eff.: maggots, luncheon meat, sweetcorn, boilies, bread & pellets. Sensible ground baiting allowed, float fishing and ledgering (ledger rigs will be checked to ensure safety), summer time good for floating baits. No artificial baits.

Town Parks Coarse Fishing Centre
Contact: Mr Paul Gammin, Town Park Farm, Totnes Road, Paignton, TQ4 7PY, 01803 523133, *Mobile:* 07800 600535, *Water:* Specimen Carp lake 1.5 acres (max 10 anglers at any one time). Match lake 2 acres (21 pegs) available for club/block bookings, phone for details. *Species:* Carp lake - Mirror and Common Carp to 35lbs. Match lake - Carp 10lbs, Crucian Carp 3lbs, Tench 5lbs, Chub 4lbs, Bream 4lbs, Roach 2lbs, Rudd 1lb, Perch 4lbs. *Permits:* No E.A. Rod licence required. *Charges:* Carp lake - Full day £7, Night (6pm - 9am) £10, Evening (4pm - Dusk) £5, 24 hrs £13. Match lake - Full day £5, Night (6pm - 9am) £7, Evening (4pm - Dusk) £4, 24 hrs £10. *Season:* 24hrs, 365 day a year, but please book night fishing in advance. *Methods:* A full list of rules are posted on site.

DEVON

Clive's TACKLE & BAIT
182 EXETER ST. (nr Cattedown roundabout), PLYMOUTH
COARSE & SEA FISHING SPECIALISTS
SHIMANO TACKLE MAIN DEALER
*** FRESH MAGGOTS DAILY ***
Good stocks of Sea Bait, Mail order supplies, Charter Boat Bookings.
Open: 6.30am-5.30pm Mon to Sat, 6.30am-7pm Fri and 6.30am-3pm Sun
Tel: 01752 228940
www.clivestackleandbaitsupplies.co.uk

STILLWATER COARSE

PLYMOUTH

Plymouth & District Angling Club
Contact: Mr Brian Morrell, 20 Pinehurst Way, Ivybridge, PL21 9UL, 01752 894199. *Water:* 3 ponds at Cadover Bridge, two at St. Germans and one at Dellamare (pure Tench) - ranging in size from 0.5 to 2 acres. *Species:* Carp to 29lb 8oz, Tench 6lb, Bream 8lb 8oz, Rudd 11lb 6oz Roach 2lb 8oz and Crucians. *Permits:* Clive's Tackle and Bait, 182 Exeter St, Plymouth. Tel: 01752 228940. *Charges:* £30 membership fee (1st January - 1st February). Other times £40 membership. Seniors £35. Juniors £10. Disabled and OAP's £15. *Season:* Open all year. St Germans and Cadover 24 hours. *Methods:* Barbless hooks. No Carp in keepnets. Unhooking mats for all Carp.

Plymouth Command Angling Association (Ponds)
Contact: Mr Vic Barnett Hon.Sec., 5 Weir Close, Mainstone, Plymouth, PL6 8SD, 01752 708206, *Water:* Two lakes of 0.75 and 1.25 of an acre for coarse fishing within ten minutes of Plymouth, plus several other accesses to associated waters in the Southwest open to members. *Species:* Carp, Tench, Bream, Perch, Roach, Rudd, Crucians, Goldfish, Eels, Golden Carp and some Koi. *Permits:* Membership is open to all serving members of HM Forces. Associate membership is also open to ex-serving members of HM Forces, no matter when the time was served. Day tickets available from Manadon Angling Supplies, Plymouth @ £5 per person, up to 5 per day. *Charges:* Costs for full membership or associate membership are available on application or enquiry to the above contact. *Season:* No close season for coarse fish. *Methods:* Barbless hooks only at the coarse fishery. Knotless keepnets to be used as per E.A. guidelines on minimum 3 metres length. No trout pellets in any form allowed. Only Carp friendly and proven pellets are to be used. All spawning fish are to be returned to the water immediately. No Carp over 2lb to be kept in keepnets.

Sunridge Fishery
Contact: RM and M Hammett, Sunridge Nurseries, Worston, Yealmpton, Plymouth, PL8 2LN, 01752 880438, *Mobile:* 07734 557212, *Water:* Approx half acre private lake that can be reserved for exclusive use. Established 30 years. *Species:* Mirror and Common Carp up to 26lb. *Permits:* From above at the Nurseries. *Charges:* £5.50 adult day, £3.50 child/OAP. *Season:* Open all year dawn to dusk, night fishing by arrangement only. *Methods:* Barbless hooks only, no keepnets (except by prior arrangement).

Warleigh Barton Fishery
Contact: Andrew Kent, Tamerton Foliot, Plymouth, PL5 4LG, 01752 771458, *Mobile:* 07811 339569, *Water:* 2 acre lake

---

Manadon Angling Supplies
11 St Erth Road, Manadon, Plymouth   Tel/Fax: 01752 79 50 60
www.manadonangling.co.uk
Off Outland Rd, Opposite Safeway
Just 200 metres from Manadon Junction of A38

PLYMOUTH'S MOST HEAVILY STOCKED TACKLE SHOP
A massive selection of **CARP, COARSE** and **MATCH** fishing gear PLUS an extensive choice for **SEA** anglers. Also **PIKE** and **CAMPING** sections

OFFICIAL AGENTS FOR: SHIMANO - GARDNER - NASH - FOX - SHAKESPEARE - SUNDRIDGE - DRENNAN - ESP - FISHRITE - JRC DAIWA - HUTCHY - FLADEN - SOLAR - DELKIM - PRESTON INNOVATIONS - MAINLINE - NUTRABAITS - SENSAS - SILLYBAITS MILO - BRILO BOXES - CARP-R-US - R. COUSINS - W.B. CLARKE - DINSMORES - D. CLEGG - WSB - JOHN ROBERTS - FISHEASY KEENETS - HIGHLANDER - ZEBCO - BLAKES - COLEMAN - KORDA - PREMIER FLOATS - COTSWOLD AQUARIUS - REUBEN HEATON MAXIMA - KRYSTON - SUFFIX - DERRI BOOTS - KAMASAN, TACKLE TERMINAL - MIRADO - ASHIMA - STARMER and many more!

VAST RANGE OF FRESH & FROZEN BAITS FOR ALL ANGLERS PLUS LIVE MAGGOTS,
PINKIES, SQUATTS, RAGWORM, SANDEELS, EARTHWORMS, PEELER & LUGWORM as available

Plymouth & District Coarse Angling Club information and memberships sold
and Plymouth Command Angling Association concessionary tickets issued.

GIFT VOUCHERS for all occasions and MAIL ORDER available

OPEN EVERY DAY with early opening SAT & SUN during summer
EASY FREE PARKING & HELPFUL FRIENDLY ADVICE

Most major Credit and Debit cards accepted

DEVON

Little Allers COARSE FISHERY
South Brent, Devon
A two acre lake in beautiful surroundings, well stocked with Carp, Bream, Tench & Roach
Day tickets collected at waters edge
Centred in the South Hams we are within easy reach of Plymouth, Torquay and Exeter
Sorry no dogs allowed
For Details phone 01364 72563

OAKTREE FISHERY
www.oaktreefishery.co.uk
info@oaktreefishery.co.uk
3 HEAVILY STOCKED LAKES
(2 pleasure, 1 specimen)
CARP 30lbs, Tench to 8lbs, Catfish 29lbs
Perch, Roach, Bream, Skimmers
Open all year, Food and Drinks, Tackle Hire, Disabled Access, B&B, Camping & Caravans, TOILET FACILITIES.
SELF CATERING COTTAGES
Set in 18 acres of beautiful countryside
'The Gateway to Exmoor and the World of Coarse Fishing'
Please phone for a brochure
Bottreaux Mill, West Anstey, South Molton, Devon EX36 3PU
Tel: 01398 341568

Mike Bolt with a Westcountry Carp.

lake & Trout fishing. *Species:* Carp, Tench, Bream. *Permits:* Self-service (No booking). *Charges:* £3.50/day, Reduced rates for O.A.Ps & Children, Children (under 15) free if accompanied by permit holding adult. *Season:* All year. *Methods:* Single rod.

SOUTH BRENT
Hatchlands Coarse Fishery
Contact: Malcolm Davies, Greyshoot Lane, Rattery, South Brent, TQ10 9LN, 01364 73500, *Water:* Two 2 acre lakes. *Species:* Carp to 22lb, Tench, Roach, Bream, Rudd and Gudgeon. *Permits:* No E.A. licence required. Block EA licence held by fishery. *Charges:* £5 per person per day. *Season:* Open all year. *Methods:* Barbless hooks only. No large Carp in keepnets.
Little Allers Coarse Fishery
Contact: M & J Wakeham, Little Allers Farm, Avonwick, South Brent, TQ10 9HA, 01364 72563, *Mobile:* 07855 427510, *Water:* 2 acre lake. *Species:* Carp, Bream, Tench, Roach, Rudd. *Permits:* On the bank. *Charges:* £5 per day adults, £3 under 16, £3.00 evening ticket after 5pm. Payments at hut in car park (correct money). *Season:* Open all year dawn to dusk. *Methods:* Barbless hooks only, no carp in keepnets. No dogs allowed.

plus 0.25 acre pond. *Species:* Mirror and Common - Now up to 30lbs. *Permits:* Day tickets. *Season:* All year. *Methods:* Barbless hooks, no keep nets.

SEATON
Horriford Fishing
Contact: Mr Pady, Horriford Farm, Colyford, Colyton, EX24 6HW, 01297 552316, *Water:* 2 ponds - 1 with access for disabled. *Species:* Bream (5lb), Roach (1lb), Tench (5lb), Carp (10lb), Perch (2lb), Rudd (1.5lb). *Permits:* From farmhouse. *Charges:* Day ticket £4. Half day ticket £2.50. *Season:* Open all year dawn to dusk. *Methods:* Barbless hooks only, no boilies.
Wiscombe Park Fishery
Contact: Mike Raynor, Wiscombe Park Fishery, Colyton, EX24 6JE, 01404 871174, *Mobile:* 07860 222342, *Water:* Half acre

SOUTH MOLTON
Oaktree Fishery
Contact: George Andrews, Bottreaux Mill, West Anstey, South Molton, EX36 3PU, 01398 341768, *Water:* 3 x 2 acre lakes. *Species:* All Carp to 30lb, Tench to 8lb, Bream, Roach, Perch to 5lb 4oz, Koi Carp, Catfish to 30lb. *Permits:* On site only from shop/reception. *Charges:* Day tickets: Adults from £5, Specimen lake £6, Junior/OAP from £4, Specimen lake £5, Eve tickets: Adult £3.50, Specimen lake £5, Junior/OAP £3.50 Specimen lake £4. *Season:* Open all year 24hrs. *Methods:* Barbless hooks only. No nut type baits. See board at fishery.

STILLWATER COARSE

DEVON

STILLWATER COARSE

TAVISTOCK
Milemead Fisheries (Coarse Lakes)
Contact: Mr Harry Dickens, Mill Hill, Tavistock, PL19 8NP, 01822 610888, *Water:* Two Lakes of 2 acres each. Match Lake available for bookings, please phone for details. Regular Sunday matches and Thursday evening matches in the summer. New 8 Peg Canal now open. *Species:* Carp to 18lb, Tench to 4lb, Bream to 4lb, Roach to 2lb, Rudd to 1.5lb, Crucians to 1lb. *Permits:* Available from lakeside tackle and bait shop. *Charges:* Adult £6, Concession £5, Evening tickets available. *Season:* All year, 7am to Dusk. *Methods:* Barbless Hooks, All nets to be dipped prior to fishing, Please read the rule boards.

TIVERTON
Bickleigh Mill
Contact: Mr Kim & Suzanne Sproat, Bickleigh Mill, Bickleigh, Tiverton, EX16 8RG, 01884 855419, *Water:* Bickleigh Mill fishing ponds. *Species:* Carp, Tench and Bream. *Permits:* Only at above. *Charges:* £4 par day. £2.50 half day. *Season:* Easter to end of September. *Methods:* Rods available.

Coombe Farm Fishponds
Contact: Mrs Curtis, Coombe Farm, Cadleigh, Tiverton, EX16 8HW, 01884 855337, *Mobile:* 07855 416369, *Water:* 3 lakes totalling 0.5 acre. *Species:* Carp to 20lb, Roach, Tench to 4lb, Bream to 1.5lb. *Charges:* £3 per day. *Season:* Open all year. *Methods:* No boilies.

Tiverton & District Angling Club
Contact: Exe Valley Angling, 19 Westexe South, Tiverton, EX16 5DQ, 01884 242275, *Water:* 11.5 Miles on Grand Western Canal, 1.25 acre mixed fishery lake at Exebridge. Various stretches on

South West Lakes Angling Association

Have you joined yet ?

Cost.
For only £10.00 (£7.50 junior/OAP) You can become a member of South West Lakes Angling Association

Benefits.
By being a member you will be entitled to a 10% discount on the cost of your season or day ticket to any of the South West Lakes Trust 14 Coarse Fisheries. You will also receive newsletters during the year. You will be entitled to fish in major competitions including the nationals run by the NFA.

Waters include.

Lower Slade - *Ilfracombe*	Squabmoor - *Exmouth*
Jennetts - *Bideford*	Old Mill - *Dartmouth*
Darracott - *Torrington*	Porth - *Newquay*
Melbury - *Bideford*	Boscathnoe - *Penzance*
Trenchford - *Nr Christow*	Argal - *Nr Falmouth*
Upper Tamar - *Bude*	Bussow - *St Ives*
Lower Tamar - *Bude*	Crafthole - *Nr Torpoint*

Application forms from most local tackle shops
or ring South West Lakes Trust on 01566 771930
Or for more information Contact
Roy Retallick on 01884 256721. Email: r.retallick@btinternet.com
Affiliated to the National Federation of Anglers

West Pitt Farm Fishery
16th Century Farmhouse and Cottages

Come fishing for the day OR stay in one of our delightful self-catering cottages and fish at your leisure.

English Tourism Council ★★★★★ SELF CATERING

- Three spring fed lakes well stocked with a wide variety of quality fish.
- Cottage guests' have their own private pond as well as access to our other lakes.
- After a day's fishing relax in our indoor heated swimming pool, sauna and solarium.
- Games' room with pool, table-tennis and table-football.
- Outdoor play area, grass tennis court and 60 acres to explore.
- Cottages will accommodate from 2 to 9 persons.
- Just five minutes' drive from Junction 27 of M5

For further information on DAY TICKET FISHING or HOLIDAYS, please contact Susanne Westgate
Whitnage, Nr Tiverton, Devon   Tel. 01884 820296   Fax 01884 820818
Email: susannewestgate@yahoo.com

DEVON

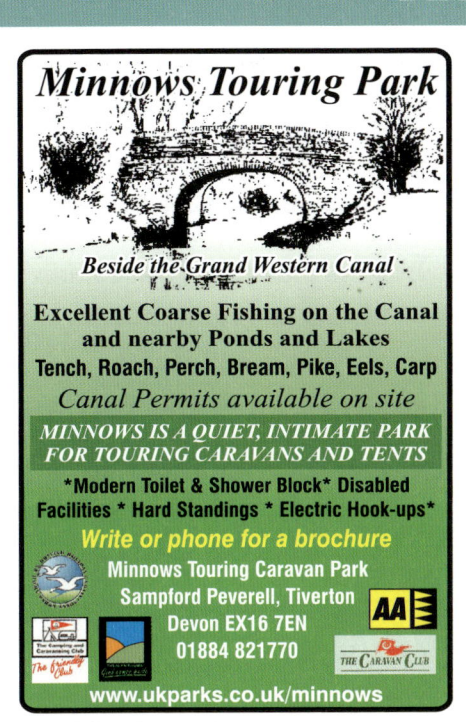

Minnows Touring Park

Beside the Grand Western Canal

Excellent Coarse Fishing on the Canal and nearby Ponds and Lakes

Tench, Roach, Perch, Bream, Pike, Eels, Carp

Canal Permits available on site

MINNOWS IS A QUIET, INTIMATE PARK FOR TOURING CARAVANS AND TENTS

Modern Toilet & Shower Block Disabled Facilities * Hard Standings * Electric Hook-ups*

Write or phone for a brochure

Minnows Touring Caravan Park
Sampford Peverell, Tiverton
Devon EX16 7EN
01884 821770

www.ukparks.co.uk/minnows

---

several rivers in Somerset. *Species:* Canal: Carp, Bream, Tench, Roach, Perch, Pike, Eels. Lakeside: Carp, Bream, Roach, Tench, Eels, Crucian Carp. *Permits:* Please ring Exe Valley for details. Also available from: Exeter Angling Centre, Enterprise Angling Taunton, Topp Tackle Taunton & Minnows Caravan Park - beside Grand Western Canal. *Charges:* Senior: Day £4, Annual £20. Conc: Junior & OAP Day £2.50, Annual £8. *Season:* Canal: Closed March 1st - May 31st inc, except 3 mile section (Basin to Halburton - ring for details). Lakeside: Open all year, Weekends full members only, Maximum five day permits per day. *Methods:* Canal Methods: Any. Restrictions: Fish from permanent pegs, no night fishing, no cars on bank, no digging of banks or excessive clearance of vegetation. Lakeside Methods: Any. Restrictions: No night fishing, no boilies, Trout pellets or nuts, one rod only, fishing from permanent pegs, no dogs, nets to be dipped. Ring Exe Valley Angling for full details.

West Pitt Farm Fishery

Contact: Susanne Westgate, Whitnage, Nr. Tiverton, EX16 7DU, 01884 820296, *Mobile:* 07855 582374, *Water:* 3 lakes up to 2.75 acres. *Species:* Common & Mirror Carp, Bream, Tench, Roach, Rudd, Crucians, Golden Tench, Chub, Golden Orfe. *Permits:* Self service day tickets £5 per day (correct money please). *Charges:* £5/day, £3.50 evenings. *Season:* All year, no closed season. Open dawn till dusk. *Methods:* No boilies. Barbless hooks only, nets to be dipped, groundbait in moderation.

STILLWATER COARSE

THE CRANFORD INN & HOLIDAY COTTAGES

ST. GILES-IN-THE-WOOD, TORRINGTON, N. DEVON.
TEL: 01805 623209. ACCOMMODATION: 01805 624697

Set in its own large grounds and well away from any traffic The Cranford Inn is both spacious and elegantly furnished, retaining its original farmhouse character. Low beamed ceilings, the original inglenook, a well stocked bar, a range of tasty bar snacks and, next door, a superb restaurant serving generous helpings of the best in traditional English Fayre.

The perfect place for your Westcountry Fishing Holiday - Coarse, Game or Sea!

The Cranford is within easy reach of the rivers Taw & Torridge and a plethora of quality Coarse and Trout Stillwaters. For Sea Anglers the Atlantic itself is close by, along with plenty of Charter Boats. The real beauty of Cranford however is its own network of large lakes, **exclusively for residents**, stocked with Carp, Perch, Tench, Roach, Rudd and Bream of the quality shown.

Phone for a free brochure and book your perfect Fishing Holiday

www.thecranfordinn.com

We're looking forward to seeing you!

DEVON

STILLWATER COARSE

TORRINGTON

Bakers Farm
Contact: Mr & Mrs Ridd, Bakers Farm, Moortown, Torrington, EX38 7ES, 01805 623260, *Water:* 1 acre lake. *Species:* Mirror & Common Carp, Tench, Roach & Rudd. *Charges:* £4/rod/day. *Season:* Open all year. *Methods:* Barbless Hooks, No large carp in keepnets.

Darracott
Contact: South West Lakes Trust, 01566 771930, *Water:* Ranger Tel: 01409 211514. *Species:* Roach up to 1lb. Mixed bags to 20lb plus of Roach, Rudd, Bream and Tench. Perch to 2.25lb. Carp to 15lb. *Permits:* See South West Lakes Trust coarse advert. *Charges:* Full day £5, Concession £4, 24 Hour £9, Season Day £90, Season Concession £70, Season Child (under 16) £35, Season Day & Night £135, Additional Fisheries £20 each. *Season:* Open all year 24 hours a day. *Methods:* No child under 14 years may fish unless accompanied by an adult over 18 years. No child under 16 may fish overnight unless accompanied by an adult over 18 years, and then only with permission of parent or legal guardian (letter to this effect must be produced).

Great Torrington Anglers Association (Coarse)
Contact: Paul Martin, 67 Calf Street, Torrington, EX38 7BH, 01805 623658, *Water:* Coarse fishing on local reservoirs, open to anglers from Torrington and surrounding areas. *Species:* Bream, Carp, Roach, Rudd. *Permits:* No day tickets sold by club. *Charges:* Annual membership Adult £5, Junior £3.

Stevenstone Lakes
Contact: Alan & Rebecca Parnell, Deer Park, Stevenstone, Torrington, EX38 7HY, 01805 622102, *Water:* Three lakes, total

East Moore Farm FISHERY
DIPTFORD TOTNES DEVON TQ9 7PE

Two acre Lake well stocked with Carp, Tench, Bream, Roach and Rudd

3 Islands - 51 Pegs
Match Bookings Welcome
Camping & Caravans by prior arrangement

Tel: 01364 73276
www.eastmoorefarm.co.uk

STAFFORD MOOR Fishery

please call for your FREE colour brochure

- Luxurious canadian lodges
- Amazing fishing
- 30 acres of stunning lakes
- Day tickets and weekly matches
- Tackle and bait shop

Stafford Moor Fishery, Toad Hall, Dolton, Winkleigh, Devon EX19 8PP
Telephone (01805) 804360   www.staffordmoor.co.uk

DEVON

Fly caught Pike. Pic - Wayne Thomas.

BRIXHAM Bait and Tackle

NEW! ONLINE SHOP

www.brixhambaitandtackle.co.uk

STILLWATER COARSE

of six acres in a parkland setting. *Species:* Mirror Carp 23lb, Common 13lb, Tench 6lb, Rudd 1lb, Eels 3lb. *Permits:* Only at Deer Park. *Charges:* Day tickets £10 per day per person. *Season:* Open 7am to sunset from 1st April to 30th September. *Methods:* Barbless hooks only, no boilies, no nut type baits, no fish over 2lb in keepnets, no dogs, no litter. Unhooking mats essential.

TOTNES
East Moore Farm Fishery
Contact: John & Kathy Bowden, Diptford, Totnes, TQ9 7PE, 01364 73276, *Mobile:* 07976 559090, *Water:* 1 lake totalling 2 acres. *Species:* Carp to 12lb, Rudd, Tench, Bream, Roach. *Charges:* On site, £5 day (2 rods per person). Under 13 half price, but must be accompanied by an adult. *Season:* Dawn to Dusk, open all year, night fishing by prior arrangement. *Methods:* No keepnets, except in matches, landing mats must be used, no boilies, barbless hooks only. Full rules at Fishery.

UMBERLEIGH
Bridleway Cottages
Contact: Mr & Mrs Fairchild, Golland Farm, Burrington, Umberleigh, EX37 9JP, 01769 520343, *Water:* 2 half acre lakes. Brook fishing for wild Brown Trout. In beautiful picture perfect surroundings. *Species:* Carp to 18lb, Tench and Roach. Quality hard fighting fish. *Permits:* Available from Farm House. *Charges:* Day tickets. *Season:* Lakes open all year, brook fishing seasonal. *Methods:* Barbless hooks only, no Carp in keep nets, no spinning.

WINKLEIGH
Okehampton Coarse Fishing Club
Contact: Mrs Paisey, 68 Moyses Meadow, Okehampton, EX20 1JY, 01837 53646, *Water:* Enclosed still water. Brixton Barton Farm. *Species:* Common Carp to 8lb, Roach, Rudd. *Permits:* Fishing only with a member. *Charges:* £3.50 Guest, £6.50 Adult, £5 Junior, £12.50 Family ticket for full membership. *Season:* 12 months, sunrise to sunset. *Methods:* Barbless hooks. No fish over 2lb in keepnets.

Stafford Moor Fishery
Contact: Andy or Debbie Seery, Dolton, Winkleigh, EX19 8PP, 01805 804360, *Water:* 8 acre specimen lake, 100 pegs match fishery (bookings available); 100 peg pleasure lake. 4 acre Carp bagging water (3lb to 10lb fish). 3 acre lake with Tench, Crucians and Bream. *Species:* Carp 30lb, Tench 5lb, Bream 5lb, Roach 2lb, Rudd 1.5lb, Eels 5lb. 208lb match record. *Permits:* At lodge at Stafford Moor. Specimen lake pre-booking only. *Charges:* £6 pleasure/day, £4.50 conc./OAP/Junior; £7.50 specimen/day (12 hours) £7.50 night (12 hours), £4.50 conc./OAP/Junior. *Season:* All year. *Methods:* The method is banned, barbless hooks (max. size 6), night fishing by arrangement.

YELVERTON
Coombe Fisheries
Contact: Mr Stephen Horn, Yelverton, Plymouth, 01822 616024, *Mobile:* 07899 958493, *Water:* Two 1 acre lakes. *Species:* Coarse fish: Rudd, Roach, Tench, Bream + various Carp (28lb). *Permits:* Local Post Office and (also mobile phone 07788 715470). *Charges:* £4/day, £2.50/evening. *Season:* No close season, dawn to dusk. *Methods:* Barbless hooks, no peanuts.

Devon Stillwater Trout

ASHBURTON
Venford
Contact: South West Lakes Trust, 01566 771930, *Species:* Brown Trout. *Charges:* Free to holders of a valid Environment Agency Licence. *Season:* 15th March - 12th October. *Methods:* Angling by spinning, bubble float & bait.

AXMINSTER
Lower Bruckland Fishery
Contact: David Satterley, Lower Bruckland Farm, Musbury, Axminster, EX13 8ST, 01297 552861, *Mobile:* 0421 429077, *Water:* 3 Large lakes and beginners pool. *Species:* Tringle Lake: Rainbows to 30lb & Wild Browns, Serpentine Lake: Rainbows. *Permits:* Available at Angler's Hut by car park. *Charges:* Tringle: £16/day, £12/half day, £10/evening - Serpentine: 4 - fish £18, 2 - fish £12.50. *Season:* All year. *Methods:* Tringle: Catch & Release, max hook 10, Barbless - Serpentine: Catch & Keep, any method except Spinners.

BARNSTAPLE
Blakewell Fisheries
Contact: Mr Richard & John Nickell, Blakewell Fisheries,

Lower Bruckland Trout Fishery

Three large lakes supplied with natural water from the Bruckland stream

Stocked with Brown & Rainbow Trout to 30lb

Corporate Day Enquiries Welcome

Hot drinks and Tackle available from the lakeside Lodge

Toilets on site

Lower Bruckland Farm, Musbury, Nr Axminster, Devon
Telephone: 01297 552861

Blakewell
Water Gardens & Trout Fishing

A well managed 5 acre lake, beautifully and exceptionally maintained, stocked with the highest quality Rainbow and Brown Trout

Fully Stocked Tackle Shop - Tackle for Hire and Sale
TUITION AVAILABLE Fish available for restocking.
Fishery open 8.30am to one hour after sunset

Muddiford, Barnstaple, N. Devon. EX31 4ET.
Tel: 01271 344533 Fax: 01271 374267
email: mail@blakewell.co.uk
www.blakewell.co.uk

DEVON

Southwood Trout Fishery

Bratton Fleming, Near Barnstaple
Tel: 01271 343608
or Kingfisher Tackle, Barnstaple 01271 344919

Beautiful 2.5 acre Lake with quality, hard fighting Rainbows to OVER 20lb!

Permits by pre-booking only

Southwood can be pre-booked for competitions, corporate days etc

Bulldog Fish Farm

SUPPLIERS OF TOP QUALITY ALL FEMALE AND TRIPLOID RAINBOW TROUT

Our delivery service includes 4WD Toyota Hi-Lux carrying up to 500lbs and a lorry carrying up to 4,400 lbs. Delivery Sizes from 12oz up to 20lb plus!

For all your requirements contact: Nigel Early
Snapper Weir, Goodleigh, Barnstaple, North Devon EX32 7JX

**on (01271) 343608
or (07767) 492800**

nigel.early@btopenworld.com

"Probably the best restocking fish in the country"
Suppliers to Anglian Water and many Scottish Fisheries

STILLWATER TROUT

DEVON

Highampton Lakes
Trout & Coarse Fishery
Established 15 years

Come and fish in peace and quiet in a secluded part of rural Devon for quality Coarse fish and Trout

3 acre Trout Lake + 1 acre Coarse Lake
Rainbow & Brown Trout to 6lb plus - Carp to 20lb plus other species
Self-service permits - Fishing from 8.30am - 9.30pm

For further details and bookings contact us on
01409 231 216
Greenacre Farm, Highampton, Beaworthy, Devon EX21 5LU

Emily with a stunning Exe Valley Rainbow.
Pic - Nick Hart Flyfishing

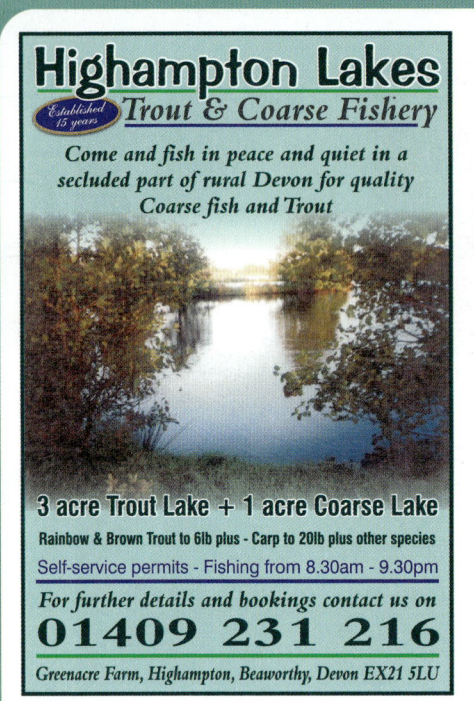

Muddiford, Barnstaple, EX31 4ET, 01271 344533, *Water:* 5 acre lake. *Species:* Rainbow to 22lb 11oz. Brown to 8lb 8oz. *Permits:* On Site. *Charges:* 5 Fish £25, 4 Fish £22, 3 Fish £20, 2 Fish £18. *Season:* All Year. *Methods:* Fly Only.

Southwood Fishery
Bratton Flemming, 01271 343608/344919, *Mobile:* 07767 492800, *Water:* 2.5 acre lake, max 10 rods. *Species:* Rainbow to 20lbs plus. *Permits:* Must be obtained in advance. Please phone numbers above or contact Kingfisher Tackle Shop, The Strand, Barnstaple, 01271 344919. *Charges:* £16 for 2 fish, £18 for 3 fish, £20 for 4 fish. £30 for a 6 fish day ticket. *Season:* Tickets to fish for 8am - 12 noon, 12 noon - 4pm, 4pm - 8pm. Open all year. *Methods:* Tickets must be pre-booked. Fly only, children under 16 must be accompanied by a fishing adult.

BEAWORTHY
South Hay Fishery
Contact: Gill and Reg Stone, South Barn Farm, South Hay, Shebbear, Beaworthy, EX21 5SR, 01409 281857, *Water:* 2 acre Trout lake, 2 miles of River Torridge. *Species:* Rainbow Trout (lake), Brown Trout, Sea Trout, Salmon (river). *Charges:* Lake £5 per day plus £1.50 per lb, River £10 per day. *Season:* Lake - all year, River - Mid March to End September. *Methods:* Fly only.

BIDEFORD
Fosfelle Country House Hotel (Game)
Hartland, Bideford, EX39 6EF, 01237 441273, *Water:* Pond approx half acre. *Species:* Rainbow & Golden Trout. *Charges:* £15 half day - 2 Trout, full day £20 - 3 fish. *Season:* Open all year. *Methods:* Displayed on site.

Torridge Fly Fishing Club
Contact: Mr A Smith (secretary), 6 Brecon Close, Bideford, EX39 4DD, 01237 478614, *Mobile:* 07816 518632, *Water:* 2 x 4 acre reservoirs situated 2 miles east of Bideford. *Species:* Stocked Rainbow Trout from 1.5 to 8lb. Natural Browns to 5lb. *Permits:* 2 day tickets allowed each day. *Charges:* Day tickets: £12.50 per day (3 fish limit) to be obtained at Summerlands Fishing Tackle, Westward Ho!, Tel. 01237 471291; Season tickets: £130 (waiting list: membership limited to 25). *Season:* 14th April - 16th December for Rainbow Trout, 14th April - 30th September for Brown Trout. *Methods:* Floating fly lines only.

CHAGFORD
Fernworthy
Contact: South West Lakes Trust, 01566 771930, *Water:* Ranger: 01647 277587. *Species:* Brown Trout. *Permits:* Self Service Kiosk. *Charges:* Full day £10, Season £130, Reduced day £8, Season £95, Child/Wheelchair £2, Season £30. *Season:* Opens 1st April 2005 - 12th October. *Methods:* Catch & Release operates. Barbless hooks only.

CHUDLEIGH
Kennick
Contact: South West Lakes Trust, 01566 771930, *Water:* Ranger Tel: 01647 277587. *Species:* Premier Rainbow Fishery Bank & Boat. 2004 average 2.8 fish per rod day. *Permits:* Self Service Kiosk - Boats may be booked in advance: 01647 277587. *Charges:* Full day £18, Season £400. Concession day £14.50,

Dave Pilkington fishing the Dart for spring Salmon

Hollies Trout Farm & Fishery
Slade Lane, Sheldon. EX14 4QS

Coarse and Fly fishing in a beautiful valley
Rainbow Trout to 14lbs, Browns to 12lbs
Light Refreshments, Bait and Rod Hire
Open dawn until dusk seven days a week
Self-catering accommodation and B&B

Tel: 0845 2267714
Email:info@holliestroutfarm.co.uk
www.holliestroutfarm.co.uk

01409 231216, *Water:* 2 Trout lakes. Also 1 Coarse Lake. *Species:* Rainbow Trout. *Permits:* Day tickets available from lakes car park. *Charges:* £20 - 4 fish, £15 - 3 fish, £10 - 2 fish. *Season:* Open all Year. *Methods:* No fish to be returned to lake.

HOLSWORTHY
Mill Leat Trout Fishery
Contact: Mr Birkett, Thornbury, Holsworthy, EX22 7AY, 01409 261426, *Water:* Two lakes totalling 3 acres. *Species:* Rainbow Trout. *Charges:* £5 plus £1.50 per lb. No Limit. *Season:* 1st April - 31st October. *Methods:* Fly only.

HONITON
Hollies Trout Farm
Contact: Fiona Downer, Sheldon, Honiton, EX14 4QS, 01404 841428 / 0845 2267714, *Water:* Spring fed lake. *Species:* Rainbow & Brown Trout. Best Rainbow 18lb 12oz (July 1993). Best Brown 11lb 14oz (May 2004). *Charges:* 2 fish - £15, 3 fish - £20, 4 fish - £25, 5 fish - £30. Concessions for O.A.P. and under 12's. *Season:* Open all year dawn to dusk.

Otter Falls (Game)
Contact: John or Carol, New Road, Upottery, Honiton, EX14 9QD, 01404 861634, *Water:* One Trout lake - circa 2.5 acres (see also entry under River Otter, Devon). *Species:* Rainbow Trout to 12lbs. *Charges:* Trout £15 day 3 fish, £10 half day - 2 fish. £60 per week. *Season:* Booking only, 8am to 1 hour after sunset. *Methods:* Barbless hooks. No keepnets.

Stillwaters Lake
Contact: Michael Ford, Lower Moorhayne Farm, Yarcombe, Honiton, EX14 9BE, 01404 861284, *Water:* 1 acre lake. 1 Sea Trout and Salmon rod and Salmon on River Axe at the Sea Pool. *Species:* Trout up to 17lb 10oz in lake (2003). Sea Trout of average size in river. 2004 - Best Brown Trout 6lb 12oz, best Rainbow 11lb. *Charges:* From £25 per day for River Axe fishing - 1 rod only. £10 per session on Stillwaters lake. *Season:* March 1st - November 1st. *Methods:* Fly only.

KINGSBRIDGE
Valley Springs Coarse and Trout Fishery (Trout)
Contact: J. Bishop, Sherford, Kingsbridge, TQ7 2BG, 01548 531574, *Water:* 2 lakes totalling approx 3 acres, Trout & Coarse. *Species:* Rainbow & Brown Trout. *Charges:* £10/Adult and £5/Child to fish plus fish caught & retained at £2.50 per lb. *Season:*

Concession Season £295, Child/Wheelchair £3, Season £90. Evening £14.50. Season Permits can be used on any Premier Fishery only. Boats £11 per day inc. 2 fish extra to bag limits. 'Wheelie Boat' available for disabled anglers (must be booked at least 48 hrs in advance). Catch and release available. *Season:* Opens 25th March 2005 - 31st October. *Methods:* No child under 14 years may fish unless accompanied by an adult over 18 years. Fly fishing only. Catch and release available.

Kennick Fly Fishers Association
Contact: Mike Boston, 5 Shirburn Rd, Torquay, TQ1 3JL, 01803 325722, *Water:* 45 acre reservoir. *Species:* Rainbow & wild Brown Trout. *Permits:* Club members able to obtain SWLT discounted tickets. *Charges:* Membership fee for club is £10 annual subscription. Under 16yrs free. *Methods:* I.A.W. SWLT byelaws.

CULLOMPTON
Goodiford Mill Fishery (Trout Lakes)
Contact: David Wheeler, Goodiford Mill, Kentisbeare, Cullompton, EX15 2AS, 01884 266233, *Water:* 2 lakes set in 20 acres. *Species:* Rainbow - 17lb 5oz, Brown Trout - 20lb 4oz, Tiger Trout. *Permits:* Rod licence required. *Charges:* £30 - 5 fish, £24 - 4 fish, £21 - 3 fish, £18 - 2 fish. Children under 14 must be accompanied by an adult. *Season:* All year. *Methods:* Max 10 longshank. Full rules on application.

HATHERLEIGH
Highampton Lakes (Trout Lake)
Contact: Greenacre Farm, Highampton, Beaworthy, EX21 5LU,

STILLWATER TROUT

STILLWATER TROUT — DEVON

HELEMOOR FISHERY & CAMPING

SET IN 11 ACRES OF BEAUTIFUL DARTMOOR COUNTRYSIDE

Two well stocked ponds
Camping on site • No licence required
Block EA licence • Open all year

RAINBOW & BROWN TROUT

North Bovey Road Moretonhampstead Devon
Tel: 01647 440338
Web: www.helemoor.co.uk

Wiscombe Park Fishery

Southleigh, Colyton, Devon
Tel: 01404 871474
Email: michael@wiscombe.co.uk

TROUT AND COARSE FISHING ALL YEAR ROUND

Three small lakes in a secluded wooded valley scheduled as an area of outstanding beauty
Record Rainbow 15lb 4oz
Day, Half Day and Season Tickets - No booking necessary

Fishing by appointment only, please telephone. *Methods:* Barbless hooks, traditional fly fishing methods only.

MORETONHAMPSTEAD
Helemoor Fishing & Camping (Trout)
North Bovey Road, Moretonhampstead, TQ13 8PB, 01647 440338, *Water:* 100 yard x 60 yard lake. *Species:* Rainbow to 12lb & Brown Trout to 5lb *Charges:* £18 for 2 fish. *Season:* Open all year. Brown Trout season applies. *Methods:* Fly only.

NEWTON ABBOT
Watercress Fishery
Contact: Mr Paul Cook or Mrs Kirsty Cook, Kerswell Springs, Chudleigh, Newton Abbot, TQ13 ODW, 01626 852168, *Mobile:* 07974 704164, *Water:* 3 spring fed lakes totalling approx 5 acres. Alder lake (specimen lake) Tiger, Brown & Rainbow. *Species:* Rainbow, Brown, Tiger Trout. *Permits:* On site. No E.A. rod licence required *Charges:* Various tickets available. Please enquire. *Season:* Open all year, 8am to 1 hour after sunset. *Methods:* Rules on notice board at fishery. Fly only.

OKEHAMPTON
Meldon
Contact: South West Lakes Trust, 01566 771930, *Water:* Ranger Tel: 01822 855700. *Species:* Brown Trout. *Charges:* Free to holders of a valid Environment Agency Licence. *Season:* 15th March - 12th October. *Methods:* Angling by spinning, fly or bait.

Roadford
Contact: South West Lakes Trust, 01566 771930, *Water:* Ranger Tel: 01409 211514. *Species:* Brown Trout Fishery - Boat & Bank (boats may be booked in advance: 01409 211514). 2004 rod average 3.93. *Permits:* Angling & Watersports Centre at Lower Goodacre. *Charges:* Full day £14, Season £300, Reduced day £12, Season £230, Child/Wheelchair £3, Season £60, Evening Mon-Fri £12. Boats £11 per day. *Season:* Opens 25 March 2005 - 12th October. *Methods:* Fly fishing only. Catch and release option - Barbless hooks only. No child under 14 years may fish unless accompanied by an adult over 18 years.

Roadford Fly Fishing Club
Contact: Rod Dibble, 25 Pine View, Gunnislake, PL18 9JF, 01822 834188, *Water:* Club fishing at Roadford Lake. *Species:* Brown Trout. *Methods:* Fly only.

SEATON
Wiscombe Park Fishery (Trout Lakes)
Contact: Mike Raynor, Wiscombe Park Fishery, Colyton, EX24 6JE, 01404 871474, *Mobile:* 07860 222342, *Water:* Two half acre lakes plus Coarse fishing. *Species:* Rainbow Trout, Brown Trout. *Permits:* Self-service (No booking). *Charges:* £17/day (8 fish limit), £12/4hrs (3 fish), £8.50/2 hrs (2 fish), Children under 15 free (accompanied by permit holding adult). *Season:* All year. *Methods:* Fly fishing (singles).

SOUTH BRENT
Avon Dam
Contact: South West Lakes Trust, 01566 771930, *Water:* Ranger Tel: 01822 855700. *Species:* Brown Trout. *Charges:* Free to holders of a valid Environment Agency Licence. *Season:* 15 March - 12 October. *Methods:* Angling by spinning, fly or bait.

Hatchlands Trout Lakes
Contact: Malcolm Davies, Greyshoot Lane, Rattery, South Brent, TQ10 9LN, 01364 73500, *Water:* 6 acres. *Species:* Rainbow, Brown, Golden, Blue and Brook Trout. *Permits:* No E.A. Permit required. *Charges:* Prices from £10 for 2 fish. Other prices on application. Sporting ticket from £18, Catch and Release £14. *Season:* Open all year. *Methods:* Barbless hooks on catch and release.

Somerswood Lake
Contact: S.A. Goodman, Brent Mill Farm, South Brent, TQ10 9JD, 01364 72154, *Water:* 2 acres in Avon valley. *Species:* Rainbow Trout. *Permits:* At farmhouse. *Charges:* Please enquire. *Season:* Open all year. *Methods:* Fly.

DEVON

Snowbee® *Prestige Fly Fishing Tackle*

Come and see the largest range of quality Game Fishing Tackle in the South West

FLY RODS ..... A full range to suit every pocket from the Snowbee Classic Range priced from £45, through the Zircon XS Rods £135 - £190 and Deep Blue Travel Fly and Spin £85-£150, to the top of the range Snowbee XS-P Trout and Spinning Rods £109-£260 and Snowbee XS-P 'Spey' Rods £355-£425. These quality rods are all built on the latest light weight High Carbon Blanks and offer exceptional value for money coupled with a performance equal to any other World-class rods. All rods come with an Original Purchaser Lifetime Guarantee. New for 2005 are the XS-P two-handed 12ft 6" #7/8 Tamar - £295 & 12ft #6/7 Torridge - £285 4pce salmon/ grilse rods. New single-handed rods include the XS-P 9ft #8 - £245 & 9ft #9 - £250, also in 4pce.

FLY REELS ... In addition to our Bar-Stock Prestige Fly Reels we are proud to offer the award winning Snowbee XS large Arbor Fly Reel. This top quality reel is built exclusively for Snowbee by British Fly Reels. It features a silky smooth Centre Disc Drag and is totally saltwater resistant. Priced between £165 and £190 the XS comes with a 5 Year Guarantee which reflects the build quality of this superb new reel. We also offer the 1112 model, the perfect choice for the salmon and saltwater fly fisherman.

WADERS .... We manufacture and stock the largest range of waders in the UK. PVC Waders from £20, Nylon Waders from £35, Neoprene Waders from £43 and our superb range of Breathable Waders from £69. This year we will be introducing the XS Neoprene Chest Waders in a choice of stocking-foot £185 or boot-foot, with a felt or Spiked sole, £195 complete with a 3yr warranty on seams.

CLOTHING .... We have introduced a completely new range of Prestige Breathable Clothing for 2005.... Breathable Wading Jacket £119, Breathable Boat Jacket £129, Breathable ¾ length Jacket £139, Breathable Bib Trousers £109. Also for 2005 is a completely new range of camouflage clothing and waders from £79.

ACCESSORIES ... Include our range of Fishing and Travel Bags, Landing Nets, Fly Boxes, Sunglasses, Leaders, Floatants, Sinkants, Smokers ...... plus a whole lot more!

IN ADDITION to our own Snowbee tackle range, we also carry one of the largest stocks of Tied Flies, Fly Tying Tools, Vices and Materials in the West Country. Over 300 patterns/sizes of Tied Flies, with over 10,000 flies in stock at any time!

STILLWATER TROUT

Full mail order service available Ring, write or e-mail for our new full colour 2005 catalogue. Trade enquiries welcome.
Tel: 01752 334933
Fax: 01752 334934
Email: flyfish@snowbee.co.uk
Website: www.snowbee.co.uk

Come and visit our showroom at Langage Business Park, just off the A38 Deep Lane Plympton Exit. Plenty of "out of town" parking

Available from Snowbee stockists or direct from ...
Snowbee (UK) ltd, Drakes Court, Langage Business Park
Plymouth, Devon PL7 5JY

Snowbee® *Tackle for the real world.*

DEVON

SOUTH MOLTON
Wistlandpound
Contact: South West Lakes Trust, 01566 771930, *Water:* Ranger Tel: 01398 371372. *Species:* Intermediate Rainbow Trout Fishery. Trout to 6lb. *Permits:* Post Office in Challacombe: (01598) 763229, The Kingfisher, Barnstaple: (01271) 344919. Lyndale News, Combe Martin: (01271) 883283, Variety Sports, Ilfracombe: (01271) 862039. Calvert Trust, Wistland Pound (01598) 763221. 'Wheelie Boat' available for disabled anglers via the Calvert Trust (01598) 763221. *Charges:* Full day £12.50, Season £210, Reduced day £11, Season £180, Child/Wheelchair £2, Season £40. *Season:* Opens 15th March - 31sth October. *Methods:* Fly fishing only. Catch and release - barbless hooks.

Wistlandpound Fly Fishing Club
Contact: Nigel Bird, 9 Kingston Avenue, Combe Martin, EX34 0AE, 01271 883252, *Water:* Fishing regular monthly competitions at Wistlandpound and other waters. Regular social events. Juniors welcome. *Species:* Rainbow Trout 1.5 to 2lb. Brown Trout 8oz to 1lb. *Permits:* Permits to fish Wistlandpound available at a reduced rate - members only. *Charges:* Subsciptions (March to March): Adults £10, Under 16s 50p. Free tuition arranged. *Season:* Seasonal at Wistlandpound. Competitions all year round.

TAVISTOCK
Milemead Fisheries (Trout Lake)
Contact: Mr Harry Dickens, Mill Hill, Tavistock, PL19 8NP, 01822 610888, *Water:* 2 acre spring fed lake, max 10 anglers at any one time. *Species:* Rainbow, Blue and Brown Trout from 1.5lb to 10lb plus. *Permits:* Available from lakeside tackle and bait shop. *Charges:* 2 fish - £12. 3 fish - £16. 4 fish - £19. 5 fish - £22 (2002

Stuart Forsyth about to release a fly caught Taw Salmon. Pic - Nick Hart Flyfishing.

STILLWATER TROUT

TAVISTOCK TROUT FISHERY
www.tavistocktroutfishery.co.uk
Parkwood Rd, Tavistock, Devon. PL19 9JW Tel: 01822 615441

OSPREY LAKE - Stocked with Trout 3lbs to VERY LARGE!

KINGFISHER & HERON LAKES - Stocked with Trout 1.5lbs to 14lbs

PLUS CHILDRENS LAKE

TACKLE SHOP! A Fly Fisherman's dream...
Rods, reels, lines, waistcoats, nets, priests, flies etc

FIVE SUPERB LAKES
Fish Gutting & Freezing   No EA Licence required
'Free' Tea & Coffee facilities for Anglers
Farm Animals & Picnic Area

Four Self Catering Holiday Lets On Site
www.tavistocktroutfishery.co.uk
JUST 200 YARDS FROM 'THE TROUT AND TIPPLE' PUB

DEVON

Prices). *Season:* Open all year 8am to dusk. *Methods:* Fly fishing only, no catch and release, please read the rule boards.

Tavistock Trout Farm & Fishery
Contact: Abigail Underhill, Parkwood Road, Tavistock, PL19 9JW, 01822 615441, *Water:* 5 lakes totalling approx 4 acres. *Species:* Rainbow Trout (3lb - huge Osprey/Kingfisher & Heron 1 1/2lb - 14lb), Brown Trout. *Charges:* Full day 6 fish permit - Osprey Lake £50, Full day 6 fish Kingfisher and Heron Lakes £27.50, other tickets available. *Season:* Open all year 8am - dusk. *Methods:* Max hook size 10.

TIVERTON
Bellbrook Valley Trout Fishery
Contact: Mr Chris Atwell, Bellbrook Farm, Oakford, Tiverton, EX16 9EX, 01398 351292, *Water:* 7 Lakes totalling 6.75 acres. *Species:* Rainbow Trout (25lb 12oz), Exmoor Blue (8lb 6oz) and Wild Brown Trout (7lb 8oz). *Charges:* Evening ticket £10, 3 fish normal £18, 2 fish specimen £22. Range of rover tickets, allowing mix of normal and specimen, start @ £25. Catch and release - £15 ticket, plus 1st fish can be taken. *Season:* Open all year 8.00am / dusk (No later than 9.00pm). *Methods:* Fly only, some catch & release available.

TORRINGTON
Great Torrington Anglers Association (Trout)
Contact: Paul Martin, 67 Calf Street, Torrington, EX38 7BH, 01805 623658, *Water:* Fly fishing on local reservoirs and canal fishing. *Permits:* No day tickets sold by club. *Charges:* Annual membership Adult £5-00, Junior £3-00.

Stephen Marks delighted with this Rainbow landed during an EA event at Innis Moor Trout Fishery in Cornwall.

STILLWATER TROUT

BELLBROOK VALLEY
TROUT FISHERY

- 4 x specimen + 3 x 'normal' lakes
- All stocked from our own fish farm
- Tuition & equipment hire
- Season tickets
- Lodge & tackle shop
- Variety of tickets available
- Corporate entertainment
- Self-catering accommodation
- Bed & Breakfast

Tel: 01398 351292
www.bellbrookfishery.co.uk

Oakford • Tiverton • Devon • EX16 9EX

DEVON

TOTNES
Newhouse Fishery
Contact: Adrian or Paul Cook, Newhouse Farm, Moreleigh, Totnes, TQ9 7JS, 01548 821426 or 01626 852168, *Water:* 4 acre lake (also see entry under River Fishing, Avon, Devon). *Species:* Rainbow Trout, Brown Trout. *Permits:* At above. No E.A. rod licence required. *Charges:* Various tickets available. *Season:* Open all year. 8am to 1 hour after sunset. *Methods:* Fly only, barbed hooks.

YELVERTON
Burrator
Contact: South West Lakes Trust, 01566 771930, *Water:* Ranger: 01822 855700 *Species:* Low Cost Rainbow & Brown Trout. *Permits:* Esso Garage, Yelverton. *Charges:* Full day £10, Season £130, Reduced day £8, Season £95, Child/Wheelchair £2, Season £30. *Season:* Opens 15 March 2005 - 12th October. *Methods:* Catch & release option. Barbless hooks only. Fly fishing only.

Burrator & Siblyback Fly Fishing & Angling Association
Contact: Derek Friend (Hon Sec), 01752 224822, *Species:* Regular fortnightly competitions fishing South West Lakes Trust waters and sea fly fishing trips. *Permits:* Open to all. *Charges:* Family membership £15, members £10. All Juniors under 18 must be accompanied by an adult. *Season:* Contact Derek at the above number.

Burrator Fly Fishers Association
Contact: Richard Adeney, 01752 218344, *Water:* BFFA is a small club running competitions during the summer and winter, with fishing trips to local still waters. Regular monthly meetings take place in the winter. *Species:* Stocked Rainbow and Brown Trout. *Permits:* From the Esso Garage at Yelverton. *Charges:* £9.25 for full day. Club membership is £10 per year, which includes membership of club insurance scheme. *Season:* 15th March to 12th October. *Methods:* Fly, barbless hooks encouraged.

Nick Hart about to return this superb Brownie to the river Exe.

Fun, Fresh Air and Fish!
Fly Fishing Courses (APGAI / STANIC / LEVEL 2)
Guided River Fishing   Saltwater Fly Fishing
www.hartflyfishing.co.uk

Nick Hart FLY FISHING

Call Nick or Pete on 01398 331660 or 07971 198559 for more information and a full colour brochure

STILLWATER TROUT

Sea Fishing

AXMOUTH
Cygnet
Contact: Paul Godfrey, 8 Prince Charles Way, Seaton, EX12 2TU, *Mobile:* 07779 040491, *Water:* Sailing from Beer in Lyme Bay area.

BARNSTAPLE
Combe Martin Sea Angling Club
Contact: Wayne Thomas, The Shippen, Loxhore Cott, Nr Barnstaple, EX31, 01271 850586, *Charges:* Family £10, Senior £6, Junior £1.

Triple Hook Club
Contact: Dennis Toleman, 32 Pilton Lawn, Barnstaple, EX31 4AA, 01271 378595, *Mobile:* 07815 009260, *Water:* Shore fishing, 8 boat trips, regular fly fishing & coarse fishing matches plus training sessions & tuition. *Permits:* Monthly meeting at Barnstaple & District Social Club (ExRBL) St Georges Road, Barnstaple, 1st Tuesday in month. New members welcome. Family orientated club, please contact Dennis on number above or come to our meetings. *Charges:* £5 membership, matches £5, Juniors £3. *Season:* All year round.

BIDEFORD
Appledore Shipbuilders Angling Club
Contact: M Horrel, 52 Devonshire Park, Bideford, 01237 474614, *Water:* Shore and boat fishing. Roving monthly competitions. Annual festive competitions. Founded in 1971, 50 plus members. South West Federation member. New members welcome. *Charges:* £5 Adult. £2 Juniors. *Season:* All year round.

Bideford & District Angling Club (Sea)
Contact: Mr B. Ackland, Honestone Street, Bideford, EX39 3DA, 01237 478846, *Water:* Bideford based club with coarse, game, boat & sea sections; fishing throughout South West. Competitions: May 28th - 31st and August 27th - 30th. Please phone for further details. *Permits:* Membership form from club, open 7pm-11pm *Charges:* £5 per annum. £2 associates. £1 for juniors/OAPs

Sanderling
Contact: Randall, Appledore, 01237 479585, *Mobile:* 07779 443472, *Water:* Estuary fishing. 2 hour trips in 'Sanderling, fully licenced and insured for 12 anglers. £10 per person. Rod and bait supplied if required. *Species:* Bass, Plaice etc. *Charges:* Two hour trip - £10 per head, rod and bait supplied.

BRIXHAM
Brixham Sea Anglers Club
Contact: Mr L.E. Turner (Secretary), Castor Road, Brixham, TQ5 9PY, 01803 853930, *Water:* Licenced Club. Holders of world record for Conger eel at 133lb 4oz. Shore fishing from Exmouth to Plymouth. Boat fishing. Wednesday night competitions on the breakwater from May to September. Bingo and social events. Junior section. *Permits:* Please telephone or write for an application form. *Charges:* £10 per year adult. £1.50 junior plus £5 joining fee (adults only).

Seaspray III & Bonnie Boys (Mackerel Fishing)
Contact: Chris Willicott, 01803 851328, *Season:* All year. Mackerel boat 1st April - 31st October.

CLOVELLY
Jessica Hettie
Contact: Clive Pearson, 01237 431405 (eve), *Mobile:* 07774 190359, *Water:* Sea Angling trips around Clovelly and Lundy. *Species:* Shark, Pollack, Mackerel, Bass. *Season:* April to October.

Ralph Atkinson Angling Charters
Contact: Ralph, Isis, Irsha Court, Irsha Street, Appledore, EX39 1RN, 01237 475535, *Mobile:* 07774 164086, *Water:* Inshore and offshore reefs, wrecks and banks and deep sea in the Bristol Channel onboard 'Hooker'. *Species:* Tope, Shark, Bass, Pollack, Rays, Congers, Huss. *Permits:* 20 mile day or night licence for up to 8 people. Fully equipped with all safety gear and tackle. *Charges:* Individuals: Adults - £33 full day, £20 half day. Under 12s £20 full day, £13 half day. Two hour trips £12 per person. To book boat £200. *Season:* Operating all year. Boat leaves Clovelly. Full day leaves 9am and returns at 5pm. Half days 9am-1pm or 1pm-5pm.

CREDITON
Crediton Inn Angling Club
Contact: NFSA Head Office: 01364 644643,

DART
African Queen
Contact: Alan Hemsley, *Mobile:* 07885 246061,

DARTMOUTH
Dartmouth Angling & Boating Association
Contact: Mervyn G Yalland (Chairman), 5 Oxford Street, Dartmouth, 01548 856254, *Mobile:* 07971 749395, *Water:* Predominantly sea fishing, some coarse fishing. *Charges:* Membership £7 individual, £13 couple, £3 Junior. (Clubhouse phone: 07977 843754).

Gemini II
Contact: Dave Harrison, 01803 851766, *Mobile:* 07968 599245,

Saltwind of Dart
Contact: Lloyd Saunders, 01803 883003, *Mobile:* 07831 315477,

Samuel Irvin
Contact: Ian Noble, Mill Pool House, 7 Market Street, Dartmouth, TQ5 9QE, 01803 834598, *Mobile:* 07780 970803, *Water:* Fishing inshore banks and reefs, mid channel wrecks and Channel Island trips. *Species:* Plaice, Turbot, Bass, Cod, Pollack, Ling, Conger, Whiting, Brill, Bream, Ray. *Charges:* From £25 per person per day. *Season:* Fishing all year round.

Two Rivers
Contact: Steve Parker, 01803 329414, *Mobile:* 07866 806585,

EXETER
Axminster Sea Angling Club
Contact: NFSA Head Office: 01364 644643,

DEVON

TACKLE DIRECT
OFFER A FULL RANGE OF DISCOUNTED TACKLE
Plus Live and Frozen Bait
10 Belgrave Promenade, Wilder Road, Ilfracombe
Tel: 01271 862363
www.tackledirect.co.uk
OPEN 7 DAYS THROUGHOUT THE SUMMER!

Variety Sports
FISHING TACKLE SPECIALISTS
SEA, COARSE & GAME
FRESH AND FROZEN BAITS
LOCAL PERMITS
23, BROAD ST., ILFRACOMBE
TEL: (01271) 862039

EXMOUTH
Blue Thunder
Contact: Mike Deem, Sandpiper Drive, Exton, Exeter, EX3 0PP, 01626 891181, *Water:* Operating from Exmouth, Devon using a 420hp 33ft Lochin angling boat. *Species:* Wreck fishing for Bass, Cod and Pollack. *Charges:* £340 for boat. £34 for individual angler. *Season:* 7.00am - 5.30pm daily.

Exmouth Sea Angling Association
Contact: NFSA Head Office: 01364 644643,

Restorick III
Contact: Colin Pike, 01363 775316, *Water:* Lyme Bay, Channel Islands.

Smuggler V
Contact: Colin Dukes, 01626 890852, *Mobile:* 07974 437740, *Water:* Channel Island, mid channel wrecking.

Starcross Fishing & Cruising Club
Contact: Mr Eddy Carter, Brunel Tower, The Strand, Starcross, EX6 8PR, 01626 89013, *Water:* Exe estuary and Lyme Bay. *Species:* Bass, Ling, Pollock, Ray, Dogfish, Bream, Flounder, Conger, Whiting plus many others. *Permits:* Not required. *Charges:* Free. *Season:* Bass have closed season on the Exe. *Methods:* No restrictions.

Stuart Line Fishing
Queens Drive, Exmouth, EX8 2AY, 01395 275882, *Mobile:* 07977 203099, *Water:* Lyme Bay. *Species:* Mackerel, Ling, Pollack, Whiting, Conger Eel. *Permits:* N/A *Charges:* Mackerel £6. Deep Sea £10. *Season:* Easter to end of October. *Methods:* Rods and reels, using feathers or hooks.

Tamesis
Contact: Nigel Dyke, 01769 580376, *Mobile:* 07970 909614,

HONITON
Honiton Sea Angling Club
Contact: Mike Spiller, 6 Charles Road, Honiton, EX14 1QG, 01404 43397, *Mobile:* 07779 308093, *Water:* A club for family membership. Regular competitions, junior matches, boat & casting competitions held. Casting tuition, member of England team. *Species:* Any sea fish. *Charges:* Senior £5, OAP £3, Junior £2. Competitions are free.

ILFRACOMBE
Ilfracombe & District Anglers Association (Sea)
Contact: David Shorney, Victoria Cottage, 8B St Brannocks Road, Ilfracombe, EX34 8EG, 01271 865874, *Water:* Beaches and rock marks. Founded in October 1929, the oldest club in North Devon. *Species:* Bass, Pollock, Conger, Mullet, Ray, Coalfish, Cod and various other species. *Permits:* From Variety Sports, Broad Street, Ilfracombe. *Charges:* Fees per year: Family £10, Adult £8, OAP £4, Junior £2. 17 competitions per year and an annual fishing festival in July/August. *Season:* January to January.

Kerry Kim
Contact: Eddie Bennellick, 01271 864143 / 01271 864143,

Osprey
Contact: Paul Barbeary, Ilfracombe, EX34 9EQ, 01271 864625, *Mobile:* 07970 101407, *Water:* Bristol Channel, Lundy Island. *Species:* Most British water species. *Charges:* On application. *Season:* All year round. *Methods:* No restrictions.

INSTOW
Betty Louise
Contact: Royston, Torridge House, Lane End, Instow, EX39 4LB, 01271 860889, *Mobile:* 07966 428189, *Water:* Licensed for 12, Shark and Tope fishing. All day and 1/2 day trips by arrangement. *Species:* Bass and Black Bream, also light line Pollacking. Between June and September, experience the fight of a life time, when we go for the Porbeagle Shark. Best day - 8 Shark weighing up to 357lb. Can weigh at local club or at local fishing CO'OP. *Charges:* £30 p/person for 12hr trip. £15 p/person for 5hr trip. £5 rod hire. £10 rod hire when sharking. Tackle can be bought on board boat. All new 2004. *Season:* Starts April - ends February. *Methods:* Drifting over 6 mile reefs with light tackle, for Bass, Pollock, Bream, Wrass. Go on anchor for Tope, Skate, Bullhuss and Conger.

IVYBRIDGE
Bridge Sea Angling Club
Contact: NFSA Head Office: 01364 644643,
Plymouth City Engineers Sea Angling Club
Contact: NFSA Head Office: 01364 644643,

KINGSBRIDGE
Kingsbridge & District Sea Anglers
Contact: Ray Carr, 17 Barnfield Walk, Kingsbridge, TQ7 1QS, 01548 853331, *Water:* Regular monthly boat and shore matches, strong junior section, matches with other clubs in region. New members welcome, contact Ray at number above. *Charges:* Seniors £10, juniors £5 (under 16), family £15 (2 adults, 2 children). Child protection policy in force.

SEA FISHING

DEVON

*Pouting fresh from the sea.
Pic by Wayne Thomas*

PAIGNTON
Charlotte Lousie
Contact: Ashley Lane, Paignton Harbour, TQ4 6DW, *Mobile:* 07767 622727, *Season:* All year round.
Our Joe-I
Contact: Simon Pedley, 01803 551504,
Paignton Sea Angling Association
Contact: NFSA Head Office: 01364 644643,
Seafield Sea Angling Club
Contact: NFSA Head Office: 01364 644643,
Tuonela
Contact: Peter Bingle, 01803 666350, *Mobile:* 07715 735842,

PLYMOUTH
British Conger Club
Contact: NFSA Head Office: 01364 644643,
D.O.E Sea Angling Club
Contact: NFSA Head Office: 01364 644643,
Dartmoor Pirates S.A.C.
Contact: NFSA Head Office: 01364 644643,
Devonport Sea Angling Club - 'The Peelers'
Contact: NFSA Head Office: 01364 644643,
Ford Hotel S.A.C. (Plymouth)
Contact: NFSA Head Office: 01364 644643,
Gypsy Mariners Angling Club
Contact: NFSA Head Office: 01364 644643,
Naval Stores Sea Angling Club
Contact: NFSA Head Office: 01364 644643,
Plymouth Command Angling Association (Sea)
Contact: Mr Vic Barnett Hon.Sec., 5 Weir Close, Mainstone, Plymouth, PL6 8SD, 01752 708206, *Water:* Boat & shore fishing. *Species:* All sea fish. *Permits:* Membership is open to all serving members of HM Forces. Associate membership is also open to ex-serving members of HM Forces, no matter when the time was served. *Charges:* Costs for full membership or associate membership are available on application or enquiry at the above contact.
Plymouth Federation S.A.C.
Contact: NFSA Head Office: 01364 644643,
Plymouth Inter Boat A.F.
Contact: NFSA Head Office: 01364 644643,
Plymouth S.A.C.
Contact: NFSA Head Office: 01364 644643,
Rodbenders S.A.C.
Contact: NFSA Head Office: 01364 644643,
Roving Rods Sea Angling Club
Contact: NFSA Head Office: 01364 644643,
Royal Naval & Royal Marines A.A.
Contact: NFSA Head Office: 01364 644643,
Scorpion
Contact: Dave Brett, Plymouth, 01752 500535,
Sea Angler
Contact: Malcolm Jones, 14 Cockington Walk, Eggbuckland, Plymouth, PL6 5QF, 01752 316289, *Mobile:* 07977 097690,
Size Matters
Contact: Graham Hannaford, Plymouth, 01752 500535,
Specimen Angling Group of Plymouth
Contact: NFSA Head Office: 01364 644643,
Stonehouse Creek Sea Angling Club
Contact: NFSA Head Office: 01364 644643,
Storm
Contact: Rod Davies, 01752 492232, *Mobile:* 07812 431982, *Season:* March to October.
Tiburon
Contact: Jim O'Donnel, 01752 330152, *Mobile:* 07855 040015, *Water:* Wreck, reef, bank Shark and Bass fishing. *Season:* Full day, half day and evening trips.

SALCOMBE
Anglo Dawn II
Contact: Chris Roberts, 16 Stentiford Hill, Kingsbridge, TQ7 1BD, 01548 854211, *Mobile:* 07967 387657, *Water:* Reef, banks inc Skerries, mid channel wrecking, Guernsey. *Species:* Cod, pollack, ling, plaice, rays, bass, conger, whiting, mackerel. *Charges:* Reefs or Banks - £265. Up to 25 mile wrecking - £350. 25 miles plus - £400. Prices are for boat for a full day, individual prices and shorter charters are available. *Season:* All year round.
Calypso
Contact: Kevin Oakman, 01548 843784, *Mobile:* 07970 651569, *Charges:* £250 Boat (minimum of 6) *Season:* Easter - October
Phoenix
Contact: Chris Puncher, 19 St Dunstans Road, Salcombe, TQ8 8AL, 01548 842840, *Mobile:* 07855 315770,
Tuckers Boat Hire
Contact: Chris Puncher, 01548 842840, *Season:* 1st April - 31st October.
Whitestrand Boat Hire
Contact: Debbie or Kevin, 01548 843818, *Water:* 32 boats.

SEATON
Beer & District Sea Angling Association
Contact: NFSA Head Office: 01364 644643,

SEA FISHING

DEVON

STARCROSS
Torbay & Babbacombe Association of Sea Anglers
Contact: NFSA Head Office: 01364 644643,

TEIGNMOUTH
Teignmouth Sea Angling Society
Contact: NFSA Head Office: 01364 644643,

TORQUAY
Dalora II
Contact: Kevin Tate, Torquay, 01626 776606, *Mobile:* 07989 527180, *Charges:* Individuals welcome. Also trips to Guernsey. *Season:* All year.
Jubrae
Contact: Geoff and Fred, 01803 213866, *Mobile:* 07860 200247,
Torbay S.A.F.A.
Contact: NFSA Head Office: 01364 644643,

TOTNES
Baywater Anglers
Contact: Martyn Green (co-ordinator), 31 Collapark, Totnes, TQ9 5LW, 01803 863279, *Water:* A light tackle sea angling club offering not only shore and boat trips but also instruction in a variety of techniques including fly fishing, beachcasting, Bassing etc. *Charges:* Membership: £10 senior, £3 junior, £15 family, £5 student aged 16-18.

WESTCOUNTRY
National Federation of Sea Anglers
Contact: Head Office, Level 5, Hamlyn House, Mardle Way, Buckfastleigh, TQ11 0NS, 01364 644643, *Water:* Sea Angling. *Species:* All sea fish. *Permits:* None apply. *Charges:* Individual membership £12 per year. Personal membership £17 per year. *Season:* None applicable.
South West Federation of Sea Anglers
Contact: Andy Alcock, 45 Newstead Road, Weymouth, DT4 0AT, 01305 772318, *Water:* South West coastal waters.

Quay Stores Ltd
23 Victoria Parade, Torquay - 01803 292080
www.tidaltackle.co.uk

DESTROYING HIGH PRICES

FOR ALL YOUR ANGLING NEEDS
Live & Frozen Bait
Open 7 days a week
Late evening opening through the summer

Sunset on the North Devon coast. Pic by Wayne Thomas

DEVON

A nice Mirror Carp taken from the margins on floating crust at Avallon Lodges.

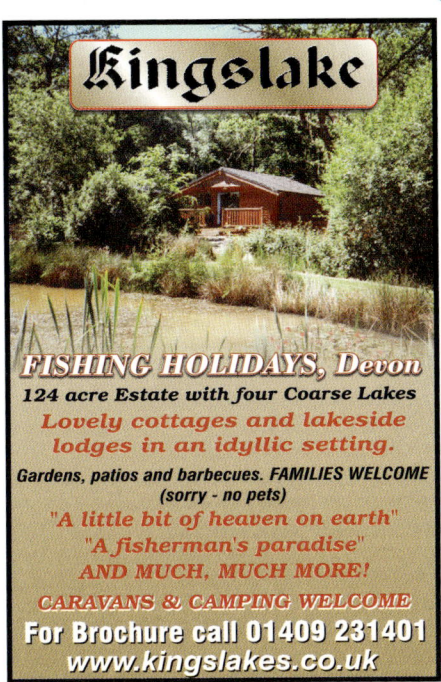

Kingslake

FISHING HOLIDAYS, Devon
124 acre Estate with four Coarse Lakes
Lovely cottages and lakeside lodges in an idyllic setting.
Gardens, patios and barbecues. FAMILIES WELCOME (sorry - no pets)
"A little bit of heaven on earth"
"A fisherman's paradise"
AND MUCH, MUCH MORE!
CARAVANS & CAMPING WELCOME

For Brochure call **01409 231401**
www.kingslakes.co.uk

Upton Lakes Fishing Holidays

Superb Fishing...

100 year old 'Top Lake'
Carp to over 26lb, Bream to over 7lb, Tench to 6lb, Perch to 3lb, Rudd and Roach to 2lb.

Purpose built 'Match Lake'
Stocked with Carp, Skimmers, Roach, Rudd, Tench and Crucians - great fishing with bags to over 90lb.

River Fishing
Just a short walk to the river Culm.

Local Attractions
Shopping in Exeter, fun for the kids at Crealy Adventure Park, Diggerland or Quadworld. Walking, Riding and Golf plus Dartmoor and both north and south coasts within easy reach

Accommodation
Superbly equipped, spacious two and three bedroomed static homes

Situated right next to the lakes with Fully equipped kitchens, bathroom, shower, modern toilets, gas heating, hi-fi, T.V. and video. Enjoy the superb countryside views from your veranda over an evening barbecue!

Now offering standard and DELUXE accommodation!

Phone for your free brochure on
07830 199690
or visit our web site...
www.upton-lakes.co.uk

Upton Lakes Fishing Holidays,
Upton Farm, Cullompton, Devon EX15 1RA

WHERE TO STAY

DEVON

Malston Mill Farm
Kingsbridge, Devon TQ7 2DR

This is one fishing holiday the wife and family will LOVE!

Lakeside luxury cottages situated in one of Devon's most beautiful valleys

Facilities include
- Indoor and outdoor swimming pools
- Outdoor Jacuzzi ❖ Snooker/Pool Room
- Fitness Room ❖ Infra Red Sauna
- Galleried Games Area ❖ Tennis Court
- Outdoor Children's Play Area

FREE Coarse Fishing for large Carp, Tench and Rudd

Telephone: 01548 852518
www.malstonmill.co.uk
Email: gresham@malstonmill.fsnet.co.uk

Kez feeding the last of the bait to seagulls after a session out of Exmouth.

HAYRISH FARM

5 & 4 STAR (ETC Rated) LUXURY ACCOMMODATION IN DEVON

Tranquil & elegant riverside properties set in a 187 acre private estate on the edge of Dartmoor National Park. 4 Self Contained Cottages & a Farm House, a Grade II listed Devon Long House with all accommodation en-suite.
Open fires, charm & character

Salmon, Sea Trout & Brown Trout fishing on private beats of the River Taw (21lb Salmon - 2004)

Simulated Game Shooting and Fishing weekends 8th April, 22nd April, 13th May and 10th June 2005.
Single Guns & Rods welcome

Regional Tourist Board
southwest tourism
MEMBER

Call Gill or David on
020 7256 9013 or 07736 628971
with any queries and for brochure.

e-mail: hayrish@easynet.co.uk or visit us at www.hayrish.co.uk

WHERE TO STAY

DEVON

Get Hooked ON THE WEB

Advertise your accommodation online in the 'where to stay' section of

www.gethooked.co.uk

3 pictures, 150 words, e-mail and website links

ONLY £60 PER YEAR*
*exc VAT

TEL: 01271 860183 or
E-MAIL: mandi@gethooked.co.uk

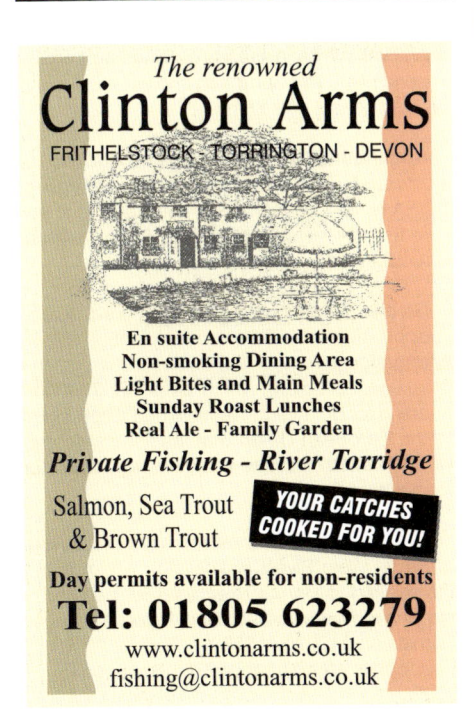

South Devon

Sunridge, Yealmpton
Idyllic rural secluded cottage set in 8 acres. Magnificent views and a well stocked Carp lake in a woodland setting, established 28 years.

Dartmoor to the north and coastal walks and beaches within 3 miles to the south. Attractive self catering converted Barn.

For Brochure Tel: 01752 880438

MYRTLE COTTAGE
INSTOW - DEVON

In a quiet location just yards from the sandy beach, this immaculate property is furnished with flair and enjoys sea views from both its sitting room and bedroom. Myrtle Cottage is within 500 yards of pubs, restaurants and shops.

Boating and fishing trips available locally, with day excursions to Lundy Island operating from Bideford (3 miles). River fishing on the Taw & Torridge, as well as Stillwater Coarse & Game fishing nearby. Tuition can be arranged along with sea fishing trips on the Betty Louise.

The cottage has one bedroom, with a fitted kitchen/dining room. On the first floor is an attractive sitting room with gas fire, twin bedded room with ensuite bathroom and W.C.

Further details available from Hoseasons on
0870 534 2342

The renowned Clinton Arms
FRITHELSTOCK - TORRINGTON - DEVON

En suite Accommodation
Non-smoking Dining Area
Light Bites and Main Meals
Sunday Roast Lunches
Real Ale - Family Garden

Private Fishing - River Torridge

Salmon, Sea Trout & Brown Trout

YOUR CATCHES COOKED FOR YOU!

Day permits available for non-residents

Tel: 01805 623279
www.clintonarms.co.uk
fishing@clintonarms.co.uk

WHERE TO STAY

South West Rivers Association in 2005

SWRA is the voice of riparian owners and game angling in the South West. It is the umbrella of the individual river associations in the South West and a powerful lobbying body regularly consulted by the Environment Agency and Government.

Its work was indirectly recognised in the 2005 Queen's New Year's Honours List when recently retired Secretary, Michael Charleston, was awarded the OBE for services to salmon and wildlife conservation. Michael's work is being carried on by Roger Furniss a former Fisheries Officer and Environmental Protection Manager whose whole career has been in the South West.

As with many aspects of modern life angling and our freedom to enjoy it are affected by an ever-growing bureaucracy. By enabling individual rivers to work together to speak with one voice SWRA continues to influence the political and environmental agenda in a number of key areas. Just some of the issues we have influenced are:-

Farm Pollution - since the Second World War, the Government's aim of national food self-sufficiency had resulted in policies which protected farming from the sorts of pollution control applied to other sectors. SWRA evidence to the Department of Food, Rural Affairs and Environment on the impact of overstocking on Bodmin Moor and the damaging effects of heavily silted run-off on fish stocks has played a part in developing more catchment sensitive policies.

Salmon Stock Assessment – to manage salmon stocks effectively it is essential to know more about their status, ie adult runs, juvenile production, vulnerable life stages. SWRA is working hard to influence the Environment Agency to adopt the best possible methods to ensure the long term improvement of our sport.

Salmon Stocking Policy – there are some situations where stocks are so threatened that artificial stocking is necessary to kick start recovery or overcome specific local problems. SWRA actively supports voluntary efforts by individual rivers to carry out scientifically based stocking and to ensure that Agency policies are not too restrictive.

River Improvements – the liberty of fishing owners and tenants was threatened by an Environment Agency proposal which would have effectively banned in-river improvements to angling waters. Strong representations from SWRA have reversed this policy to one which is no longer anti-angling improvement.

The Threat of Abstraction – SWRA has been active in ensuring that new Environment Agency policies on managing abstraction from rivers are not at the expense of fish stocks and angling. This watchdog role is vital against a background of ever growing demand for water.

National Byelaw Review – In 1999 the Government approved a national byelaw restricting the killing of rod-caught salmon to after 16 June. This byelaw is due for review in 2008 and SWRA believes it should be replaced by individual river byelaws tailored to meet the different needs of each river. We have already obtained agreement in principle to this approach and will be working on its practical achievement.

Angling in 2015 – the Agency is drawing up a new strategy to widen participation in Angling. SWRA is very supportive and is working to ensure that the key part played by fishing owners is recognised.

On the international front SWRA continues to support the work of the North Atlantic Salmon Foundation to remove the drift net fishery off the West coast of Ireland which takes many salmon heading for our rivers. We have had a complaint to the European Union that the fishery contravenes the EU Habitats Directive registered for formal investigation.

If you would like to know more about the work of South West Rivers Association why not join the mailing list for its Newsletter, or become a supporter. Please contact the Secretary, Roger Furniss on 01392 841235
or email: email@furniss2733.fsnet.co.uk

The role of the ACA in protecting rivers, lakes, ponds and streams

The Formation and History of the Anglers Conservation Association

The ACA was established in 1948 with the aim of protecting the lakes and rivers of the United Kingdom from pollution. ACA members each pay a subscription and are either individual members, angling clubs, riparian owners, fisheries or federations.

The ACA's legal team represents the member clubs and riparian owners in seeking compensation from offenders who cause pollution damage or other harm to fisheries, or injunctions preventing activities which threaten to damage fisheries from going ahead. The ACA legal team also advises clubs and riparian owners across the whole range of angling and related law. Over the years, the ACA has taken on many thousands of cases against polluters and those who damage fisheries, recovering well over £1 million pounds in damages. At any one time, the ACA has approximately 50 cases in progress as well as hundreds of advice matters.

The ACA's most notable achievement in the early years was an action against three defendants in the case of The Pride of Derby Angling Association v British Celanese [1952] 1 All E.R. 1326. After 17 days in the High Court and 6 days in the Court of Appeal, damages were awarded against all the defendants. The City Corporation was forced to spend £1.8 million (the equivalent of £30 million today) on new sewage treatment works. Likewise, the Electricity Authority had to spend £180,000 (the equivalent of £3 million today) on improving its cooling apparatus.

The ACA's legal team has teeth and bites hard. In the face of an ACA challenge, many cases have settled both before and after the issue of proceedings. The ACA uses specialist methods to calculate damages payable and these have been accepted by insurance companies, loss adjusters, solicitors and judges. In addition, the ACA employs environmental economists to verify its methods. The ACA also employs the leading fisheries biologists and experts to advise on the effect of the pollution and other damage on fish and waterways.

The ACA has built up an enviable reputation for its resolve in representing ACA members. Many controversial issues have been addressed head-on in the Courts. The ACA has achieved changes in environmental legislation and is constantly pushing at the boundaries of common law to improve the protection it offers to rivers, lakes, streams and ponds.

The ACA is unique in that not only do ACA club or riparian owner members not pay a penny for legal representation when the ACA takes a court action on their behalf to recover compensation, but the member also gets to keep all the damages to use to protect and improve the affected fishery. This is something no other organisation does in the same way.

Some Further Examples of the Successful Work of the ACA

In the 1980s, the ACA began the first private prosecution of a water authority bringing to the public's attention the combination of the poacher/gamekeeper role under the pre-privatisation days of the water industry where water authorities regulated themselves.

In the early 1990s, the ACA initiated a private prosecution under the Water Resources Act 1991 against British Coal for pollution from abandoned mines, specifically the River Rhymney in Glamorgan, an issue the then National Rivers Authority had, at that stage, avoided.

In 1999, the ACA embarked upon a groundbreaking mediation to break the deadlock in litigation arising from pollution of the River Eden, Cumbria, in 1994. The £415,000 we recovered resulted in the establishment of a Rivers Trust devoted to protecting the habitat of that river.

THE GET HOOKED GUIDE

The ACA is currently tackling other forms of damage caused to fisheries, such as the increasing problem of escapee rainbow trout from trout farms, diffuse agricultural pollution and overabstraction of water.

The ACA is also examining how to formulate a damages claim after an invertebrate kill has occurred. While it is obvious to anglers that this kind of damage will ultimately affect the fish, proving this to the satisfaction of the Courts has never been easy. The ACA is always exploring new ways of testing the common law framework to its limits.

Expansion of the ACA's Role in Providing New Legal Services

The ACA has also expanded its role into offering a general legal helpline to member clubs and riparian owners on all aspects of fishery law and fisheries in general. This list is by no means exhaustive, but the advice service covers areas such as:

- setting up a fishery
- ownership of stocks
- advising on leases
- whether to incorporate or not
- insurance
- abstraction licences
- discharge consents
- navigation
- public liability and rights of way
- bailiffing and poaching
- land drainage
- fish passes
- club rules

Consultation and Lobbying

The ACA also lobbies hard on behalf of members in other areas such as water resources management and takes any opportunity to respond to consultation and debate on the aquatic environment.

The ACA has very close links with other organisations, such as the individual Rivers Trusts and is asked to attend many important angling events, as well as being available at all major angling shows around the country to meet members and answer questions.

If you wish to contact to our legal department – call 01568-620447 or e-mail either Karen Capper or Guy Linley-Adams on karen@a-c-a.org or guy@a-c-a.org.

ACA
Eastwood House
6 Rainbow Street
Leominster
Herefordshire
HR6 8DQ
01568-620447

Anglers' Conservation Association

Picture - Westcountry Rivers Trust

Carp on a Dry Fly

Mike Weaver

Unhooking a 14 pounder from Spires Lakes.

When I started fishing over half a century ago, carp had an almost mythical quality. Carp fisheries were few and far between – and when you found them their inhabitants had a reputation for being almost impossible to catch.

All of that has now changed. Wherever you live, there are likely to be several carp lakes within a short drive. The popularity of carp fishing has encouraged numerous fishery entrepreneurs to dig a lake, stock it with carp and open up for fishing – as this publication readily demonstrates. Check virtually any of the stillwater coarse fisheries in Get Hooked and you will find lakes that are stocked with a variety of carp, including common, mirror, ghost, koi or grass – and the good news is that they will all readily take a dry fly in the right conditions.

And the ideal conditions for catching a carp on a dry fly are just when fly-fishing gets really tough on the rivers. In the dog days of summer when high temperatures, brilliant sunshine and low water make trout and salmon fishing increasingly difficult, that is the time to have a go for carp. Indeed, when the temperature hovers around 30 degrees C on a cloudless day your chances of finding the carp in just the mood to suck in a dry fly are at their best.

Go to any carp lake between mid morning and mid afternoon on such a day and you are likely to find the carp cruising or just basking at the surface. So right from the word go you have solved one of the basic challenges of fishing – locating the fish. In any branch of fishing, once you have found a fish you are well on the way to catching it.

However, as countless anglers have discovered, having located a fish you have to employ the right tackle and tactics to bring it to the net. First the tackle and anyone who fishes a fly for trout on lakes and reservoirs is already equipped for carp. All you need is a fly rod of around 9 ft, a standard fly reel, a 7 or 8 weight floating line and a leader of about 7 ft of 8 lb nylon and you are ready to go.

The choice of a dry fly offers endless opportunities for experimentation, but I have found an egg fly very effective. This is the pattern so popular with fly fishers on the Pacific coast of North America, where trout and other species take the eggs of Pacific salmon, and this simple fly is produced by tying Glo Bug yarn to a size 10 or 12 hook, my favourite colour being pink. The only problem is that the egg fly is not inherently buoyant, and on many carp fisheries there is no space for false casting to dry the fly. Fortunately, if you tie your own flies, this problem is easily overcome by tying in a bowtie of closed-cell foam at the head.

If there are plenty of carp at the surface, some will take readily if you simply cast the fly to them, but a bit of ground baiting with Pedigree Chum Mixer will usually get the fish feeding and willing to take the fly more readily. The snag is that I can

THE GET HOOKED GUIDE

cast a fly much farther than I can throw a dog biscuit, so this year I intend to get a catapult for long-distance ground baiting.

If all goes well, the carp will come up to the fly, suck it in and a lift of the rod will set the hook. Some fish, however, will stop and then start mouthing the fly without actually taking it. Those carp that stop to "taste" the fly hardly ever take it so save your time and look for another fish. When you do hook a fish, the first screaming run on a simple fly reel is an experience to savour.

Get everything right and you will be amazed at how many carp you will catch on a dry fly. A three-hour session in the middle of a hot still day can easily produce 10, 15 or even more carp and after playing that many fish on a single-handed rod in really hot conditions you will be ready to call a halt and go home for a rest.

A final word about choosing the right day. I usually fly fish for carp on a weekday when there are not too many other anglers on the lake. You want plenty of space for successful fly fishing, and the last thing that other anglers who have settled down for a few hours relaxed and peaceful bait fishing really need is a fly fisherman charging around constantly hooking and playing fish. Enjoy your fly-fishing but don't wear out your welcome.

Nice Common on an egg fly

What Actions are Needed for Healthy Fly life?

Management to meet requirements for fly life – provide water quality, quantity and habitat.

Decrease and limit abstraction, silt, road runoff, endocrine disruptors, pesticides, invasive species, flood damages, storm discharges.

More anglers to join in the S&TA flylife survey, which is 'live' and updated annually & support efforts to influence national environment policy.

A 'Canary Test' is required for anglers to use to detect 'invisible pollution' that kills flylife.

What Conditions are Needed for Abundant Fly Life?

Water Quantity - Flow and temperature are critical.

Water Quality – Poor water quality from diffuse pollution from agriculture, inadequately treated sewage, endocrine disrupters, run-off from roads are all detrimental.

Habitat - Weed growth cover for invertebrates and fish - buffer strips, fencing protection from cattle poaching to produce natural channel widths and meanders.

Contributed by the Salmon & Trout Association – Fighting for the Future of Game Angling.

To learn more about flylife and how to help visit www.salmon-trout.org or call the S&TA at 0207 283 5838.

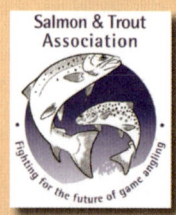

Salmon & Trout Association

DORSET

- RIVER FISHING
- STILLWATER COARSE
- STILLWATER TROUT
- SEA FISHING
- WHERE TO STAY

Dorset Game Road Directions

101. Amherst Lodge
From the A35 Bridport to Honiton road, take the Hunter's Lodge turning at Raymonds Hill onto the B3165 towards Lyme Regis. After 1.4 miles turn right down Cathole Lane. Keep to the right into St Marys Lane and you will come to Amherst. Tel: 01297 442773.

102. Flowers Farm Fly Fishery
Situated midway between Dorchester and Yeovil off A37. From Dorchester take A37, travel for approx 7 miles look out for green dome on right, 0.5 mile turn right to Batcombe, 0.5 mile turn right at T junction marked to the Friary, take second left at fishing sign, then right at bottom of hill. The fishery is at the side of St Francis Friary. From Yeovil take A37 for approx. 6 miles, turn left at crossroads marked Batcombe, take 3rd left along top Batcombe Downs at fishing sign, right bottom of hill. Continue 0.5 mile to Fishery. Tel: 01300 341351.

Dorset Coarse Road Directions

103. Christchurch Angling Club (Coarse & Game)
Please enquire at local Tackle Shops or telephone 01202 490014 or 07720 671706.

104. Gold Oak Fisheries
Hare Lane, Cranborne. Please telephone 01725 517275 for directions.

105. Mangerton Valley Coarse Lake
From Bridport take A3066 North for approx. two miles. Continue straight across mini roundabout, then turn immediately right. Look out for our sign after one mile. Telephone 01308 458482.

106. Ringwood & District Anglers Association
Please contact Tackle shops in Ringwood area or Telephone Ken Broddle on 01202 871496.

107. Wood Farm Caravan Park
7 miles west of Bridport on A35, entrance off roundabout with A3052 (access to fishing through caravan park). Tel: 01297 560697.

108. Woolsbridge Manor Farm
Please telephone 01202 826369 for directions.

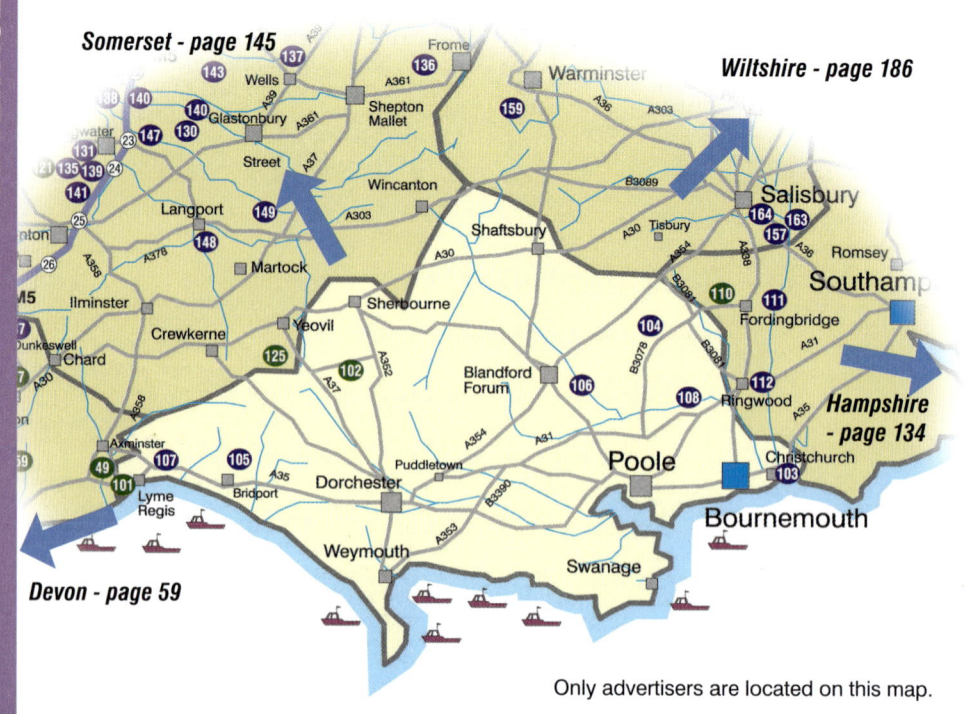

Only advertisers are located on this map.

Dorset River Fishing

THE 'HAMPSHIRE' AVON
For detailed description of the Hampshire Avon and tributaries, see under Hampshire River fishing.

RIVER AVON PEWSEY - CHRISTCHURCH
Fisheries located between Pewsey and Salisbury are predominantly managed for Brown Trout fly fishing. A mixture of Coarse, Salmon and Trout fishing is available on the main river between Salisbury and Christchurch.

Bournemouth's Simon Ebborn with a fit 6lb 7oz chub taken from Throop on feeder fed maggots. Pic by Steve Martin. Courtesy Southern Angler.

Christchurch Angling Club (Game)
Contact: John Cheetham, 19b Willow Way, Christchurch, BH23 1JJ, 01202 490014, *Mobile:* 07720 671706, *Water:* Largest club on the river Avon, mainly mid/lower Avon, Burgate - Christchurch, also Fishing on River Stour between Gains Cross and Christchurch. Stillwater Coarse fishing at Whitesheat. Various other stillwaters. Sea Trout at Christchurch Harbour. Please telephone the secretary for full details. *Species:* Salmon, Sea Trout, Rainbow Trout & Brown Trout. *Permits:* Ray Goodman (Membership Secretary) Tel: 01202 475173 or Local Tackle shops. *Charges:* Adult £140, Junior £51, OAP/Concession £105. Salmon £262. All prices are inclusive of joining fees. *Season:* Rainbow Trout all year round. Brown Trout: 1st April to 15th October. Salmon 1st February to 31st August. Sea Trout 1st July - 31st October. *Methods:* See rules for individual waters.

Royalty Fishery
Contact: John Cheetham, 19b Willow Way, Christchurch, BH23 1JJ, 01202 490014, *Mobile:* 07720 671706, *Water:* Approx 1 mile of double bank fishing. Lowest beat on the river. Controlled by Christchurch Angling Club. *Species:* Roach 3lb, Chub 8lb, Dace 1lb, Barbel 14lb, Pike 38lb, Bream 11lb, Perch 4lb, Carp 31lb, Tench 7lb, Salmon 40lb, Sea Trout 15lb *Permits:* Tickets available from Davis Tackle only. *Charges:* Tel: 01202 485169. Free for Christchurch Angling Club members. Day tickets Adults Summer £10 / Winter £8. *Season:* Coarse: 16th June - 14th March. Sea Trout 15th April - 31st October. Salmon 1st February - 31st August. *Methods:* No spinning, no night fishing. No Barbel, Carp or game fish to be kept in keepnets.

Winkton Fishery
Contact: John Cheetham, 01202 490014, *Mobile:* 07720 671706, *Water:* Approx 1 mile of fishing. Lower river near Christchurch *Species:* Roach to 3lb 10oz, Chub to 6lb, Dace to 1lb, Barbel 13lb, Pike to 30lb, Perch to 3lb. *Permits:* Davis Tackle only as above. *Charges:* £10 per day (2 rods per day, coarse only), Block bookings for clubs available. Please call 01202 490014. *Season:* June 16th - March 14th, 7am to 2 hours after sunset. *Methods:* No spinning. Coarse only: No Barbel or game fish to be placed in keepnets.

FROME
The Frome rises through chalk on the North Dorset Downs near Evershot, and flows south east through Dorchester, and finally Wareham, where it confluences with the River Piddle in Poole harbour.
The River Frome is well known for its excellent Salmon, Brown Trout and Grayling fishing. There are also good numbers of coarse fish in certain areas; although access is limited sport can be very rewarding. Salmon and Trout fishing is generally controlled by syndicates and local estates.

Dorchester Fishing Club
Contact: Mr J.Grindle (Hon. Sec.), 36 Cowleaze, Martinstown, DT2 9TD, 01305 889682, *Mobile:* 07810 555316, *Water:* Approx 6.5 miles of double bank on the Frome near Dorchester, Brown Trout fly fishing. *Species:* Brown Trout, Grayling. *Permits:* John Aplin, Dorchester (01305) 266500 john@river-keeper.co.uk. *Charges:* Day tickets and membership available. Please telephone John Aplin for day tickets and John Grindle for membership details. *Season:* April 1st - October 14th. *Methods:* Dry fly and Nymph only. Barbless hooks are encouraged.

Frome, Piddle & West Dorset Fishery Association
Contact: R.J. Slocock, 01929 471274, *Water:* An amalgamation of of riparian owners with an interest in the welfare of river fisheries in their locality. Information can be obtained concerning estate waters from the contact above.

River Frome (Town Section)
Contact: Purbeck Angling Centre / Deano or Barry, 28 South Street, Wareham, BH20 4LU, 01929 550770, *Water:* One mile stretch of the River Frome. *Species:* Roach, Dace, Grayling, Eels, Pike, Salmon, Trout, Sea Trout, Mullet, Bass, Flounder, Carp and Perch. *Permits:* Enquiries to Purbeck Angling Centre. *Charges:*

DORSET

RIVER FISHING

CHRISTCHURCH ANGLING CLUB

Superb fishing available on the South's finest waters including Hampshire Avon
including the Royalty Fishery,
Dorset Stour, River Frome, Mature Gravel Pits and well managed Lakes and Ponds
Night Fishing and Day Tickets available
Offering easy access for disabled people - Toilets on most fisheries

Carp to 41lb plus
Tench to 9lb plus
Perch to 4lb plus
Rainbow Trout to 10lb plus
Barbel to 14lb 10oz
Chub to 7lb plus
Roach to 3lb plus
Pike to 33lb plus

For further details phone John Cheetham on
01202 490014 or 077 2067 1706
or visit our web site at www.christchurchac.org.uk

DORSET

Free fishing on public section. Enquiries to Purbeck Angling Centre. *Season:* Normal closed seasons apply. *Methods:* This stretch is run as a Coarse Fishery only. All Game and Saltwater fish are to be returned immediately.

Wessex Chalk Streams Ltd. (Frome)
Contact: Richard & Sally Slocock, Lawrences Farm, Southover, Tolpuddle, Dorchester, DT2 7HF, 01305 848360, *Water:* 5 Lakes & Pools totalling 4 acres for Rainbow Trout. Plus 16 Beats on Rivers Piddle & Frome for Brown Trout. *Species:* Brown Trout. Some beats with all wild fish, other beats with stocked browns to augment the wild fish. *Permits:* From the above address. *Charges:* From £27 to £70 day. Generous discounts for large bookings. *Season:* 1st April - 15th October. *Methods:* Barbless hooks, catch and release.

PIDDLE AND WEST DORSET STREAMS

'West Dorset' streams include the River Brit, Asker, Bride and Char. These streams are relatively short, 'steep' water courses supporting populations of mainly Brown Trout and Sea Trout.

The River Piddle rises at four major springs near Alton St. Pancras, initially flowing south before turning east at Puddletown towards Poole Harbour, where it confluences with the River Frome. This small chalk stream offers excellent Brown Trout fishing, with Salmon, Sea Trout and coarse fish in the lower reaches. The Agency operates a salmon and sea trout rod fishery in this area. Other fish species can be found in the River Piddle including, Roach, Dace, Pike and Perch. Much of the fishing is controlled by local syndicates and estate waters; further information about these groups can be obtained from the aforementioned Frome, Piddle and West Dorset Fishery Association.

Environment Agency - Piddle Fishery
Contact: Fisheries Recreation & Biodiversity Officer, Environment Agency, Rivers House, Sunrise Business Pk, Higher Shaftesbury Rd, Blandford, DT11 8ST, 08708 506506, *Water:* 3km of bank fishing on Lower Piddle. *Species:* Salmon & Sea Trout. *Permits:* 14 permits per annum. *Charges:* £205 plus vat (£35.87), subject to annual review.

Manor of Wareham
Contact: Guy Ryder, The Estate Office,, Manor of Wareham, Cow Lane, Wareham, BH20 4RD, 01929 552666, *Water:* Stretch on river Piddle single bank fishing. *Species:* Brown Trout and Sea trout. *Charges:* Season tickets only. Price on application. *Season:* E.A. Byelaws. *Methods:* E.A. Byelaws.

Wessex Chalk Streams Ltd. (Piddle)
Contact: Richard Slocock, Lawrences Farm, Tolpuddle, Dorchester, DT2 7HF, 01305 848360, *Water:* 5 Lakes & Pools totalling 4 acres for Rainbow Trout. Plus 16 Beats on Rivers Piddle & Frome for Brown Trout. *Species:* Lakes: Rainbow Trout, Rivers: Brown Trout. *Permits:* At above address. *Charges:* Minimum £19 day, Max £65. *Season:* April 1st to October 15th. *Methods:* Fly Fishing only, most river beats are catch & release using barbless hooks.

STOUR

The River Stour in Dorset is well known by anglers across the country for the quality of its fishing. Over the years many British record captures have been made here, for example, the current Roach record stands at 4lb 3oz, taken from the Stour near Wimborne.

The Stour rises on the Greensand at St. Peters Pump in Stourhead Gardens and flows through Gillingham. Nearby it is joined by the Shreen Water and the River Lodden. The Stour stretches out for 96 km, passing through the Blackmoor Vale down to the sea at Christchurch; the total fall over this distance is approximately 230m. Other notable tributaries along its length include the River Tarrant confluencing near Spetisbury, the River Allen at Wimborne and the Moors River coming in near Christchurch. The Stour confluences with the River Avon at the 'Clay Pool' in Christchurch, before flowing into the harbour area and ultimately out into the English Channel.

Blandford & District Angling Club
Contact: Peter Brundish (Sec.), 10 Windmill Road, Blandford Forum, DT11 7HG, 01258 453545, *Water:* 4 miles of Dorset Stour (Crown Meadows and Nutford) and 1 mile of river at Bugs Water between Blandford and Charlton Marshell A350. We also swap books with four local clubs, giving access to five lakes. *Species:* Roach to 1.5lb, Bream to 8lb 10oz, Perch to 3lb 2oz, Carp to 17lb, Chub & Pike to 25lb. Common Carp 28lb 12oz (Crown Meadows 2002). *Permits:* Conyers Tackle Shop, Market Place, Blandford Tel 01258 452307. Todber Manor Fishing Tackle Shop, Tel: 01258 820384. Or from the secretary, Peter Brundish. *Charges:* Senior £30, O.A.P. £16.50, Junior £8.50, Day tickets: Senior £4, junior £2. Please enquire for family membership. *Season:* Normal coarse season. *Methods:* Boilies can be used in small amounts. Carp over 5lb to be weighed and released, not kept in keepnets. Only members are permitted to night fish.

Dorchester & District Angling Society
Contact: J.W.Smith, Secretary, 11 Kings Road, Dorchester, DT1 1NH, 01305 268674, *Water:* 4 miles on Dorset Stour, 1.5 miles Dorset Frome plus lakes at Kingcombe and West Knighton. R. Brue Somerset plus water sharing agreements and Federation waters on Somerset Levels. *Species:* Roach, Dace, Chub, Pike, Gudgeon, Perch, Eels, Carp, Bream, Grayling. *Permits:* 'Reels & Deals', Weymouth, Aplins Tackle Dorchester, Weymouth Angling Centre, Surplus International, Dorchester. *Charges:* Adult members £43. Reductions for Juniors & Spouses. Members guest tickets, no day tickets, half-year membership from December 1st. *Season:* June 16th - March 14th, Stillwater open all year. *Methods:* Various, specific to particular waters.

Durweston Angling Association
Contact: Mr Vernon Bell (secretary), Endcote, Durweston, DT11

DORSET

RIVER FISHING

OQE, 01258 451317, *Water:* 2 miles River Stour. *Species:* Bream, Roach, Rudd, Gudgeon, Dace, Eels, Chub, Pike, Perch. *Permits:* From the Mill House, Durweston. *Charges:* Day tickets: £3, River permit £30/adult, £5/under 16. Prices may change in 2005. *Season:* Close season 14th March - 16th June. *Methods:* Children under 10 years must be accompanied by an adult.

Gillingham & District A A (Stour)
Contact: Simon Hebditch (Hon. Secretary), 8 Maple Way, Gillingham, SP8 4RR, 01747 821218, *Mobile:* 07990 690613, *Water:* 7 miles Upper Stour - Gillingham to Marnhull. Also Turners Paddock lake at Stourhead. Mappowder Court 4 lakes at Mappowder. *Species:* Roach 3lb, Chub 4lb 8oz, Barbel 6lb, Pike 21lb, Dace 1lb, Bream 6lb, Gudgeon 3oz, Perch 3lb 4oz, Tench 3lb, Carp 10lb, Eels 4lb. Trout, Grayling 2lb 8oz. *Permits:* Mr P Stone (Treasurer) The Timepiece, Newbury, Gillingham, Dorset, SP8 4HZ. Tel: 01747 823339. Mr J Candy, Todber Manor Fisheries Shop, Tel: 01258 820384. *Charges:* £4 day ticket, £25 season ticket. £12 juniors and concessions. (probable charges for 2005). *Season:* June 16th to March 14th. *Methods:* Best stick float with maggot casters and bread. Large lump of bread for Chub. Sweetcorn also very productive for Chub. Feeder for Bream.

Muscliffe & Longham
Contact: Nev Cooke, 904 Wimborne Road, Moordown, Bournemouth, BH9 2DW, 01202 514345, *Water:* 1.5 miles river Stour at Muscliffe and quarter mile at Longham. *Species:* Chub, Barbel, Roach, Dace, Pike, Eels, Minnow, Gudgeon and Perch. *Permits:* Free (owned by Bournemouth Council). *Charges:* Free. E.A. licence required. *Season:* 16th June to 14th March. *Methods:* No restrictions.

Ringwood & District A.A. (Stour)
Contact: Mr Steve Martin, 2 Oakmead Road, Creekmoor, Poole, BH17 7XN, 01202 777892, *Mobile:* 07812 360278, *Water:* 11 stretches on Stour including total control of Throop fishery and various stretches upstream to Stourpaine. *Species:* Throop - Barbel to 16lb, Chub 8lb. Middle regions good general Roach, Chub, Bream, Pike, Perch, some Trout, Grayling and Carp. *Permits:* Local tackle shop or contact Ken Broddle (Membership Secretary) on: 01202 871496. *Charges:* Adult £100, Junior £40, concessions for OAP's and disabled; Throop day tickets £8.00. Concessions, O.A.P's, Disabled and Juniors available from local tackle dealers. *Season:* As per coarse season. *Methods:* All on reverse of ticket.

Stalbridge Angling Association (Stour)
01963 250311, *Water:* 2.5 miles Stour, Lanshire Lake, Stalbridge. *Species:* Bream, Tench, Roach, Dace, Pike, Chub, Rudd. *Permits:* C.C. Moores Ltd (animal foods), Stalbridge, 01963 362254. Bernie Ackland, 4 Russel Ave., Milborne Port, 01693 250311. *Charges:* Senior Annual £22 no joining fee, Junior (under 17 years) £8 & Concessions (Reg. Disabled & OAPs) £12 no joining fee. Husband and wife ticket £30. Day Tickets £5 senior, £2.50 junior. *Season:* Normal river closed season.

Sturminster & Hinton A.A
Contact: Mr R. Brown (membership sec.), Uplands Close, Broad Oak, Sturminster Newton, DT10 2HL, 01258 473178, *Water:* 14 miles mid River Stour, 3 small lakes (Stokewake Lake & Highbench Lake) members only. Plus joint fisheries at Lodden Lake. *Species:* Roach, Chub, Tench, Bream, Perch, Carp, Pike. *Permits:* Kev's Garage, The Bridge, Sturminster Newton (opposite The Bull pub). www.s-haa.co.uk (new members). *Charges:*

Stephanie Martin landed this 6lb Carp at Whitemoor Lakes

£5/day, £10/week, Juniors season £3, Adults season £22. *Season:* March 14th - June 16th. *Methods:* No dogs, radios, no live baiting. One rod, second rod only for Pike. Barbless hooks at lakes. No night fishing. Always carry your membership permit.

Throop Fisheries
Contact: Ringwood & District Angling Club, Mr Steve Martin, 2 Oakmead Road, Creekmore, Poole, BH17 7XN, 01202 777892, *Mobile:* 07812 360278, *Water:* See entry under Coarse Fisheries - Bournemouth. 10 miles on Dorset Stour. *Species:* Barbel to 16lb, Chub to 8lb, Bream and Roach. *Permits:* Local tackle shop (Christchurch Angling Centre - 01202 480520) or contact Ken Broddle (Membership Secretary) - 01202 871469. *Charges:* Day tickets £8, to be obtained before fishing. *Season:* 16th June - 14th March inclusive. *Methods:* See reverse of tickets.

Wareham & District Angling Society
Contact: Deano Watts, c/o Purbeck Angling Centre, 28 South Street, Wareham, BH20 4LU, 01929 550770, *Water:* River waters on North Dorset Stour, Piddle and the Frome. 5 lakes Wareham area plus 9 near Dorchester. *Species:* Coarse. *Permits:* Wessex Angling, Poole, Dorset Tel: 01202 668244, Dennings Tackle, Wyke Regis. Purbeck Angling Centre Tel: 01929 550770 *Charges:* Senior £40, Ladies / O.A.P's £20, Junior £10. Membership runs from June 1st to May 31st (2004 prices). *Season:* Two lakes at Wareham and nine at Dorchester open during Coarse closed season. *Methods:* Barbless, no litter, no cans, variations as per membership book.

Wimborne & District Angling Club (Stour)
Contact: S. Batts (secretary), 8 Bullfinch Close, Creekmoor, Poole, BH17 7UP, 01202 658033, *Water:* 10 miles River Stour, 17 lakes, 1 mile River Avon *Species:* Trout & Coarse Fisheries. *Permits:* Certain waters are available on Guest Tickets £6 from Wessex Angling Centre, 321 Wimborne Rd, Oakdale, Poole, Dorset. Guest tickets to members only. *Charges:* £80 plus £10 joining fee. OAP and disabled concessions. Junior £25, under 12 accompanied by an adult free. *Season:* Coarse - all year round. Sea Trout - April 16th to Oct 31st. Salmon - 1st Feb to 30th Sept. 4 x Trout Lakes - 1st Mar - 31st Oct. *Methods:* Barbless hooks on Coarse Stillwaters, no floating baits.

Dorset Stillwater Coarse

BEAMINSTER
Higher Kingcombe Coarse Fishing
Contact: Mr Crocker, Higher Kingcombe, Dorchester, DT2 0EH, 01300 321079, *Water:* 5 lakes - approx 4 acres of water in total. *Species:* Carp (Mirror, Common & Ghost), Perch, Roach, Rudd, Bream, Tench. Specimen lake - Carp to 27lb *Charges:* Day ticket £5, Evening (after 6pm) £3, Night (10pm - 6am) £4, 24hrs ticket £7.50, Juniors (16 and under) £2.50 per day. *Season:* Open all year. *Methods:* Max 2 rods per person, barbless hooks only, under 14's must be accompanied by an adult.

BLANDFORD
Milton Abbas Lakes
Contact: Wayne Little / Lesley Woodcock, Milton Abbas, Blandford, DT11 0BW, 01258 880919, *Mobile:* 07780 966117, *Water:* 8 acre syndicate lake - waiting list - phone for application form. 3 acre day ticket lake (new for 2003). *Species:* Carp 10lbs up to 18lbs, Grass Carp to 16lbs, Tench to 6lbs, Roach to 2lbs, Crucian Carp, Bream , Tench, Perch & Eels. *Permits:* Telephone Bookings only. Maximum of 10 anglers per day. Tickets on the bank. *Charges:* Adult £10.00 per day, £15 - 24 hours. Juniors £5 per day, £10 - 24 hours (Must be under 16 and accompanied by an adult). *Season:* Day ticket lake opening April 2003. No close Season. Fishing times 7am until Sunset. *Methods:* No keep nets or Carp sacks, 2 rods only. No peas, nuts or beans, a suitable landing net and unhooking mat if Carp fishing, no dogs, fires, swimming or bait boats.

BOURNEMOUTH
East Moors Lake
Contact: Mr. Nicolas Hoare, East Moors Farm, East Moors Lane, St. Leonards, Ferndale, Bournemouth, 01202 872302, *Water:* 1.5 acre lake. *Species:* Carp: Common, Mirror, Ghost, Leather, Purple Blushing; Tench, Gold Tench, Roach, Perch, Rudd, Chub & Pike. *Charges:* Members only, Country/Holiday membership available - Please telephone for details. *Methods:* Barbless hooks only, no boilies, no keepnets, no dogs. Children under 14 must be accompanied by adult.

Throop Fisheries (Coarse Lake)
Contact: Ringwood & District Angling Club, Mr Steve Martin, 2 Oakmead Road, Creekmore, Poole, BH17 7XN, 01202 777892, *Mobile:* 07812 360278, *Water:* Northern edge of Bournemouth. 10 Miles of river bank on Dorset Stour & Stillwater Mill Pool. *Species:* Barbel, Chub, Carp, Roach, Tench, Perch, Dace, Pike. *Permits:* Ringwood Tackle - Tel. 01425 475155, Bournemouth Fishing Lodge - Tel. 01202 514345 or contact Ken Broddle (Membership Secretary) 01202 871469 *Charges:* Prices on application & list. *Season:* 16th June - 14 March (Open every day between these dates). *Methods:* No night fishing.

BRIDPORT
Highway Farm
Contact: John & Pauline Bale, West Road, Bridport, DT6 6AE, 01308 424321, *Water:* 2 small lakes in quiet, secluded valley. *Species:* Carp, Tench, Roach, Rudd. *Permits:* From the Post Office. *Charges:* £5 day / £3 half day. *Season:* Open all year, dawn to dusk. No night fishing. *Methods:* No boilies or keep nets. Barbless hooks only. No dogs.

Mangerton Valley Coarse Fishing Lake
Contact: Clive & Jane Greening, New House Farm, Mangerton Lane, Bradpole, Bridport, DT6 3SF, 01308 458482, *Water:* 1.6 acre lake. *Species:* Carp to 26lb (Common and Mirror), Roach, Tench. *Permits:* From Post Office. *Charges:* £5 day, £3.50 half day, £2.50 evening. *Season:* Possibly closed March - April - May (please ring first). *Methods:* Barbless hooks. No boilies or beans. No nuts, no dogs. Night fishing by arrangement. All children under 12 to be accompanied by an adult.

Washingpool Farm Fishing
West Bay Watersports, 10a West Bay, Bridport, DT6 4EZ, 01308 421800, *Water:* 2 lakes (1 x 1.5 acre, 1 x 1.75 acre). *Species:* Carp to 10lb, Mirror Common Crucian, Ghost 15lb, Wild Carp, Tench, Roach, Rudd & Bream. *Charges:* Limited Day tickets in advance from West Bay Watersports. £5 per day 2 rods *Season:* Open all year dawn to dusk. *Methods:* Barbless hooks only, no keepnets.

CHRISTCHURCH
Avon Tyrrell Lakes
Contact: Dave Clarke, Avon Tyrrell House, Bransgore, Christchurch, BH23 8EE, 01425 672347, *Water:* Two lakes totalling approx 2.5 acres. *Species:* Carp, Tench, Roach, Bream, Perch and Rudd. *Permits:* On site from reception. *Charges:* £6 Day Tickets Adults. £3 Juniors(Under 16). Season Tickets also available, please note Night Fishing only available on a season ticket. *Season:* Open mid June to mid March - 8.30 to 17.00hrs on day ticket from June 2005. *Methods:* Barbless Hooks, No keepnets, No nut baits. See rules on site.

Christchurch Angling Club (Coarse Ponds)
Contact: John Cheetham, 19b Willow Way, Christchurch, BH23 1JJ, 01202 490014, *Mobile:* 07720 671706, *Water:* Various coarse ponds including Blashford, Somerley and Cranebrook lakes. Please telephone the secretary for full details. See entry under Hampshire Avon. *Species:* Carp to 42lbs, Pike to 36lbs, Bream 14lbs, Perch 4lbs, Tench 10lbs, Roach, Rudd. *Permits:* Ray Goodman (Membership Secretary) Tel: 01202 475173

DORSET

or Local Tackle shops. *Charges:* Adult £140, Junior £51, OAP/Concession £105. *Season:* 16th June - 14th March. Night fishing available with prepaid permit. *Methods:* See individual fishery rules.

Hordle Lakes
Contact: M.F. Smith, Hordle Lakes, Hordle Lane, Hordle, Lymington, SO41 0GD, 01590 672300, *Mobile:* 07778 954799, *Water:* Seven spring fed lakes set in 11 acres. *Species:* Double figure Carp, Tench, Roach, Rudd, Bream and Perch. *Permits:* At the fishery. Can also issue EA rod licences on site. *Charges:* Adults £7.50 per day. OAPs £5. Kiddies pool £3. *Season:* Open all year 8am to dusk. Night fishing by arrangement. *Methods:* All fish to be returned immediately. No groundbaiting, loose feeding only. Barbless hooks only, no larger than size 6. No boilies, beans, nuts, trout bait or floating crust/biscuit. Full rules at the fishery.

Orchard Lakes
Contact: Mr R Southcombe, New Lane, Bashley, New Milton, BH25 5TD, 01425 612404, *Mobile:* 07973 963304, *Water:* 3 small lakes, largest 2 acres. 50 peg match lake. *Species:* Carp, Tench, Bream, Roach, Rudd, Perch. *Permits:* Day tickets on the bank. *Charges:* All lakes - £6 per day. *Season:* Open all year 7am to dusk. *Methods:* Barbless hooks only. No keepnets.

Sopley Farm PYO
Contact: Sopley Farm PYO, Sopley, Christchurch, 01425 475155, *Water:* 8 acre lake. 1000 yard perimeter. *Species:* Carp, Bream, Roach, Rudd. *Permits:* At local Tackle shops. *Charges:* Membership of Ringwood & District Anglers Association. *Season:* All year.

Whirlwind Lake
Contact: Mr & Mrs Pillinger, Whirlwind Rise, Dudmore Lane, Christchurch, BH23 6BQ, 01202 475255, *Water:* Secluded lake. *Species:* Common, Crucian and Mirror Carp, Roach, Rudd, Tench, Chub etc. *Permits:* On site and local fishing tackle shops. Davis Tackle, 75 The Bargates, Christchurch: 01202 485169. Pro Tackle, 258 Barrack Road, Christchurch: 01202 484518. Advanced booking advisable, limited number available. *Charges:* Adults £7.50 day ticket. £5 half day (Limited places). Children (must be accompanied) £5 day. *Season:* Open all year. *Methods:* Barbless hooks only, no keepnets, no boilies.

CORFE
Arfleet Mill Lakes
Contact: Mr B Charron, Dairy Cottage, Knitson, Corfe Castle, BH20 5JB, 01929 427421, *Water:* 1 acre spring fed lake, 1 acre deep water lake and a young anglers pool. Situated off the B3351 near Corfe Castle. *Species:* Carp to 29lb 3oz, Roach, Rudd, Tench, Perch and Eel. *Permits:* Local Tackle shops or on Telephone number above. *Charges:* £6.50 day - 2 rods, £3.95 1/2 day and concessions for children under 16. *Season:* Opens April 29th 2004. Night fishing by arrangement only - please phone. *Methods:* No Trout pellets, no keepnets, barbless hooks only, no ground bait.

CRANBORNE
Gold Oak Fishery
Contact: Mr J Butler, Gold Oak Farm, Hare Lane, Cranborne, BH21 5QT, 01725 517275, *Water:* 7 small lakes. *Species:* Carp to 20lb, Green + Golden Tench to 5-6lb, Perch 2.5lb, Roach 2lb, Chub 4lb, Bream 3lb. *Charges:* Summer day - £7 Adult, £5 Junior. 1/2 day - £5 Adult, £3 Junior. Eve - £3 Adult, £1 Junior.

Winter day - £5 Adult, £3 Junior. 1/2 day - £3 Adult, £2 junior. *Season:* All year. *Methods:* No large fish in keepnets, barbless hooks, dogs on lead.

Martins Farm Fishery
Contact: Mr Ball, Martins Farm, Woodlands, Verwood, 01202 822335, *Water:* 2.5 acre spring fed lake. *Species:* Carp to 26lb, Tench to 5lb, Perch, Roach, Rudd. *Permits:* Tel: 01202 822335. *Charges:* £8 Adult day ticket, £4 Juniors (under 14). *Methods:* No keepnets, barbless hooks, no hemp. Boilies in moderation.

Wimborne & District Angling Club (Coarse Lakes)
Contact: S. Batts (secretary), 8 Bullfinch Close, Creekmoor, Poole, BH17 7UP, 01202 658033, *Water:* 12 coarse lakes, 10 miles river Stour, 1 mile river Avon. 5 Trout lakes. See also entry under Stour. *Species:* Mixed Coarse. *Permits:* Certain waters are available on guest tickets. £6 from Wessex Angling, 321 Wimborne Rd, Oakdale, Poole. Guest tickets to memebrs only. *Charges:* £80 plus £10 joining fee. OAP and disabled concessions. Junior £25, under 12 accompanied by an adult free. *Season:* All year round. *Methods:* Barbless hooks on Coarse Stillwaters, no floating baits.

DORCHESTER
Dorchester & Dist. Angling Society (Coarse Lake)
Contact: J.W.Smith, Secretary, 01305 268674, *Water:* See entry under Stour. Coarse lakes at Kingcombe and West Knighton. *Species:* Carp, Tench, Perch and Roach. *Season:* Lakes open all year. *Methods:* Barbless hooks only. No boilies or bivvies on lakes.

Gillingham & District A.A. (Mappowder Court)
Contact: Simon Hebditch (Hon. Secretary), 8 Maple Way, Gillingham, SP8 4RR, 01747 821218, *Mobile:* 07990 690613, *Water:* Mappowder Court Fishing Complex (4 lakes), Mappowder Nr Dorchester. (see also entry under river fishing Stour). *Species:* Crucian/Crucian cross 2lb, Carp 22lb, Tench 4lb, Eels 3lb, Roach 2lb, Rudd 1lb, Gudgeon, Perch 2lb, Bream 3lb, Barbel 1lb, Grass Carp 8lb. *Permits:* Mr P Stone (Treasurer) The Timepiece, Newbury, Gillingham, Dorset, SP8 4HZ. Tel: 01747 823339. Mr J Candy, Todber Manor Fisheries Shop, Tel: 01258 820384. Kings Stag Garage, Kings Stag, Nr Hazelbury Bryan. *Charges:* £4 day ticket, £25 season ticket. £12 juniors and concessions. (probable charges for 2005). *Season:* Open all year. *Methods:* Barbless hooks. Mainly pole fishing. Big baits for double figure Carp on Pheasant lake. Pole on Spring lake for mixed bags.

Hermitage Lakes (Coarse)
Contact: Nigel Richardson, Common Farm, Hermitage, Cerne

DORSET

TOP FLOOR TACKLE
Above Surplus International, 12 Hardye Arcade, South St, Dorchester
SEA • COARSE • GAME
Stockists of ABU, Nash, ESP, Dynamite Baits,
Elite Baits, Mainline, Fox, D.T. Baits, Badger *and lots more!*
Quality Outdoor Wear & Camping Equipment
EXCELLENT PRICES ON GORETEX CLOTHING
LIVE RAG & LUG / AMMO BAITS
Specialists in Carp Fishing with over 15 years
invaluable experience and local knowledge
TICKETS AVAILABLE FOR RADIPOLE LAKE
Phone Ali or James on **01305 250 200**

Wessex Angling
FOR ALL YOUR ANGLING NEEDS
Coarse - Sea - Game
www.wessexangling.co.uk
All the major names at competitive prices
319-321 Wimbourne Rd., Poole, Dorset. Tel/Fax: 01202 668244

STILLWATER COARSE

Abbas, Dorchester, DT2 7BB, 01963 210556, *Water:* Half acre lake. *Species:* Carp. *Charges:* Day ticket £4. *Season:* Closed 14th March - 16th June. *Methods:* Barbless hooks, no keepnets.

Luckfield Lake Fishery
Contact: John Aplin, 1 Athelstan Road, Dorchester, DT1 1NR, 01305 266500, *Mobile:* 07889 680464, *Water:* 1.5 acre clay pit in beautiful surroundings. *Species:* Carp to 23lb, Tench to 9lb plus, Roach to 3lb plus. *Permits:* As above. *Charges:* Day £6, Night £10, half season £45. *Season:* Open all year. *Methods:* No keepnets, barbless hooks.

Lyons Gate Fishing Lakes
Contact: Stuart Jones, Lyons Gate, Nr Cerne Abbas, Dorchester, DT2 7AZ, 01300 345260, *Water:* Four lakes totalling approximately 3.5 acres. *Species:* Carp to 25lb, Tench to 8lb, Chubb, Barbel, Bream, Golden Orfe, Roach, Rudd. *Charges:* £5 p/day (2 rods), night fishing can be arranged. *Season:* Open all year dawn to dusk. *Methods:* Barbless hooks only. No groundbaiting - loose feed only. Full details at the fishery.

Pallington Lakes
Contact: Mr Simon or Mrs Tini Pomeroy, Pallington, Dorchester, DT2 8QU, 01305 849233, *Mobile:* 07887 840507, *Water:* 3 lakes and a stretch of the river Frome. *Species:* Lakes: Carp to 35lb 10oz, Tench to 12lb 3oz, Perch to 4lb 13oz, Grayling to 3lb 12oz, Roach 3lb, Bream 10lb, Rudd 3lb. *Permits:* Lakes are private club water - members only. *Charges:* Lakes: All year round season ticket. River limited rod ticket £25 per day. *Season:* All year round. Shop open daily 8 to 9am. Members & their guests fishing only. River fishing by appointment. *Methods:* Barbless hooks, No keepnets. No nut baits. All anglers must be in possession of a fish antiseptic. All Carp anglers must have minimum 36 inch landing net and a unhooking mat. Nets to be dipped. All anglers must observe fishery rules.

GILLINGHAM
Culvers Farm Fishery
Contact: V.J. Pitman, Culvers Farm, Gillingham, SP8 5DS, 01747 822466, *Water:* One 1.5 acre lake. One 3 acre lake. *Species:* Carp, Bream, Roach and Tench. *Charges:* Day £6. Half Day £4. OAP's and under 16 £4 all day. *Season:* Open all year. No night fishing. *Methods:* Barbless hooks only. No Boilies. No keepnets allowed on Middle Mead. Lower Mead - keepnets permitted.

LYME REGIS
Wood Farm Caravan Park
Contact: Jane Bremner, Axminster Road, Charmouth, DT6 6BT, 01297 560697, *Water:* 2 ponds totalling approx 1 acre. *Species:* Carp, Rudd, Roach, Tench & Perch. *Permits:* Rod licences sold. *Charges:* £4 day ticket. £17 week. £40 season. *Season:* All year. *Methods:* No boilies, keepnets. Barbless hooks only.

POOLE
Alder Hills Fishery
Sharp Road, Talbot Heath, Poole, SP6 1JG, 07939 514346, *Water:* Mature 2.5 acre clay pit situated on the Poole / Bournemouth border. *Species:* Carp (common, Mirror and Koi) to 20lb plus, Tench 6lb plus, Roach 2lb plus, Pike 10lb plus, Perch, Eels and Rudd. *Permits:* Day tickets must be puchased in advance from: Wessex Angling Centre, Castaways Tackle, AC Angling, Bournemouth Fishing Lodge or the Dorset Knob Pub at the end of Sharp Road. All are situated locally. Annual tickets from 07939 514346. *Charges:* Adult day ticket (16-64 years) £5. Junior day (under 16-over 65) £2.50. Annual tickets from £15. Please call 07939 514346. *Season:* Open 16 June to 14 March from 7am to dusk. Night fishing by arrangement only. *Methods:* Barbless hooks only. 2 rods per person maximum. Tickets in advance only. All litter must be taken home.

STALBRIDGE
Stalbridge Angling Association (Coarse Lake)
01963 250311, *Water:* Lake at Lanshire Lane, Stalbridge. See also entry under Stour. *Species:* Carp (12lb), Perch (2lb), Chub, Roach. *Permits:* C.C. Moores Ltd (animal foods), Stalbridge, 01963 362254. Bernie Ackland, 4 Russel Ave., Milborne Port, 01693 250311. *Charges:* Senior £22. Disabled/OAP £14. Junior £10. Day Ticket Senior £5, Junior £2.50. *Season:* No closed season on lake. *Methods:* No Boilies or Nuts. No fixed method feeders or fixed leads. No keepnets. Barbless hooks only to be used.

STURMINSTER NEWTON
Sturminster & Hinton A.A (Coarse Lakes)
Contact: Mr R. Brown (membership sec.), Uplands Close, Broad Oak, Sturminster Newton, DT10 2HL, 01258 473178, *Water:* 3 small lakes (Stoke Wake Lake & High Bench Lake) members only. Also see entry under river fishing - Stour.

DORSET

STILLWATER COARSE

Todber Manor Fisheries
Contact: John Candy, Manor Farm, Todber, Sturminster Newton, DT10 1JB, 01258 820384, *Mobile:* 07974 420813, *Water:* Two 1 acre Carp Lakes. 3 acre cnal style mixed fishery. 4 acre Bream and Carp water. 2 acre specimen Carp lake. *Species:* Carp, Tench, Bream, Skimmers, Crucians, Perch, Roach and Barbel. Specimen lake has Common Carp to 27lb 8oz and Mirror Carp to 27lb 12oz. *Permits:* From the address above. *Charges:* £5 per day. Specimen Lake -£8 per day, £15 for 24 hours (3 rods). *Season:* Open all year. *Methods:* Barbless hooks only. Specimen lake must use 42" landing net and unhooking mats.

WAREHAM
Wareham & District Angling Society (Coarse Lakes)
Contact: Deano Watts, c/o Purbeck Angling Centre, 28 South Street, Wareham, BH20 4LU, 01929 550770, *Water:* See entry under River Fishing, Stour. 14 lakes including Breach Pond, Pitmans Pond & Lily Pond.

WEYMOUTH
Osmington Mills Holidays
Contact: Reception, Osmington Mills, Weymouth, DT3 6HB, 01305 832311, *Water:* 1 acre lake. *Species:* Carp, Tench, Bream, Roach. *Permits:* Caravan Park reception, on bank. *Charges:* £6 per day Adults, £3 under 16, £3.50 Evening ticket after 5pm. *Season:* May 23rd - March 15th. *Methods:* Barbless hooks, no keepnets, no particle bait.

Radipole Lake
Contact: Mr D.Tattersall, Council Offices, North Quay, Weymouth, DT4 8TA, *Mobile:* 07980 730045, *Water:* 70 acres plus. *Species:* Carp to 20lb, Eels, Roach to 2lb, Dace, Pike, Mullet. *Permits:* Reels and Deals, 61b St. Thomas Street, Weymouth: 01305 787848. Weymouth Angling Centre, 24 Trinity Road, Weymouth: 01305 777751. *Charges:* Day - Junior £2, Adult £4, 60 plus £3; Monthly - Juniors £5, Adult £16, 60 plus £10; Annual - Adult £38, 60 plus £28, Junior £12. *Season:* 16th June - 14th March. *Methods:* 2 rod max, barbless hooks only, no bivvies.

Warmwell Holiday Park
Contact: John Aplin - Fishery Manager, Warmwell, Nr Weymouth, DT2 8JE, 01305 257490, *Mobile:* 07889 680464, *Water:* 3 lakes. 2 acre Carp lake (fish to 20lb+) - 20 swims pre-booking only. 2 mixed fishing lakes. *Species:* Carp to 20lb+, Perch to 4lb, Pike to 20lb, Rudd, Crucians, Eels. *Permits:* Day tickets available all year, but must be purchased in advance. Contact fishery manager on number above. *Charges:* Residents £3 for 24 hour ticket. Non residents £4 all lakes - fishing dawn to dusk only. Prices may change in 2005. *Season:* Open all year. *Methods:* Specimen Lakes: Barbless hooks. No nuts, beans or pulses. 2 rods max. No keepnets. No remote control boats. Unhooking mats must be used. Minimum 10lb line.

WIMBORNE
Crooked Willows Farm
Contact: Mr & Mrs VJ Percy, Mannington, Wimborne, BH21 7LB, 01202 825628, *Water:* 1.5 acres. *Species:* Carp to 20lb, Tench to 6lb, Chub 4lb, Roach, Rudd & Crucians. *Permits:* Available on bank. *Charges:* £5/day, Juniors £3. *Season:* Dawn to Dusk all year round. *Methods:* Barbless hooks only, no groundbait, no keepnets.

Environment Agency - Little Canford Ponds
Contact: Fisheries Recreation & Biodiversity Officer, Environment Agency, Rivers House, Sunrise Business Pk, Higher Shaftesbury Rd, Blandford, DT11 8ST, 08708 506506, *Water:* Approx. 2 acres with facilities for the Disabled including fully accessible fishing platforms. *Species:* Carp, Bream, Roach, Perch Tench, Rudd, Pike. *Charges:* 2004 prices: Adult £43, Conc. £21.50, Junior £21.50, under 12 years free (subject to annual review).

Riverside Lakes
Contact: Tony Perkins, Riverside Farm, Slough Lane, Horton, BH21 7JL, 01202 821212, *Water:* 3 lakes over 6 acres. *Species:* Carp, Koi, Rudd, Tench, Perch, Roach, Bream, Orf & Eels. *Permits:* Bailiff collects money & issues tickets on-site. *Charges:* £6.50 Day ticket, £4.50 Senior & under 14. *Season:* All year. *Methods:* No barbs, no night fishing, no keepnets, no improper equipment, no boilies.

Whitemoor Lake
400 Colehill Lane, Colehill, Wimborne, BH21 7AW, 01202 884478, *Water:* 2 acre lake with 44 pegs and half acre canal with 20 pegs. Ladies, gents and disabled toilets. *Species:* Carp 25lb, Tench 7lb, Perch 4 to 9lbs, Roach 2lb, Rudd 1 to 8lbs. *Permits:* Tickets on the bank. Night fishing by arrangement. *Charges:* Adults £6, Juniors £3.50, O.A.P's £4. Evenings £3. *Season:* No close season. *Methods:* No barbed hooks, no keepnets, no braid.

West Bay WATER SPORTS
10a Westbay, Bridport, Dorset
TEL 01308 421800

Permits for Local Clubs and Day Ticket Waters
www.anglingmailorder.com
Large selection of
SEA - COARSE - GAME
FISHING TACKLE & BAITS

EXE VALLEY ANGLING
19 Westexe South, Tiverton, Devon
TEL 01884 242275

www.gethooked.co.uk
Check out our Web Site! Get HOOKED ON THE WEB

Dorset Stillwater Trout

BRIDPORT
Mangerton Mill
Contact: Mr Harris, Mangerton Mill, Mangerton, Bridport, DT6 3SG, 01308 485224, *Water:* 1 acre lake. *Species:* Rainbow Trout. *Permits:* Post Office. *Charges:* £5 to fish. £8 up to 2 fish. £11.50 up to 3 fish. £15 up to 4 fish. *Season:* 1st April - 31st December. *Methods:* Max hook size 10.

CRANBORNE
Wimborne & District Angling Club (Trout Lakes)
Contact: Mr J Burden (game secretary), 35 Hardy Crescent, Wimborne, BH21 2AR, 01202 889324, *Water:* 5 Trout lakes plus Brown Trout on the river Avon. See also entry under Stour. *Charges:* £75 plus £8 joining fees.

DORCHESTER
Flowers Farm Fly Fishers
Contact: Alan.J.Bastone, Flowers Farm, Hilfield, Dorchester, DT2 7BA, 01300 341351, *Water:* 5 lakes total 3.75 acres. *Species:* Rainbow & Brown Trout. Best fish in 2003 - 13lb 4oz Rainbow and 5lb 8oz Brown. *Permits:* Some 25 and 50 fish tickets available. Prices on request (Tel/Fax: 01300-341351). *Charges:* £23 per day, £17 half day, £13 evening. *Season:* Open all year 5.30am to dusk. *Methods:* Single fly, max size 10, Bank fishing only.

Hermitage Lakes (Trout)
Contact: Nigel Richardson, Common Farm, Hermitage, Cerne Abbas, Dorchester, DT2 7BB, 01963 210556, *Water:* 3 half acre lakes. *Species:* Rainbow & Brown trout. *Charges:* Day (4 fish) £15, Half day (3 fish) £12, Evening (2 fish) £9. *Season:* Open all season. *Methods:* Max size 10 longshank.

Wessex Fly Fish. Trout Lakes & Chalk Streams Ltd.
Contact: Richard & Sally Slocock, Lawrences Farm, Southover, Tolpuddle, Dorchester, DT2 7HF, 01305 848460, *Water:* See entries under Piddle and Frome. 5 clearwater lakes and pools totalling 4 acres. *Species:* Lakes: Rainbow Trout only. Rivers: Brown Trout only. *Permits:* From the above address. *Charges:* Lakes: Day £26, £22/6hrs, £18/4hrs, £15/evening, conc.(OAP) £18 (3 fish - usual £18 ticket only 2 fish) and favourable hours. *Season:* Lakes: March 1st - January 2nd. *Methods:* Fly only. Lakes: Max 10 h/s. Rivers: Barbless or de-barbed.

LYME REGIS
Amherst Lodge
Contact: Darren Herbert (Baliff) or B Stansfield, Amherst Lodge, St Mary's Lane, Uplyme, Lyme Regis, DT7 3XH, 01297 442773, *Mobile:* 07765 817206, *Water:* 6 stream fed Trout lakes totalling 4 acres. *Species:* Rainbow to 7lb, Brown Trout to 4lb (catch and release only), Tiger Trout to 1lb. *Permits:* Go to rod room on arrival. *Charges:* From £15 for two fish bag. Catch & release £15 day or £10 up to 4 hours. Prices may change in 2005. *Season:* Open all year 9am to dusk. Must book if arriving before 9am.

Methods: Small imitative patterns only. Barbless for catch & release. In season upper lakes are dry fly only.

WIMBORNE
Whitesheet Trout Lakes
Contact: John Cheetham, 19b Willow Way, Christchurch, BH23 1JJ, 01202 490014, *Mobile:* 07720 671706, *Water:* 3 lakes totalling 7 acres. See Christchurch Angling Club main entry under River Avon, Hampshire. *Species:* Rainbow & Brown Trout. *Permits:* Davis Tackle Shop: 01202 485169 *Charges:* 5 fish £12 club members. 5 fish £22 non club members. Check with Davis Tackle. *Season:* Open all year dawn to dusk. *Methods:* Fly only.

DORSET

Sea Fishing

BOURNEMOUTH
Bay Angling Society
Contact: NFSA Head Office: 01364 644643,
Boscombe & Southbourne S.F.C.
Contact: NFSA Head Office: 01364 644643,
Bournemouth & District S.A.A.
Contact: NFSA Head Office: 01364 644643,
Christchurch & District Fishing Club
Contact: Christopher Amos, 59 Pauntley Road, Mudeford, Christchurch, BH23 3JH, 01202 490309, *Mobile:* 07759 590444, *Charges:* Adults £8. Family £16 (2 adults and dependant children). Senior £4. Junior £4.
Dorset Police Sea Angling Club
Contact: NFSA Head Office: 01364 644643,
Pokesdown & Southbourne Ex SMC
Contact: NFSA Head Office: 01364 644643,
Post Office Angling Group (Bournemouth)
Contact: NFSA Head Office: 01364 644643,
Winton Workmens A.C.
Contact: NFSA Head Office: 01364 644643,

BRIDPORT
Channel Warrior
Contact: Chris Reeks, 01460 242678, *Mob:* 07785 730504,
West Bay Sea Angling Club
Contact: c/o Westbay Watersports, 10a Westbay, Bridport, DT6 4EL, 01308 421272, *Mobile:* 07977 365068, *Water:* Regular competitions throughout year, many on world famous Chesil Beach. Boat and Junior sections. *Charges:* Seniors & OAP's £12 p/a, Juniors £6 p/a.

CHRISTCHURCH
Christchurch Royal British Legion
Contact: NFSA Head Office: 01364 644643,
Christchurch Shore Fishing Club
Contact: NFSA Head Office: 01364 644643,
Mudeford Mens Club S.A.A.
Contact: NFSA Head Office: 01364 644643,

DORCHESTER
Blandford Sea Angling Club
Contact: NFSA Head Office: 01364 644643,

LYME REGIS
Amaretto 11
Contact: Steven Sweet, 01297 445949, *Mob:* 07836 591084,
Blue Turtle
Contact: Douglas Lanfear, 01297 34892, *Mobile:* 07970 856122,
Lyme Regis Sea Angling Club
Contact: Ron Bailey, 6/26 Broad Street, Lyme Regis, DT7 3QE, 01297 443674, *Mobile:* 07850 180331, *Water:* Club restarted in 2002, new members welcome. Boat & shore fishing. Regular monthly matches. Tuition available. Contact Ron at number above. *Charges:* Membership £12, Juniors £5.

Marie F
Contact: Harry May, 01297 442397, *Mobile:* 07974 753287, *Water:* Lyme Regis *Charges:* 1hr Mackerel fishing trips, children welcome - Adults £7, Children £5 (all tackle included). Daily deep sea fishing, 8.30 - 11.30, £18 Adult, £15 Children (rod/bait inc). *Season:* Easter to the end of October.
Neptune
Contact: Peter Ward, 01297 443606, *Mobile:* 07768 570437,
Susie B
Contact: Ron Bailey, 01297 443674, *Mobile:* 07850 180331,

POOLE
Albion Sea Angling Club
Contact: NFSA Head Office: 01364 644643,
Aries II
Contact: Duncan Purchase 01425 278357, *Mobile:* 07759 736360,
Hamworthy Royal British Legion Sea Angling Club
Contact: NFSA Head Office: 01364 644643,
Lady Betty Charters
Contact: Ade Ponchaud, 30 Stockbridge Close, Poole, BH17 8SU, 01202 600731, *Mobile:* 07939 531009, *Water:* Between St. Aldhelms Head and The Needles, up to 6 miles offshore. Also Poole Harbour. *Species:* Mackerel, Bream, Rays, Tope, Conger, Flatfish, Bass, Cod, Whiting. *Charges:* 4hr trip from £120, 8hr trip from £200 - more details available from www.pooleangling.co.uk *Season:* All year, Daytime and evenings.
Lychett Bay Angling Club
Contact: NFSA Head Office: 01364 644643,
Mistress Linda
Contact: Phil Higgins, 11 Lyell Road, Parkstone, Poole, 01202 741684, *Mobile:* 07860 794183,
North Haven Yacht Club (Fishing)
Contact: NFSA Head Office: 01364 644643,
Our Gemma
Contact: Mervyn Minns, 01425 274636, *Water:* Under 20 mile radius. *Season:* All year.
Poole & District Sea Angling Association
Contact: NFSA Head Office: 01364 644643,
Poole Bay Small Boat Angling Club
Contact: Martin Burt, c/o 32 Alton Road, Poole, BA14 8SH, 01202 721955, *Mobile:* 07771 748486, *Water:* Club waters are from St Catherines on the Isle of Wight to Portland Bill in the west. *Species:* NFSA Wessex Division specimen sizes adopted. *Permits:* None needed. *Season:* Fishing all year.
Poole Charter Skippers Association
Contact: NFSA Head Office: 01364 644643,
Poole Dolphins Sea Angling Club
Contact: NFSA Head Office: 01364 644643,
Reel Action
Contact: Stuart, 01202 256182, *Mobile:* 07813 345143, *Water:* Wreck, Shark, Conger and Bass fishing.
Tango Bravo
Contact: Steve Porter, 01202 665482, *Mobile:* 07967 598669, *Water:* Fast angling boat, fishing out of Poole.

SWANAGE
San Gina Charter Boat
Contact: Swanage Angling Centre, 6 High Street, Swanage, BH19 2NT, 01929 424989, *Water:* Deep sea fishing trips. Fully licenced for 10 anglers. Experienced Skipper.

DORSET

Swanage and District Angling Club
Contact: Swanage Angling Centre, 01929 424989, *Water:* Fishing around Swanage and Purbeck coast with good fishing on Swanage pier. Open 24 hours a day. *Species:* Bass, Pollack, Rays, Dogfish, Pouting, Mackerel, Plaice, Turbot, Congers, Bream, Flounder.

WEYMOUTH
Atlanta
Contact: Dave Pitman, 01305 781644, *Mob:* 07721 320352,
Autumn Dream
Contact: Len Hurdiss, 01305 786723, *Mob:* 07966 361961,
Bonwey
Contact: Ken Leicester, 01305 821040, *Mob:* 07831 506285,
Channel Chieftain IV
Contact: Pat Carling, 01305 787155, *Mobile:* 07976 741821, *Season:* All year.
Flamer III
Contact: Colin Penny, 47 Ferndale Road, Weymouth, DT4 8N, 01305 766961, *Mobile:* 07968 972736, *Water:* English Channel. *Species:* All species. 47 different species landed in 2003. *Charges:* Boat booking- £290 to £390. Individuals £35 to £50. Price dependant on type/length of trip. *Season:* Fishing all year round.
Lady Go-Diver
Contact: David Gibson, 10 Portwey Close, Weymouth, DT4 8RF, 01305 750823, *Mobile:* 07766 145054, *Water:* English Channel and Channel Islands. *Species:* Bass, Cod, Pollack, Bream, Turbot, Plaice, Brill, Shark and others. *Charges:* £300 to charter the boat for a day. *Season:* All year. *Methods:* Uptide, downtide, anchored and drifting over sandbanks and wrecks.
MV Freedom
Contact: Peter, *Mobile:* 07976 528054, *Water:* Disabled Angling. Totally wheel chair accessible. Also available as angling charter.
Offshore Rebel
Contact: Paul Whittall, 01305 783739, *Mob:* 07860 571615,
Out-Rage
Contact: Rod Thompson, 01305 822803, *Mobile:* 07970 437646,
Peace & Pleanty
Contact: Chris Tett, 01305 775775, *Mobile:* 07885 780019,
Top Cat
Contact: Mr Wellington, 01305 823443, *Mob:* 07966 133979,
Valerie Ann
Contact: Ron Brown, 01305 779217, *Mobile:* 07976520607, *Water:* Reef bank and wreck fishing. *Season:* All year round.
Weymouth Angling Society
Contact: R.D. Stewart, Commercial Road, Weymouth, DT4 8NF, 01305 785032, *Water:* All shore line from Lyme Regis to Christchurch harbour. *Species:* Bass, Pollack, Plaice, Flounder, Cod, Sharks, Ray, Wrasse, Conger, Gurnard, Pouting, dogfish and a variety of Sharks. *Permits:* N/A. *Charges:* N/A. *Season:* Open. *Methods:* Restrictions in competitions only.

WIMBORNE
Marden - Edwards Sea Angling Association
Contact: NFSA Head Office: 01364 644643,

SWANAGE ANGLING CENTRE

PENN REELS · Shakespeare SINCE 1897 · Abu Garcia FOR LIFE

A GOOD SELECTION OF SEA, COARSE, AND GAME FISHING TACKLE SUPPLIED

Friendly staff and advice at all times

FRESH & FROZEN BAITS

Just 200 yards from Swanage Pier!

6 High Street, Swanage   Tel 01929 424989
email: swanageangling@brewer8779.freeserve.co.uk

WEYMOUTH ANGLING CENTRE

THE OLD HARBOUR HOUSE, 24 TRINITY ROAD, WEYMOUTH, DORSET DT4 8TJ

Opposite Charter Fleet Moorings & Town Bridge
Fishing Instruction at Chesil Beach Including the use of Shimano Rod & Reels

- Ragworm/Lugworm ◆ Devon Peeler/Hermit
- Ammo Frozen Baits ◆ Terminal Tackle ◆ Boat Bookings
- Carp Tackle & Bait ◆ Maggots/Dendras ◆ Rods & Reels
- Coarse/Game ◆ Mail Order ◆ No Charge on Cancelled Bait
- Permits for Radipole Lake

OPEN 7 DAYS A WEEK UNTIL 6PM
6.30am in the summer / 7.30am from Nov-Mar

We don't have to say we are the cheapest, biggest or best... Our customers say it for us!
Voted the TOP SHOP in Sea Angler and Sea Angling News

Email: wac@deepsea.co.uk
www.deepsea.co.uk
Fax: 01305 788881

TEL: 01305 777771

SEA FISHING

DORSET

Woolsbridge Manor Farm CARAVAN PARK

Level and sheltered pitches (all with electric hook ups) on a family run farm in the heart of Dorset

Many modern facilities including:
Toilets, hot and cold showers and basins, baby changing area, laundry room, washing up area. Separate shower room including toilet for family/disabled use. Shop on site, calor gas, public telephone. Play area with climbing equipment, sand pit and tree house.

AA ▶▶ | HOLIDAY PARK | SILVER CaSSOA silver award

Email: woolsbridge@btconnect.com
Tel: 01202 826369
Fax: 01202 820603

It's not just about catching fish. Sights like this swimming grass snake are much more familiar to the angler. Pic - Nick Hart.

WOOD FARM
CARAVAN AND CAMPING PARK

CHARMOUTH • DORSET DT6 6BT
TEL: 01297 560697 www.woodfarm.co.uk

- Breathtaking countryside views
- Sheltered, level tent pitches on grass
- Touring van all-weather pitches (electric hook ups)
- Peaceful Holiday Homes in old orchard
- Superb indoor swimming pool
- Idyllic fishing lake and dog walking area
- Tennis court and large children's play area
- Well equipped indoor recreation area
- Immaculate toilet & shower blocks

★★★★★ TOURING PARK | DAVID BELLAMY CONSERVATION AWARD | The Best of British | THE CARAVAN CLUB

WHERE TO STAY

Who are the BDAA?

Coarse - Sea - Game - Specimen

The British Disabled Angling Association (BDAA) was founded in 1996 to help develop opportunities for people with disabilities to access the sport of angling. In the early days the Registered National charity had just 18 eager members on its books, so great was the demand that in just 9 years the membership has grown to a staggering 23,000, with calls from all over the globe requesting help and advice.

New structures

With help & advice from its consultants the BDAA has now secured a respected position within angling and government to become a representative body for all disability issues within angling, the organisation is inclusive and empowers disabled people into its management structure to offer the very best in advice, support and events.

- Patrons
- Trustees
- Management Teams
- Competitions Development Team
- Disability Projects Team
- Coaching Team
- Access Team
- Disability Awareness Team
- Web site Development Officer
- Volunteer Liaison Officer

National coverage

So what do they actually do? the list is endless. BDAA offer a fully supportive National networking approach through its regional representatives who are available to offer advice, help and support not only to disabled people but non disabled people, fisheries, clubs, schools, community centres, policy, education, coaching and more.

- Introduction to fishing road shows,
- Professional angling Coaching,
- Access advice,
- Competitions,
- Children's days,
- Community and residential visits,
- Specialised equipment,
- Disability awareness courses

Authorities use the BDAA to offer advice on how angling can improve its environment and give more open opportunities for people with disabilities to access the sport.

In the UK 54,000 disabled people hold a fishing licence, of whom 1,000 fish competitively and the majority for pleasure, we firmly believe that many more would fish if they realised the possibilities.

BDAA want to inform people how accessible angling is becoming an activity which has no discrimination regardless of your disability, gender or age. You can visit the outdoors in a healthy environment, just for enjoyment or competing up to national or world level.

The BDAA is funded by public donations and the disability project funded by the Environment Agency and the English Federation of Disability Sport; we provide free membership to 22,000 members ensuring that we reach the maximum number of people with minimal cost.

The charities activities include advising fisheries and local authorities on access, and producing a booklet 'Inclusive Angling' on how to improve access and platform design. The booklet explains how to create accessible pathways, platforms and car parking areas, and provide the extra services that make fisheries inclusive for anglers with disabilities.

Just as important, the booklet is supported by 'The Specialised Equipment Guide', another BDAA booklet which lists ways to get around a range of problems. It includes equipment for Wheelchair users, Amputees, Stroke, Head injuries, Visual and other disabilities helping them to find an alternative activity to the mainstream: from rod-holders to audible and flashing-light bite-indicators for people with sensory impairments; and from wheelchair accessory frames to remote controlled reels imported from the USA.

THE GET HOOKED GUIDE

The BDAA caters for disabled coarse, sea and game anglers. It has its own Salmon fishing rights on the River Doon in Ayrshire Scotland, offers help for disabled people who want to try specimen angling, provides sea fishing aboard the adapted catamaran MV Freedom in Weymouth, and fly fishing through the Wheelyboat Trust, a charity who design and provide specially developed accessible boats and much more.

Fishing is especially attractive to young disabled people and aids their development. The BDAA offers educational visits to special schools, hospitals, residential and community centres to encourage the disabled and newly disabled either to try fishing for the first time or come back into fishing after disability. Our educational introduction to fishing gives both teachers and children an insight to what fishing can offer as a therapeutic activity. We have proven that fishing increases attention spans, offers social inclusion, a sense of achievement and aids motor skills development.

By contacting the BDAA, we can arrange a visit to your centre or, if an individual, post you an introductory pack giving information on all types of fishing and what it involves. The BDAA has a comprehensive web site which receives 2.5 million hits per year from visitors seeking information on fishing with disabilities, the website has a mass of information that is constantly accessed and downloaded by people all over the world.

From 5 to 95 years the BDAA can help you to go fishing, why not give it a try?

British Disabled Angling Association (BDAA)
9 Yew Tree Road,
Delves, Walsall,
West Midlands
WS5 4NQ.
Tel: 01922 860912
email terry@bdaa.co.uk
or visit the web site www.bdaa.co.uk

Rainbow Trout. Pic - The Editor

The Match Fishing Scene

Tony Rixon

As a match angler of nearly 30 years I have seen changes to the sport I could never have envisaged when I started. From catching Roach, Bream and Chub from a sluggish Bristol Avon to the sometimes frantic sport encountered on the modern-day commercial waters.

I have not fished a river for about 4 years, not because they are not as good as they used to be (as there still seems to be plenty of fish in them) and I see many anglers in my shop who still fish rivers every week - with some good returns. As with a lot of the nation's rivers the Avon seems to have had an upsurge of fish to specimen proportions. Carp to over 30 pounds, Barbel to 15 pounds plus and chub to 6 pounds seem commonplace. Bream are regularly caught to nearly 10 pounds throughout its entire length.

What is worrying is the apparent absence of smaller specimens of the above and, apart from about 4 months of the year between mid-summer and late autumn, the shoals of roach seem to do a disappearing act, so for most of the year big fish usually decide the top spots in a lot of the matches. With big fish playing such a part on the rivers many match anglers have deserted the rivers in favour of the more consistent sport available on the still waters. To see the popularity of these venues you only have to look at the match bookings to find they are frequently booked for up to 2 years in advance by many of the clubs and associations that would normally have been fishing the rivers.

The benefits are many, such as safe parking - with no car crime, easy access to the water, many fisheries boasting good facilities for disabled anglers, with flat stable platforms to fish off, toilets/shops available on site and, of course, the quality of sport is absolutely cracking.

As far as matches go on these venues you would generally have to catch Carp to win. The weights now being achieved, in even the coldest weather, are over 100 pounds and, in warmer conditions, up to and over 200 pounds is regularly required.

Another interesting aspect is the introduction of the silver fish pool. If you think that you have no chance of winning from your draw, and it can become apparent very quickly which anglers around you are catching well, it is possible to change your attack and target the smaller species such as Crucians, Tench, Bream, Roach and Rudd. All these fisheries are stuffed with these smaller fish and, as they go largely uncaught, you will usually need between 20 and 90 pounds to win the silver fish pool. This is a good to brilliant day by anybodys' standards. So, rather than going home empty-handed, it is possible to get a brown envelope from a mediocre to sometimes bad draw and recoup some of your expenses for the day.

By and large, match and pleasure anglers

THE GET HOOKED GUIDE

have never had it so good, with easily accessible and prolific fishing. Even for those amongst us who still feel that running water is the place to be, good sport can be achieved with a little more preparation and homework. So keep an eye on angling weeklies for pointers as to where to go, but most importantly pay a visit to your local tackle shop for the most up-to-date information. Information in the weeklies can at times be two weeks out of date.

Even if you only class yourself as a pleasure angler, if you get the chance, go and watch some matches on your local waters. You can often learn an awful lot by watching for a couple of hours. This, in turn will help you catch bigger and more fish in ways you might not have thought about.

One word of warning though, is give the anglers in these matches every respect. Do not ask too many questions while they are fishing, and always wait until they have finished what they are doing or they turn to talk to you. Most importantly, keep back from the waters edge. Avoid stepping over their tackle, as a lot of anglers pegs look like bomb-sites, with pole sections, rods and various other pieces of tackle strewn all over the place. Any breakages which occur can be very costly!

At the end of the day all any of us want is a good days sport, with a few fish and the chance of a 'few bob' back for our troubles. Also we must learn to appreciate what we have. This means don't leave litter. Most fisheries have waste bins and if they don't always take your rubbish home with you as there is no excuse for leaving any waste behind. Be aware of wildlife and treat it with the respect it deserves as it has as much right to be there as you do! Always be civil and respectful to other anglers and bankside users as all we want is an enjoyable days sport - SO BE LUCKY.

Cam Clearie looks really pleased with this superbly conditioned 11lb 11oz Dorset Stour Barbel caught on legered maggot. Picture by Steve Martin - courtesy Southern Angler.

HAMPSHIRE

- RIVER FISHING
- STILLWATER COARSE
- STILLWATER TROUT
- SEA FISHING
- WHERE TO STAY

Hampshire Game Road Directions

109. Dever Springs Trout Fishery
From Exeter: At the A303 turn off the turning for Dever Springs is signposted Barton Stacey approximately five miles on the left after passing Andover. After turning left from the A303 onto the slip road, there is a 'T' junction where you need to take a right towards Barton Stacey, travelling over a bridge. After approximately 1 mile, you will see a sign for Dever Springs to your right. From London: Turn off at the A303 turning. Dever Springs is signposted Barton Stacey approximately two miles on the left after travelling over the Bullington Cross A34 intersection, and is just before the Little Chef pull-in on the left. Then follow directions as above. Tel: 01264 720592.

110. Rockbourne Trout Fishery
Please telephone 01725 518603 for directions.

Hampshire Coarse Road Directions

111. Christchurch Angling Club (Coarse & Game)
Please enquire at local Tackle Shops or telephone 01202 490014 or 07720 671706.

112. Ringwood & District Anglers Association
Please contact Tackle shops in Ringwood area or Telephone Ken Broddle on 01202 871496.

Please note..
All of the information on fisheries, clubs and charters in this guide is published in a fully searchable format on our web site at

www.gethooked.co.uk

The web site includes additional information that does not appear in the guide. There is also a database of tackle shops and further information on accommodation.

Hampshire River Fishing

THE 'HAMPSHIRE' AVON

The River Avon is one of England's most famous rivers, and is revered by all anglers for the quality of fish that live in it. This river creates a certain mystique that captivates the attentions of fishers from all walks of life. The River Avon rises in the Vale of Pewsey and, with its tributaries the Bourne and Wylye, drains the chalk of Salisbury Plain. The River Nadder, which is joined by the Wylye near Salisbury, drains the escarpment of the South Wiltshire Downs and the Kimmeridge clays of the Wardour Vale. The River Ebble and Ashford Water also drain the South Wiltshire Downs and join the Avon downstream of Salisbury and Fordingbridge respectively.

Below Fordingbridge, a number of streams drain the New Forest area. The Avon finally drains into Christchurch harbour, where it is joined by the Rivers Stour and Mude before discharging into the English Channel.

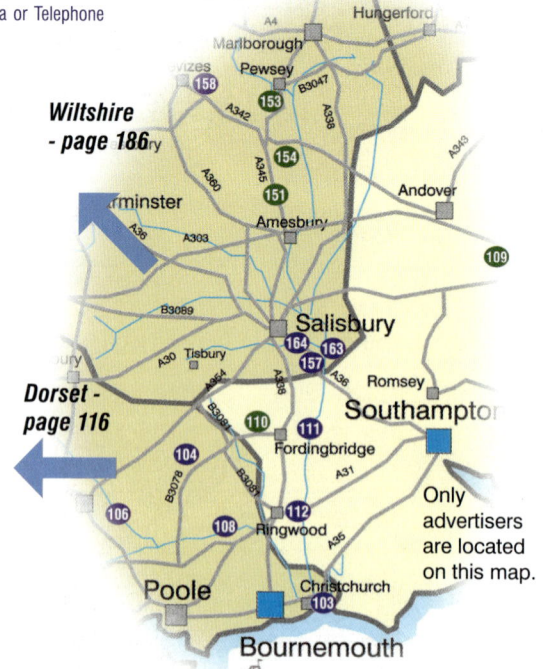

Wiltshire - page 186

Dorset - page 116

Only advertisers are located on this map.

HAMPSHIRE

Britford (Coarse)
Contact: London Angler's Association, Izaak Walton House, 2A Hervey Park Road, E17 6LJ, 0208 5207477, *Water:* Several stretches of the Hampshire Avon. *Species:* Roach 4lb, Barbel 10 lb, Chub 7 lb, plus specimen Dace, Grayling, Perch & Pike. *Permits:* Day membership tickets available from Fishery Keeper on the bank - £5 Seniors per rod, maximum of 2 rods. £2.50 Juniors & OAPs per rod, maximum of 2 rods. *Charges:* Senior: £39 - Junior: £21 - OAP/Reg. Disabled: £22 - Husband & wife: £58 - Club affiliated membership available on request. Prices may change in 2005. *Season:* Current EA byelaws apply. *Methods:* See members handbook.

Britford (Game)
Contact: London Angler's Association, Izaak Walton House, 2A Hervey Park Road, E17 6LJ, 0208 5207477, *Water:* Several stretches of the Hampshire Avon. *Species:* Trout & Salmon. *Permits:* Salmon & Sea Trout - Day membership permit available from Fishery Keeper on bank - £20 per day. Trout fishing - £10 per day (available from Fishery Keeper on bank). *Charges:* Prices may change in 2005. *Season:* Current EA byelaws apply. *Methods:* See members handbook.

Christchurch Angling Club (Coarse River)
Contact: John Cheetham, 19b Willow Way, Christchurch, BH23 1JJ, 01202 490014, *Mobile:* 07720 671706, *Water:* Largest club on the river Avon, mainly mid/lower Avon, Burgate - Christchurch, including the Royalty Fishery as of 1.4.01, also Fishing on River Stour between Gains Cross and Christchurch plus various coarse ponds including Blashford, Somerly and Whitesheat lakes. Please telephone the secretary for full details. *Species:* Roach (3lb), Chub (7lb), Dace (1lb), Barbel (14lb), Pike (36lb), Bream (11lb), Perch (4lb), Carp (40lb), Eels (5lb), Crucian Carp (4lb), Grayling (3lb), Tench (9lb). *Permits:* Ray Goodman (Membership Secretary) Tel:01202 475173 or for rivers and stillwaters enquire at Local Tackle shops. *Charges:* Adult £140, Junior £51, OAP/Concession £105. *Season:* Coarse: 16th June to 14th March. Salmon: 1st Feb to 31st August. Rainbow Trout all year round. Brown Trout: 1st April to 15th October. *Methods:* See rules for individual waters.

Fordingbridge Park Day Ticket Fishing
Fordingbridge Recreation Ground, Fordingbridge, 07939 514346, *Water:* 500 yards of fishing on the Hampshire Avon. *Species:* Chub 6lb 2oz, Roach 3lb 6oz, Dace 1lb, Rainbow Trout 6lb, Eels 1lb, Pike 23lb, Perch 1lb, Carp 16lb. *Permits:* Day Tickets must be purchased in advance from one of the following outlets: Fordingbridge Service Station (Q8 Garage, 500 yds from fishery). Ringwood Tackle. Avon Angling Centre (Ringwood). Fordingbridge Tourist Information Centre. *Charges:* £5 Adults per Day age 16-64. £2.50 per day for Juniors (15 and under) and Senior Citizens (65 plus). *Season:* Coarse Fishing June 16th, March 14th 7.30am - Darkness. Trout Fishing April to June by arrangement only - Contact 07939 514346. *Methods:* Max 2 rods per person. No fishing under power lines or in play area. Tickets must be purchased in advance.

Middle Avon
Contact: Simon Cooper, Fishing Breaks, The Mill, Neatham Street, Nether Wallop, Stockbridge, SO20 8EW, 01264 781988, *Water:* Hampshire Avon south of Amesbury. Very lightly fished with good Mayfly hatch. *Species:* Brown Trout. *Permits:* By phone or e-mail from Fishing Breaks. *Charges:* £95 per rod per day inc. vat. *Season:* May to September. *Methods:* Dry fly & Nymph only.

RIVER FISHING

Ringwood & District Anglers Association
www.ringwoodfishing.co.uk

Many miles of excellent fishing on some of the best waters in the South of England on the Hampshire Avon and Dorset Stour including the famous Throop Fishery.

Chub to 8lb, Barbel to 16lb, Bream to 11lb, Carp to 39lb, Tench to 12lb

For more details contact Ken Broddle on 01202 871496 or visit a local Tackle Shop

Day Tickets available for Throop, Severals and our Stillwaters

135

HAMPSHIRE

Ringwood & District A.A. (Hampshire Avon)
Contact: Mr Steve Martin, 2 Oakmead Road, Creekmoor, Poole, BH17 7XN, 01202 777892, *Mobile:* 07812 360278, *Water:* Between - Severals fishery at Ringwood upstream to Fordingbridge including Ibsley. *Species:* Barbel to 14lb, Chub to 7lb, Roach 3lb plus, Pike 30lb plus, Bream 10lb plus, Perch, Carp, Dace, Salmon, Sea Trout, Brown Trout. *Permits:* Local tackle shop or contact Ken Broddle (Membership Secretary) on: 01202 871496. *Charges:* Adult £100, Junior £40, Concessions, O.A.P's, Disabled £62 (Joining fee-£15 adult, £5 junior). Severals day tickets £7.50. Concessions for O.A.P's, Disabled, Juniors. Prices subject to seasonal review. *Season:* Slight variations to coarse season due to Salmon fishing, Current E.A. byelaws apply.

Wessex Salmon and Rivers Trust
Contact: B.G.Marshall, 63 Forestside Gardens, Poulner, Ringwood, BH24 1SZ, 01425 485105, *Water:* WSRT is a charitable trust restoring and conserving salmon to the lowland southern rivers.

DUN
Holbury Lane Lakes (River Dun)
Contact: Tim Weston / Jerry Wakeford, Holbury Lane, Lockerley, Romsey, SO51 0JR, 01794 341619, *Water:* 1000yds of river Dun, a tributary of the river Test, plus four Trout Lakes (see Stillwater Trout, Romsey). *Species:* Brown Trout 1 1/2lb average. *Permits:* 10 or 25 fish tickets. *Methods:* Single fly, max size 10, no catch and release, priest and net must be carried by anglers.

TEST
Boreham Mill
Contact: Simon Cooper, Fishing Breaks, The Mill, Neatham Street, Nether Wallop, Stockbridge, SO20 8EW, 01264 781988, *Water:* 1.7 miles double bank fishing on Wallop Brook. *Species:* Brown Trout. *Permits:* By phone or e-mail from Fishing Breaks. *Charges:* £100 per day plus VAT May to July. £90 August to September. *Season:* May to September. *Methods:* Dry fly & Nymph only.

Stillwater Coarse

FORDINGBRIDGE
Cranborne Fruit Farm
Contact: Cranborne Fruit Farm, Alderholt, Fordingbridge, 01425 475155, *Water:* 3 acre lake. *Species:* Carp, Bream, Roach, Rudd. *Permits:* At all local tackle shops. *Charges:* Membership of Ringwood & District Anglers Association. *Season:* January to November.

Lake Farm Fishery
Contact: P.S. Birch, Lake Farm, Sandleheath, Fordingbridge, SP6 3EF, 01425 654106, *Water:* 3 acre lake. *Species:* Carp to 25lb. *Charges:* Day tickets £6 at lakeside. *Season:* Open all year 8am to sunset. *Methods:* Barbless hooks only, no keepnets.

RINGWOOD
Blashford Lakes
Contact: John Cheetham, 19b Willow Way, Christchurch, BH23 1JJ, 01202 490014, *Mobile:* 07720 671706, *Water:* Series of former Gravel Pits. Fishing available to members of Christchurch Angling Club. See entry under Hampshire Avon. Includes Spinnaker lake. *Species:* Carp to 42lb, Pike to 36lb, Bream to 14lb, Perch to 4lb, Roach, Tench & Rudd. *Permits:* Ray Goodman (Membership Secretary) Tel: 01202 475173 or local tackle shops. *Charges:* Adults - £140 Junior - £51 OAP/Concession - £105. *Season:* 16th June - 14th March. Night fishing available with prepaid permit from Tackle shops. *Methods:* See individual fishery rules.

Hurst Pond
Contact: Ringwood Tackle, 01425 475155, *Water:* 1.5 acre pond at Hedlands Business Park, Blashford, Ringwood, Hants. *Species:* Carp 18lb, Tench 6.5lb, Roach 2.5lb, Rudd 2lb, Perch 3lb 12oz, Crucians 2.5lb, Eels 5lb. *Charges:* £5 per day. Limited night fishing, £10 - 24hr ticket. *Season:* Open all year.

Moors Valley Country Park
Contact: Clare Gronow, Horton Road, Ashley Heath, Nr Ringwood, BH24 2ET, 01425 470721, *Water:* The Moors Lake covers an area of 9 acres. Maximum depth 2 meters. *Species:* Tench to 6lb, Roach to 2lb, Perch to 2lb, Rudd 2lb, Pike to 20lb. Most river species ie Dace/Gudgeon etc. *Permits:* Fishing is from the bays marked by wooden posts on the west bank and has disabled access. Permits from visitor centre. *Charges:* £3.50 Adults (17 - 65yrs), £3 65yrs plus, £2.50 Junior (Up to 16yrs). Car park charges vary throughout the year, pay on foot system. *Season:* Moors lake from 16th June to 14th March. *Methods:* Rod licence for 12yrs plus, one ticket per rod, fishing from 8-30am to dusk, no keepnets, no boilies, barbless hooks, wooden bays only, float/ledger/feeder/dead bait for Pike.

Ringwood & District A.A. (Coarse Lakes)
Contact: Mr Steve Martin, 2 Oakmead Road, Creekmoor, Poole, BH17 7XN, 01202 777892, *Mobile:* 07812 360278, *Water:* 3 lakes at Northfield, plus 1 at Hightown on the outskirts of Ringwood. *Species:* Hightown - Mixed fishery with Carp to 38lb 14oz, Tench, Bream, Roach, Rudd, Pike, Eels. Northfield - Big Carp to 30lb, Tench to 12lb, Bream, Roach, Rudd, Pike. *Permits:* Local tackle shop or contact Ken Broddle (Membership Secretary) on: 01202 871496. *Charges:* Adult £100, Junior £40, concessions for OAP's and disabled. Available at Ringwood Tackle, West St., Ringwood, 01425-475155. Prices may change for 2005, please enquire. *Season:* All year fishing available. *Methods:* All on reverse of ticket.

Turf Croft Farm Fishery
Contact: Keith, Stephen, Christine Duell, Forest Road, Burley, Nr Ringwood, BH24 4DF, 01425 403743, *Mobile:* 07850 086021, *Water:* 8 acre lake - naturally spring fed. *Species:* Ghost Carp to 19lbs, Mirror Carp to 28lbs, Tench to 6lbs, Bream to 4lbs, Perch to 2lb, Rudd, Red Rudd, Golden Tench to 5lb, Roach & Crucians to 2.5lbs. *Permits:* Day ticket only. No Night fishing. *Charges:* £7 per two rods maximum. *Methods:* No boilies, no nut baits, no hemp, no keepnets, natural bait.

HAMPSHIRE

Stillwater Trout

FORDINGBRIDGE
Damerham Fisheries
Contact: Mike Davies, The Lake House, Damerham, Fordingbridge, SP6 3HW, 01725 518446, *Water:* 6 lakes. 1.5 mile Allan River. *Species:* Rainbow Trout (Sandy, Lavender, White & Electric Blue Rainbow Trout). *Permits:* Season Rods. *Charges:* Full Rod £1,700 (30 days), 1/2 Rod £1000 (15 days), 1/4 Rod £650 (10 days). Guest Rod £70. Please phone to confirm prices. *Season:* March - October. *Methods:* Fly only.

Rockbourne Trout Fishery
Contact: Rockbourne Trout Fishery, Rockbourne Road, Sandleheath, Fordingbridge, SP6 1QG, 01725 518603, *Mobile:* 07802 678830, *Water:* 6 Spring fed lakes & 3 chalkstream beats on the Sweatford water. *Species:* Rainbow / Brown Trout, Triploids. *Permits:* From the fishery. *Charges:* 5 fish day £48. 4 fish day £40. 3 fish half day £33. 2 fish (4 hrs) £25. Sporting ticket £35 - 8hrs fishing, keep first brace then catch and release. *Season:* Open all year except Xmas. *Methods:* Fly only, max hook size 10lb, no droppers, tandem/double/treble hooks, no dogs.

ROMSEY
Holbury Lane Trout Lakes
Contact: Tim Weston / Jerry Wakeford, Holbury Lane, Lockerley, Romsey, SO51 0JR, 01794 341619, *Water:* 4 lakes totalling 7.5 acres plus 1000yds on the river Dun (see River Dun entry). *Species:* Rainbow Trout to 2lb to 5lb, Blue Trout 2lb to 5lb and Brown Trout 3lb plus. *Permits:* 10 or 25 fish ticket. *Charges:* 2 fish half day £25. 4 fish full day £37. *Season:* 9am to dusk. *Methods:* Single fly, max size 10, no catch and release, priest and net must be carried by anglers.

STOCKBRIDGE
John O' Gaunts
Contact: Mrs E Purse, 51 Mead Road, Chandlers Ford, Southampton, SO53 2FB, 01794 388130, *Mobile:* 02380 252268, *Water:* 2 Lakes approx 7 acres in Test Valley. *Species:* Rainbow Trout (various sizes). *Permits:* Available from Fishery Tel: 02380 252268 or 01794 388130. *Charges:* £36/day -4-fish, £19/half day - 2-fish. *Season:* February 1st - November 30th inclusive, Wednesdays & Saturdays throughout December and January. *Methods:* Fly and Nymph only.

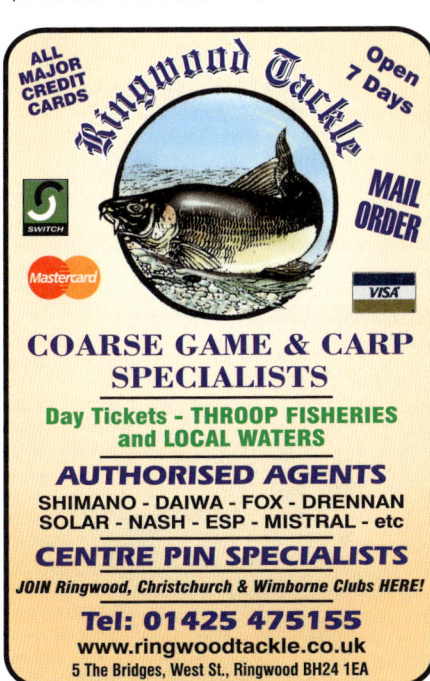

HAMPSHIRE

Dever Springs Trout Fishery

Barton Stacey, Nr Winchester, Hampshire, SO21 3NP

Legendary Big Fish Water!

Two crystal clear, spring fed lakes totaling 6 acres
Half mile of the River Dever
Prolific Natural Fly Life

A STALKER'S PARADISE!

Minimum stock size 3lb average weight 5lb

British Record Brown - 28lb 1oz

Call now for an unforgettable day's fishing

Booking Recommended!

01264 720592

www.deversprings.freeserve.co.uk

Hampshire Sea Fishing

BOURNEMOUTH
Individuals Sea Angling Club
Contact: Trevor Sutch, 67 Windmill Grove, Portchester, Fareham, PO16 9HU, 02392 201696, *Water:* Hampshire and Dorset coast line. *Species:* All sea fish. *Charges:* None *Season:* All year *Methods:* Promoter of the Hants and Dorset Premier League.

LYMINGTON
Challenger II
Contact: Mike Cottingham, 01425 619358, *Mobile:* 07884 394379,
Lymington & District Sea Fishing Club
Contact: Fishing Club HQ, Bath Road, Lymington, SO41 9SE, 01590 674962, *Water:* Boat and shore fishing, with strong Junior section. Fishing for trophies throughout the year. New members welcome. *Charges:* Adults - £6.50 joining fee, plus £13 p/a subs. Juniors - £2 joining fee, plus £4 p/a subs.
Sundance
Contact: Roger Bayzand, 01590 674652,

WINCHESTER
Dever Springs
Contact: Mr N. Staig and Miss P. Bull, Barton Stacey, Winchester, SO21 3NP, 01264 720592, *Water:* Two lakes totalling 6 acres plus a half mile stretch of the river Dever. *Species:* Cultivated Rainbow Trout - British record holder at 36lb 14oz. Cultivated Brown Trout - British record holder at 28lb 1oz. *Permits:* EA rod licence required. *Charges:* 4 fish £60. 3 fish £48. 2 fish £35. Father & son permit - 5 fish, £75. *Season:* Open all year. *Methods:* Fly only. Max hook size 12, single wet or dry fly. No catch and release.

Get HOOKED! ON THE WEB
Fully searchable Fisheries Directory - over 800 Entries!
www.gethooked.co.uk

Spinning for Bass.
Pic - Wayne Thomas

STILLWATER TROUT / SEA FISHING

138

Will 2004 go down in history as the year that Recreational Sea Angling became recognised?

A pivotal event for sea angling took place in 2004. The Prime Minister's Cabinet Office Strategy Unit produced a 220 page report called 'Net Benefits' that thoroughly examined the fisheries sector focusing on a sustainable and profitable future for UK fishing.

The single most powerful message that came out of this report was the recommendation that: "the over arching aim of fisheries management should be to maximise the return to the UK of the sustainable use of fisheries resources and protection of the marine environment". Who would argue with that?

Readers may well be asking, wouldn't that objective already be part of existing policy? Regrettably nothing could be further from the truth. Our publicly owned fish stock resources have been managed by DEFRA, who have been the sponsors of commercial fishing and the entire management philosophy has had nothing to do with 'best value'.

There have been many studies conducted around the world that show how recreational sea angling generates far higher socio-economic impacts than most realise. Such studies however, have been regarded as out side reasonable consideration by UK politicians/decision makers. Then in 2001, the National Assembly for Wales commissioned a study into the fisheries sector and it was found that recreational sea angling in Wales was a bigger earner than commercial fishing. Meanwhile, angling organisations lobbied the government and eventually in 2002 a study to evaluate recreational sea angling throughout England and Wales was commissioned. The results confirmed what anglers had expected. Sea angling is big business. Comparing the economic impact of commercial and recreational fishing is difficult and even economists have different takes on this issue. However to give some perspective to the two sectors it was found from the DEFRA funded study that recreational sea anglers directly spent into the English and Welsh economy, £538 million in 2003. According to the DEFRA 2003 statistics the entire value of all fish landed in English and Welsh ports by UK fishing boats was £144 million.

There are of course economic downstream values from quayside landings for commercial fish, but significant proportions of species that are important to commercial fishing are of no direct interest to sea angling. Species such as hake, lemon sole, cuttle, shellfish etc. are neither targeted nor caught by anglers. When the commercial first hand sale value of all those species that are of direct interest to recreational angling are totted up, it amounts to less than £50 million. Those same resources support £538 million annual expenditure by sea anglers.

Yet further evidence showing how important recreational sea angling is to the South West, was provided by a study of sea angling conducted as part of the 'Invest in Fish South West' project. 'Invest in Fish South West' is an ambitious £1.6 million project involving all stakeholders to decide which fisheries management options would best benefit the region socially, economically and environmentally. Visit www.investinfish.org .

The study of sea angling in the South West showed the South West offers some of the finest and most diverse sea angling opportunities in the UK. 240,900 residents of the SW go sea angling and visitors spend 750,000 days angling in the SW. this activity generates £165 million expenditure within the region each year and supports over 3,000 jobs. The most popular species is bass with nearly half of all sea anglers choosing it as their favourite. For anglers, abundance of target species is important and the availability of older and larger fish is even more so than the number of fish. The message is clear. For some species, the best return can be generated by utilising them as sport fish.

THE GET HOOKED GUIDE

GET HOOKED ON THE WEB

GET NOTICED ONLINE ADVERTISE WITH

www.gethooked.co.uk

3 pictures, 150 words, e-mail and website links

ONLY £60 PER YEAR*

*exc VAT

TEL: 01271 860183 or
E-MAIL: mandi@gethooked.co.uk

Despite the apparent unwillingness within the marine fisheries management regime throughout Europe to face up to this fact, the same is much better understood for fresh water. The summary report of the EIFAC symposium, held in Budapest in June 2000, read; "inland fisheries management in most European and North American countries tends increasingly to emphasize recreation and conservation, rather than the older function of food production. Many of the problems currently facing managers lie in the transition from commercial to recreational fishing. Recreational fishing is thought to have growing socio-economic benefits to society through increased rent and through the development of tourism."

Back to the Strategy Unit report 'Net Benefits': This report repeatedly highlighted the importance of recreational angling and in a section devoted to the recreational sea angling sector, recommended that fisheries departments should review the evidence for re-designating commercially caught species for wholly recreational sea angling, beginning with bass.

Such recomendations confront many historical assumptions and mindsets and many individuals in our archaic fisheries management regime regard such results as nothing short of blasphemy. However the message is clear, we need to look beyond what has simply been done previously and select the direction that provides the greatest good for the greatest number of stakeholders.

Will the UK government be able to adapt to the necessary sea change in thinking? Well believe it or not it has already done so! The Turks and Cacaos Islands are a British protectorate ninety miles north of the Dominican Republic. Throughout the 70's and 80's whilst most developed nations were busy destroying fisheries by underwriting un-needed commercial expansion and ignoring the evidence that stocks were plummeting, the Turks and Cacaos Islands shunned those poor models. Trawling is banned in the Islands as are purse seining, gill netting and dredging. Commercial fishermen here are small business artisans relying on free diving for conch and lobster and hand lining over the reefs. The Islands government recognising that fishery resources have many uses, have focused on sport fishing tourism. The UK Government made a conservation grant to the Islands in 1998 of $1.5 million.

There is no doubt that UK decision makers are beginning to recognise potential socio-economic benefits from the development of recreational sea angling and there are signs that the message is percolating through to the EU. As I write this article, the EU fisheries commission have published an invitation to tender for an evaluation of recreational sea angling throughout Europe.

Of particular relevance to the South West, is the formulation of a Strategy for development of the fisheries sector by the South West Regional Development Agency. The report of a conference held in Exeter during January this year to address the requirements of such a Strategy, attended by the Fisheries Minister Ben Bradshaw, drew attention to the recreational sea angling industry and gave the value of the recreational sector as broadly equivalent to that of the commercial sector.

Will I one day be able to pick up my rod and

THE GET HOOKED GUIDE

whether I choose to fly fish, cast a plug or bait fish, will I be able to go fishing in the South West, confident of catching four, five and six pound bass with a realistic chance of a number of larger fish including the magic double figure 10 pound specimen during the course of a season? Or will I have to rely on my annual pilgrimage to places with ever so familiar names such as Barnstaple, Plymouth, Truro and Falmouth in Massachusetts, where their enlightened approach to managing striped bass supports a multi billion dollar sustainable industry?

Perhaps the most poignant twist to the restoration story of striped bass comes from an article in a US commercial fishing magazine. The article focuses on how the commercial fishermen in Virginia are celebrating the "re-birth" of the striped bass fishery. They are now able to catch more and bigger bass, in a far more profitable fishery, as a direct result of the management measures that have been implemented from the involvement of the recreational sector.

I believe the Southwest could become to England, what Massachusetts is to North America and if so, it is entirely down to the dedication of a handful of committed anglers working together through organisations like the NFSA, BASS and SACN, who have taken up the political cudgel on behalf of the painfully silent majority, researching the facts, articulating the case to politicians, to fisheries departments and many other decision makers.

If you're an angler, a tackle dealer, a charter boat operator, a recreational boat builder, chandlery supplier or a part of the tourism sector who would benefit from South West fish stocks being managed differently, support the work of the NFSA, BASS and SACN.

Malcolm Gilbert
National Federation of Sea Anglers
Bass Anglers Sportfishing Association
Sea Anglers Conservation Network

www.nfsa.org.uk
www.ukbass.com
www.anglers-net.co.uk/sacn

Saltwater fly fishing on the North Devon Coast. Pic - Nick Hart

Anglers helping Flylife

Fly life need anglers' help now more than ever.

By observing and recording changes in fly life numbers, anglers are monitoring the quality of the aquatic environment. The flylife alarm bell started ringing even more loudly when anglers around the country shared their historical flylife observations. The results of the Salmon & Trout Association National Riverfly Survey showed a dramatic flylife decline to one third of those species and numbers observed in the 1950s and 1960s.

Mayfly Spinner

Where to Start Helping? Participate in the S&TA National Flylife Survey

Salmon & Trout Association (S&TA) wants more anglers to join in the survey. It is live and updated annually. Anyone can participate – member, non-member, novice, and experienced angler. If starting out, then simply limit recorded observations to "fly in general". The simplest data is still valuable. Those people with extensive fly identification knowledge can distinguish between, for example, Large Dark Olives or Medium Olives.

Why Participate?

The observations of anglers from around the country provides river specific, regional and national snapshots of what is happening to fly life populations and shows trends and pinpoints problem areas.

Flylife are the miner's canary of the aquatic environment. There is no way of knowing when or why our canaries are dying without observations. Anglers are the best placed people to do that work. While, the Environment Agency (EA) does flylife monitoring, they do not survey every waterbody, nor do they do any summer flylife monitoring. Thus, for these and other weaknesses in the EA monitoring system, the combined stresses on flylife of, for example, water abstraction and pollution concentration increases go unrecorded and unknown unless anglers point them out!

How will the results be used?

Already, the results have helped make the flylife decline impossible to dismiss or ignore. Working together with many organisations, the S&TA presses for sensible, urgent actions to sort out the many causes of the decline. A positive step: the EA will use the Flylife Survey results to better identify where problems are occurring and take action to find the causes and implement remedies. The Salmon & Trout Association will be monitoring the Environment Agency to see that action happens.

New for this year

will be the S&TA National Stillwater Flylife Survey, allowing anglers on stillwaters to monitor and record their observations of stillwater flylife. The format will be similar to the Riverfly survey, only with different species of flylife. It will be ready for anglers in autumn.

Without flylife there would be no flyfishing. Support the organisations that are working to protect the future of your sport and the aquatic environment it depends on.

The 2005 survey form will be available from the S&TA on 0207 283 5838 and via the website on salmon-trout.org. Please return responses by the beginning of January 2006.

SOMERSET

- RIVER FISHING
- STILLWATER COARSE
- STILLWATER TROUT
- SEA FISHING
- WHERE TO STAY

Somerset Game Road Directions

113. Blagdon
Bristol Water fisheries are well signposted from major roads. Tel: 01275 332339.

114. Burton Springs Fishery (Game & Coarse)
From junction 23 or 24 of the M5 follow signs for Bridgwater. Take the A39 out of Bridgwater heading for Minehead. After approx 3 miles you will come to Cannington Roundabout. Follow the brown signs for Hinkley Point visitor centre. At the Cannington war memorial turn right following the Hinkley Point visitor centre signs. After approx six miles turn left to Burton. We are exactly one mile down this road on the left. Look for our sign. Tel: 01278 732135.

115. Cameley Trout Lakes
Situated 10 miles between Bristol, Bath & Wells. Off A37. Telephone 01761 452423.

116. Chew Valley
Bristol Water fisheries are well signposted from major roads. Tel: 01275 332339.

117. Clatworthy
Wessex Water fisheries. Tel: 0845 600 4 600.

118. Combe Sydenham Fishery
From Taunton: Take the A358 road towards Minehead. After the Bishop's Lydeard bypass, take the left hand turning under the railway bridge. Follow the road for 7 miles until you reach the crossroads at the bottom of the hill. Turn right and you will find Combe Sydenham on the left after about 1 mile. From Minehead: Take the A39 towards Williton and turn right at the Washford radio masts. When you reach the crossroads at the top of the hill, turn left and stay on that road, through Monksilver and you will find the fishery on the right.

119. Exe Valley Fishery
M5 exit 27 to Tiverton on A361. Take A396 towards Minehead at Black Cat Junction, continue on A396 towards Minehead, at Exebridge turn left at garage on B3222, over bridge at the Anchor Inn take first right to fishery. Tel: 01398 323328.

120. Fly Fishing in Somerset
Please contact Robin Gurden on 01643 851504. Based in Winsford. Somerset. Exmoor.

121. Hawkridge
Wessex Water fisheries. Tel: 0845 600 4 600.

122. Lance Nicholson
River Fishing Permits & directions available from Lance Nicholson, 9 & 11 High Street, Dulverton, Somerset. Tel: 01398 323409 - Trout & Salmon fishing on the Exe, Barle & Haddeo.

123. Litton
Bristol Water fisheries are well signposted from major roads. Tel: 01275 332339.

124. Nick Hart Fly Fishing
J27 from M5 . A361 on to A396 Tel: 01398 331660 or 07971 198559.

125. Sutton Bingham
Wessex Water fisheries. Tel: 0845 600 4 600.

126. The Barrows
Bristol Water fisheries are well signposted from major roads. Tel: 01275 332339.

127. Wimbleball
South West Lakes Trust fisheries are well signposted from major roads. Tel: 01398 371372.

Somerset Coarse Road Directions

128. Airsprung Angling Association
Please contact local Tackle Shops or Tel: 01225 862683.

129. Alcove Angling Club
Please telephone 0117 9025737 or 07941 638680 for directions.

130. Avalon Fisheries
Please phone 01278 456429 or 07855 825059 for directions.

131. Bridgwater Angling Association
Please Telephone Mr John Hill 01278 424023 or Mr Mike Parnell 01278 459032

132. Bristol, Bath & Wilts Amalgamated Anglers
Please phone 0117 9672977.

133. Bullock Farm Lakes
From Junction 20, M5 follow B3133 for Yatton. Drive through village of Kenn, turn right for Kingston Seymour. Follow signs for Bullock Farm Fishing Lakes. Tel: 01934 835020.

134. Diamond Farm
Fishing is on river Axe at Brean. Site can be found from M5 junction 22. Follow signs for Burnham-on-Sea, Brean. On reaching Brean turn right at junction for Lympsham and Weston Super Mare on the Weston road. Diamond Farm is approx half mile from junction on left hand side. Tel: 01278 751041 / 751263.

135. Durleigh Reservoir
Wessex Water fisheries. Tel: 0845 600 4 600

136. Edney's Fisheries
Signed off Mells to Vobster road. Turn into Popples Lane, leading to Edney's Farm. Grid ref 72/50.5 Please telephone 01373 812294 or mobile 07941 280075.

137. Emborough Ponds
Please contact Thatchers Pet & Tackle, 18 Queen Street, Wells, Somerset. Tel: 01749 673513.

138. Emerald Pool Fisheries
Off the A38 at West Huntspill, turn into Withy Road by the Crossways Inn. Take the next right Puriton Road. Travel for approx. 0.5 mile, over Huntspill river, take the next track on the left. Pool on the right at the top of the track. Tel: 01278 794707 or 685304.

139. Follyfoot Farm Fisheries
We are on main A38, on the Taunton side of North Petherton. Entrance to lake in first layby on the right heading south. Tel: 01278 662979 or 07748 400904.

140. Godney Moor Ponds
Please telephone 01458 447830 for directions.

SOMERSET ROAD DIRECTIONS

141. HBS Fisheries
From J25 M5 come back through Bathpool on the A38. Pick up the A361 towards Glastonbury. At Durston Elms garage turn left. After one mile turn left again at crossroads, the fishery is half a mile on the right hand side. Tel: 01823 412389.

142. Laburnum House
Please Tel: 01278 781830 for directions.

143. Lands End Fishery
From M5 junction 22, turn left at first roundabout, then first left and follow road to T junction, turn left signposted Wedmore, continue through village of Mark, then into Blackford where you turn right by the school signposted Heath House, follow road to crossroads, turn right, then second right, fishery is at bottom of lane. Tel: 07977 545882.

144. Northam Farm
Leave the M5 at junction 22. Follow signs to Burnham-on-Sea, Brean. Continue through Brean village and Northam Farm is on the right half a mile past Brean Leisure Park. Tel: 01278 751244.

145. Plantation Leisure Ltd
From Bristol - Weston-Super-Mare A370. Turn towards Yatton on B3133 at Congresbury traffic lights. Go right through Yatton. Turn left towards Kingston Seymour just after the Bridge Inn. At village take middle lane. From M5 junction 20 Clevedon. Turn left at both roundabouts onto B3133 towards Yatton, after approx 3 miles turn right towards Kingston Seymour. At village take middle lane. Tel: 01934 832235.

146. Tan House Farm Lake
M4 exit Junction 18 onto A46 Stroud to Chipping Sodbury on to B4060 Wickwar. Continue until see Rangeworthy sign, turn left into Bury Hill Lane. Alternatively M5 to junction 14 to Wickwar to Chipping Sodbury B4060 for 1.5 miles. Take 3rd road on right to Rangeworthy and Bury Hill Lane. Tel: 01454 228280.

147. The Sedges
Exit M5 at J23 continue to Puriton Hill heading for Street/Glastonbury. When reach T junction turn right, continue for approx. 3 miles. Cross motorway bridge take 1st left through housing estate watch out for sleeping policemen! when exit Eastern Avenue take left turn, then first right into Dunwear lane. You will see our sign. Please telephone 01278 445221 or mobile 07967 398045 for directions.

148. Thorney Lakes
Directions from A303 to Muchelney. Turn off A303 dual carriageway signposted Martock Ash. Follow signs to Kingsbury Episcopi, at the T junction in village turn right, through the village of Thorney, over river bridge & disused railway. Lakes are on right.

149. Viaduct Fishery
From Yeovil take the A37 north towards Ilchester and then the B3151 to Somerton. Turn left onto the B3153 (Signposted Somerton) and go up hill to mini roundabout. Go straight over roundabout and take first right through housing estate to T-junction. Turn left and almost immediately first right onto track to fishery. Tel: 01458 274022.

150. Warren Farm Holiday Centre
Leave the M5 at junction 22 and follow the B3140 past Burnham on Sea to Berrow & Brean. We are situated 1.5 miles past Brean Leisure Park Tel: 01278 751227.

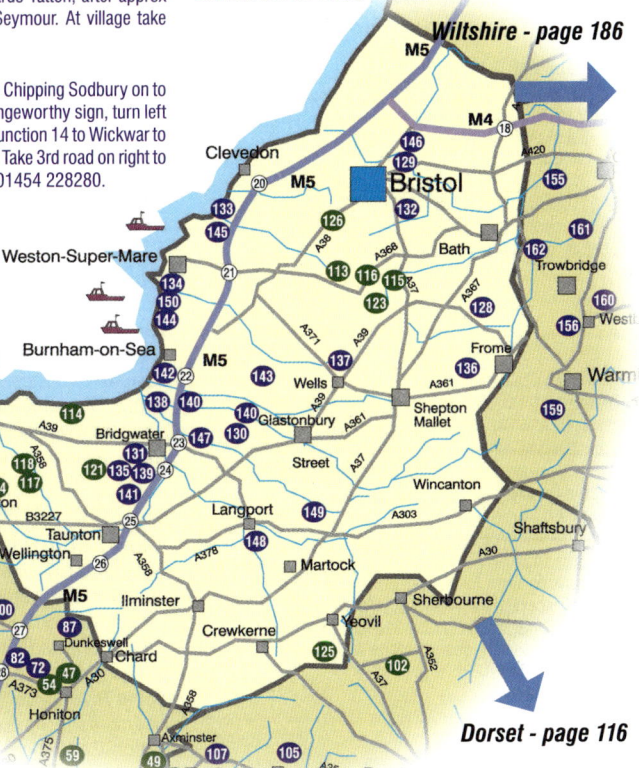

ADVERTISERS ROAD DIRECTIONS

Wiltshire - page 186
Devon - page 59
Dorset - page 116

Only advertisers are located on this map.

Somerset River Fishing

AVILL

Fly Fishing in Somerset (Avill)
Contact: R.M. Gurden, 3 Edbrooke Cottages, Winsford, Nr Minehead, TA24 7AE, 01643 851504, *Mobile:* 07814 243991, *Water:* 2/3rds mile on River Avill between Timberscombe and Dunster. *Species:* Wild Brown Trout. *Charges:* On application. *Season:* March 15th - September 30th *Methods:* Fly only. EA byelaws apply.

AXE

The River Axe emerges from the Mendip Hills at Wookey Hole and from here to below Wookey the river is Trout water. The river deepens as it crosses low lying land at the foot of the Mendips to the sluices at Bleadon and Brean Cross, the tidal limit. Fish species in the lower reaches include Bream, Roach, Tench, Dace and Pike.

Weston-super-Mare A.A
Contact: Weston Angling Centre, 25a Locking Road, Weston-super-Mare, BS23 3BY, 01934 631140, *Water:* River Axe, River Brue, South Drain, North Drain. Summer Lane Pond, Locking Pond. *Species:* Bream, Tench, Roach, Carp, Gudgeon, Perch, Rudd, Chub & some Dace. *Permits:* Weston Angling Centre. *Charges:* Season £23, Week £10, Day £4. *Season:* Old River Axe, Summer Lane and Locking Ponds - year round. *Methods:* No boilies, no nuts, no cat foods.

BARLE

See under Devon - Exe and tributaries.

Fly Fishing in Somerset (Barle)
Contact: R.M. Gurden, 3 Edbrooke Cottages, Winsford, Nr Minehead, TA24 7AE, 01643 851504, *Mobile:* 07814 243991, *Water:* 2 miles on the Barle. *Species:* Wild Brown Trout, Salmon. *Season:* March 15th to September 30th. *Methods:* All waters fly only.

Paddons
Contact: Mrs M. McMichael or Mr P. Jones, Northmoor Road, Dulverton, TA22 9PW, 01398 323514, *Water:* 400 yards single bank on River Barle. *Species:* Brown Trout & Salmon. *Permits:* Lance Nicholson Gun Shop, Gloster House, High Street, Dulverton, Somerset. Tel: 01398 323409. *Charges:* Day ticket - Adults £5, Juniors £1. *Season:* March 15th to September 30th. *Methods:* Fly fishing.

River Barle fishing
Contact: George Prodrick, Millhams Mead, Millmills Lane, Dulverton, TA22 9HQ, 01398 323409, *Mobile:* 07971 699247, *Water:* 2.5 Miles of double bank fishing on the River Barle. *Species:* Brown Trout to 3.5lbs plus. Salmon - 15lbs. Rainbow

Fly Fishing in Somerset
Tuition
Tackle Hire
Guide/Ghillie Service
Fishing Holidays Arranged
Day Tickets on Exclusive Waters
Tel: 01643 851504 & 07814 243991
Email: complete.angling@virgin.net
http://freespace.virgin.net/complete.angling

Lance Nicholson
9 & 11 High Street, Dulverton, Somerset TA22 9HB
Phone: 01398 323409   Fax: 01398 323274
COUNTRY SPORTS & CLOTHING
For all your Game Fishing, Shooting and outdoor needs...
Barbour, Tilley, Bob Church, Maxima, Leeda, Orvis etc.
GUNS - AMMUNITION - RIFLES - REPAIRS
Trout & Salmon Fishing available
www.lancenich.co.uk

Trout - 3lbs. *Permits:* Trout and Salmon licence required. Fishing permits from Lance Nicholson, 9-11 High St., Dulverton. Tel: 01398 323409. *Charges:* £10 per day for Trout and £20 per day for Salmon. *Season:* Trout: March to Sept. Salmon: 15 Feb to end Sept. *Methods:* Fly and Spinner ONLY.

BRIDGWATER AND TAUNTON CANAL

Cut in 1827 the canal provided a good commercial waterway between the two towns. The canal has been recently restored for navigation but there is only infrequent boat traffic. The canal offers excellent coarse fishing from the towpath for Roach, Bream, Tench, Rudd, Perch & Pike.

HUNTSPILL RIVER / SOUTH DRAIN / CRIPPS RIVER / NORTH DRAIN

The Huntspill River is a man made drainage channel, excavated in the 1940s and connected to the River Brue and South Drain via the Cripps River. The North Drain was dug c1770 to drain low lying moors to the north of the River Brue. The Huntspill is a notable coarse fishery and is often the venue for national and local match fishing competitions. Catches consist primarily of Bream and Roach.

SOMERSET

Bridgwater Angling Association
For a Superb Selection of Coarse Fishing!
6 miles on the Bridgwater & Taunton Canal. Fishing on the rivers Cripps, Brue, North & South Drain, King's Sedgemoor Drain, Langacre Rhine & The Huntspill. Stillwater fishing at Combwich, Walrow, Dunwear & Screech Owl & Bridgwater Docks.
Day Permits from local Tackle Shops
For further information and membership details contact
Mr M Pople, 14 Edward Street, Bridgwater TA6 5EU
www.bridgwaterangling.co.uk
Tel: 01278 422397   Mobile: 07903 950019

The North and South Drain and Cripps River contain similar species and also offer good sport for the coarse angler.

Bridgwater Angling Association
Contact: Mr M Pople, 14 Edward Street, Bridgwater, TA6 5EU, 01278 422397, *Mobile:* 07903 950019, *Water:* 6 miles on the Bridgwater & Taunton Canal, Fishing on the rivers Cripps, Brue, North & South Drain, King's Sedgemoor Drain, Langacre Rhine & The Huntspill. Stillwater fishing at Combwich, Walrow, Dunwear & Screech Owl and Bridgwater Docks. *Species:* All types of Coarse Fish. *Permits:* Available from Tackle outlets throughout Somerset area including Somerset Angling, 74 Bath Rd, Bridgwater, Tel: 01278 431777 & Thyers Tackle, 1a Church Street, Highbridge, Tel: 01278 786934. Veals Fishing Tackle, 61 Old Market Street, Bristol 0117 9260790. Topp Tackle, 63 Station Road, Taunton 01823 282518. Further information on Bridgwater A.A. available from Watts News, Edward Street, Bridgwater. Open: Mon-Sat 5am-7pm, Sunday . 5am-4pm. Tel: 01278 422137. *Charges:* Adult season: 2 rods £27, 3 rods £46, 4 rods £54. Senior Citizens: 2 rods £10, 3 rods £17, 4 rods £20. Junior (7-11yrs) 2 rods only £4. (12 to 17yrs) 2 rods only £7. Day tickets £5, enquire at outlets. *Season:* E.A. byelaws apply. Bridgwater and Taunton Canal open all year. *Methods:* Full rules and map with permits.

Taunton Angling Association (Bridgwater & Taunton Canal)
Contact: Mike Hewitson, 56 Parkfield Road, Taunton, TA1 4SE, 01823 271194, *Water:* 6 miles on Bridgwater & Taunton Canal (also see entries under Stillwater Coarse). *Species:* Roach 2lb, Bream 8lb, Eels 3lb, Rudd 2lb, Perch 3.5lb, Pike 27lb, Tench 7lb, Carp 23.5lb, Grass Carp 19.5lb. *Permits:* Topp Tackle, Taunton, (01823) 282518. Enterprise Angling, Taunton (01823) 282623. Somerset Angling, Bridgwater (01278) 431777. Street Angling, Street (01458) 447830. Wellington Country Sports, Wellington (01823) 662120. Thyer's Tackle, Burnham-on-sea (01278) 786934. Yeovil Angling Centre, Yeovil (01935) 476777. Planet Video & Angling, Chard (01460) 64000. Exe Valley Angling, Tiverton (01884) 242205. Exeter Angling Centre, Exeter (01392) 436404. Thatcher's Pet & Tackle, Wells (01749) 673513. West Coast Angling Centre, Watchet (01984) 634807. *Charges:* Season £28.50. Day tickets £5 Senior, £2 Junior. *Season:* Closed 14th March - 16th June, Ponds and canal open all year. *Methods:* Barbless hooks on stillwaters. All fish (including Pike and Eels) to be returned alive.

BRISTOL AVON
The River Avon flows from its sources near Sherston and Tetbury to its confluence with the Severn at Avonmouth some 117 kilometers and is fed by many tributaries on its way. The headwaters of the River Avon, the Tetbury and Sherston branches join at Malmesbury. Both are important Trout streams where fishing is strictly preserved and there is little opportunity for the visiting angler to fish these waters.

Malmesbury to Chippenham
Coarse fisheries predominate in this section, although Trout are stocked by fishing associations in some areas. Arguably one of the best fisheries in the country, this section contains a wide range of specimen fish. Local records include: Roach 3lb 2oz, Perch 3lb 3oz, Tench 8lb 5 1/2oz, Bream 8lb 8oz, Dace 1lb 2oz, Chub 7lb 10oz, Carp 20lb 8 1/4oz and Pike 33lb 3oz. Also many Barbel to 12lb have been reported.

Chippenham to Bath
Upstream from Staverton to Chippenham the Avon continues to be an important coarse fishery, both for the pleasure angler and match fisherman. The river flows through a broad flood plain and provides a pastoral setting. In the faster flowing sections chub, Roach, Dace and Barbel can be caught in good numbers.

Bath to Hanham
Between Hanham and Bath much of this length retains a rural character and is an important coarse fishery used by pleasure and match anglers. The National Angling Championships have been held here. Roach, Bream and Chub are the main catches and, in some favoured swims, Dace. Very good catches of Bream are to be had with specimen fish. 'Free' fishing is available through Bath from the towpath side between Newbridge and Pulteney Weir. Carp of 20lb have been reported caught downstream of Pulteney and Keynsham Weirs.

Hanham to Avonmouth
Between Netham Dam and Hanham Weir the river is affected by spring tides. The water has a very low saline content and this length of river provides reasonable coarse fishing. Below Netham Dam the river contains mostly estuarine species but some sea Trout and Salmon have been seen.

Avon Valley Country Park (River Avon)
Bath Rd, Keynsham, Bristol, BS31 1TP, 0117 9864929, *Water:* 1.5 miles on River Avon. *Species:* Tench & Coarse fish. *Permits:*

RIVER FISHING

SOMERSET

From above. *Charges:* £5 Adult entrance to park (includes ticket to fish), £4 Child, £4.50 Senior Citizen. *Season:* Park open: Easter - 1st November 10am - 6pm. Current E.A. Byelaws apply on the river.

Bathampton Angling Association (Box Brook)
Contact: Dave Crookes, 25 Otago Terrace, Larkhall, Bath, BA1 6SX, 01225 427164, *Water:* 3 miles of Box brook (tributary of Avon). Split into 2 beats at Middle Hill and Shockerwick. *Species:* Brown Trout (occasional Rainbows) Grayling. *Permits:* Local fishing tackle shops. *Charges:* Adults £25, combined lady and gent £35, juniors £8, O.A.P £7. Registered disabled £7, Under 12's free. To year end 31/12/05. Members only special day permits must be purchased before fishing. *Season:* Fishing from 1st April to 15 October inclusive. *Methods:* Traditional Fly/Nymph only.

Bathampton Angling Association (Bristol Avon Claverton)
Contact: Dave Crookes, 25 Otago Terrace, Larkhall, Bath, BA1 6SX, 01225 427164, *Water:* 2.5 miles of Bristol Avon up and downstream from Claverton. *Species:* Bream to 6lbs, Chub to 5lbs, Roach to 2.5lbs, Pike to 25lbs, Barbel to 13lbs. *Permits:* Local fishing tackle shops. *Charges:* Adults £25, combined lady and gent £35, juniors £8, O.A.P £7. Registered disabled £7, Under 12's free. To year end 31/12/05. Members only. *Season:* Standard river close season, night fishing on application. *Methods:* Club byelaws apply.

Bathampton Angling Association (Bristol Avon Kelston)
Contact: Dave Crookes, 25 Otago Terrace, Larkhall, Bath, BA1 6SX, 01225 427164, *Water:* 2 miles of Bristol Avon at Kelston. *Species:* Bream to 8lbs, Roach to 2lbs, Pike to 20lbs, Chub to 3lbs, Barbel to 8lbs. *Permits:* Local fishing tackle shops. *Charges:* Adults £25, combined lady and gent £35, juniors £8, O.A.P £7. Registered disabled £7, Under 12's free. To year end 31/12/04. £3 day tickets available to Non-Members. Tickets must be purchased before fishing. *Season:* Standard river close season. *Methods:* Club byelaws apply.

Bathampton Angling Association (Bristol Avon Newbridge)
Contact: Dave Crookes, 25 Otago Terrace, Larkhall, Bath, BA1 6SX, 01225 427164, *Water:* 1.5 miles of Bristol Avon at Newbridge, downstream of Bath. *Species:* Bream to 10lbs, Chub to 4lbs, Roach to 2.5lbs, Pike to 16lbs. *Permits:* Local fishing tackle shops. *Charges:* Adults £25, combined lady and gent £35, juniors £8, O.A.P £7. Registered disabled £7, Under 12's free. To year end 31/12/04. £3 day tickets available to Non-Members. Tickets must be purchased before fishing. *Season:* Standard river close season. *Methods:* Club byelaws apply.

Bathampton Angling Association (Bristol Avon Saltford)
Contact: Dave Crookes, 25 Otago Terrace, Larkhall, Bath, BA1 6SX, 01225 427164, *Water:* 1.5 miles of Bristol Avon at Saltford. *Species:* Bream to 8lbs, Roach to 2lbs, Chub to 3lbs. *Permits:* Local fishing tackle shops. *Charges:* Adults £25, combined lady and gent £35, juniors £8, O.A.P £7. Registered disabled £7, Under 12's free. To year end 31/12/05. £3 day tickets available to Non-Members. must be purchased before fishing. *Season:* Standard river close season. *Methods:* Club byelaws apply.

Bristol & West Federation of Anglers
Contact: Hon Sec. B Lloyd, 386 Speedwell Road, Kingswood, Bristol, BS15 1ES, 0117 9676030, *Mobile:* 07831 311582, *Water:* Bristol and West waters are; Swineford to Keynsham, Jack Whites Cottage (Londonderry Farm) all right hand bank down stream. *Species:* Roach, Chub, Carp, Barbel, Pike. *Permits:* Open to affiliated clubs, including Bristol, Bath and Wilts amalgamation.

Jason with a 18lb 6oz Carp caught in tutorial at Combwich Pond on Bridgwater AA Water

Bristol Avon
Contact: Avon Aquatics & Water Gardens, Jarrets Garden Centre, The Park, Bath Road, Willsbridge, Bristol, BS15 6EE, 0117 932 7659, *Water:* Free stretch from Crews Hole Road - Chequers - Hanham mills, 2.5 miles approx. *Species:* All coarse fish. *Permits:* EA licence required. *Charges:* Free fishing (Further details contact Avon Aquatics). *Season:* Closed season applies.

Bristol City Docks Angling Club
Contact: Bob Taylor, 118 Northcote Road, Downend, Bristol, BS16 6AR, 01179 040261, *Mobile:* 07990 573831, *Water:* 3 miles on Bristol Avon from Chequers Weir to Netham. Feeder canal (Netham - docks), Bristol Docks system. *Species:* Skimmers, Bream, Roach, Dace, Chub, Pike, Eels, Carp, Tench and Perch. *Permits:* All Bristol tackle shops and Harbour Masters office, or from secretary above on 01454 773990 or 07790 573831. *Charges:* Season: Senior & 2 Juniors under 12 £15, Seniors £12.50, Concessions, Disabled, Juniors, O.A.P's £6.50, Day tickets in advance: Seniors £2.50 + Concessions £1, Day tickets on the bank issued by Bailiff: Seniors £5, Juniors/Conc £2. Prices may change in 2005. *Season:* 1st April - March 31st inclusive, River - normal close season applies; Docks and Feeder Canal open all year. *Methods:* Docks: Pole and Feeder. Pole & Waggler on Feeder Canal. All normal river tactics on the Avon. Daily update information from Tony on 0117 9517250.

Bristol PSV Club
Contact: Mike Wilson, Bristol, *Mobile:* 07850 731137, *Water:* Well established club, fishing waters in Hereford, Gloucester, Bristol, Bath & Somerset. 25 matches a year. Meeting 1st Tuesday of every month in the Midland Spinner on Wick road, Kingswood. *Charges:* Membership £10 per year. Juniors welcome. Please contact Matt on number above or call in to the Midland Spinner.

SOMERSET

Bristol, Bath & Wiltshire Amalgamated Anglers
Contact: Jeff Parker, 16 Lansdown View, Kingswood, Bristol, BS15 4AW, 0117 9672977, *Water:* Approx 80 miles Coarse Fishing on Bristol Avon & Somerset Rivers & Streams. Stillwaters at Lyneham, Calne, Malmesbury, Bath and Pawlett near Bridgwater. Trout only water on Cam Brook. Too much to list here, please contact the secretary for full details. *Species:* All coarse species. *Permits:* Full Membership available from the Secretary. Veterans over 70 years contact the secretary for details of discounted membership. Full members only may fish at Tockenham Reservoir, Burton Hill lake at Malmesbury & Shackells Lake. Day Tickets for all waters except Burton Hill & Tockenham are available at Tackle Shops. Limited night fishing. *Charges:* Adults £30 (discount for early purchase). Adult and child £35. Concessions £10. Night fishing full members £50 per season. *Methods:* No metal cans or glass bottles in possession, no fresh water fish as livebait, maximum 2 rods per angler, full rules on application.

Frys Match Group
Contact: Ray Cooper, *Mobile:* 07811 256627, *Water:* 45 Pegs - 2 mile stretch single bank fishing. *Species:* Carp, Barbel, Bream, Roach. *Permits:* Membership available to all, please contact Ray. *Charges:* £10 season ticket. Under 16 fish for free if accompanied by adult. *Season:* E.A. Byelaws apply.

BRISTOL FROME
The Bristol Frome rises at Dodington and offers a fair standard of coarse fishing on the lower sections. The upper section contains limited stocks of Brown Trout, Roach and Perch. This tributary of the River Avon is culverted beneath Bristol and discharges into the Floating Harbour.

Frome Angling Association (River)
Contact: Gary Collinson, 94 Nunney Road, Frome, BA11 4LD, 01373 465214, *Water:* 12 miles River Frome - 10 acre lake. See entry under stillwater coarse, Frome. *Species:* River: Roach, Chub, Bream. Lake: Tench, Carp, Roach, Pike. *Permits:* Haines Angling, Tel: 01373 466406. *Charges:* £15 Senior, £7 Junior Under 16 and O.A.P's. Day tickets £3. *Season:* 16th June to March 14th, unless changes in legislation occur. *Methods:* No restrictions.

Farleigh Wood Fishery (River)
Wood Cottage, Tellisford, Bath, BA2 7RN, 01373 831495, *Water:* Brook with several pools plus 1 acre coarse fishing lake (see Stillwater Coarse, Bath). *Species:* River: Brown Trout to 2lb. *Charges:* Day ticket 2 fish £19, 1 fish £17, half a day 2 fish £15, Evening or sporting ticket £10. *Season:* EA season for river fishing. *Methods:* List of rules at fishery.

Frome Vale Angling Club
Contact: Nigel Vigus (Secretary), 32 Rock Lane, Stoke Gifford, Bristol, BS34 8PF, 01179 759710, *Water:* 1 mile river Frome; half acre lake (Winterbourne). *Species:* Carp, Roach, Bream, Tench, Pike, Perch, Chub. *Permits:* As above. *Charges:* Per season: Seniors £15 - Juniors £7 - OAP's/Disabled £5. Day tickets not available. *Season:* From June 16th - March 14th. Closed season March 15th - June 15th. *Methods:* Barbless hooks on all waters. Lakes: barbless hooks, no floating baits, no keepnets, hooks no larger than size 10, no cereal ground baits.

RIVER FISHING

Bristol, Bath & Wiltshire Amalgamated Anglers
www.amalgamatedanglers.co.uk

Approx 80 miles of superb COARSE FISHING

on the Bristol Avon & Somerset Rivers
Tockenham Lake - Lyneham, Sword and Sabre Lakes - Calne, Shackell's Lake near Bath, Brickyard Ponds - Pawlett near Bridgwater, Burton Hill Lake - Malmesbury

DAY TICKETS AVAILABLE ON ALL RIVERS & SOME LAKES
Limited night fishing for full members at £50 per season
Full Adult Membership £30. Concessions £10. Adult & Child £35. Discount for early purchase

Contact Jeff Parker on 0117 9672977

SOMERSET

RIVER BOYD
The River Boyd rises just south of Dodington and joins the Bristol Avon at Bitton. In the middle and lower reaches coarse fish predominate. The upper reaches above Doynton contain Brown Trout.

BY BROOK
The Broadmead and Burton brooks together form the By Brook which flows through Castle Combe and is joined by several smaller streams before entering the River Avon at Bathford. Brown Trout predominate above the village of Box, mostly small in size but plentiful in number. At Box and below the fishery is mixed and Dace to 14oz and Roach of 2lb are not uncommon.

RIVER MARDEN
The River Marden is fed by springs rising from the downs above Cherhill and joins the river Avon upstream of Chippenham. Brown Trout occur naturally in the upper reaches. Downstream of Calne coarse fish predominate and weights of more than 30lb are regularly caught in matches. The Marden Barbel record stands at over 10lb.

SOMERSET FROME
The Somerset Frome is the main tributary of the Bristol Avon. It drains a large catchment area which is fed from the chalk around Warminster and limestone from the eastern end of the Mendips. There are numerous weirs and mills mostly disused. The tributaries above Frome provide ideal conditions for Brown Trout with fishing on the River Mells. The middle and lower reaches provide excellent coarse fishing.

Airsprung Angling Association (Frome)
Contact: Ian Stainer, 61 Poulton, Bradford-on-Avon, BA15 1EA, 01225 862683, *Water:* River Frome at Stowford Farm (near Farleigh Hungerford). See also entry under Wiltshire, river fishing, Kennet & Avon Canal. *Species:* Carp, Bream, Chub, Roach, Rudd, Dace, Tench, Perch, etc. *Permits:* Wiltshire Angling, 01225 763835; West Tackle, Trowbridge, 01225 755472. Haines Angling, Frome. Trowbridge Road Post Office, Bradford-upon Avon. Melksham Angling Centre, Melksham. *Season:* Subject to normal close season. *Methods:* Details from Association.

Avon & Tributaries Angling Association
Contact: Andrew T Donaldson, 104 Berkley Road, Bishopstone, Bristol, BS7 8HG, 01179 442518, *Water:* Somerset Frome, Cam, Wellow, Midford Brooks. *Species:* All Coarse species and Trout. *Permits:* No day tickets, guest ticket from individual members. *Season:* In rules. *Methods:* In rules.

Russel Richards with a 30lb 1oz Common from Bagwood Lake. Pic - Bristol Angling Centre.

MIDFORD BROOK
The Midford Brook runs through well wooded valleys with mostly mixed fishing on the lower reaches and Trout fishing in upper reaches. The largest Brown Trout recorded weighed 5lb 6oz.

KENNET AND AVON CANAL
There are some 58 kilometres of canal within the Bristol Avon catchment area which averages one metre in depth and thirteen metres in width. The Kennet & Avon Canal joins the River Avon at Bath with the River Kennet between Reading and Newbury. The canal was opened in 1810 to link the Severn Estuary with the Thames. The canal, now much restored, provides excellent fishing with Carp to 25lb, Tench to 5lb also Roach, Bream, Perch, Rudd, Pike and Gudgeon.

Bathampton Angling Association (Kennet & Avon Canal)
Contact: Dave Crookes, 25 Otago Terrace, Larkhall, Bath, BA1 6SX, 01225 427164, *Water:* 6.5 miles of Kennet and Avon canal. From Bath to Limpley Stoke Hill. *Species:* Bream to 4lbs, Chub to 3.5lbs, Roach to 2lbs, Pike to 10lbs, Carp to 24lbs, Tench to 3lbs. Perch to 2.5lbs. *Permits:* Local fishing tackle shops. *Charges:* Adults £25, combined lady and gent £35, juniors £8, O.A.P £7. Registered disabled £7, Under 12's free. To year end 31/12/05. £3 day tickets available to non-members must be purchased before fishing. *Season:* Open all year. *Methods:* Club bye-laws apply.

SOMERSET

BRUE

The River Brue is a Trout fishery from its source above Bruton to Lovington. From here to Glastonbury a number of weirs provide areas of deep water and coarse fish predominate, notably Chub and Roach, together with Bream, Dace and Pike. Similar species may be found between Glastonbury and Highbridge where the river is channelled across the Somerset Levels and connected with a number of drainage channels such as the Huntspill River and North Drain.

Glaston Manor Angling Association
Contact: Adam Mitchell, NFU Office, 1 Sadler Street, Wells, BA5 2RR, 01749 673786, *Water:* Brue - approx. 15 miles both banks; Lydford on Fosse to Westhay. 3 miles on River Sheppey plus South Drain from Catcott Bridge back to source. Also see entry in Stillwater Coarse, Street. 1.75 miles approx. on North Drain. *Species:* Roach, Chub, Bream, Dace, Perch, Gudgeon, Pike, Tench and Carp. *Permits:* Thatchers Tackle, Wells. Street Angling, High St, Street, Somerset Tel: 01458 447830. *Charges:* Day ticket £4, Junior membership £8, Senior membership £24, OAP and disabled £12. 28 day permit £10. *Season:* Current E.A. byelaws apply. *Methods:* No live bait permitted, full rules on day ticket and annual permit.

Highbridge Angling Association (River)
Contact: Mr C Brewer, 8 Willow Close, East Huntspill, Near Highbridge, TA9 3NX, 01278 786230, *Water:* Basin Bridge, East Huntspill *Species:* Carp to 33lb, Pike to mid 20's, all other coarse species. *Permits:* Thyers Tackle, Highbridge - 01278 786934. Also available from other local tackle shops. *Charges:* Day tickets £3, 7 day ticket £10 or season ticket £20. Senior citizen £10. *Season:* March 15th - June 16th closed season. *Methods:* No live baiting, full list with ticket.

Merry Farm Fishing
Contact: Mr.Peter Dearing, Merry Farm, Merry Lane, Basonbridge, TA9 3PS, 01278 783655, *Water:* 600 yards on the River Brue. *Species:* Pike 20lb plus, Bream 10lb, Tench 5lb, Chub, Carp, Roach 1.5lb, Gudgeon, Ruffe, Perch 4lb. *Permits:* Day tickets. *Charges:* £1 per day. *Season:* 16th June to 14th March. *Methods:* No restrictions.

Mill House
Contact: Mr & Mrs M Knight, Mill Road, Barton St. David, Nr. Somerton, TA11 6DF, 01458 851215, *Water:* Mill stream off river Brue - owners rights to fish. *Species:* Chub, Trout, Eels. *Permits:* Available at fishing and tackle shop in Street, for whole of the river Brue. Street Angling Centre, 160 High St, Street. 01458 447380. *Charges:* £4 for day pass. £10 for monthly pass. *Season:* Season starts around mid june.

Walleden Farm Fishery
Contact: Mr Andrew Wall, East Huntspill, Highbridge, TA9 3UP, 01278 786488, *Water:* Section of river Brue. See also entry under stillwater trout. *Species:* Trout. *Permits:* From the above. *Season:* Open all year. *Methods:* Any legal method.

RIVER FISHING

CUT OUT POLLUTION NOW!

Telephone 0800 80 70 60 anywhere in England and Wales to report:
- Damage or danger to the natural environment
- Pollution
- Poaching
- Risks to wildlife
- Fish in distress
- Illegal dumping of hazardous waste
- Flooding incidents (for reporting flooding only)

ENVIRONMENT AGENCY INCIDENT HOTLINE

0800 80 70 60

CALL FREE, 24 HRS A DAY, 7 DAYS A WEEK

Help us to protect the environment.

Environment Agency

Cut out this card and keep it close to your telephone

DON'T IGNORE IT! REPORT IT!

Environment Agency

SOMERSET

RIVER FISHING

CAM AND WELLOW BROOKS

The Cam and Wellow Brooks, rising on the north side of the Mendip Hills, flow through what was a mining area and now provide good quality Trout fishing controlled by local fishing associations.

Cameley Lakes (River Cam)
Contact: J. Harris, Hillcrest farm, Cameley, Temple Cloud, Nr Bristol, BS39 5AQ, 01761 452423, *Water:* Fishing on River Cam. See also entry under Stillwater Trout, Bristol. *Species:* Rainbow and Brown trout, wild Trout. *Permits:* Details on request. *Charges:* Details on request. *Season:* Details on request. *Methods:* Details on request.

CHEW

The River Chew rises near Chewton Mendip and flows through the Bristol Waterworks Reservoirs at Litton and Chew Valley Lake. The river continues through Chew Magna, Stanton Drew, Publow, Woolard and Compton Dando to its confluence with the River Avon at Keynsham. A mixed fishery for most its length and is particularly good for Roach, Dace and Grayling below Pensford.

Bathampton Angling Association (River Chew)
Contact: Dave Crookes, 25 Otago Terrace, Larkhall, Bath, BA1 6SX, 01225 427164, *Water:* One mile of river Chew at Compton Dando, near Keynsham. *Species:* Roach, Chub, Grayling, Brown Trout, Rainbow Trout, Dace, Perch. *Permits:* Local fishing tackle shops. *Charges:* Adults £25, combined lady and gent £35, juniors £8, O.A.P £7. Registered disabled £7, Under 12's free. To year end 31/12/04. Members only. *Season:* Open all year. Fly only for trout from 15 March to 15 June inclusive . *Methods:* Club bye-laws apply.

Keynsham Angling Association
Contact: Mr K. N. Jerrom, 21 St Georges Road, Keynsham, Bristol, BS31 2HU, 01179 865193, *Water:* Stretches on the rivers Avon and Chew. *Species:* Mixed. *Charges:* Members only fishing. Membership details from secretary or Keynsham Pet & Garden Centre, tel: 01179 862366. Adult membership £12. Juniors, OAPs, disabled £4. *Season:* Current E.A. Byelaws apply. *Methods:* Details in members handbook. On rivers Chew and Avon there are no restrictions other than current E.A. Byelaws.

Knowle Angling Association (River Chew)
Contact: Keith Caddick, 41 Eastwood Crescent, Brislington, Bristol, BS4 4SR, 01179 857974, *Mobile:* 0794 634 7581, *Water:* 5 miles of upper and lower river Chew, 2.5 miles river Yeo. 2 lakes - Publow and Ackers lake at Pensford. Plus fishing at Chew Magna reservoir (see Stillwater Trout, Bristol). *Species:* Brown and Rainbow Trout. *Permits:* From Kieth Caddick. *Charges:* £80 annual membership. New members pay extra £5 entrance fee. *Season:* All rivers 1 April - 15 October. Lower Chew open all year. Trout 1st April to 15 October. Coarse Fish and Grayling 16 June to 14 March. *Methods:* Fly only on upper Chew. Any method on Lower Chew. Any method on river Yeo.

EXE & TRIBUTARIES

See description under Devon.

Beasley Mill
Contact: P. Veale, Lance Nicholson, 9 High Street, Dulverton, TA22 9HB, 01398 323409, *Water:* Approx 1 mile double bank on Barle at Dulverton. *Species:* Trout and occasional Salmon. *Permits:* As above. *Charges:* £10 Trout, £25 Salmon. *Season:* 15th March - 30th September. *Methods:* Any legal method.

Broford Fishing
Contact: P. Veale, Lance Nicholson Fishing, Tackle & Guns, 9 High Street, Dulverton, TA22 9HB, 01398 323409, *Water:* Approx 5 miles bank fishing on Little Exe. *Species:* Wild Brown Trout with occasional Salmon. *Permits:* As above. *Charges:* £10 per day - Trout. £25 per day - Salmon. *Season:* 15th March - 30th September. *Methods:* Fly Only for Trout. Any legal method for Salmon.

Dulverton Angling Association
Contact: P. Veale, Lance Nicholson Fishing, Tackle & Guns, 9 High Street, Dulverton, TA22 9HB, 01398 323409, *Water:* Approx. 5 miles bank on Exe & Haddeo. Membership open to all. *Species:* Brown Trout & Salmon. *Permits:* No charge - Members only. *Charges:* Adults £20. Junior £1 (all juniors under 16 must be accompanied by an adult). *Season:* 15th March - 30th September. *Methods:* Any legal method.

Exe Valley Fishery (River Exe)
Contact: Andrew Maund, Exebridge, Dulverton, TA22 9AY, 01398 323328, *Water:* Half a mile of single bank. *Species:* Salmon Trout and Grayling. *Permits:* Day Tickets from Exe Valley Fishery. *Charges:* Contact for details. *Season:* EA Byelaws apply. *Methods:* Trout and Grayling fly only. Salmon fly or spinner.

Fly Fishing in Somerset (Little Exe)
Contact: Mr Robin Gurden, 3 Edbrooke Cottages, Winsford, Nr Minehead, TA24 7AE, 01643 851504, *Mobile:* 07814 243991, *Water:* Upper Exe 2.5 miles, Barle 2 miles. *Species:* Wild Brown Trout, Salmon early and late season. *Season:* March 15th to September 30th. *Methods:* All waters fly only.

Nick Hart Fly Fishing (Exe)
Contact: Nick Hart, The Cottage, Benshayes Farm, Bampton, Tiverton, EX16 9LA, 01398 331660, *Mobile:* 0797 1198559, *Water:* 1.5 miles of Upper Exe, 3 miles of Middle Exe (see also entries under Devon, Taw and Torridge). *Species:* Upper Exe: Trout to 1lb, Middle Exe: Salmon to double figures. *Permits:* From Nick Hart Fly Fishing. *Charges:* Trout: £15/day, Salmon: £30/day . *Season:* Trout Season: 15th March - 30th September. Salmon Season: 14th February - 30th September. *Methods:* Upper Exe: Fly only, barbless hooks, compulsory catch & release - Middle Exe: Spin or fly fish year round.

ISLE

The River Isle rises near Wadeford and soon after its source is joined by a tributary from Chard Lake. Trout are found as far as Ilminster but below the town coarse fish predominate. The profile of the river is fairly natural though a number of shallow weirs provide increased depth in places. Species caught in the lower stretches include Chub, Dace and Roach.

SOMERSET

The Barle, a tributary of the Exe. Pic - Bryan Martin

RIVER FISHING

THE KINGS SEDGEMOOR DRAIN
The Kings Sedgemoor Drain is an artificial drainage channel dug c1790. As well as draining a large area of moor it also carries the diverted water of the River Cary and excess flood flows from the River Parrett. The KSD is a very well known coarse fishery and is used for both local and national match fishing competitions. Fish species present include Roach, Bream, Tench, Perch and Pike.

PARRETT
The River Parrett rises in West Dorset and there is some Trout fishing as far as Creedy Bridge upstream of the A303. Below this point a number of weirs and hatches result in deeper water and slower flows. The resulting coarse fishery contains a wide variety of species including Roach, Bream, Rudd, Chub, Dace, Carp, Crucian Carp and Pike. Similar species are found in the lowest freshwater section at Langport where the Rivers Isle and Yeo join the Parrett to form a wide deep river which becomes tidal below Oath Sluice.

Chard & District Angling Club
Contact: Mr Braunton, Planet Video & Angling, 19a High Street, Chard, TA20 1QF, 01460 64000, *Water:* Approx 1.5 miles on the river Isle. Also Chard Reservoir and Perry Street Pond, see entry under coarse fishery. *Species:* Dace, Roach, Chub, Perch, Bream, Gudgeon. *Permits:* Planet Video & Angling, 19a High Street, Chard, Somerset TA20 1QF. Tel: 01460 64000. *Charges:* Membership £15 per year, Juniors £8, OAP's & Concessions £10; includes coarse stillwater Perry Street Pond. No day tickets Perry Street or on river. *Season:* Closed season 14th March to 16th June on river.

Ilminster & District A.A. (River Isle)
Contact: P. Lonton, Marshalsea, Cottage Corner, Ilton, Ilminster, 01460 52519, *Water:* Approx 6 miles on the river Isle. *Species:* Roach, Chub, Perch, Bream, Dace. *Permits:* Day tickets from Ilminster Warehouse. Membership details from the secretary. Annual membership tickets from Ilminster Warehouse, Yeovil Angling Centre, The Tackle Shack, Chard Angling, Enterprise Angling, Taunton. *Charges:* £16 annual membership. Day tickets £4. Junior £3. *Season:* Current E.A. Byelaws apply. *Methods:* Club rules apply.

Newton Abbot Fishing Association (River Isle)
Contact: Clive Smith (membership secretary), PO Box 1, Bovey Tracey, Newton Abbot, TQ13 9ZE, 01626 836361, *Water:* 1 mile stretch of the river Isle at Hambridge. Popular winter venue. See entry under Devon, Stillwater Coarse, Newton Abbot *Species:* Pike, Roach, Rudd, Bream, Tench and Dace. Pike fishing can be frantic. *Season:* Rivers are controlled by the national close season for coarse fish.

KENN AND BLIND YEO
The New Blind Yeo is an artificial drainage channel which also carries some of the diverted water of the River Kenn. Both waters contain good Roach with Bream, Rudd, Carp, Perch, Tench and Pike.

Clevedon & District F.A.C.
Contact: Mr Newton, 64 Clevedon Rd, Tickenham, Clevedon, BS21 6RD, 01275 856107, *Water:* 6 miles - Blind Yeo / River Kenn. *Species:* Roach, Bream, Rudd, Eels, Perch, Pike & Tench. *Permits:* NSAA Permit at all local tackle shops. *Charges:* Season: Seniors: £20, Juniors/OAP: £10; Weekly £10; Daily £3. *Season:* June 16th - March 14th inc. *Methods:* Waggler/Stick, Pole, Ledger, no live baits, no coarse fish to be used as dead bait.

Langport & District Angling Association
Contact: Den Barlow, Florissant, Northfield, Somerton, TA11 6SJ, 01458 272119, *Water:* 5 miles on the river Parrett. Coombe Lake - 2.75 acres, no closed season. *Species:* All common coarse species except Barbel. *Permits:* Fosters Newsagency, Bow Street, Langport. *Charges:* Annual £12, junior £5, disabled/OAP £6. Weekly £5. Senior day £3, junior day £1.50. *Season:* Closed season on river only. Membership from 16th June to 15th June inc. Night fishing permitted on river only from Langport A.A. controlled banks. *Methods:* Lake: Barbless hooks, No boilies, No Carp in keepnets.

Somerset Levels Association of Clubs
Contact: Newton Abbot Fishing Association, Clive Smith (Membership Secretary), PO Box 1, Bovey Tracey, Newton Abbot, TQ13 9ZE, 01626 836661, *Water:* See entry under Newton Abbot Fishing Association Devon, Stillwater Coarse. Rights to numerous parts of the Parret, Brue, Isle and other stretches of drain in the Langport area. *Species:* All coarse species.

Stoke Sub Hamdon & District A.A. (River)
Contact: Mr Derek Goad (Secretary), (H.Q. at Stoke Working Mens Club), 2 Windsor Lane, Stoke-Sub-Hamdon, TA14 6UE, 01935 824337, *Water:* Upper Stretches River Parrett approx 10km. Long Load Drain (Shared Water) also see entry under Stillwater Coarse, Yeovil, Bearley Lake. *Species:* Carp, Tench, Roach, Rudd, Bream, Perch, Dace, Chub, Pike, Eel, Gudgeon, Ruffe. Trout Fishing also available. *Permits:* Season permits only. Available from Stax Tackle, Montacute and Yeovil Angling Centre, Yeovil. Also available from secretary. *Charges:* Season tickets: Senior £12, Juniors/OAPs £6 (Bearley Lake). Juniors under 14 must be accompanied by an adult. *Season:* Trout 1st April - 31st October. Lake all year. Coarse (River & Drain) 16th June - 14th March. *Methods:* Trout: No maggot. River Coarse: No restrictions.

SOMERSET

RIVER FISHING

Tiverton & District Angling Club (River Parret)
Contact: Exe Valley Angling, 19 Westexe South, Tiverton, EX16 5DQ, 01884 242275, *Water:* Various stretches on several rivers in Somerset including Isle, Brue and North Drain. See also entry under stillwater coarse, Devon, Tiverton. *Permits:* Please ring Exe Valley for details. Also available from: Exeter Angling Centre, Enterprise Angling Taunton, Topp Tackle Taunton & Minnows Caravan Park - beside Grand Western Canal *Charges:* Senior: Day £4, Annual £20. Conc: Junior & OAP Day £2.50, Annual £8 *Season:* Coarse: closed 15th March to 16th June. Trout: open from 15th March to 30th September. Salmon: open 14th February to 30th September.

TONE

The River Tone rises on the edge of Exmoor National Park and not far from its source it feeds into and out of Clatworthy reservoir. From here to Taunton there are some twenty miles of fast flowing Trout river, though Grayling, Dace and Roach appear near Taunton where weirs provide increased depth. Through the town and just below, Chub, Dace and Roach predominate but at Bathpool the river becomes wider, deeper and slower. Roach, Bream, Carp, Tench and Pike are the typical species in this stretch which continues to the tidal limit at New Bridge.

Taunton Angling Association (Tone)
Contact: Mike Hewitson, 56 Parkfield Road, Taunton, TA1 4SE, 01823 271194, *Water:* 6 miles on River Tone (See also entry under Taunton and Bridgwater Canal & Stillwater Coarse). *Species:* Roach 2lb, Pike 36lb, Dace 1lb, Bream 10lb, Tench 5lb, Perch 3lb, Carp 30lb, Grayling 2.5lb, Chub 6.5lb. *Charges:* Season £28.50. Day tickets £5 senior, £2 junior. *Season:* Closed from 14th March to 16th June. *Methods:* All fish (including Pike and Eels) to be returned alive.

Wellington Angling Association
Contact: M Cave, 60 Sylvan Road, Wellington, TA21 8EH, 01823 661671, *Water:* Approx 2 miles on River Tone. Both banks from Nynhead weir to Wellington. *Species:* Brown Trout. *Permits:* Membership only. *Charges:* Joining fee £10, annual membership £12. *Season:* As E.A. season. *Methods:* No spinning.

WEST SEDGEMOOR DRAIN

This artificial channel was excavated in the 1940s on the lines of existing watercourses. Coarse fish species present include Bream, Roach, Tench and Carp.

Taunton Angling Association (W. Sedgemoor Drain)
Contact: Mike Hewitson, 56 Parkfield Road, Taunton, TA1 4SE, 01823 271194, *Water:* 2 miles of West Sedgemoor Drain, easy access for disabled anglers (also see entries under Stillwater Coarse). *Species:* Bream 7lb, Roach 2.5lb, Eels 2lb, Tench 8lb, Pike 29lb, Perch 2lb, Rudd 2lb, Carp 26lb. *Charges:* Season £28.50. Day tickets £5 senior, £2 junior. *Season:* Closed from 14th March to 16th June. *Methods:* All fish (including Pike and Eels) to be returned alive.

YEO

The River Yeo rises near Sherborne and between here and Yeovil the river is a coarse fishery, though tributaries such as the River Wriggle have Brown Trout. Below Yeovil a number of weirs produce areas of deep water and the resulting fishery contains good Dace together with Roach, Chub, Bream and Pike.

Ilchester & District A.A.
Contact: Mr B Bushell (Chairman), 1 Friars Close, Ilchester, Yeovil, BA22 8NU, 01935 840767, *Water:* River Yeo above and below Ilchester. *Species:* Chub, Roach, Dace, Bream, Gudgeon, Tench, Perch and Carp. *Permits:* Tackle shops in Yeovil. Yeovil Angling Centre. Ilchester Post Office. Newsagents, Ilchester, or from Club Chairman at above address. *Charges:* Season ticket £12. OAP/junior £6. Weekly ticket £5. *Season:* Open 16th June to 15th March. *Methods:* Current E.A. Byelaws apply. Club rules on ticket and fishery map.

Mudford Angling Club
Water: 3.5 miles double bank on river Yeo. *Species:* Chubb, Bream, Dace, Roach. *Charges:* Club membership available from Yeovil District Angling Centre: 01935 476777 and Stax Tackle at Montacute: 01935 822645.

N. Somerset Association of Anglers
Contact: Mr Newton, 64 Clevedon Rd, Tickenham, Clevedon, BS21 6RD, 01275 856107, *Water:* Blind Yeo, Kenn, Brue, Apex Lake, Newtown Ponds & Walrow Ponds, Tickenham Boundry Rhyne, North Drain (also see entry Stillwater, Coarse, Highbridge). *Species:* Roach, Bream, Eels, Perch, Rudd, Carp, Pike, Tench. *Permits:* NSAA Permits available at all local Tackle Shops. *Charges:* Season: Seniors £20. Juniors/OAP/ Disabled £10. Weekly: £10. Day £3. *Season:* June 16th - March 14th inclusive. Apex Lake & Newtown Ponds: closed March 1st - 31st inclusive. *Methods:* Apex Lake and Newtown Ponds: Barbless hooks, No live or dead baits, no floating baits, min. breaking strain line 2.5lb.

Northover Manor Water
Contact: Mark Haddigan, Ilchester, BA22 8LD, 01935 840447, *Water:* 50 yards single back fishing on the Yeo. *Species:* Roach, Bream and Carp. *Charges:* Please enquire at Reception. *Season:* E.A. Byelaws.

Yeovil & Sherborne Angling Association (Yeo)
Contact: Pete Coombes, 44 Monksdale, Yeovil, BA21 3JF, 01935 427873, *Water:* 4 miles rivers, Sherborne Castle Lake & discounted tickets Viaduct Fishery. Long Load Drain. *Species:* Roach, Bream, Carp, Dace Chub, Perch, Rudd, Tench. *Permits:* Membership details from above & local tackle shops. *Charges:* No day tickets. River Club card £12, £2 off cost of day ticket at Viaduct. contact the above or local tackle shops. *Season:* 16 June to 14 March on non enclosed stillwaters.

Somerset Stillwater Coarse

BATH

Bath Anglers Association
Contact: Andy Smith, 68 Bloomfield Rise, Odd Down, Bath, BA2 2BN, 01225 834736, *Water:* Regular matches, open to all in region. Fishing amalgamation waters. *Charges:* Contact above, or Dave Bacon at Bacons Tackle - 01225 448850. Membership free, but must be member of Bristol, Bath & Wiltshire Amalgamated Anglers. Adults & Children welcome.

Bathampton Angling Association
Contact: Dave Crookes, 25 Otago Terrace, Larkhall, Bath, BA1 6SX, 01225 427164, *Water:* Small pond at Weston village in Bath. *Species:* Carp to 10lb, Roach to 1.5lb, Bream to 2lb, Hybrids to 1lb, Tench to 4lb. *Permits:* Bacons Tackle Box, 83 Lower Bristol Road, Bath. Avon Aquatics, Willsbridge Rd., Bristol. Scott Tackle, 42 Soundwell Rd., Bristol. *Charges:* Adults £25, combined lady and gent £35, juniors £8, O.A.P £7. Registered disabled £7, Under 12's free. To year end 31/12/05. Members only special day permits must be purchased in advance at £2 p/day. *Season:* Open all year. *Methods:* Special rules apply. Available from secretary, on website, from shop.

Bathampton Angling Association (Huntstrete Ponds)
Contact: Dave Crookes, 25 Otago Terrace, Larkhall, Bath, BA1 6SX, 01225 427164, *Water:* 3 lake complex at Hunstrete, near Pensford. Total 11 acres 120 pegs. *Species:* Bream to 8.5lbs, Chub to 2.5lbs, Roach to 2.5lbs, Pike to 22lbs, Carp to 28lbs, Tench to 9lbs, Perch to 2.5lbs, Crucians to 2lbs, Eels to 7lbs. *Permits:* Local fishing tackle shops (members only). *Charges:* Adults £25, combined lady and gent £35, juniors £8, O.A.P £7. Registered disabled £7, Under 12's free. To year end 31/12/05. Additional special day permit at £2.50 must be obtained before fishing. *Season:* Open all year fishing times vary according to time of year. No night fishing. *Methods:* Copies of rules available from secretary and tackle shops. Also displayed on notice boards at lakeside, and on website.

Bathampton Angling Association (Newton Park Pond)
Contact: Dave Crookes, 25 Otago Terrace, Larkhall, Bath, BA1 6SX, 01225 427164, *Water:* 2.5 acre lake at Newton Park, near Bath. *Species:* Bream to 2.5lbs, Chub to 7lbs, Roach to 2lbs, Pike to 24lbs, Carp to 27lbs. *Permits:* Local fishing tackle shops (members only). *Charges:* Adults £25, combined lady and gent £35, juniors £8, O.A.P £7. Registered disabled £7, Under 12's free. To year end 31/12/05. Additional special day permit at £3 must be obtained before fishing. Members only. *Season:* Open all year fishing times vary according to time of year. No night fishing. *Methods:* Copies of rules available from secretary and tackle shops. Also displayed on notice boards at lakeside, and on website.

Farleigh Wood Fishery (Coarse)
Wood Cottage, Tellisford, Bath, BA2 7RN, 01373 831495, *Water:* 1 acre coarse fishing lake plus brook fishing (see entry River Frome, Bristol). *Species:* Carp to double figures. *Charges:* Price on application. *Season:* All year coarse fishing. *Methods:* List of rules at fishery.

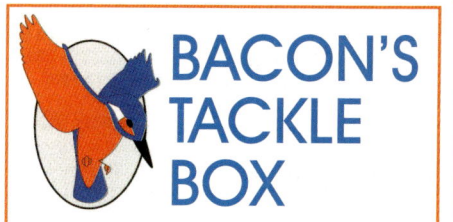

BACON'S TACKLE BOX

83 LOWER BRISTOL RD, BATH
Tel: 01225 448850

Quality Tackle
Quality Bait
Local Permits
Local Advice

COARSE • GAME • SEA

Open 7 days from 7am
(She won't let me open on Xmas Day!)

BRIDGWATER

Beeches Fishery
Contact: Andrew Bradbury, 01278 423545, *Water:* 9 ponds set in 5 acres of designated county wildlife site. *Species:* Carp (Crucians, Common, Mirror), Roach, Rudd, Tench, Perch and Eels. *Permits:* Limited day tickets, only available in advance from Andrew Bradbury on the above telephone number. *Charges:* Valid EA rod licence required. *Season:* Close season - March to June. No night fishing.

Bridgwater Angling Association (Coarse Lakes)
Contact: Mr M Pople, 14 Edward Street, Bridgwater, TA6 5EU, 01278 422397, *Mobile:* 07903 950019, *Water:* See entry under Taunton and Bridgwater Canal. Various stillwaters. Stillwater fishing at Combwich, Walrow, Dunwear & Screech Owl *Species:* All types of Coarse Fish. *Permits:* Available from Tackle outlets throughout Somerset area including Somerset Angling, 74 Bath Rd, Bridgwater, Tel: 01278 431777 & Thyers Tackle, 1a Church Street, Highbridge, Tel: 01278 786934. Veals Fishing Tackle, 61 Old Market Street, Bristol 0117 9260790. Topp Tackle, 63 Station Road, Taunton 01823 282518. Further information on Bridgwater A.A. available from Watts News, Edward Street, Bridgwater. Open: Mon-Sat 5am-7pm, Sunday . 5am-4pm. Tel: 01278 422137. *Charges:* Adult season: 2 rods £27, 3 rods £46, 4 rods £54. Senior Citizens: 2 rods £10, 3 rods £17, 4 rods £20. Junior (7-11yrs) 2 rods only £4. (12 to 17yrs) 2 rods only £7. Day tickets £5, enquire at outlets. *Season:* Open all year except Screech Owl (traditional Coarse close season). *Methods:* Disabled access at all lakes except Screech Owl. No reserving swims.

Bridgwater Sports & Social Club
Contact: Duncan, Danny or Nick, Bath Road, Bridgwater, TA6

SOMERSET

STILLWATER COARSE

4PA, 01278 446215, *Water:* 3 large ponds. *Species:* Carp to 30lb, Crucian to 3lb, Bream to 4lb, Roach to 1.5lb, Perch to 4lb, Tench to 6.5lb. *Charges:* £25/person - private members fishing. *Season:* Normal open season. *Methods:* No night fishing.

Browns Pond
Contact: Phil Dodds, Off Taunton Rd (A38), Bridgwater, TA6 4QE, 01278 444145, *Water:* 2.5 acres. *Species:* Carp to 22lb, Tench to 5lb, Bream to 6lb, Perch to 2lb & Roach. *Charges:* On site. £2 per day. *Season:* Closed May, open June 1st - April 30th; dawn to dusk. *Methods:* No night fishing, barbless hooks only, no live bait, no Carp sacks.

Burton Springs Fishery (Coarse Lake)
Contact: Tony Evans, Lawson Farm, Burton, Nr Stogursey, Bridgwater, TA5 1QB, 01278 732135, *Mobile:* 07866 026685, *Water:* Approx 2 acre lake. *Species:* Mirror, Common, Leather Carp, Ghost Carp to 30lb, Tench to 5 lb, Perch to 3.5lbs. *Permits:* Self Service at fishing lodge. *Charges:* £6 per day, 2 rods - Day Ticket. £12 - 5pm to 9am next day. £15 for 24hrs. Night fishing strictly by arrangement. *Season:* Open all year 8am - 9pm or dusk. Night fishing by arrangement. *Methods:* Barbless hooks only, no nuts.

Durleigh Reservoir
Contact: Wessex Water, 0845 600 4600, *Water:* 80 acre reservoir *Species:* Carp, Roach, Bream, Perch, Tench and Pike *Permits:* Contact Ranger Paul Martin on 01278 424786 *Charges:* Day Ticket £6, Day Concession £4, Evening Ticket £4, Book of Tickets £45 for 10 *Season:* Open all year except Christmas day, Boxing day, New Years Eve and day.

Plum Lane Fishery
Contact: Mrs J. Goodland, Plum Lane, Dunwear, Bridgwater, TA6 5HL, 01278 421625, *Water:* 1 acre pond. *Species:* Predominately Carp to 10lb plus Tench. Roach and Skimmers. *Permits:* On site. *Charges:* £5 per adult (1 rod). *Season:* Open all year. *Methods:* Barbless hooks only. No keepnets. No Braid. Advice available on site.

Summerhayes Fishery
Contact: Peter Wakelin, Somerset Bridge, Bridgwater, TA6 6LW, *Mobile:* 07866 557896, *Water:* Several lakes - totalling 6 acres. *Species:* Carp to 22lb, Bream, Tench, Roach, Rudd, Perch, Ghost Carp to 16lb. *Charges:* On bank £5 day, £3.50 Concessions. Disabled access. *Season:* Open all year dawn to dusk. *Methods:* Barbless hooks, no nuts. Maximum 2 rods.

Taunton Road Ponds
Contact: Phil Dodds, Off Taunton Rd (A38), Bridgwater, 01278 444145, *Mobile:* TA6 4QE, *Water:* 3.5 acres. *Species:* Large carp to 32lb, Tench to 6lb, Bream to 13lb 6oz, Perch to 3lb, Rudd to 2lb, Skimmer Bream to 12oz & Roach to 8oz. *Charges:* On site, £2 per day. *Season:* Closed May, open June 1st - April 30th. Dawn to dusk. *Methods:* No night fishing, barbless hooks only, no live bait, no Carp in keepnets, no Carp sacks.

The Sedges
Contact: Pat & John, River Lane, Dunwear, Bridgwater, TA7 0AA, 01278 445221, *Mobile:* 07967 398045, *Water:* 3 lakes totalling 7.5 acres, including 2 match lakes. *Species:* Tench, Rudd, Roach, Bream, Chub, Carp to 32lb. *Charges:* On bank: £5 adult day, children accompanied by adult £4. *Season:* Open all year dawn to dusk. *Methods:* No keepnets in summer months, no carp sacks, barbless hooks, unhooking mats. Strictly no cat meat or nuts.

Trinity Waters
Contact: John Herring, Hopfield Fish Farms, Straight Drove,

The Sedges
Three superb lakes situated just outside Bridgwater on the Somerset levels

Brick Lake - 2 acre general coarse lake stocked with Tench, Roach, Bream, Chub & Carp.
Tile Lake - 3 acres with Carp to 32lb and over 100 doubles!
CANAL MATCH LAKE - 36 pegs with Bream, Carp, Rudd & Roach

Static Caravans 2 mins from the waters edge

Contact Pat & John, The Sedges, River Lane, Dunwear, Bridgwater TA7 0AA. Tel 01278 445221 / Mob 07967 398045

ALCOVE ANGLING CLUB
Quality Coarse Fishing in the Bristol Area
FOUR COARSE LAKES WITH PARKING
Extensive stocking programme
Match & Pleasure angling
Established, friendly club
Open all Year
OPEN MEMBERSHIP - NO WAITING LIST
CONTACT KEN DAVIS mobile 07941 638680
Email: alcove.a.c.bristol@blueyonder.co.uk

Chilton Trinity, Bridgwater, 01278 450880, *Mobile:* 0772 0542141, *Water:* Currently 3 lakes: 6.5 acres, 2 acres and 1 acre. *Species:* Rudd to 2lb. Roach to 2lb. Perch to 3lb. Tench to 6lb. Golden Tench to 5lb. Bream to 11lb. Mirror, Common to 20lb and Grass Carp to 12lb. Mirror and Common to 30lb in specimen lake. *Permits:* On site only. *Charges:* £5 per day, £7.50 for two rods. £3 juniors and concessions. Match rates on request. *Season:* Open all year dawn to dusk. *Methods:* Barbless hooks. No keepnets. No fixed rigs.

BRISTOL

Alcove Angling Club
Contact: Mr K.Davis (Membership Secretary), 6 Ashdene Ave, Upper Eastville, Bristol, BS5 6QH, *Mobile:* 07941 638680, *Water:* 4 lakes in Bristol & South Glos. *Species:* Carp, Bream, Roach, Tench, Rudd, Pike, Perch. *Permits:* As above. *Charges:* Adult £40, OAP/Disabled £25. *Season:* No close season. *Methods:* As specified in membership card, Night fishing at Alcove Lido only.

Bagwood Lake
Contact: Woodland Golf Club - David Knipe, Trench Lane, Almondsbury, Bristol, BS32 4JZ, 01454 619319, *Water:* One coarse lake. *Species:* Carp. *Permits:* On site, pay in shop. *Charges:* £7 - 12 hour ticket. £13 - 24 hour ticket. *Season:* Open all year - night fishing by arrangement.

Bitterwell Lake
Contact: Mr C.W. Reid, The Chalet, Bitterwell Lake,, Ram Hill, Coalpit Heath,, Bristol,, BS36 2UF, 01454 778960, *Water:* 2.5 Acres. *Species:* Common, Mirror, Crucian Carp, Roach, Bream, Rudd, Perch. *Charges:* £5.00 -1 rod. £2.50 second rod, O.A.P's

156

SOMERSET

Superb 7lb 2oz Tench from Lands End.

Avon Angling Centre

Extensive knowledge of all local waters and coastline

Efficient and friendly service   All credit cards accepted

348 Whitehall Rd, St George, Bristol. BS5 7BW
Tel: 0117 9517250 or **Mob:** 07974 807941

SCOTT TACKLE

An Excellent Range of Tackle & Baits
SPECIAL DEALS ALWAYS AVAILABLE
42 Soundwell Rd, Staple Hill, Bristol. Tel 0117 9567371
Email: scottackle@madasafish.com

STILLWATER COARSE

etc, Reg. disabled and arrivals after 4 pm. *Season:* Closed for spawning 4 - 6 weeks May - June. *Methods:* Barbless hooks size 8 max, no bolt rigs, no boilies, no nuts, hemp or groundbait.

Boyd Valley Lake
Contact: Avon Aquatics, Jarrets Garden Centre, The Park, Bath Road, Willsbridge, Bristol, BS15 6EE, 01179 327659, *Water:* 1.5 acre lake. *Species:* Carp to 9lb, Tench, Roach and Bream. *Permits:* Dat tickets from Jarrets Garden Centre. *Charges:* £5 per day. *Season:* Open all year.

Bristol, Bath & Wiltshire Amalgamated Anglers (Lakes)
Contact: Jeff Parker, 16 Lansdown View, Kingswood, Bristol, BS15 4AW, 0117 9672977, *Water:* See entry under Bristol Avon - Various stillwaters, too much to list here, please contact the secretary for full details; Stillwaters at Lyneham, Calne, Malmesbury, Bath and Pawlett near Bridgwater. *Species:* All coarse species. *Methods:* Maximum 2 rods, no metal cans or glass allowed on banks, no freshwater fish to be used as livebait. Full rules and maps available.

Carps Angling Club
Contact: John Bennett, 30a Church Road, Hanham, Bristol, BS15 3AL, 0117 9601597, *Water:* Match orientated club (57 matches per 2004). Open to all. Fishing in Carp lakes in the region. *Charges:* Contact John at number above. Annual membership fees: Seniors £10, OAP's £7.50, Disabled £7.50, Juniors £5.00, Ladies £5.00. No match fees for juniors and ladies. *Methods:* All matches under fishery rules.

Cross Hands Angling Club
Contact: Phillip Bond - Secretary, 25 North Street, Down End, Bristol, BS16 5FW, 01179 754218, *Water:* The Crest lake - 30 pegs. Hunters lake at Clutton - 20 pegs. *Species:* Carp to 16lb. *Permits:* Members only - Limited membership available from above, junior section. *Charges:* Junior £20 p/year, OAP £20 p/year, Seniors £45 p/year. *Season:* Open all year. Hunters Lake - closed March 14th to June 16th.

Duchess Pond
Contact: Wayne Tooker (Leaseholder), 0117 9372001, *Mobile:* 07980 091286, *Water:* 2 acre pond. *Species:* Mixed fishery plus Carp to 28lb. *Permits:* Limited day tickets from Jarrats Garden Centre, Bitton - 01179 327659. Bristol Angling Centre - 01179 508723. Or direct from Wayne. *Charges:* £5 Adults, £2.50 under 16. £60 season ticket. £70 Parent & Child season ticket. *Season:* Open all year Dawn to Dusk. Night Fishing available to syndicate members only. Please enquire. *Methods:* Full rules displayed at Fishery.

Foresters Angling Club
Contact: Chris Gay, Bristol, 01179 095105, *Water:* Around 40 members meeting at Foresters Arms, Downend. *Species:* Carp. *Charges:* £10 membership, pools money on the day, £15 inclusive. Juniors welcome. *Season:* If interested in starting fishing matches at a friendly club, please telephone Chris.

Ham Green Fisheries
Contact: Mr Hunt, Ham Green, Chapel Lane, Pill, BS20 6DB, 01275 849885, *Mobile:* 07818 640227, *Water:* Two lakes. 1 acre 25 peg. 2 acre open bank. *Species:* 1 acre lake stocked with Carp, Roach, Rudd, Perch, Pike, Bream, Skimmers, Chub, Golden Tench and Golden Orfe. 2 acre lake all the above with Carp to 35lb. *Permits:* Mr Hunt, 21 Station Rd, Portishead, Bristol; also on lake side from Baliff. Veals Tackle Shop, 61 Old Market St, Bristol. *Charges:* £5 in advance from Veals Tackle or £5 on the bank. *Season:* No closed season. 7am to 8pm from 16 June to 13 October. 8am to 5pm from 1 November to 30 April. Night fishing strictly by arrangement, booking essential by telephone to Mr Hunt. *Methods:* No live bait, barbless hooks preferred, no keepnets for fish over 1lb, Carp sacks allowed. Children must be accompanied by an adult.

SOMERSET

BILL PUGH Fishing Tackle
COARSE · FLY · SEA
Local Permits - Easy Parking
Open 6 days a week - 8 to 5.30
410 Wells Road, Red Lion Hill, Knowle, Bristol
Telephone: 0117 977 0280

STILLWATER COARSE

King William IV Angling Association
Contact: Jerry Pocock, 86 Tower Road South, Warmley, Bristol, BS30 8BP, 01179 492974, *Mobile:* 07761 799876, *Charges:* £3 joining fee. Juniors free of charge. Further details from Jerry. *Season:* Open to all in the area. Regular meetings and matches.

Kingswood Disabled Angling Club
Contact: Trebor Mearns, 22 Newland Road, Withywood, Bristol, BS13 9ED, 0117 9641224, *Mobile:* 07766 347829, *Water:* Bristol based Coarse fishing club meeting monthly. New members welcome. Must be registered disabled at local Social Services Office. Regular fishing trips and matches organised. Please phone for further information. *Charges:* £7.50 adults annual membership.

Mardon Angling Club
Contact: Mr Austin, 65 Grange Avenue, Hanham, Bristol, BS15 3PE, 0117 9839776, *Water:* Open to all. Regular monthly meetings, full match calendar. *Charges:* Please contact above. Charges £10 per annum, children under 16 free. *Season:* All year.

Paulton Lakes
Contact: John Wiles, Ruthin Villa, High Street, High Littleton, Bristol, BS39 6JD, 01761 472338, *Mobile:* 07709 471414, *Water:* Two lakes located off Bristol Road, Paulton. Approx 2.5 acres. with a total of 25 swims (two new lakes planned). *Species:* Island Lake: Carp 31lb, Roach 3lb, Chub 10lb plus, Tench 6lb, Eels 6lb. King Lake: Carp 12lb, Grass Carp, Crucian Carp, Tench 6lb, Chub 8lb, Roach 3lb, Rudd. *Permits:* Day tickets available from A.M. Hobbs, The Island, Midsomer Norton. Tel: (01761) 413961and from Central Garage, High Street, Paulton. Tickets MUST be purchased in advance - not available on the bank. *Charges:* £6 per day ticket. Concessions for juniors/seniors. Season tickets available. *Season:* Closed Easter Monday to June 16th. Fishing from dawn to one hour after dusk. Night fishing by syndicate members only. *Methods:* Full details on ticket. Barbless hooks, no Carp in keepnets, unhooking mats must be used, no pre-baiting or ground baiting.

Ridgeway & District AA
Contact: Steve Dumbleton, Bristol, 01179 603193, *Water:* Open to all. Match fishing every fortnight in Summer, less frequent in Winter months. *Charges:* Annual membership £8, Juniors welcome. Please telephone Steve on number above.

Royal British Legion Kingswood
Contact: Mr Lloyd, 386 Speedwell Road, Kingswood, Bristol, BS15 1ES, 0117 9676030, *Mobile:* 07831 311582, *Water:* Open to all Royal British Legion members, regular matches.

Tan House Farm Lake
Contact: Mr & Mrs James, Tan House Farm, Yate, Bristol, BS37 7QL, 01454 228280, *Water:* Quarter mile lake. *Species:* Roach, Perch, Carp, Bream, Tench, Rudd. *Permits:* Day tickets from Farm House. *Charges:* Adult £3 per rod or £5 for 2 rods, Children & O.A.Ps £2. *Season:* Closed April 8th - May 26th. *Methods:* No Ground bait, dog & cat food, boilies, barbless hooks only. No trout pellets.

Westcountry Disabled Angling Association
Contact: Carey Sutton, 01275 830541, *Water:* Open to all adult disabled anglers and children (must be accompanied by an adult). Fishing different venues throughout the south west region and taking part in national competitions. Alternative contact Ian Darke on 01225 336371. *Charges:* £5 p/a membership, plus peg fees.

BURNHAM-ON-SEA

Highbridge Angling Association (Apex Lake)
Contact: Mr C Brewer, 8 Willow Close, East Huntspill, Near Highbridge, TA9 3NX, 01278 786230, *Water:* Apex lake, Marine drive, Burnham-on-sea. *Species:* Mixed coarse fish. Carp to 20lb, Bream to 8lb, Roach to 3lb and Chub to 5lb. *Permits:* From local tackle dealers. *Methods:* No night fishing.

CHARD

Chard & District Angling Club (Coarse Lakes)
Contact: Mr Braunton, Planet Video & Angling, 19a High Street, Chard, TA20 1QF, 01460 64000, *Water:* Perry Street Pond - 1.5 acres. Chard Reservoir - 48 acres. Also 1.5 miles on Isle see entry under associations. *Species:* Roach, Bream, Carp, Tench, Perch, Eels, Rudd. *Permits:* Planet Video & Angling, 19a High Street, Chard, Somerset TA20 1QF. Tel: 01460 64000.. Perry Street Ponds - members only, details from secretary. *Charges:* Chard reservoir £6 per day (£4 club members). Perry Street ponds members only, membership £15. *Season:* Open all year. *Methods:* Full list of rules from fishery notice board and membership book.

CHEDDAR

Cheddar Angling Club
Contact: Cheddar Angling Club, P.O. Box 1183, Cheddar, BS27 3LT, 01934 743959, *Water:* 200 acre Cheddar reservoir. *Species:* Pike, Perch, Tench, Roach, Eels, Carp. *Permits:* Permits are NOT available at the reservoir. Only from: Broadway House Caravan Park, Axbridge Road, Cheddar, Somerset. Bristol Angling Centre, 12-16 Doncaster Road, Southmead, Bristol. Thatchers Pet and Tackle, 18 Queen St, Wells. Veals Fishing Tackle, 61 Old Market St., Bristol. Thyers Fishing Tackle, Church St., Highbridge. *Charges:* Seniors season permit £40, Juniors season permit £20, Seniors day permit £5, Juniors day permit £3. *Season:* No closed season. *Methods:* No live baiting, Moderate ground baiting, No dead baiting 16th June - 30th September. No night fishing. Dawn to dusk only. Unhooking mats recommended. Rod limits: seniors maximum 3 rods, juniors one rod only.

Stone Yard Fisheries
Contact: Thatchers Angling, 18 Queen St, Wells, BA5 2DP, 01749 673513, *Water:* Small Ponds (15 Anglers) at Litton near Chewton Mendip. *Species:* Carp to approx 18lb, small Tench. *Permits:* Thatchers Angling 01749 673513. 5 tickets per day

SOMERSET

Kelly Inglis with a net full from Bullock Farm.

NORTHAM FARM

Spend your holiday with us in Somerset and enjoy our first class facilities, including a well stocked Coarse Fishing Lake, for Caravanners and Campers. Nightly rate starts from £5.50 for two persons.

Northam Farm Caravan Park, Brean Sands, Burnham on Sea, Somerset TA8 2SE

www.northamfarm.co.uk
enquiries@northamfarm.co.uk

For our full colour brochure please
Tel: 01278 751244 Fax: 01278 751150

WARREN FARM
Holiday Centre
For your touring holiday in Somerset
Our Fishing Lakes are well stocked with a variety of coarse fish - 3 acre main lake!
Fishing to competition level across the moors
Sea Fishing opposite the park
Please phone for a brochure
01278 751227   www.warren-farm.co.uk
Warren Farm Holiday Centre, Brean Sands, Somerset TA8 2RP

STILLWATER COARSE

available from A.M. Hobbs Angling 01761 413961. *Charges:* Day £5 Senior, £2.50 Junior. *Season:* March 1st - October 31st. *Methods:* Barbless hooks only. No Boilies.

COLEFORD
Breach Valley Fishing
Contact: Lower Vobster, Coleford, Radstock, BA3 5LY, 01373 812352, *Water:* 2 ponds totalling 1.5 acres approx. *Species:* Carp 28.25lb, Roach, Tench, Perch and Bream. *Charges:* Day tickets on bank, £6 per day. *Season:* Open June 11th to end of March, dawn to dusk. *Methods:* No keepnets, no boilies, barbless hooks.

CONGRESBURY
Silver Springs Fish Farm
Contact: Liz Patch, Silver Street Lane, Congresbury, BS49 5EY, 01934 877073, *Mobile:* 07837 809005, *Water:* General coarse lake: 4.5 acres. Specimen Carp lake: 2.5 acres. *Species:* General: Carp to mid twenties, Rudd, Roach to 3lbs, Tench, Chub and Bream. Specimen: Mirrors and commons to high 20's/low 30's. *Permits:* General & specimen: On site. *Charges:* General: £5 / £3.50 conc. Specimen: £8 & £5 full and concessionary respectively. *Season:* General: All year dawn till half hour before dusk. Specimen: All year *Methods:* General: Barbless hooks. Specimen: No poles, no keepnets, no nuts, barbless hooks only.

CORFE
Taunton Angling Association (Wych Lodge Lake)
Contact: Mike Hewitson, 56 Parkfield Road, Taunton, TA1 4SE, 01823 271194, *Water:* Wych Lodge Lake, 3 acre large carp lake (also see entries under River & Canal Fishing). *Species:*

Large Carp up to 12lb, Grass Carp 12lb, Roach, Tench 2lb, Rudd and Perch all to 2lb. *Permits:* Only from Topp Tackle, Taunton (restricted to 10 pegs). Please bring season ticket as proof of membership when purchasing day permit. Separate day ticket available for non season ticket holders. *Charges:* £3 per day. £6 for non season ticket holders. *Season:* Open all year. *Methods:* Barbless hooks, no Carp in keepnets, no lighting of fires, no litter.

CREWKERNE
Highlands Dairy Lake
Contact: J.Wyatt, Highlands Dairy Farm, Hewish, Crewkerne, TA18 8QY, 01460 74180, *Water:* 2 x one acre lakes. *Species:* Carp, Tench, Rudd, Roach, Perch. *Permits:* At house. *Charges:* £4 per day. £5 to include night fishing. *Season:* Open all year. *Methods:* No keepnets for Carp. Barbless hooks only.

Manor Farm
Contact: Mr A. Emery, Wayford, Nr Crewkerne, TA18 8QL, 01460 78865, *Mobile:* 07767 620031, *Water:* 3 large ponds. *Species:* Carp - Mirror, Common and Ghost, Tench, Rudd, Gudgeon, Roach, Perch, Bream, Eels. *Permits:* As above. *Charges:* £5 per day. *Methods:* Barbless hooks.

Water Meadow Fishery
Contact: Mr. Pike, Trindlewell Cottage, North Perrott, Crewkerne, TA18 7SX, 01460 74673, *Water:* 2 coarse lakes totalling approx 1.75 acres. *Species:* 16 different varieties of coarse fish. *Charges:* On site - £5 day. £3 morning/afternoon. £2 half day/evening. *Season:* Open all year - dawn to dusk. *Methods:* No boilies or keepnets, barbless hooks only, ground baiting in moderation.

SOMERSET

STILLWATER COARSE

EDNEY'S FISHERIES
Edney's Farm, Mells, Nr Frome, Somerset.
Tel: 01373 812294. Mobile 07941 280075
Three well stocked lakes, heated by natural springs, in the heart of the Countryside
e-mail: john.candy@jandscandy.co.uk
Carp (mirror, common, ghost, linear and leather) to 30lb. Also Tench Roach and Rudd. **100lb BAGS COMMON!**
Hard Track with Lakeside Parking
CARAVAN & CAMPING ON SITE

AVALON FISHERIES
ALLAN TEDDER (TED)
Tel: 01278 456429
9 acre - 70 peg
Match and Coarse Lake
Just 15 mins from Bridgwater & Burnham on Sea
Mobile: 07855 825059
www.avalon-fisheries.co.uk

FROME

Barrow Farm Pond
Contact: John Nicholls, Barrow Farm, Witham Friary, Frome, BA11 5HD, 01749 850313, *Mobile:* 07734 978988, *Water:* Half acre lake. *Species:* Carp, Perch and Tench. *Charges:* £5 adult. £3.50 children and OAPs. *Season:* February to September. Phone for details. *Methods:* No restrictions.

Edneys Fisheries
Contact: Richard Candy, Edneys Farm, Mells, Frome, BA11 3RF, 01373 812294, *Mobile:* 07941 280075, *Water:* 3 lakes. Hard standing and parking at all lakes. *Species:* Carp to 30lb, Tench to 9lb, Roach, Rudd, Golden Rudd, Perch, Common, Mirror, Linear, Leather and Ghost Carp. Golden Orf and Blue Orf to 6lb in lake 2. In lake 2 and 3 there are Chub. *Permits:* Yearly tickets £85 Adults, £65 Under 14 *Charges:* Adults £5, Under 14 yrs £3.50. Night tickets available at £5 for all. *Season:* 24hrs a day, 365 days a year. *Methods:* Barbless hooks, no nuts, no feeding of boilies, no fish over 2lb in keepnets.

Frome Angling Association (Coarse Lake)
Contact: Gary Collinson, 94 Nunney Road, Frome, BA11 4LD, 01373 465214, *Water:* 10 acre lake. 12 miles river Frome - see entry under River Fishing Somerset. *Permits:* Hainer Angling. Tel: 01373 466206.

Mells Pit Pond
Contact: Mr M.Coles, Lyndhurst, Station Road, Mells, Frome, BA11 3RJ, 01373 812094, *Water:* 1 acre lake. *Species:* Various Carp, Rudd, Roach, Tench, Perch. *Permits:* Tickets issued at bankside. *Charges:* £5/day, season tickets £60. *Season:* March to November. *Methods:* Barbless hooks. No keepnets.

Parrots Paddock Farm
Contact: Mr. Baker, Wanstrow Rd., Nunney Catch, 01373 836505, *Mobile:* 07931 273758, *Water:* 90yd x 75 yd pond. *Species:* Crayfish, Catfish, Tench, Roach, Bream & Carp. *Permits:* Please phone first. *Charges:* £5 p/day Adult, £5 p/day OAP, £3 p/day Children, Disabled and Under 10 free. Night fishing £15. *Season:* Open all year, dawn to dusk. *Methods:* No night fishing, keepnets only for small fish, barbless hooks only, ground bait in moderation.

Witham Friary Lakes
Contact: Mr. Miles, Witham Hall Farm, Witham Friary, Nr Frome, BA11 5HB, 01373 836239, *Water:* Two lakes totalling approx. 2 acres. *Species:* Carp, Roach, Tench, Perch, Gudgeon. *Permits:* On site. *Charges:* £4 a day - £6 night ticket (dusk - 8 am). *Season:* All year. *Methods:* Barbless hooks only.

GLASTONBURY

Avalon Fisheries
Contact: Allan Tedder (Ted), 7 Coronation Road, Bridgwater, TA6 7DS, 01278 456429, *Mobile:* 07855 825059, *Water:* 9 acre Match & Coarse lake approximately 70 pegs. *Species:* Carp to mid 20's, Tench 8.5lb, Bream 9lb 2oz, Perch 3lb, Roach, Rudd. *Permits:* Site office and on the bank. Mobile Phone 07855 825059. *Charges:* £6 Adult, £4 Junior / O.A.P. / Disabled. *Season:* No closed season - Open dawn to dusk. *Methods:* No floating or boilie baits permitted in the match lake. Keepnets permitted - No Carp in keepnets, all nuts banned, barbless hooks, night fishing by appointment only.

Glaston Manor Angling Association (Moorland Fishery)
Contact: Adam Mitchell, NFU Office, 1 Sadler Street, Wells, BA5 2RR, 01749 673786, *Water:* Moorland Fishery (stillwater), Meare and Burtle Ponds, Burtle (3 ponds in about 12 acres). See also entry under river fishing, Brue. *Species:* Tench, Carp, Bream, Roach, Rudd, Perch (no Carp at Burtle Ponds). *Permits:* Thatchers Tackle, Wells. Street Angling, High St, Street, Somerset Tel: 01458 447830. *Charges:* No day tickets on stillwaters, Junior membership £8, Senior membership £24, OAP and disabled £12. *Season:* Current E.A. byelaws apply. *Methods:* No live bait permitted, full rules on day ticket.

HIGHBRIDGE

Emerald Pool Fishery
Contact: Mr Alan Wilkinson, Emerald Pool Fishery, Puriton Road, West Huntspill, Highbridge, TA9 3NL, 01278 794707, *Water:* 4 lakes in total. 1.5 acre lake, plus 'Sapphire Lake' - 20 peg disabled angler friendly pool for adults and juniors. New match and new specimen lake (25 anglers). *Species:* Bream, Golden Orfe, Roach, Rudd, Tench, Perch, Barbel 5lb. Emerald Lake - Small Carp to 7lb, plus Sturgeon to 4 feet long. Specimen Lake - fish to 40lb. Sapphire Lake - fish to 4lb. Match Lake - 1 to 2lb Carp. *Permits:* Enviroment Agency rod licence required on this water. *Season:* All year. *Methods:* Barbless hooks only, no Carp sacks, no peanuts or ground bait, all Sturgeon to be released immediately, no fish over 3lb to be retained at all.

Highbridge Angling Association (Coarse Lakes)
Contact: Mr C Brewer, 8 Willow Close, East Huntspill, Near Highbridge, TA9 3NX, 01278 786230, *Water:* 3 Lakes at Walrow. *Species:* Carp to mid 20's, Pike to mid 20's, Bream to 12lb, Tench to double figures and all other coarse species. *Permits:* Thyers Tackle, Highbridge - 01278 786934. Also available from

SOMERSET

Emerald Pool *Fishery*

Quality fishing on four varied and well managed lakes

Emerald - 1.5 acre lake stocked with Carp to 22lb, Sturgeon to 4' long, Tench, Perch, Bream, Golden Orfe, Barbel to 5lb, Roach and Rudd

Sapphire - 20 peg pool, stocked with the same fish as Emerald, with the exception of Barbel

Specimen - heavily stocked with Carp from 7lb to 40lb and Barbel

Match - stocked with Common and Mirror Carp

Excellent Disabled Facilities

Self Catering Holiday Cottage beside the lake.

Sleeps four - disabled friendly

For further details contact
Mr Alan Wilkinson, Emerald Pool Fishery, Puriton Rd, West Huntspill, Highbridge, Somerset.
Tel: 01278 794707 or 0797 486 2503

STILLWATER COARSE

SOMERSET

PLANTATIONS Lakes & Cafe
Carp & Coarse Fishing

0.75 acre Carp Lake
Well stocked with Common, Mirror & Ghost Carp

2.5 acre Coarse Lake
Stocked with Tench, Roach, Rudd, Golden Rudd, Bream, Dace, Perch, Chub, Golden Tench, Gudgeon, Crucian Carp, Barbel

Day ticket - Adult £6, Junior/OAP/Disabled £4, Extra Rod £1
Half Days - Adult £4, Junior/OAP/Disabled £2.50

HORSESHOE MATCH LAKE
Local Country Walks, Camping & Caravan Club Site

For more information Tel: **01934 832325**
Middle Lane, Kingston Seymour, Clevedon, North Somerset
Email: watravis@plantations.freeserve.co.uk

A nice Common from Plantations.

other local tackle shops. *Charges:* Day tickets £3, 7 day ticket £10 or season ticket £20. Senior citizen £10. Night fishing £5 per night by prior arrangement only. Telephone Mr A Hardwick - 01278 765941 *Season:* Open all year.

N. Somerset Association of Anglers (Coarse Lakes)
Contact: Mr Newton, 64 Clevedon Rd, Tickenham, Clevedon, BS21 6RD, 01275 856107, *Water:* See also entry under Yeo. Apex lake: 6 acre lake, Newtown: 3 acre lake, Walrow ponds: 2 acre lake, 3 acre lake and 6 acre lake. *Species:* Apex: Carp to 18lbs, Bream to 7lb, Pike to 15lb, Roach, Rudd. Newtown: Carp to 24lb, Pike to 27lb, Bream 7lb, Roach, Rudd, Perch. Walrow: Carp to 26lb, Bream 11lb, Tench 10lb, Pike 24lb, Roach, Rudd, Perch. *Permits:* Local tackle shops, purchased in advance of fishing. *Charges:* £3 day, £10 week, £20 season, junior/OAP/disabled £10. *Season:* Apex & Newtown Lakes - closed March 1st - 31st inlcusive. Walrow Pond - open all year. *Methods:* Apex & Newtown Lakes: Barbless hooks, min. 2.5lb BS line, no live or dead bait, no floating bait.

ILMINSTER

Ilminster & District A.A. (Coarse Lake)
Contact: P. Lonton, Marshalsea, Cottage Corner, Ilton, Ilminster, 01460 52519, *Water:* Dillington Estate Pond. *Species:* Carp, Roach, Chub, Perch, Bream, Tench. *Permits:* Ilminster Warehouse, Yeovil Angling Centre, The Tackle Shack, Chard Angling, Enterprise Angling, Taunton. Membership details from the secretary. *Charges:* Day tickets £4. £16 annual membership. £9 Oap/disabled. Junior £6.. *Season:* Open all year. *Methods:* Club rules apply.

KEYNSHAM

Avon Valley Country Park (Coarse Pond)
Bath Rd, Keynsham, Bristol, BS31 1TP, 0117 9864929, *Water:* Small Coarse pond. *Species:* Carp to 12lb. *Permits:* From above. *Charges:* £5.50 Adult entrance to park (includes ticket to fish), £5 Child, £5 Senior Citizen. *Season:* Park open: Easter - 1st November 10am-6pm. *Methods:* Barbless hooks only, no keepnets.

Keynsham Angling Association (Coarse Lake)
Contact: Mr K. N. Jerrom, 21 St Georges Road, Keynsham, Bristol, BS31 2HU, 01179 865193, *Water:* Century ponds 0.25 acres, see also entry under river Chew. *Species:* Mixed fishery. *Charges:* Day ticket for club members £2.50. *Season:* Open all year dawn to dusk. Closed alternate Sunday mornings until 1pm. *Methods:* Barbless hooks and no boilies.

KINGSTON SEYMOUR

Bullock Farm Fishing Lakes
Contact: Philip & Jude Simmons, Bullock Farm, Back Lane, Kingston Seymour, BS21 6XA, 01934 835020, *Water:* 5 Lakes totalling 6.25 acres, including specialist Carp lake. *Species:* Carp - Common, Mirror, Ghost, Crucian, Grass, Purple and Koi. Tench, Roach, Rudd, Chub, Bream, Skimmer Bream, Golden Orfe, Golden Tench. *Permits:* Only at lakeside. *Charges:* £6 day ticket, £4 O.A.P's / Under 14s / Disabled. Season tickets & Match rates available. *Season:* Open all year round Dawn - Dusk. *Methods:* No boilies, Barbless hooks, Fish friendly keepnets only, No dogs, under 14's to be accompanied by an adult. Common sense!

Plantations Lake
Contact: Mr or Mrs W.Travis, Middle Lane Farm, Middle Lane, Kingston Seymour,, Clevedon, BS21 6XW, 01934 832325, *Water:* 0.75 acre Carp lake, 2.5 acre coarse lake, 1.75 acre match lake open. *Species:* 12 Species of coarse fish incl. Barbel, Crucian Carp. 3 Species of Carp in Carp lake. *Charges:* £6 Adult (£1 extra rod), £4.00 Juniors/O.A.P's/Disabled. Half days (from 2pm) available: adult £4, juniors/OAPs £2.50. Please enquire for membership details. *Season:* All year. *Methods:* No boilies, barbless hooks.

SOMERSET

LANGPORT
Langport & District Angling Association (Coarse Lake)
TA11 6SJ, *Water:* Coombe Lake - 2.75 acres. See entry under Parrett. *Species:* Carp to 30lb, Tench 6.5lb, Roach 1.5lb, Perch 2lb plus, Bream 7lb, Chub 4lb. *Permits:* See entry under Parrett. *Charges:* See entry under Parrett. *Season:* No closed season. No night fishing. *Methods:* Barbless hooks, no boilies, no Carp in keepnets.

Thorney Lakes
Contact: Richard or Ann England, Thorney Farm, Muchelney, Langport, TA10 0DW, 01458 250811, *Water:* Two 2 acre lakes. *Species:* A selection of coarse fish including large Carp. *Permits:* On the bank. *Charges:* £5/day, £3/half day after 4 p.m, £3 for O.A.Ps & Children under 16. *Season:* 16th March - 31st January. *Methods:* Barbless hooks, no boilies, nuts or pulses, all nets to be dipped on site, no night fishing.

MARTOCK
Ash Ponds
Contact: Pat Rodford, Ash Ponds, Burrough Street, Ash, Martock, 01935 823459, *Water:* Four 1 acre ponds. *Species:* Carp to 30lb, Tench to 6lb and Bream. *Permits:* On the bank. *Charges:* £5 for 12 hours. *Season:* No closed season.

SHEPTON MALLET
Bridge Farm Fishery
Contact: Jon Thorners, Bridge Farm Shop, Pylle, Shepton Mallet, BA4 6TA, 01749 830138, *Water:* 0.25 mile long x 30m wide lake, approx 3 acres. *Species:* Common Carp to 15lb, Roach, Rudd and other coarse fish. *Permits:* From farm shop on arrival. *Charges:* Adults £5, Juniors under 16 £2.50. *Season:* Open all year, dawn to dusk. *Methods:* Barbless hooks only, no keepnets, for Carp, no night fishing.

SOMERTON
Viaduct Fishery
Contact: Mr Steve Long, Viaduct Fishery, Cary Valley, Somerton, TA11 6LJ, 01458 274022, *Water:* Six Coarse Lakes including one specimen lake. *Species:* Mirror Carp 27lb, Crucian Carp, Common Carp 23lb, Perch 4lb, Roach 1.5lb, Bream 6lb, Tench 8lb and Golden Tench, Rudd, Ruffe. *Permits:* Fishery Shop or Pre-Payment Office; E.A. Rod licences available. *Charges:* Day ticket £5, Under 16 £4, Summer Evening ticket £3.50, Winter Half day ticket £3. £2 charge for second rod; Match bookings taken. *Season:* All year. *Methods:* All nets to be dipped, no nuts or boilies, barbless hooks size 10 max, no fixed rigs, no braid, fishing from pegs only.

STREET
Godney Moor Ponds
Contact: Nick Hughes, Street Angling Centre, 160 High Street, Street, BA16 0NH, 01458 447790, *Water:* Approx 4 acres. *Species:* Coarse fish including Carp. *Permits:* Only from Street Angling Centre. *Charges:* £5 per day (All genders). *Season:* April to February inclusive. Sunrise to sunset only. *Methods:* No nuts, 2 rods max. Carp fishing in large pond only. Barbless hooks only. No boilies in small pond.

Taunton Angling Association (Walton Ponds)
Contact: Mike Hewitson, 56 Parkfield Road, Taunton, TA1 4SE,

THORNEY LAKES
Coarse Fishing
Camping & Caravans

A Beautiful spot to fish, even better to stay in an inspiring landscape in the secret Somerset Levels

FULL FACILITY SITE FOR CAMPING & CARAVANS
MUCHELNEY, LANGPORT, SOMERSET.
Tel: 01458 250811
Email: enquiries@thorneylakes.co.uk   www.thorneylakes.co.uk

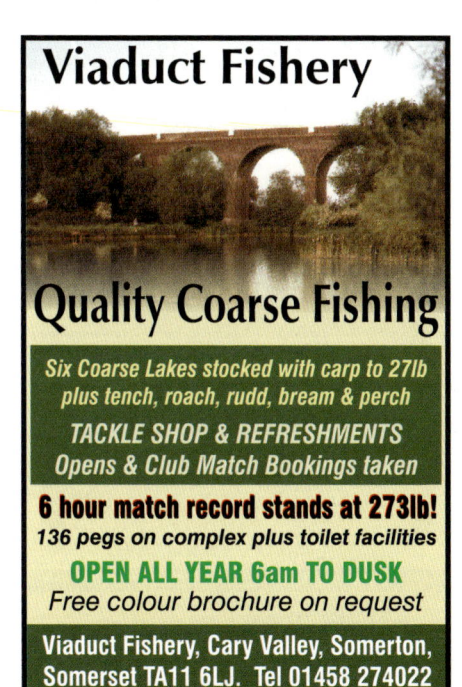

Viaduct Fishery

Quality Coarse Fishing

Six Coarse Lakes stocked with carp to 27lb plus tench, roach, rudd, bream & perch
TACKLE SHOP & REFRESHMENTS
Opens & Club Match Bookings taken
6 hour match record stands at 273lb!
136 pegs on complex plus toilet facilities
OPEN ALL YEAR 6am TO DUSK
Free colour brochure on request

Viaduct Fishery, Cary Valley, Somerton, Somerset TA11 6LJ. Tel 01458 274022

STREET ANGLING CENTRE

NICK HUGHES
For all your fishing needs in Coarse, Game and Sea Tackle
ROD REPAIR AND RENOVATION SERVICE
160 High St, Street, Somerset. Tel/Fax 01458 447830
Godney Moor Ponds, Langport, Bridgwater, Taunton, Cheddar and Glaston Manor A.A. coarse fishing permits available

STILLWATER COARSE

SOMERSET

STILLWATER COARSE

Follyfoot Farm
Heavily Stocked 3 acre lake
Koi, Mirror and Common Carp to 30lb
ON-SITE CAFE & BAIT SHOP
Professional Tuition available
Taunton Rd, North Petherton, Somerset
Tel; 01278 662979 or 07748 400904
www.follyfootfishery.co.uk

HBS Fisheries

SPECIMEN LAKE
Around 2.5 acres with depths ranging from 2-15ft.
Every swim has underwater features designed and built for big carp.
The stock at the moment is 43 fish between 10-28lbs.

MATCH LAKE
Mature match lake of half an acre with depths to 10ft.
Stocked with roach, rudd, tench, bream, golden orfe and carp to 15 lbs.
BOTH LAKES AVAILABLE ON DAY AND NIGHT TICKETS.
Car park, toilet and other facilities
HBS FISHERIES ADSBOROUGH Near Taunton
Tel: 01823 412389 for further details

Lands End Farm Fishery
Heath House, Wedmore, Somerset
Match Lake & Specimen Lake
Open all year - Dawn to Dusk
NEW - 30 PEG MATCH LAKE NOW OPEN
Stocked with Carp to 23lb, Tench and Bream to 8lb, Grass Carp to 17lb, Roach, Rudd, Golden Rudd, Barbel, Perch, Ide, Chub and Golden Orfe.
Disabled Facilities - Toilets - Refreshments
Please Telephone 07977 545882

HBS Fishery
Contact: Mr Richard Bult, HBS Fishery, Adsborough, Near Taunton, TA7 0BZ, 01823 412389, *Water:* Two lakes of 2.5 acres and half an acre. *Species:* Match Lake: Roach, Rudd, Carp, Tench, Bream (Carp to 15lb). Specimen Lake: 45 Carp between 10lb and 31lb. *Permits:* Day and night tickets sold on the bank. *Charges:* Match Lake: £4 for 12 hours, £6 for 24 hours. Specimen Lake: £6 for 12 hours, £10 for 24 hours. *Season:* Open all year except a 1 month close season to allow fish to spawn. *Methods:* No nuts. Barbless hooks etc. Full rules at fishery.

Taunton Angling Association (King Stanley Pond)
Contact: Mike Hewitson, 56 Parkfield Road, Taunton, TA1 4SE, 01823 271194, *Water:* King Stanley Pond (also see entries under River & Canal Fishing). *Species:* Carp 18lb, Roach 1lb, Tench 3lb, Rudd 1lb, Perch 1lb. *Permits:* Topp Tackle - Taunton: 01823 282518 or Enterprise Angling - Taunton: 01823 282623. *Charges:* Season £28.50. Day tickets £5 senior, £2 junior. *Season:* Open all year. *Methods:* Barbless hooks only. No Carp in keepnets.

Taunton Angling Association (Maunsel Ponds)
Contact: Mike Hewitson, 56 Parkfield Road, Taunton, TA1 4SE, 01823 271194, *Water:* Three Ponds together comprising Maunsel Ponds (also see entries under River & Canal Fishing). *Species:* Carp 21lb, Tench 5lb, Roach 1lb, Bream 3lb, Crucians 1lb. *Charges:* Season £28.50. Day tickets £5 senior, £2 junior. *Season:* Open all year. *Methods:* Barbless hooks, no Carp in keepnets.

WEDMORE
Lands End Farm Fishery
Contact: Michael Duckett, Heath House, Wedmore, BS28 4UQ, 07977 545882, *Water:* Match lake and specimen lake, total 3 acres. Now open, new 30 peg match lake. *Species:* Carp to 22lb (Common, Mirror, Ghost, Crucian) Grass Carp to 17lb, Bream to 8lb, Tench and Roach 2lb, Rudd, Chub, Ide, Perch, Barbel, Golden Orfe to 4lb. *Permits:* From offfice on site. *Charges:* £5/day, £3 after 4pm, £4 juniors, £4 conc. *Season:* Open all year. 7am to dusk in the summer. *Methods:* Barbless hooks only, no keepnets, no dog biscuits, boilies or nuts.

WELLINGTON
Langford Lakes (coarse lakes)
Contact: Mr. Hendy, Middle Hill Farm, Langford Budville, Wellington, TA21 0RS, 01823 400476, *Water:* 4 lakes, one Carp specimen lake. *Species:* Carp, Roach, Perch, Tench, Bream. *Charges:* Prices on application. *Season:* Open all year dawn to dusk. *Methods:* No keepnets allowed, children under 16 must be accompanied by fishing adult.

WELLS
Emborough Ponds
Contact: Thatchers Tackle, 18 Queen Street, Wells, BA5 2DP, 01749 673513, *Water:* 3.5 acre lake. *Species:* Carp to 25lb, Tench 8lb, small Roach. *Charges:* Limited membership, please enquire at Thatchers Tackle. *Season:* 1st March - 31st December.

01823 271194, *Water:* Walton Ponds, 2 ponds (also see entries under River & Canal Fishing). *Species:* Carp 25lb, Tench 3lb, Roach 1lb, Rudd 2lb, Pike 22.5lb. *Charges:* Season £28.50. Day tickets £5 senior, £2 junior. *Season:* Open all year. *Methods:* Barbless hooks, no Carp in keepnets.

TAUNTON
Follyfoot Farm
Contact: Rupert Preston, Follyfoot Farm, North Petherton, TA6 6NW, 01278 662979, *Mobile:* 07748 400904, *Water:* Three acre Carp lake. *Species:* Mirror, Koi and Common to 30lb. *Permits:* On the bank - self service. *Charges:* £6 per day. Night fishing £12. *Season:* Open all year dawn to dusk. Night fishing by prior arrangement only. *Methods:* No keepnets, barbless hooks only, no dogs or radios. Full rules at the fishery.

SOMERSET

WINTERBOURNE
Frome Vale Angling Club (Coarse Lake)
Contact: Nigel Vigus (Secretary), 32 Rock Lane, Stoke Gifford, Bristol, BS34 8PF, 01179 759710, *Water:* Half acre lake at Winterbourne. See entry under Bristol Frome.

WIVELISCOMBE
Oxenleaze Farm Caravans & Coarse Fishery
Contact: Richard & Marion Rottenbury, Chipstable, Wiveliscombe, TA4 2QH, 01984 623427, *Water:* 3 lakes 2 acres. *Species:* Carp 30lb, Tench 9lb, Roach 2lb 6oz, Rudd 2lb 3oz, Bream 8lb. *Permits:* At above address. *Charges:* £8/person/day (2 Rods max), Spectators £1/person/day. NO night fishing. *Season:* 1st April - 30th September. *Methods:* Barbless hooks, no ground bait.

YEOVIL
Ashmead Lakes
Contact: Steve Maynard, Stone Farm, Ash, Martock, TA12 6PB, 01935 823319, *Water:* 11 acres. *Species:* Mirror and Common Carp to over 30lb. *Charges:* Syndicate water. Please phone for details. *Season:* Closed January to mid February. *Methods:* No restrictions.

Stoke Sub Hamdon & District AA (Coarse Lake)
Contact: Mr Derek Goad (Secretary), (H.Q. at Stoke Working Mens Club), 2 Windsor Lane, Stoke-Sub-Hamdon, TA14 6UE, 01935 824337, *Water:* Bearley Lake, see also entry under River Parrett. *Permits:* Season permits only. Available from Stax Tackle, Montacute and Yeovil Angling Centre, Yeovil. Also available from secretary. *Charges:* Season tickets: Senior £12, Juniors/OAPs £6 (Bearley Lake). Juniors under 14 must be accompanied by an adult. *Season:* Lake open all year. *Methods:* Lake, no boilies or nut baits (lake rules apply). No night fishing.

The Old Mill Fishery
Contact: Mike Maxwell, Tucking Mill Farm, Stoford, Yeovil, BA22 9TX, 01935 414771, *Water:* Four 1.5 acre lakes plus fishing on a tributary of the river Yeo and a canal. *Species:* 21 different species of coarse fish. River contains Roach, Dace, Chub and Barbel. *Permits:* On the bank. *Charges:* Permit for lakes and river £6/day (£4 under 16yrs and OAP). £3 evening ticket 4pm onwards in summer. Club bookings taken. *Season:* Open all year 7am to dusk. *Methods:* Barbless hooks only. Keepnets allowed, but no Carp to be retained in keepnets.

Yeovil & Sherborne Angling Association (Coarse Lakes)
Contact: Pete Coombes, 44 Monksdale, Yeovil, BA21 3JF, 01935 427873, *Water:* Sherborne Castle Lake & discounted tickets Viaduct Fishery. Also see River Yeo entry. *Species:* Roach, Bream, Carp, Perch, Rudd, Tench. *Permits:* Membership details from above & local tackle shops. *Charges:* No day tickets. River Club card £12, £2 off cost of day ticket at Viaduct. *Season:* Open all year.

THATCHERS TACKLE
(Props R. & A. Miles)
18 Queen Street, Wells, Somerset
Telephone: (01749) 673513

In the heart of Somerset, for all your angling needs

SEA ANGLING BAITS • LURES/TACKLE • RODS & REELS

- Try Us -

WESTON Angling Centre
LARGE SELECTION OF FRESHWATER, SEA AND GAME TACKLE
Full selection of fresh & frozen coarse and sea baits always available
Stockists of Abu, Daiwa, Drennan, Shakespeare, Preston, Ron Thompson, Okuma and many more...
Friendly advice always at hand - Local licences sold
All credit cards welcome
25a Locking Road, Weston Super Mare
Call Robert on 01934 631140

Richworth
Where Quality Counts
- Freezer Baits
- Shelf Life Boilies
- Base Mixes
- Flavours
- Colours & Additives
- Pellets and Paste
- Groundbaits
- Active Xtracts
- Leads & Accessories
- 1st Contact Rig Components
- Clothing and Videos

For a free colour brochure containing all Richworth Products please send your name and address with a 1st class stamp to:
Streamselect Ltd, Island Farm Avenue, West Molesey, Surrey KT8 2UZ
www.richworth.com

Check out our Web Site!
Get HOOKED!
ON THE WEB
www.gethooked.co.uk

STILLWATER COARSE

Cadbury Angling

Cadbury Garden & Leisure, Smallway, Congresbury

Tel: 01934 875733

Email: cadburyangling@hotmail.com

We Stock Sea, Fly, Coarse & Carp Tackle

Live and Frozen Baits
Maggot, Caster, Pinkie & Squat, Rag, Lug and a Range of Frozen Sea Bait

All the terminal tackle you require and helpful friendly advice on all aspects of fishing

Tackle From Top Manufacturers

Fox	Shimano	Daiwa
Korda	Abu Garcia	Airflo
Drennan	Century	Orvis

And many many more.....

Stillwater Trout

BRIDGWATER

Burton Springs Fishery (Trout Lake)
Contact: Tony Evans, Lawson Farm, Burton, Nr Stogursey, Bridgwater, TA5 1QB, 01278 732135, Mobile: 07866 026685, Water: Approx 2 acre lake. Species: Brown, Rainbow, Tiger & Blue Trout. Permits: Self service at fishing lodge. Charges: 4-fish ticket £22, 2-fish/ 6hr £17, sporting ticket £12 (catch & release permitted after limit). Season: Open all year 8am - 9pm or dusk. Methods: Fly only. Barbless hooks only, only Rainbow Trout may be taken.

Hawkridge Reservoir
Contact: Wessex Water, 0845 600 4 600, Water: 32 acre reservoir. Species: Brown and Rainbow Trout. Permits: Gary Howe (Ranger) Tel: 01278 671840. Charges: Day Ticket £15, Season Ticket £340, Day Concession £13, Evening Ticket £8 (no concessions). Book of Tickets - £78 for 6 available only from the ranger. Concession book of tickets £68. Boat (rowing) per day per boat £13, Boat (evening) £6. Season: 16th March -9th October 2005.

BRISTOL

Avon Fly Fishers Club
Contact: Bill Pugh, Bill Pugh Pets & Fishing, 410 Wells Road, Red Lion Hill, Knowle, BS14 9AF, 0117 9770380, Water: Fishing competitions, video and social evenings, plus members public liability insurance.

Blagdon Lake
Contact: Bob Handford, Bristol Water Fisheries, Blagdon Lake, Park Lane, Blagdon, BS40 7UD, 01275 332339, Water: 440 Acre Lake. Celebrating 100 years of public fishing. Species: Rainbow Trout best 16lb 4oz, Brown Trout best 10lb 4oz. Total catch last season over 25,000. Average weight 2lb 2oz. Permits: Woodford Lodge, Chew Valley Lake and Blagdon Lodge, Blagdon Lake. Charges: Day bank £15.50, O.A.P. £13.50, Junior £8, Evening Bank £11.50 - Day boat £23.50, O.A.P. £21.50, Junior £16, Afternoon £19.50, Evening £16 - Season £555, O.A.P. £350 (Valid at Chew and Barrows also). Season: 24 March - 30 November 2005. Methods: Fly fishing only.

Bristol Reservoir Flyfishers Association
Contact: Martin Cottis (Sec.), 3 Hillhouse Road, Downend, Bristol, BS16 5RR, 0117 9877285, Mobile: 07747 843548, Water: Fishing on Bristol Waterworks reservoirs. Blagdon,

---

Burton Springs Fishery

Two lakes each of approx 2 acres, set in peaceful countryside and overlooked by the Quantock Hills

Trout Lake for fly fishermen, with crystal clear water, Rainbow, Brown, Blue & Tiger Trout. Average size of two pounds plus.

Toilets on site

Coarse Lake contains many double figure Carp to 30 lbs, Tench Bream and Perch.

Phone 01278 732 135

www.burtonspringsfishery.co.uk   Email:- burtonsprings@aol.com

Burton Springs Fishery, Burton, Stogursey, Nr Bridgwater, Somerset TA5 1QB.

IT'S BEAUTIFUL *fishing at* **BRISTOL WATER**

For a start it's superb sport from bank or boat on our well stocked lakes at Chew, Blagdon and Barrows, just south of Bristol. Over 61,000 fighting fit, beautiful trout were caught last year at fisheries as natural as nature herself.

Forget those overstocked 'ponds', test yourself on a real fishery. And our knowledgeable staff are on hand to advise you on tactics, the best spots to fish and supply any tackle you may need.

For more information and a free copy of 'The Buzzer' magazine visit our website or call 01275 332339.

- Superb fishing lodge and restaurant at Chew plus well-stocked tackle shop (open 8.30am - 5pm daily)
- Season opens 17th March

BRISTOL WATER fisheries

Woodford Lodge, Chew Stoke, Nr Bristol BS40 8XH.
www.bristolwater.co.uk

SOMERSET

Cameley Lakes
Fishing for Rainbow & Brown Trout on 5 acres of lakes
Open from 8am to dusk
Hillcrest Farm, Cameley, Temple Cloud, Nr. Bristol
Tel: 01761 452423

Get Hooked On The Web
Fully searchable Fisheries Directory - over 800 Entries!
www.gethooked.co.uk

Bristol Angling Centre
...are one of the largest Tackle Shops in Europe!
We sell all the local permits and can give you all the advice you need
Tel 0117 9508723
12-16 Doncaster Road, Southmead, Bristol BS10 5PL
5 mins from M4 and M5
www.bristolangling.co.uk
Email: info@bristolangling.co.uk

STILLWATER TROUT

Chew Valley and Barrows. Competitions organised from bank and boat. Tuition offered. Full winter programme of activities including: tackle auctions, fly tying sessions, beginners and improvers casting sessions. *Species:* Rainbow and Brown Trout, fly fishing for Pike. *Permits:* Day tickets direct from Bristol Water. Club does not sell day tickets. *Charges:* £3 joining fee. Annual membership £7.50 full members, £5 pensioners and registered disabled, joining fee £1 juniors - annual membership fee juniors free. *Season:* End March to end of October (extension of season on banks and at Barron Tanks). *Methods:* Fly fishing only.

Cameley Lakes
Contact: J. Harris, Hillcrest Farm, Cameley, Temple Cloud, BS18 5AQ, 01761 452423, *Water:* One 2.5 acre lake and three 1 acre lakes plus fishing on the river River Cam. *Species:* Rainbow Trout, Brown Trout 1 - 5lb. *Permits:* Car park. *Charges:* £25 incl VAT Day ticket 4 fish. £20 incl VAT Half Day ticket 2 fish. *Season:* Open all year - 8.00 till sundown. *Methods:* Fly fishing only. Hooks no larger than 1 inch.

Chew Valley Lake
Contact: Bob Handford, Bristol Water Fisheries, Woodford Lodge, Chew Stoke, Nr.Bristol, BS40 8XH, 01275 332339, *Water:* 1,200 Acre lake. 32 motor boats for hire. *Species:* Rainbow Trout to 14lb 6oz, Brown Trout to 12lb 3oz. Pike to over 38lb. Total catch last season - over 28,000. Average weight 2lb 5oz. *Permits:* Woodford Lodge, Chew Lake. *Charges:* Day bank £13.50, O.A.P. £11.50, Junior £7, Evening bank £10.50 - Day boat £29.50, O.A.P. £27, Junior £20.50, Afternoon £24, Evening £18.00 - Season £455, O.A.P. £295 (Valid at Barrows also). *Season:* 17 March - 30 November 2005. *Methods:* Fly fishing only. Pike trials October-November.

Jacklands Trout Fishery
Contact: Mr H Waygood, Jacklands Bridge, Clevedon Road, Nailsea, Bristol, BS21 6SG, 01275 810697, *Water:* 1 acre lake. *Species:* Rainbow Trout from 1.5 - 12lbs. *Permits:* On site. *Charges:* Fish @ £1.90 per lb. *Season:* Open all year dawn to dusk. *Methods:* Fly only, no catch & release.

Knowle Angling Association (Trout Lakes)
Contact: Keith Caddick, 41 Eastwood Crescent, Brislington, Bristol, BS4 4SR, 01179 857974, *Mobile:* 0794 634 7581, *Water:* 2 lakes - Publow and Ackers lake at Pensford. Plus fishing at Chew Magna reservoir, (also see entry in River Fishing, Chew). *Species:* Rainbow and Brown Trout up to 8lb. Restocking for 2004 season. *Charges:* £80 annual membership. New members pay extra £5 entrance fee. *Season:* Chew Magna Reservoir open all year for Rainbows. Brown Trout from 1 April to 15 October. Lakes open all year. *Methods:* Fly only on lakes and upper Chew.

Litton Lakes
Contact: Bob Handford, Bristol Water Fisheries, 01275 332339, *Water:* 7 acre lake and 11 acre lake at Coley, Nr Chewton Mendip. *Species:* Brown & Rainbow Trout. Total catch last year season - over 1,000. Average weight 2lb 9oz. *Permits:* Woodford Lodge, Chew Valley Lake. *Charges:* £100 permit for two rods upwards, fishing both lakes exclusively. Bag limit 5 fish per person. Corporate packages with tuition available. *Season:* Open all year. Available Thursday to Sunday. *Methods:* Fly fishing only.

The Barrows
Contact: Bob Handford, Bristol Water Fisheries, Bristol, 01275 332339, *Water:* Three lakes of 25 acres (No. 1) 40 acres (No. 2) 60 acres (No.3) at Barrow Gurney, Nr. Bristol. Arguably the best

bank fishing of all the Bristol Water Fisheries. *Species:* Rainbow Trout (10lb 10oz) Brown Trout (9lb 1oz). Total catch last season over 7,000. Average weight 1lb 11oz. *Permits:* Permit kiosk at the reservoir. *Charges:* Day bank £11, O.A.P. £9.50, Junior £6, Evening bank £8.50, Season £340, O.A.P. £225. *Season:* 17th March - 30th November 2005. *Methods:* Fly fishing only.

DULVERTON
Exe Valley Fishery
Contact: Andrew Maund, Exebridge, Dulverton, TA22 9AY, 01398 323328, *Water:* 3 Lakes fly only (2 + 1 + 3/4 acre lakes), 1 small lake any method half acre. *Species:* Rainbow Trout. *Permits:* Day Tickets. *Charges:* Day ticket £5.50 5 fish limit, plus £3.50 per kilo, rod hire £5. *Season:* All year.

Fly Fishing in Somerset (Winsford)
Contact: R.M. Gurden, 3 Edbrooke Cottages, Winsford, Nr Minehead, TA24 7AE, 01643 851504, *Mobile:* 07814 243991, *Water:* Small stillwater at Winsford. *Species:* Rainbow Trout. *Charges:* By prior arrangement only, please contact above. *Season:* Open all year, Dawn to Dusk.

Wimbleball
Contact: South West Lakes Trust, 01566 771930, *Water:* Information Office Hours: 01398 371372. *Species:* Premier Rainbow Fishery - Boat & Bank (boats may be booked in advance: 01398-371372). Average for 2004: 3.7 per rod day. Biggest fish: Rainbow 11lb 13oz (caught 2004). *Permits:* Self service at Hill Barn Farm. *Charges:* Full day £18, Season £400. Reduced day £14.50, Season £295, Child/Wheelchair £3, Season £90. Evening £14.50. Season Permits can be used on any Premier Fishery only. Boats £11 per day inc. 2 fish extra to bag limits, catch & release ticket available. 'Wheelie Boat' available for disabled anglers (must be booked at least 48 hrs in advance). This venue may be booked for competitions. *Season:* Opens 25th March 2005 - 31st October. *Methods:* Fly fishing only. No child under 14 years may fish unless accompanied by an adult over 18 years.

Wimbleball Fly Fishing Club
Water: Regular fishing days, bank and boat. Fishing Wimbleball and other stillwaters. Strong junior section, tuition can be arranged for juniors. *Permits:* All details available from Wimbleball Fishing Lodge.

HIGHBRIDGE
Walleden Farm Fishery
Contact: Andrew Wall, East Huntspill, Highbridge, TA9 3UP, 01278 786488, *Water:* 2.2 acre trout lake. Also section of river Brue. See entry under river fishing. *Species:* Trout. *Permits:* From the above. *Season:* Open all year. *Methods:* Any legal method.

TAUNTON
Combe Sydenham Fisheries
Contact: Jim Laver, Merry Cottage, Monksilver, TA4 4JA, 01984 656273, *Water:* Three spring fed woodland lakes of just over one acre each. Two catch and take and one catch and release. *Species:* Rainbows to 16lb. Browns to 2lb, Blue and Tiger Trout to 4lb. *Permits:* Self service from fishing lodge. *Charges:* £30 for four fish ticket. £20 for two fish. £15 single fish evening ticket. £15 for a four hour session on the catch and release pond. *Season:* Open every day from 8am to half hour before dusk. Please note the fishery is closed on certain days between October and

---

TOPP TACKLE LTD
63 Station Rd., Taunton, Somerset TA1 1PA
Tel: 01823 282518
COARSE - GAME - SEA
Permits for local waters
Maggots, Worms, Ammo Frozen Pike and Sea Baits in stock all year round
We are just 5 minutes from the M5 (junction 25) Head for the cricket ground - Railway Station. Do not follow town centre signs.

EXE VALLEY FISHERY LTD
FISH FOR TROUT
Fly fishing in 3 lakes - 2, 1, 3/4 acres
Any method lake - 3/4 acre
No individual Rod Licence required

* Day tickets £5.50
* Rod Hire £5
* Catch @ £3.50 per kg
* 5 bag limit.
* Tackle, Salmon and Trout for sale
* Refreshments available

SHOP & FISHING OPEN ALL YEAR
Exebridge, Dulverton, Somerset TA22 9AY
Tel: (01398) 323328   Fax: (01398) 324079
Email: info@exevalleyfishery.co.uk
Web: www.exevalleyfishery.co.uk

Somerset's Newest Trout Fishery!
Come and enjoy some fantastic sport!
Rainbows, Blues, Tigers and Browns, ranging from 2 – 16lbs. 3 stunning ponds set in the unrivalled, wooded surroundings of Exmoor National Park
Combe Sydenham Fisheries
Monksilver, Taunton, Somerset
Open 7 days – Please phone before travelling
Tel: 01984 656273 / 07795 096020

STILLWATER TROUT

SOMERSET

February. *Methods:* Fly only on barbless hooks.
Fly Fishing in Somerset (Trout Lake)
Contact: R.M. Gurden, 3 Edbrooke Cottages, Winsford, Nr Minehead, TA24 7AE, 01643 851504, *Mobile:* 07814 243991, *Water:* 2 acre lake, which can accommodate groups of up to 10. 1.5 acre lake in Quantock. *Species:* Rainbow Trout. *Charges:* On application. *Season:* Open all year.

Hawkridge Fly Fishing Club
Contact: Mr & Mrs Salter, 3 Dunster Close, Taunton, TA2 8EE, *Water:* Primarily fishing on Hawkridge Reservoir. Club meetings 8pm first Tuesday of the month at The Blake Arms, Bridgwater. Visiting speakers & monthly competitions in season. Club trips, fly tying and social evenings. *Species:* Rainbow and Brown Trout. *Permits:* From the fishing lodge at Hawkridge Reservoir. *Season:* New fly fishermen welcome, old and new. *Methods:* Fly fishing only. Boats available.

WIVELISCOMBE
Clatworthy Fly Fishing Club
Contact: Mr F Yeandle, 51 Mountway Rd, Bishops Hull, Taunton, TA1 3LT, 01823 283959, *Water:* 130 acre Clatworthy reservoir on Exmoor. *Species:* Rainbow and Brown Trout. *Permits:* On site from Lodge. *Charges:* Day Ticket £15/5-fish limit, Concessions £13 OAP's. Evening Ticket £8. 6 Days £78, Concessions £68. Season £340/4-fish limit (only 4 visits/week allowed), no concession on season tickets. Boats £13/day, £6 evening. *Season:* Open 17th March -10th October. *Methods:* Fly fishing only.

Clatworthy Reservoir
Contact: Wessex Water, 0845 600 4 600, *Water:* 130 acre reservoir. *Species:* Rainbow and Brown Trout. *Permits:* Contact ranger Dave Pursey on 01984 624658. *Charges:* Day Ticket £15, Season Ticket £340, Day Concession £13, Evening Ticket £8 (no concessions). Book of Tickets - £78 for 6, available only from the ranger. Concession book of tickets £65. 'Wheelie' boat available for wheelchair users. Boat (rowing) per day per boat £13, Boat (evening) £6. *Season:* 16th March - 9th October 2005.

YEOVIL
Sutton Bingham Fly Fishers Association
Contact: Dave Stacey or Colin Greenham, 01935 423223/824714, *Water:* Hold regular competitions throughout the season. For members only. Tuition available. Fly tying classes held during the close season. *Species:* Brown Trout to 16lb, Rianbows to 18lb. *Permits:* Day tickets on site. *Charges:* New members always welcome. Adult and junior £3 per year. *Season:* March to October.

Sutton Bingham Reservoir
Contact: Wessex Water, 0845 600 4 600, *Water:* 142 acre reservoir. *Species:* Rainbow and Brown Trout. *Permits:* Contact ranger Ivan Tinsley on 01935 872389. Advisable to book boats in advance. *Charges:* Day Ticket £15, Season Ticket £340, Day Concession £13, Evening Ticket £8 (no concessions). Book of Tickets - £78 for 6, available only from the ranger. Concession book of tickets £68. "Wheelie" boat available for wheelchair users. Boat (rowing) per day per boat £13, Boat (evening) £6. *Season:* 16th March - 9th October 2005.

STILLWATER TROUT

Fishing and more...

ring 0845 600 4 600

Wessex Water
a YTL company

Somerset Sea Fishing

BATH
Gannet Sea Angling Club
Contact: NFSA Head Office: 01364 644643,

BRISTOL
Bath & Bristol Civil Service Sea Angling Club
Contact: NFSA Head Office: 01364 644643,
Bridgwater Sea Angling Club
Contact: Clive Hooper, 48 Chilton Street, Bridgwater, TA6 3HU, 01278 457221, *Water:* Shore angling. *Charges:* Club membership.
Bristol Channel Federation of Sea Anglers
Contact: Keith Reed, 27 St Michaels Avenue, Clevedon, BS21 6LL, 01275 872101, *Water:* Bristol Channel, Hartland Point. North Devon to St Davids Head, Dyfed (all tidal waters eastwards). *Species:* All sea fish, both boat and shore records, yearly update. 52 different species recorded in major (over 1lb) rec.list, 16 different species in minor (under 1lb) rec.list. *Charges:* £50 per CLUB per year inclusive of shore activities insurance. *Season:* All year round activities, shore and boat contests, small boat section with inter-club activities. *Methods:* Fishing to specimen sizes, all specimen fish awarded certificate, best of specie annually, plus fish of the month. Team & Individual annual awards. New for 2003 - Charter Boat contests only. Touch Trace rules. All fish returned alive.
Clevedon Breakaways Sea Angling Club
Contact: J. Aspinall, 6 Lydford Walk, Bedminster, Bristol, BS3 5LJ, 0117 9669869, *Mobile:* 07977 393397, *Water:* Boat, Shore and Competitions in the Bristol Channel and South West. Affiliated to B.C.F.S.A. and N.F.S.A. *Species:* All species. *Charges:* Adult £20 plus £2 joining fee. Juniors £6. OAP £6 per year.

BURNHAM-ON-SEA
Burnham on Sea Boat Owners S.A.A.
Contact: Mr Simon Stroud, 4 Ham Lane, Burnham-on-Sea, TA8 1QA, 01278 794573, *Water:* Up tide fishing. *Species:* Conger, Skate, Dogfish, Flounder. *Permits:* Jetty permits, annual charge £10. Available fron Sedgemoor District Council. *Charges:* Car and trailer parking £6 for 12 hours. *Season:* All year.
Kelly's Hero
Contact: Dave Saunders, 01278 785000, *Mobile:* 07970 642354,
Three B's Sea Angling Society
Contact: NFSA Head Office: 01364 644643,

CLEVEDON
Clevedon Pier S.A.C.
Contact: Paul Holliday, *Mobile:* 07986 855368, *Water:* Shore fishing from Portishead to Kingston Seymour. *Species:* Regular meetings, matches twice monthly at weekends plus one Wednesday match per month. New members, adult and junior welcome. Please contact Paul on the number above.

DULVERTON
Dulverton & District Sea Angling Society
Contact: L A Mace (Sec), Mounsey Farm, Dulverton, TA22 9QE, 01398 323718, *Water:* 40 members, junior and senior's welcome. Boat and shore fishing competitions once a month. Fishing both coasts, beginners welcome. *Charges:* £6 Senior / £3 Junior.

MINEHEAD
Alykat Charters and Images
Contact: Dave Roberts, 102 Periton Lane, Minehead, TA24 8DZ, 01643 703892, *Mobile:* 07764 150648, *Water:* Bristol Channel
Bishops Lydeard S.A.C.
Contact: Allen Thompson, 24 Boobery, Sampford Peverall, Tiverton, EX16 7BS, 01884 821067, *Mobile:* 07970 108577, *Water:* Beach casting, boat trips - Bristol channel. *Charges:* Annual membership.
Brunel S.A.C.
Contact: Keith Reed, 27 St Michaels Avenue, Clevedon, BS21 6LL, 01275 872101, *Water:* General deep sea angling. *Season:* Meetings at village hall in Coalpit Heath.
Fulmar
Contact: Steve Pilbrow, 25 Marley Close, Minehead, TA24 6DS, 01643 706627, *Mobile:* 07836 350741, *Water:* 28ft vessel, licensed for 9 people. Charter, beginners welcome. Tackle available. *Species:* Deep sea fishing on reefs and wrecks. Conger, Cod, Whiting, Tope, Bull huss, Pollock, Mackerel, Dogfish and many more. Seasonal fish. *Charges:* Boat charters and individuals. *Season:* All year round from Minehead harbour.
Minehead & District Sea Angling Club
Contact: Steve Pilbrow, 25 Marley Close, Minehead, TA24 6DS, 01643 706627, *Mobile:* 07836 350741, *Water:* Established 1950. Membership open to all adults and juniors. Monthly boat fishing competitions and some shore fishing. Tuition given, beginners and infirm welcome. *Species:* Conger, dogfish, Tope, Cod, Whiting, Huss, Rays, Whiting Smooth Hound and many more. *Charges:* Joining fee: £15 Adults and £10 OAP's/Juniors. *Season:* All year round.
Taunton Sea Angling Club
Contact: Bob Bugg, 8 Leigh Road, Taunton, TA2 8HQ, 01823 335342, *Water:* North Somerset Coast.

Colin's — 258 Milton Road, Weston Super Mare
The only Tackle Shop in Weston worth a visit
FREE PARKING
Friendly, Professional advice given freely
Sea & Freshwater Bait always in stock
Late night Friday until 6.30pm
Closed Wednesdays
Tel: 01934 644296

SOMERSET

Tor Sea Angling Club
Contact: Bob Musgrave, 18 Mildred Road, Walton, Nr Street, BA16 9QR, 01458 442957, *Water:* Boat / shore fishing. *Season:* Meet 3rd Monday each month, 8pm at Globe Inn, Summerton.
West Coast Tackle
Contact: Steve, The Quay, Minehead, TA24 5UL, 01643 705745, *Water:* Choice of 9 charters. Trips arranged for individual or parties.

WATCHET
Scooby Doo Too
Contact: Stephen Yeandle, 01984 631310, *Mobile:* 07778 750939, *Water:* 07778 750939 (boat)

WELLINGTON
Blackdown Sea Angling Club
Contact: Andy Fudge, 11 Parklands Road, Wellington, TA21 8RS, 01823 665320, *Water:* Monthly meetings 1st Tuesday of the month, at the Dolphin Inn, Wellington - 8pm onwards. *Species:* Fishing from shore and boat (mainly Bristol Channel). Monthly competitions, plus open competitions. *Permits:* New members welcome, please contact Andy or come to our meetings. *Charges:* £6 p/a membership, £3 juniors and OAP's.

WELLS
Wells & District Sea Angling Club
Contact: NFSA Head Office: 01364 644643,

WESTON-SUPER-MARE
Birnbeck Breakaways S.A.C.
Contact: Matt Bishop, 125 Berbena Way, 78 Locking Road, Weston - Super -Mare, BS22 4RW, 01934 513422, *Mobile:* 07717 882567, *Water:* Beach casting. *Season:* All year.
Weston Outcasts S.A.C.
Contact: Steve Moore, Hill View, Stoke Street, Rodney Stoke, Cheddar, BS27 3UD, 01749 870712, *Mobile:* 07977 228133, *Water:* Meeting monthly at the Bridge Inn, Yatton, 2nd thursday of the month - 8pm. Primarily shore angling, with regular competitions and two open matches fishing Bristol channel. *Permits:* Adults and juniors welcome, please contact Steve or come to our meetings.
Weston-Super-Mare Sea Angling Association
Contact: NFSA Head Office: 01364 644643,

YEOVIL
Royal British Legion (Yeovil) Sea Angling Club
Contact: NFSA Head Office: 01364 644643,
Three Counties Sea Angling Association
Contact: NFSA Head Office: 01364 644643,
Yeovil & District Sea Angling Club
Contact: NFSA Head Office: 01364 644643,

Perfect peace as the sun sets. Pic - Wayne Thomas

SOMERSET

Get Hooked on the Web

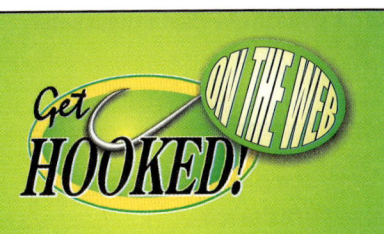

Advertise your accommodation online in the 'where to stay' section of

www.gethooked.co.uk

3 pictures, 150 words, e-mail and website links

ONLY £60 PER YEAR*

*exc VAT

TEL: 01271 860183 or
E-MAIL: mandi@gethooked.co.uk

TAN HOUSE Farm Lake

Private Coarse Fishing

Roach, Perch, Bream, Tench, Rudd & Carp

THE CARAVAN CLUB

Day Tickets Only - £3 per rod, £5 - 2 rods. Children/OAP's £2

Self Catering Cottage and 5 Unit Touring Caravan Site adjacent to lake

Tan House Farm, Yate, Bristol BS37 7QL
Telephone: 01454 228280
www.daltonsholiday.com

'DIAMOND FARM'

CARAVAN AND CAMPING PARK
Weston Rd, Brean, Somerset TA8 2RL

Riverside site ideally situated for a quiet family holiday only 5 minutes away from 7 miles of sandy beach

Facilities include showers, electric hook up, play area, shop, cafe & laundry.

Fishing on the River Axe on site
Bungalow also for hire

SEND S.A.E. OR PHONE FOR MORE DETAILS

Tel: 01278 751041/751263
www.diamondfarm.co.uk

Bullock Farm & Fishing Lakes

Two self-catering 17th century barn-conversion holiday cottages in award-winning village. Each sleeps 4/5 with free fishing. Regret no pets, no smoking.

5 heavily stocked lakes - specimen carp record 27.5lbs. Open dawn to dusk. Regularly featured in national angling press, *come and see why!*

Tel: 01934 835020
Web: www.bullockfarm.co.uk
E-mail: info@bullockfarm.co.uk
Kingston Seymour, North Somerset, BS21 6XA

SELF-CATERING

Laburnum House Lodge Hotel

Superb Facilities for Fishermen and Families - all year round

The banks of the Nationally famous River Huntspill are situated a mere 100 yards from the Hotel; a rich and diverse waterway teeming with a variety of freshwater fish.

Superb Restaurant, Indoor Heated Pool, Tennis Court, Clay Pigeon Shooting, Sauna and Jacuzzi, Skittle Alley, Darts & Pool, Walks through "Scenic Somerset"!
Water Skiing or Jet Skiing within 5 minute's drive
Nature reserve within 500 yards of premises.

Phone us now for a superb angling break
01278 - 781830

Email laburnumhh@aol.com   www.laburnumhh.co.uk
Sloway Lane, West Huntspill, Highbridge, Somerset. TA9 3RJ

WHERE TO STAY

Game Fishing Contacts

For the Salmon & Trout Association

S&TA has the influence to change Government policy, legislation, and management practices to protect and improve the water environment. Stay informed and take action. Join Today and make your voice heard where it matters. Join the fight for the future of game angling and the environment

Cornwall Branch
Mr A G Hawken
Tel: 01208 75513
Email: alan@aghawken.freeserve.co.uk

North Devon Branch
Lt Col J D V Michie
Tel: 01837 87115
Email: duncmcnen@aol.com

South & East Devon & Tamar Branch
Mr C Hall
Tel: 01837 840420
Email: hall@skaigh.freeserve.co.uk

Somerset Branch
Mrs S Pizii
Tel: 01460 281370
Email: pizii@supanet.com

North Wiltshire & South Gloucester
Mr R Moore
Tel: 01793 610437
Email: bmoore@baxglobal.com

Bristol & West Branch
Mr J S Tennant
Tel: 01278 683621

Hampshire Branch
Mr E P Morgan
Tel: 01730 263843

North Wilts & South Gloucester Branch
Mr R Moore
Tel: 01793 610437
Email: bmoore@baxglobal.com

West Sussex Branch
Mr B Burbidge
Tel: 01903 873878
Email:blackwaterob@gonefishing.ie

Wessex Branch
Mr B Ricketts
Tel: 01985 850884
Email: barry.rickets@btinternet.com

For further S&TA information
Tel. 0207 283 5838
Email: hq@salmon-trout.org
Website: www.salmon-trout.org

Small Spurwing

The Wheelyboat Trust

The Wheelyboat Trust has been operating since 1985 and used to be known as the Handicapped Anglers Trust. Its Wheelyboat has probably been the single most important innovation to help disabled anglers get on the water and fish.

Reservoirs, lakes and ponds are, by their nature, pretty inaccessible to wheelchair users and others with mobility problems: the banks are often steep and unmade and where there is access it may be limited and offer little opportunity to fish the water effectively. Traditional boats are difficult to get into and once on board the angler is totally reliant on a boat partner.

Wheelyboats overcome all these difficulties – they make the entire water accessible, are simplicity itself to board and the flat deck provides access throughout thus giving the angler the dignity of their own independence. In short, Wheelyboats enable disabled anglers to fish on equal terms with their able-bodied counterparts.

The Trust's 100th Wheelyboat was built in January 2005. The original design has been superseded by a new model, the Mk II. Whereas the Mk I has a flat bottom like a punt, the Mk II has a tridhedral hull and drifts and steers like a traditional boat. Both models are extremely stable and virtually unsinkable but the Mk II is a more substantial craft and is better suited to larger, more open waters. It is much better looking, too.

The Wheelyboat Trust is working closely with South West Lakes Trust to improve angling opportunities for disabled people in the region and is exploring possibilities to increase the numbers of Wheelyboats available. There was a new Mk II Wheelyboat on Wistlandpound Reservoir last year and a new Mk II should follow at Wimbleball Reservoir in the near future.

A new 20' Wheelyboat for angling and pleasure boating will be supplied to Roadford Reservoir in the spring. This is being funded by The Hedley Foundation, Lloyds TSB and the Environment Agency.

Wheelyboats are hired like any other angling boat except that fisheries tend to prefer 24 hours notice for a booking. For more information on the work of the Trust, contact the Director or visit the website.

THE WHEELYBOAT TRUST
(Formerly Handicapped Anglers Trust)
Reg charity 292216
Andy Beadsley, Director
North Lodge, Burton Park, Petworth
West Sussex, GU28 0JT.
Tel/fax 01798 342222,
e-mail: wheelyboats@tiscali.co.uk,
Web site: www.wheelyboats.org

Wheelyboat locations list for the region

# indicates Mk II Wheelyboat

Avon	Blagdon Lake Blagdon	Trout fishing	01275 332339
Cornwall	Stithians Reservoir Redruth	Trout fishing	01209 860301 www.swlakestrust.org.uk
Devon	Roadford Reservoir # Okehampton	Trout fishing	01409 211514 www.swlakestrust.org.uk.
Somerset	Clatworthy Reservoir Taunton	Trout fishing	01984 624658 www.wessexwater.co.uk/recreation
Somerset	Sutton Bingham Reservoir Yeovil	Trout & coarse fishing	01935 872389
Somerset	Wimbleball Reservoir Brompton Regis	Trout fishing	01398 371372 www.swlakestrust.org.uk
Wiltshire	Coate Water Swindon	Trout & coarse fishing	01793 522837, 01793 433165

BRISTOL WATER fisheries

Tuition
Anyone can learn to fly fish and it's not as hard as you may think. You don't need to have any tackle or expensive equipment to start with and Bristol Water supply tutors, helpers and experts to make sure that everyone can enjoy a day at the water.

Our Chief Instructor, Mike Gleave, is STANIC* qualified and a REFFIS* guide. These nationally recognized qualifications, and his long experience both of teaching and practising the art of flyfishing, make him the ideal person to introduce newcomers to the sport. As well as running the courses listed here, Mike is available for private instruction, and we can thoroughly recommend his services.

*Salmon and Trout Association National Instructor's Certificate; Register of Experienced Fly Fishing Instructors and Schools

Tagged Fish
Win a days boat fishing and the chance of free fishing in 2006!

Throughtout the season tagged fish are released in all of our Lakes. If you catch one of these fish we will give you a free days fishing for two persons in a boat. At the end of the season the names of the lucky captors will go into a draw for a free All Waters Season Permit for next season.

Casting Tuition
We offer two-hour casting tuition sessions for beginners and near beginners most Saturday mornings from 11am to 1pm during the fishing season. The cost is £10 per person; tackle is provided if needed; groups are kept small and advance booking is essential.

Fly Fishing Tuition
Once a month, normally on the last Saturday, we offer a fishing class with carefully supervised bank fishing. The four hour course also covers fly selection, entomology and safety and costs £20 per person; groups are small and advance booking is essential. Two half-price bank visits may be taken after completing this course. Boat Fishing instruction for one or two persons can also be organised. A four hour session costs £25 - the date and time to be arranged by mutual agreement with the instructor.

Beginners' Days
We offer beginners a chance to try fly fishing on Saturday afternoon sessions throughout the fishing season and some weekdays during August. Here they will learn the basics of fly casting and fishing, as well as have the chance to bank fish, and if available, boat fish during the session. Tackle can be supplied and the cost is just £10.00 per person. Minimum age for juniors is 12 years. Advance booking is essential as there will be limited places on each session.

Apply to Woodford Lodge.

Free Tuition with John Horsey
John Horsey, our local professional guide, has fished here for many years and is well qualified to give advice and help to newcomers and regulars to the fisheries. This advice is available to anglers **Free Of Charge!** On six occasions during the season John will be available at Chew Valley to give assistance from boat or bank. You can book him for an hours free tuition. Just ring

Woodford Lodge to reserve your place on one of the following dates: 5th April, 2nd May, 13th June, 18th July, 2nd Aug, 2nd Sept.

Competitons
Youth Competition.

Bristol Water host many competitions each season including local Club events and National & International contests. We also arrange various competitions for local anglers and teams.

There is an evening league held at Chew Valley throughout the spring & early summer. The ten event series is very popular and there are prizes in each round and for the overall champion. The best five results of each anglers are used to decide the winner of the league. after each event there is a complimentary buffet and drink.

The Bristol Water Teams Challenge is for teams of six local or regular BW customers. This is a fun event taking place from the boats on Chew Valley. There are no prizes, just the honour of having your teams name on the carved wood fish trophy. The event finishes with a free buffet for all the competitors.

Todays Flyfisher European Open.

2005 will again see the English Final of the TFEO Teams competition held at Chew Valley. Over six days 33 teams of six anglers will compete for places in the International Final. This year will also see the Grand Final of the TEFO Individual contest held at Chew Valley in August. For details of all the above events contact us on the telephone number below.

Enquiries and Bookings.

Phone or write to Bristol Water Fisheries, Woodford Lodge, Chew Stoke, Bristol. BS40 8XH. Telephone or fax: 01275 332339 for a free brochure, for all enquiries and for bookings.

Weekly update by web or direct via email.

Visit our web site for regular updates on the fishing at www.bristolwater.co.uk

If you would like the weekly fishing results and news to be emailed to you, email: bob.handford@bristolwater.co.uk to be added to the list.

Chew sunset. Pic - Nick Hart

TUITION

KEY
- **Name**
- Contact details
- Qualifications
- Area covered
- Equipment available
- Specialities

- Game
- Coarse
- Sea

There's a Coach Near You!

There are numerous opportunities to learn how to fish from trained, experienced angling coaches, either in one-to-one or group sessions.

In addition, every year there are hundreds of local "try it" events, junior matches and special angling courses throughout the region.

Generally coaches affiliated to angling clubs and associations operate without payment for the benefit of members. Others are linked to specific fisheries or tackle shops and are freelance. They usually levy a small fee for their services. Some coaches also act as angling guides at specific fisheries.

Further information is available from:

Coarse Angling
Glyn Williams
National Federation of Anglers
Halliday House
Egginton Junction
Derby DE65 6GU
Tel: 01283 734735
www.nfadirect.com

Roger Cannock
Newquay, Cornwall
Tel 01637 879330. Mobile 07961 916900
Email: rogercan2001@yahoo.co.uk
Professional Anglers Ass. coach since 2000
Available across the West Country.
All equipment available. Seat boxes, poles, beachcasters and fly rods. Tackle hire available. Rod Licences.

Coarse fishing techniques specialist.
Match angling techniques.
Guiding and tuition on the Counties festival venues.

Gary & Annie Champion
Tel 01872 863551. Mobile 07968 380716
Email: champsflyfish@btopenworld.com
APGAI/STANIC
Devon & Cornwall
Rods, Reels, Flys etc.

Enjoy your sport more by improving your techniques. Professional instruction in all aspects of fly fishing. Single and Double handed fly casting. Fresh water and salt.
Also fly dressing, traditional and modern methods.

Roy Buckingham
Arundell Arms, Lifton, Devon PL16 0AA
Tel 01566 784666 / Fax 01566 784494
Email: reservations@arundellarms.com
www.arundellarms.com
Full member APGAI. STANIC qualified instructor.
Lifton area of Devon. Based at The Arundell Arms Hotel.
Rods, Reels Flies etc.

Individual tuition and courses. Beginners and refresher courses, including Spey casting. All aspects of fly fishing.

David Pilkington
Arundell Arms, Lifton, Devon PL16 0AA
Tel 01566 784666 / Fax 01566 784494
Email: reservations@arundellarms.com
www.arundellarms.com
Full member APGAI. STANIC qualified instructor.
Lifton area of Devon. Based at The Arundell Arms Hotel.
Rods, Reels Flies etc.

Individual tuition and courses. Beginners and refresher courses, including Spey casting. All aspects of fly fishing.

Robert Jones
South Lodge, Courtlands Lane, Exmouth EX8 3NZ
Tel 07020 902090 Mobile 0797 0797 770
Email: robertjones@eclipse.co.uk
FRICS. EA Beginners Licence Agent.
The West Country centred on East Devon and rivers Otter, Axe, Teign, Exe, Avon and Camel.
All equipment including EA Licence.

Rivers. Sea Trout by fly at night. Guiding. Bass.
For age 10 and over.

Nick Hart Fly Fishing
The Cottage, Benshayes Farm, Bampton,
Nr Tiverton, Devon EX16 9LA
Tel 01398 331660. Mobile 07971 198559
Email: nick@hartflyfishing.co.uk
www.hartflyfishing.co.uk
APGAI, STANIC Level 2
North and South Devon, Somerset.

Experience fun, fresh air and fish! Learn to fly fish from scratch or improve your skills. Courses tailored to your requirements. Full colour brochure available.

TUITION

Pete Tyjas
Nick Hart Fly Fishing, The Cottage, Benshayes Farm, Bampton, Nr Tiverton, Devon EX16 9LA
Tel 01398 331660. Mobile 07780 530953
Email: pete@hartflyfishing.co.uk
www.hartflyfishing.co.uk
Level 2
North and South Devon, Somerset.
Equipment can be provided

Experienced River Fishing Guide. Novice anglers, one, two and three day courses. Learn to double haul.

Sea Angling
David Rowe
National Federation of Sea Anglers
Hamlyn House
Mardle Way
Buckfastleigh
Devon TQ11 ONS
Tel: 01364 644643

Game Angling
Malcolm Hanson
PO BOX 1270
Marlborough
Wiltshire SN8 4WD
Tel: 01627 511628

All Angling Styles
Professional Anglers Association
Trenchard
Lower Bromstead Road
Moreton
Newport
Shropshire TF10 9QD
Tel: 01952 691595
www.paa.uk.com

R.E.F.F.I.S Fly Fishing Instructors
Tel: 01305 848460
www.reffis.co.uk

John H Dawson
29 Bourchier Close, Bampton, Tiverton, EX16 9AG.
Tel 01398 331498   Mobile 07816 453474

STANIC - Salmon, Trout and Fly Dressing
Devon and Somerset.
All tackle (no clothing).

Fly fishing and casting tuition on rivers, stillwaters and sea. Guiding service. Fly dressing tuition. Fly fishing and fly dressing classes at East Devon College. Overseas fishing holidays.

Devon, Wilts & UK Fly Fishing School
Tom Hill. 25 Little Week Close, Dawlish EX7 0RA
Tel: 01626 866532   Email: tom.hfly@btinternet.com
GAIA / REFFIS
UK and Worldwide inc. Australia and New Zealand
All tackle available

Single and double Spey casting. Stillwater Tuition. Double haul and snake roll. Wild Brown Trout, Salmon and Sea Trout. One, two and three day courses available for beginners or advanced students. Please Note: Children to be accompanied by an adult.

Phil & Jo Hyde
37 Church Street, Paignton, Devon TQ3 3AJ
Tel 01803 409127. Mobile 0780 3080 284
Email: philthefish@eurobell.co.uk
NFSA, S&TA, PAA, JAGB Licenced
Level II Coaches/Instructors
Westcountry, Eire, Florida, USA
All angling equipment available (custom built rods).

Surf casting, marine spin, bait and fly casting for distance & accuracy. Stillwater and river trout fly fishing and fly tying. Beginners, families & children.

Colin Nice
17 Lawn Vista, Sidmouth, Devon EX10 9BY.
Tel 01395 577517   Mobile 07989 402650

Over 40 years experience in game fishing in the West Country, fly tying, sea fishing in East Devon
Throughout the West Country. Based East Devon.
All tackle for fly fishing and sea fishing (bait/lure/fly). Plus all equipment for fly tying.

Tying Brown & Sea Trout flies for rivers Axe, Otter, Exe and Sid. Saltwater fly fishing for Bass. Plugging.

Bryan Martin
South Molton, Devon.
Tel: 01769 550840   Mobile 07759 352194
Email: bryan@devonflyfishing.co.uk
www.devonflyfishing.co.uk
APGAI / STANIC
North Devon and West Somerset.
All tackle.

Salmon, Sea Trout and Trout fishing on rivers and stillwaters. Beginners and experienced. Saltwater fly fishing

KEY
Name
Contact details
Qualifications
Area covered
Equipment available
Specialities

— Game
— Coarse
— Sea

TUITION

APGAI *Bob Wellard APGAI*

The game angling Instructors association (GAIA) which is the parent body for all qualified angling instructors confer and administer all the examinations and qualifications of GAIC and APGAI. All the assessors for all GAIA qualifications are trained APGAI examiners.

APGAI can be attained in three separate disciplines: Trout & Sea Trout, Fly dressing and Salmon. Before instructors can be considered for APGAI assessment they will already need to possess a suitable intermediate qualification such as GAIC, STANIC, SGAIC or SANA in the discipline, for which they wish to be assessed.

All APGAI qualified instructors are fully insured and have gained certificates in Health & Safety, Child Protection and First Aid.

APGAI members are all committed to Continuing Professional Development and hold regular workshops for members to ensure that standards are retained and are continually improving.

APGAI members are in demand due to their technical skills and their ability to teach others. They hold regular casting clinics at all the major Game Fairs and also figure prominently at fly dressing demonstrations at these events.

KEY
- Name
- Contact details
- Qualifications
- Area covered
- Equipment available
- Specialities

Game / Coarse / Sea

Lechlade & Bushyleaze Trout Fisheries (Tim Small)
Lechlade, Gloucestershire GL7 3QQ
Tel: 01367 253266
Email: trout@star.co.uk
www.lechladetrout.co.uk
Team of three Instructors
On site at the fishery
Rods, reels, lines etc.
Stalking and beginners a speciality.
Please telephone to book.

Mike Gleave
Dresden, 7 Dundry Lane, Dundry, N, Somerset BS40 8JH
Tel 01275 332339 / 01275 472403
www.bristolwater.co.uk
STANIC & REFFIS
Bristol & the South West, Bristol Water Fisheries.
All Tackle, not clothing.

Stillwater techniques. Fly Tying. Guiding from boat and bank at Blagdon and Chew.

Tuition and Guiding with the REFFIS network in the Westcountry

Simon Cooper	02073 598818
Mike Gleave	01275 472403
Tom Hill	01626 866532
Tony King	01305 789560
Sally Pizii	01823 480710
Roddy Rae	01837 54731
Richard Slocock	01305 848460
Simon Ward	01489 579295
Jim Williams	01666 822905

REFFIS   www.reffis.co.uk

Roy Buckland
8 Millington Drive, Trowbridge BA14 9EU
Tel 01225 760465. Mobile 07967 558772
Email: roy@buckland-1.freeserve.co.uk
STANIC Trout.
West Wiltshire and the Chew Valley
Rods, reels, lines etc.

Beginners. Roll casting. Double hauling

The Total Fly Fishing Company Ltd
David Griffiths, James Mills & John Hotchkiss
Tel 01747 871856
Email: d.griffiths@freenet.co.uk   www.totalflyfishing.co.uk
APGAI/STANIC Trout, Salmon, Sea Trout.
Exclusive private lake in Wiltshire. Chalk Streams.
All tackle available

The Total Experience for:
Expert Casting Tuition (APGAI/GAIA)
Unforgettable escorted trips - U.K. and abroad
Bespoke Corporate days

SECTAS For the Kids

Tony Savage

As a teacher in a secondary school in Cornwall I was approached 4 years ago to run an activities day event, being a keen angler I agreed to take 20 pupils fishing one day and another 20 the next. Extra staff were drafted in to help and a lake was booked. It soon became apparent from looking at the list of names that a good few of the kids were the lively ones to say the least, the naughty ones.

The day arrived and the pupils were deposited in the car park by their parents and they made their way to the lake. Despite the assorted array of angling equipment, mainly sea angling with 15 to 20 lb line, the two-day event was a huge success all the kids were brilliant and the touch fuse was lit.

I decided that it would be a great idea to set up an angling club to cater for all children in South East Cornwall, that was the easy part. A coaching course was called for, the NFA contacted and the course completed, a club name was decided upon, a child protection policy written the clubs aims outlined and then the important bit, funding.

We, being a committee that was made up of friends who all expressed an interest, decided that as the area we live in is designated an area of social depravation all the kids should have good quality tackle to use, £2,500 was raised and tackle was bought over a period of 12 months. Some of the major tackle manufacturers were contacted and this resulted in one donating 2 poles to the club, fantastic, others donated bait boxes and end tackle. Some however refused outright, talk about biting off the hand that feeds you.

With all the tackle acquired I discovered my car was not big enough to carry it all so we decided to purchase club transport.

We collected £1000 from various sponsors to obtain a vehicle and with a little extra from my pocket we purchased a Land Rover. We decided upon a Land Rover as some of the fisheries have tracks to get to the waters edge, easy to dump the mountains of tackle, and after fishing in the wet all the mud can get hosed out, simple.

So the fishing club got started and SECTAS, South East Cornwall Taught Angling Society, was formed to promote social inclusion and to get the kids away from drugs and anti social behaviour. With all the tackle transported to the lakeside, the fishing began. I thought about teaching the kids all about the basics, rod set up, poles rigs etc but all they wanted to do was fish. Luckily most had casting experience albeit beach fishing and knew how to cast for miles. Still within minutes they were fishing. A lot of my own tackle was used in the early days but to see the look on a 13 year old as you show him how to use a pole at 14.5m is fantastic. The only drawback is that now my pole has more electricians tape on it than carbon.

The approach I take is very laid back and relaxed, I let the kids' enthusiasm set the pace for the session and I always endeavour to get the kids catching fish. We talk about everything and anything, fishing to football.

THE GET HOOKED GUIDE

I see fishing as an escape for some of the kids who come from troubled home lives and something they can share with their friends and families. Others are just keen and want to improve. I have some kids who will not listen, who know best and who's dad is a better fisherman than I will ever be but these are the kids traits and the aim of the club is not to change the kids into perfect people but to introduce them to fishing and nurture their interest.

I have only ever had one kid fall in, that was on a school trip and no harm was done, he actually liked being the centre of attention. I have had another kid who's first fish was a 3 lb Tench, I have sat and watched one of the clubs whips glide gracefully across a lake, attached to a 6lb Carp, and sat and helped two girls count their afternoon haul of 75 small silver fish. The memories that I have gained and that the kids hopefully will remember as they grow older are irreplaceable and priceless.

I generally take 4 kids fishing at a time, so they all benefit from individual tuition and gain something from the session. They all have their individual goals. SECTAS has never turned a kid away from a days fishing and regularly get enquires for taster sessions to see if kids wish to take up angling.

So what for the future? I work full time as does my wife so time is precious, and as the only coach I feel that to take on someone and train them as a coach would be good to allow the kids even more time fishing and someone else to talk to apart from me. Tom Pickering has agreed to be the clubs patron so to get him down for a day would be great, as would any other recognised anglers.

The ultimate dream is for the club to own a lake; the kids can manage it and the surrounding area and involve other kids not so fortunate, the local probation service has expressed an interest. An outdoor education centre with angling as the main activity. I have recently been given a boat that needs a lot of work but upon its completion I may take members sea or estuary fishing.

We have been going for only 18 months and the possibilities for the future are limitless but as a not for profit club we rely on other peoples generosity, both monetary and with equipment. We have a wish list.

The people I would like to thank are too many to list but I must thank my wife Anna for her patience and support.

www.sectas.netfirms.com

20th to 29th August 2005

Sponsored by Royal Bank of Scotland, Environment Agency and Sportsmatch, National Fishing Week 2005 seeks to attract up to 200,000 first time or 'lapsed' anglers to join Britain's 4 million regular anglers in a 'Celebration of Angling".

It is hoped that there will be many events that will provide expert tuition by approved coaches. Many venues will offer easy access from the road network and public transport. In addition, it is hoped to encourage venues that are able to accommodate access for people with disabilities.

To find out where the nearest National Fishing Week event is to you, use the search facilities on the website at www.nationalfishingweek.co.uk, type in your postcode and check for details.

Safe Sea Fishing from the Shore

Essential advice for anglers

Wayne Thomas

The diverse South West shore line has a wealth of opportunities to be enjoyed by the angler. Sadly the coastline has also been the location for several angling related tragedies over recent years. The sea can give great pleasure but can be cruel and unforgiving if not treated with due respect.

Plan

The vast majority of accidents that occur would have been avoided if those involved had been fully aware of the dangers they faced and taken avoiding action. An awareness of tidal state, weather conditions and local topography are essential if planning a trip to the coast.

If visiting an area for the first time try to obtain information from tourist information centres, local fishing tackle shops or local angling clubs. Purchase a tide-table that covers the region you intend to fish. Check the weather forecast and consider how this is likely to affect the venue you plan to visit. Open coast venues can be extremely dangerous when strong winds cause rough seas. Remember that low pressure systems far out in the Atlantic can also cause large ground swells to roll inshore. The North Cornish coast is particularly prone to these swells that have swept many an angler from a position high above the water.

Many rock marks used by anglers involve a steep descent down cliffs on tracks more suited to mountain goats. Remember that what is easily negotiated during dry weather becomes treacherous after rain when each rock feels like it has been coated with grease.

Always study a tide table and ensure that you can escape from the mark you intend to fish. Many visitors to the seashore are cut off by the rising tide each year. It is also important to be aware of the size of the tide as spring tides will come far higher up the shoreline than neap tides.

Be aware of the dangers posed by soft mud found in many estuaries that can trap the unwary or hamper retreat from a flooding tide. Remember that the Bristol Channel has one of the highest tidal rise and falls anywhere in the world which results in some awesome tidal flows.

Be Prepared

Having planned where to go taking into consideration tide, weather and geographical nature you will need to ensure you are dressed appropriately. When fishing from rocks stout footwear with a good grip is essential. When fishing adjacent to deep water a flotation suit is a wise investment which will improve your chances of survival if you do fall into the water and will also ensure you remain warm in even the coldest conditions.

Self inflating buoyancy aids are also a wise precaution especially when wading.

During hot weather drink plenty to avoid dehydration and during cold weather take a hot drink in a flask. If it is sunny apply sun cream to exposed skin and wear a hat.

A mobile phone is a useful tool which may enable you to summon help in an emergency. Try to avoid fishing alone. If you do, ensure that someone knows where you have gone and your expected time of return.

A small first aid kit packed into the rucksack can prove beneficial.

Ensure that you have planned how to land the fish you hook. A long handled gaff or landing net will enable fish to be successfully landed without going too near the water line. In some instances a drop net will be required.

A rope with a suitable floating ring that can be thrown to someone in the water is well worth carrying.

Be Aware

Be constantly aware of the weather conditions and the state of the tide. Always keep a close eye on the sea, do not turn your back as that freak wave could surge in at any time.

The most vulnerable time for many anglers is

THE GET HOOKED GUIDE

when attempting to land a big fish. At this time it is easy to get too close to the waters edge with adrenalin surging through the veins risks are taken. Remember no fish however big is worth loss of life.

Whilst fishing be aware of the presence of others particularly when casting and ensure that you have a shock leader to avoid crack offs that can result in heavy leads travelling at speed in any direction.

Safety is a broad topic and I could broaden this article to cover other risks such as hooks, sharp knifes and dangerous fish but for now I will summarise:-

- Be aware of the hazards and risks.
- Plan your trip taking into account weather, tide and topography.
- Be prepared with the right clothing and equipment.
- Take precautions in case things go wrong.
- Remember! At best an Accident will spoil a days fishing at worst your life!
- Do not become one of next year's grim statistics.

Get HOOKED! ON THE WEB

Advertise your fishery online in the 'featured fishery' section of
www.gethooked.co.uk

3 pictures, 150 words, e-mail and website links

ONLY £60 PER YEAR*
*exc VAT

TEL: 01271 860183 or
E-MAIL: mandi@gethooked.co.uk

Fern enjoying an afternoon boat fishing off Exmouth

WILTSHIRE
and Gloucestershire

WILTSHIRE

- RIVER FISHING
- STILLWATER COARSE
- STILLWATER TROUT
- SEA FISHING
- WHERE TO STAY

WILTSHIRE ROAD DIRECTIONS

Wiltshire Game Road Directions

151. Avon Springs
Please phone 01980 653557 or 07774 801401 for road directions.

152. Lechlade & Bushyleaze Trout Fisheries
GLOUCESTERSHIRE Lechlade and Bushyleaze Trout Fisheries lie near the headwaters of the River Thames, half-a-mile east of the town of Lechlade. They are clearly signposted on the A361 Swindon to Burford road. Within easy travelling distance of Oxford, Birmingham and Bristol, and only 1 1/2 hours from London, the fisheries are a short drive from either the M4 or the M40. Tel: 01367 253266.

153. Manningford Trout Fishery
The Fishery is 2 miles north of Upavon on the A345. Phone 01980 630033 for more details.

154. Upavon Farm Fishing
From centre of Upavon take the Salisbury road A345 & access to River is on the left within walking distance from village pub. Tel: 01980 630008 or Mob: 07770 922544.

Wiltshire Coarse Road Directions

155. Airsprung Angling Association
Please contact local Tackle Shops or Tel: 01225 862683.

156. Brokerswood Country Park
Please telephone 01373 822238.

157. Green Hill Farm
Travel from Salisbury on the A36 road to Southampton, after about 10 miles east out of Salisbury, take the B3079, signposted Landford. About 1 mile along road is Landford Bakery on right, then at the next crossroads turn left, a brown sign indicates the camp site and we are about 400 yards on the right hand side at the foot of a small hill.

158. Lakeside Rendezvous
Easily accessed off the A342 & is approximately a 20 minute drive from Chippenham exit off the M4 motorway. We are 1 1/2 hours from London. Nearest train station is Chippenham with direct links to Bristol & London. Tel: 01380 725447.

159. Longleat & Shearwater
From Warminster take 362 towards Frome, follow signs to Longleat. Further information from the bailiff, Nick Robbins on 01985 844496 or 07889 625999.

160. Rood Ashton Lake
Leave A350 heading through West Ashton Village. Take next left signed Rood Ashton, continue past East Town Farm, turn left. Home Farm is 0.5 mile on left, you will see a sign. Tel: 01380 870272.

161. Silverlands Lake
From M4 Junction 17 take the A350 south (Chippenham bypass) continue for approx. 8 miles, still on the A350, you will be on the Laycock bypass. After passing a turn on the left for Lacock and on right for Whitehall Garden Centre, take the next turn on the right Folly Lane West, continue along this lane, under railway bridge to the no through road where you will see the sign for Wick Farm. Tel: 01249 730244.

162. Tucking Mill
Wessex Water fisheries. Tel: 0845 600 4 600.

163. Waldens Farm Fishery
Off the A36 Salisbury to Southampton road near Whaddon. Phone for futher details 01722 710480 or 07766 451123.

164. Witherington Farm Lakes
2 miles out of Salisbury on A36 fork right as dual carriageway starts, then first right again after about 0.5 miles. Follow signs for Downton and Stanlynch. Witherington Farm is about 3 miles on the right. Tel: 01722 710021 / 710088.

Only advertisers are located on this map.

Wiltshire River Fishing

AVON HAMPSHIRE
For detailed description of the Avon, see under Hampshire river fishing

Calne Angling Association
Contact: Miss J M Knowler, 123a London Road, Calne, 01249 812003, *Water:* River Avon, River Marden and a lake. *Species:* Barbel to 8lb, Pike to 8lb, Carp to 10lb, Bream to 6lb, Rudd to 8oz, Roach to 2.5lb; Wild Carp in lake. *Permits:* T.K.Tackle. *Charges:* Please enquire at T.K.Tackle. *Season:* River: June - March, Lake: open all year. *Methods:* No restrictions.

Salisbury & District Angling Club
Contact: Rick Polden - Secretary, 29a Castle Street, Salisbury, SP1 1TT, 01722 321164, *Water:* Several Stretches on River Avon at Little Durnford (premium Trout fishery & Grayling), Amesbury, Ratfyn Farm & Countess Water. Also fishing on Dorset Stour (mixed fishery), River Wylye (premium Trout & Grayling), Nadder (Trout & Coarse), Bourne & Ratfyn Lake at Amesbury. Premier stocked chalkstream fishing. *Species:* All species Coarse and Game. Carp to 30lbs plus, Tench to 5lbs, Roach to 2.5lbs, Chub to 6lbs plus, Barbel to 10lbs plus, Pike to 20lbs plus. *Permits:* Enquire via Secretary at sdacsec@onetel.com or club address. Day ticket available for certain waters. *Charges:* Membership £62. Game membership £130. More details from the secretary. New members £15 registration on joining. *Season:* Lakes: 1st June - 31st March. Rivers: 16th June - 14th March - Coarse. 15th April - 15th October - Trout. 1st February - 30th September - Salmon. *Methods:* As per rules for each fishery.

Services Dry Fly Fishing Association
Contact: Major (Retd) CD Taylor - Hon Secretary, c/o G2 Sy,HQ 43 (Wessex) Brigade, Picton Barracks, Bulford Camp, Salisbury, SP4 9NY, 01980 672161, *Water:* 7 miles on River Avon from Bulford upstream to Fifield. *Species:* Brown Trout & Grayling. *Permits:* Fishing Restricted to Serving & Retired members of the Armed Forces and MOD civilians. for membership details apply to Secretary. *Charges:* On application. *Season:* 24 April - 14 October. Grayling until 31st December. *Methods:* Only upstream fishing permitted, dry fly exclusively during May & dry fly/nymph thereafter.

Wroughton Angling Club
Contact: Mr T.L.Moulton, 70 Perry's Lane, Wroughton, Swindon, SN4 9AP, 01793 813155, *Water:* 1.25 miles Rivers Avon and Marden at Chippenham, Reservoir at Wroughton. *Species:* Roach, Perch, Bream, Pike, Barbel, Chub, Carp, Tench. *Permits:* Mr M. Shayler, 20 Saville Crescent, Wroughton, Swindon, Wilts, Tel: 01793 637313. *Charges:* £17 per season. No day tickets (2004 prices - may change in 2005). *Methods:* Restrictions - No Boilies, peanuts, particle baits, dog biscuits or nuts of any description.

AVON WILTSHIRE
See under BRISTOL AVON

The Hampshire Avon at Upavon, Wilts

This is a select chalk stream renowned for it's wild Brown Trout and Grayling fishing. We offer a 3/4 mile stretch which is open to both day and season ticket holders.

The river is ideally suited to a 8.5ft rod (max river width 40ft, min 20ft). Waist waders are advisable with depths between 18 inches and 3ft. Average fish are 1 to 1.5lb. Last season's largest fish was a 3lb plus brown.

Access to the river by car is no problem.

Season tickets are £500 and day tickets are £45 Grayling day ticket £20

BED & BREAKFAST AVAILABLE

Tel 01980 630008
Mobile: 07770 922 544
Email: fly@fishinglessons.co.uk

Avon Springs Fishing Lake (River)
Contact: BJ Bawden, Recreation Road, Durrington, Salisbury, SP4 8HH, 01980 653557, *Mobile:* 07774 801401, *Water:* 1 mile Wiltshire Avon at Durrington. Two Trout lakes, see entry under Stillwater Trout, Salisbury *Species:* Brown Trout and Grayling. *Charges:* £40 day ticket. River and Lake ticket £50. *Methods:* Fly only.

Upavon Farm
Contact: Peter C Prince, No 3, The Old Tractor Yard, Rushall, Near Pewsey, SN9 6EN, 01980 630008, *Mobile:* 07770 922544, *Water:* 0.75 miles on Hampshire Avon in Wiltshire. *Species:* Brown Trout, both stocked and Wild, up to 3lb average 1.5lb. Wild Grayling to 2lb average 1lb. *Permits:* Day, Season Permits. *Charges:* Day ticket £45, Grayling day rate £20. *Season:* Brown Trout commences 15th April, ends 30th September. Grayling fishing thereafter. *Methods:* Catch and release, barbless hooks excepting annual season ticket holders.

Wiltshire Fishery Association
Contact: Richard Archer (Hon Sec.), 01722 717990, *Water:* An association of riparian owners and fishing club representatives. The association covers the River Avon catchment above Salisbury and it's tributaries.

BRISTOL AVON
Malmesbury to Chippenham
Coarse fisheries predominate in this section, although Trout are stocked by fishing associations in some areas. Arguably one of the best fisheries in the country, this section

WILTSHIRE

RIVER FISHING

John Eadie's
Ultimate Tackle Dealer
Game, Coarse & Sea Fishing Supplies
Freshwater & Frozen Baits
Local Permits
Open 9-5 Monday to Saturday
20 Catherine St, Salisbury - Tel: 01722 328535
5B Union St, Andover - Tel: 01264 351469

Airsprung Angling Association
NFA registered Coarse Fishery
for bookings call
Ian Stainer 01225 862683
Roger Green 01225 765009

contains a wide range of specimen fish. Local records include: Roach 3lb 2oz, Perch 3lb 3oz, Tench 8lb 5 1/2oz, Bream 8lb 8oz, Dace 1lb 2oz, Chub 7lb 10oz, Carp 20lb 8 1/4oz and Pike 33lb 3oz. Also many Barbel to 12lb have been reported.

Airsprung Angling Association (Barton Farm)
Contact: Ian Stainer, 61 Poulton, Bradford-on-Avon, BA15 1EA, 01225 862683, *Water:* Barton Farm. From Bradford Upon Avon to Avoncliff. *Species:* Tench, Bream, Chub, Rudd, Perch, Pike. *Permits:* Wiltshire Angling, 01225 763835; West Tackle, Trowbridge, 01225 75547. Trowbridge Road Post Office, Bradford-upon Avon.Also from Ian Stainer. *Charges:* £3 per day. Special rates for club bookings. *Season:* Subject to normal close season. *Methods:* No night fishing. No fishing in pegged areas on match days. No radios. No fishing within 25 metres of locks etc. No bloodworm or joker. Beware of overhead cables.

Airsprung Angling Association (Bristol Avon)
Contact: Ian Stainer, 61 Poulton, Bradford-on-Avon, BA15 1EA, 01225 862683, *Water:* See also entry under Kennet & Avon Canal. Bristol Avon at Bradford on Avon, Pondfields, Staverton Meadows, and between Holt and Melksham. *Species:* Carp, Pike, Bream, Chub, Roach, Rudd, Dace, Tench, Perch, etc. *Permits:* Wiltshire Angling, 01225 763835; West Tackle, Trowbridge, 01225 755472. Haines Angling, Frome. Trowbridge Road Post Office, Bradford-upon Avon. Melksham Angling Centre, Melksham. *Charges:* On application. *Season:* Subject to normal close season. *Methods:* Details from Association.

Avon Angling Club (Bristol Avon)
Contact: R.P. Edwards, 56 Addison Road, Melksham, SN12 8DR, 01225 705036, *Water:* 4 miles of Bristol Avon. See also entry under Kennet and Avon Canal. *Species:* Roach, Bream, Tench, Chub, Barbel, Perch, Pike, Eels. *Permits:* Robbs Tackle, Chippenham; Wiltshire Angling, Trowbridge or call 01225 705036. *Charges:* Day ticket £3. Full Licence £14. Junior/OAP Licence £5. *Season:* Current EA Byelaws apply. *Methods:* No blood worm or joker to be used.

Chippenham Angling Club
Contact: Mr Duffield, 95 Malmesbury Road, Chippenham, SN15 1PY, 01249 655575, *Water:* 8 miles on River Avon. Carp lakes at Corsham. *Species:* Barbel 15.5lb, Chub 5lb, Roach 2.5lb, Bream 10lb, Perch 4lb, Pike 33lb, Carp 20lb (all weights approximate). *Permits:* Premier Angling, Chippenham: 01249 659210. *Charges:* Please telephone for prices. *Season:* June 16th - March 14th. *Methods:* No boilies or keepnets on Carp lake.

Haydon Street Angling Society (Bristol Avon)
Contact: Mike Cottle, Silver Greys, 43 Dayhouse Lane, Badbury Wick, Chiseldon, 01793 644748, *Water:* Bristol Avon at Dauntsey, Dodford Farm. *Species:* Mixed including Chub, Barbel and Roach, Tench. *Permits:* Members only. No day tickets. *Charges:* Full membership £30. Family membership (Husband, wife & two chldren) £30. Concessions £10. *Season:* Subject to statutory close season on rivers.

Swindon Isis Angling Club (Bristol Avon)
Contact: Peter Gilbert, 31 Havelock St, Swindon, SN1 1SD, 01793 535396, *Water:* Two miles of the Bristol Avon at Sutton Benger near Chippenham. See also entry under Thames. *Species:* Bream 9lb 9oz, Perch 4lb, Tench 9lb, Barbel 14lb, Pike 28lb, Roach 2lb 7oz and usual species *Permits:* Tackle shops in Swindon, Chippenham, Cirencester and Calne. *Charges:* As per Thames entry. *Season:* From 16th June to 14th March. *Methods:* No bans.

KENNET AND AVON CANAL

There are some 58 kilometres of canal within the Bristol Avon catchment area which averages one metre in depth and thirteen metres in width. The Kennet & Avon Canal joins the River Avon at Bath with the River Kennet between Reading and Newbury. The canal was opened in 1810 to link the Severn Estuary with the Thames. The canal, now much restored, provides excellent fishing with Carp to 25lb, Tench to 5lb also Roach, Bream, Perch, Rudd, Pike and Gudgeon.

Airsprung Angling Association (Kennet & Avon)
Contact: Ian Stainer, 61 Poulton, Bradford-on-Avon, BA15 1EA, 01225 862683, *Water:* Two kilometres on Kennet and Avon Canal from Beehive Pub to Avoncliffe aquaduct at Bradford-on-Avon. Kings Arms Hilperton Road Bridge to Crossguns, Avoncliff. *Species:* Carp, Bream, Chub, Roach, Rudd, Dace, Tench, Perch, etc. *Permits:* Wiltshire Angling, 01225 763835; West Tackle, Trowbridge, 01225 755472. Haines Angling, Frome. Trowbridge Road Post Office, Bradford-upon Avon. Melksham Angling Centre, Melksham. *Charges:* Day ticket £2. Full licence

WILTSHIRE

Superb bag of Rainbows from Manningford

RIVER FISHING

Pewsey & District Angling Association
Contact: Jim Broomham, 85 Broad Fields, Pewsey, SN9 5DU, 01672 563690, *Water:* 4 Miles Kennet & Avon canal. Milkhouse Bridge (East) to Lady's Bridge (West). *Species:* Roach, Tench, Carp, Bream, Perch, Pike, Rudd and Chub. *Permits:* The Wharf, Pewsey (Day tickets only). *Charges:* Day tickets Senior £3 / Junior/OAP £2. £5 on bank. *Season:* No closed season. *Methods:* Rod and line.

NADDER

The River Nadder rises near Tisbury draining the escarpment of the South Wiltshire Downs and Kimmeridge Clay of the Wardour Vale. The River Wylye joins the Nadder near Wilton before entering the main River Avon at Salisbury.

The Nadder is well known as a mixed fishery of exceptional quality; there is a diverse array of resident species including Chub, Roach, Dace, Bream, Pike, Perch, Brown Trout and Salmon. Much of the fishing is controlled by estates and syndicates although two angling clubs offer some access to the river.

Compton Chamberlayne
Contact: Simon Cooper, Fishing Breaks, The Mill, Neatham Street, Nether Wallop, Stockbridge, SO20 8EW, 01264 781988, *Water:* Seven beats on part of the Compton Chamberlayne Estate. *Species:* Brown Trout. *Permits:* By phone or e-mail from Fishing Breaks. *Charges:* £95 per day plus VAT May 1 to May 13. £110 May 14 to June 19. £95 June 20 to September 20. *Season:* May to September. *Methods:* Dry fly & Nymph only.

Nine Mile Water
Contact: Simon Cooper, Fishing Breaks, The Mill, Neatham Street, Nether Wallop, Stockbridge, SO20 8EW, 01264 781988, *Water:* Seven beats on part of the Compton Chamberlayne Estate. *Species:* Brown Trout. *Permits:* By phone or e-mail from Fishing Breaks. *Charges:* £95 per day plus VAT May 1 to May 13. £110 May 14 to June 19. £95 June 20 to September 20. *Season:* May to September. *Methods:* Dry fly & Nymph only.

Tisbury Angling Club
Contact: Mr E.J.Stevens, Knapp Cottage, Fovant, Salisbury, SP3 5JW, 01722 714245, *Water:* 3 miles on River Nadder. 3.5 acre lake and 2.5 acre lake. *Species:* Roach, Chub, Dace, Pike, Bream, Perch, Carp, Brown Trout. *Permits:* £5 per day Guest tickets. *Charges:* Adult £4 joining fee and £24 per season. Juniors £7.50 per season. OAPs £12.50 per season. Seniors £5 per day (dawn to dusk) Juniors £3 per day (dawn to dusk). New members welcome. *Season:* 16th June to 14th March. *Methods:* General.

SEMINGTON BROOK

The Semington Brook is spring fed from Salisbury Plain and flows through a flat area to its confluence with the River Avon downstream of Melksham. In the upper reaches and in some of its tributaries Brown

price on application. *Season:* Open all year *Methods:* No night fishing, No fishing on match days in pegged areas. No radios etc. No fishing within 25 metres of locks etc. No bloodworm or joker; be aware of overhead cables !

Avon Angling Club (Kennet and Avon)
Contact: R.P. Edwards, 56 Addison Road, Melksham, SN12 8DR, 01225 705036, *Water:* 2.5 miles of Kennet and Avon Canal. See also entry under Bristol Avon. *Species:* Bream, Tench, Roach, Carp. *Permits:* Wiltshire Angling, Trowbridge; Robbs Tackle, Chippenham or call 01225 705036. *Charges:* Day ticket £3. Full licence £14. Junior/OAP licence £5. *Season:* All year.

Devizes A.A. (Kennet & Avon Canal)
Contact: T.W. Fell, 21 Cornwall Crescent, Devizes, SN10 5HG, 01380 725189, *Water:* 15 miles from Semington to Pewsey, also 6.5 acre lake. *Species:* Carp 15 - 23lb, Roach, Tench, Pike to 26lb, Bream. *Permits:* Angling Centre, Snuff St., Devizes, Wiltshire. Tel: 01380 722350. Local tackle shops in Devizes, Melksham, Trowbridge, Chippenham, Calne, Swindon. Wiltshire Angling: 01225-763835. *Charges:* Adult £20 per season. Junior £7.50. Day tickets £3.50 (not sold on the bank). 14 day ticket £8. Prices may change in 2005. *Season:* E.A. byelaws apply. *Methods:* Anglers must be in possession of current Environment Agency rod licence.

Marlborough & District A.A
Contact: Mr.M.Ellis, Failte, Elcot Close, Marlborough, SN8 2BB, 01672 512922, *Water:* Kennet & Avon Canal (12 miles approx). *Species:* Roach, Perch, Pike, Tench, Bream, Carp. *Permits:* Mr M Ellis, 'Failte', Elcot Close, Marlborough, Wilts, SN8 2BB. *Charges:* Full membership £30 plus £5 joining fee, Junior up to 16 £5, Ladies £5, O.A.P's £10. *Season:* Open all year. Membership from 1st Jan - 31st Dec. *Methods:* No live baiting, no bloodworm or joker.

189

WILTSHIRE

Trout predominate. Downstream of Bulkington coarse fish prevail with sizeable Bream, Chub, Roach, Dace and Perch.

STOUR
See description under Dorset, river fishing.

Stourhead (Western) Estate
Contact: Sonia Booth, Estate Office Gasper Mill, Stourton, Warminster, BA12 6PU, (01747) 840643, Water: 10 ponds and lakes, largest 10 acres, on the headwaters of the Stour. Species: Wild Brown Trout. Permits: Weekly permit £30. Charges: Season permit for fly fishing £100, no day tickets. Season: April to October - no time restrictions.

THAMES

Haydon Street Angling Society (Hannington)
Contact: Mike Cottle, Silver Greys, 43 Dayhouse Lane, Badbury Wick, Chiseldon, 01793 644748, Water: Hannington: a prime stretch of the upper Thames. Species: Mixed including Chub to 6lb and Barbel to 12lb. Permits: Members only. No day tickets. Charges: Full membership £30. Family membership (Husband, wife & two chldren) £30. Concessions £10. Season: Subject to statutory close season on rivers.

Haydon Street Angling Society (Ingelsham)
Contact: Mike Cottle, Silver Greys, 43 Dayhouse Lane, Badbury Wick, Chiseldon, 01793 644748, Water: Ingelsham: a prime stretch of the upper Thames. Species: Mixed including Chub, Bream and Roach. Permits: Members only. No day tickets. Charges: Full membership £30. Family membership (Husband, wife & two chldren) £30. Concessions £10. Season: Subject to statutory close season on rivers.

Swindon Isis Angling Club (Thames)
Contact: Peter Gilbert, 31 Havelock St, Swindon, SN1 1SD, 01793 535396, Water: 2 mile of river Thames at Water Eaton near Cricklade, Swindon. Species: Barbel 9lb, Chub 4.5lb, Roach 2lb, Bream 7lb, Perch 2lb. Permits: Tackle shops in Swindon, Chippenham, Cirencester and Calne. Charges: Club Permits: Senior £34.50. OAP and disabled £12. Juniors £8. The club permit contains two free day tickets and more day tickets can be obtained for £5 each; 1/2 year starts 1 November, £12 & £6 all others. Season: From 16th June to 14th March. Methods: No bans.

WYLYE

The River Wylye rises near Kingston Deverill and flows off chalk, draining the western reaches of Salisbury Plain. The river confluences with the River Nadder at Wilton near Salisbury, then joins the main River Avon which flows south to Christchurch.

This river is best described as a 'classic' chalk stream supporting predominantly Brown Trout; hence most fisheries here are managed for fly fishermen. The fishing is predominantly controlled by local syndicates and estates.

Roy Buckland with a bag of Blagdon opening day Rainbows to 5lb.

Langford Lakes (River Wylye)
Contact: Wiltshire Wildlife Trust, Duck Street, Steeple Langford, Salisbury, SP3 4NH, 01722 792011, Water: Wylye - half mile. Species: Brown Trout, Grayling. Charges: £30 Trout, £20 Grayling per rod. Season: April 15th - Oct 14th Trout season. Oct 15th - March 14th Grayling season. Methods: Full details at Fishery.

Sutton Veny Estate
Contact: Mr & Mrs A.Walker, Eastleigh Farm, Bishopstrow, Warminster, BA12 7BE, 01985 212325, Water: 4 miles on River Wylye. 2 miles of only wild Trout. Species: Brown Trout and Grayling. Charges: £50/day plus VAT (no beats), Season tickets upon request. Sutton Veny Fishing Syndicate - details on request. Season: 15th April - 15th October. Methods: Dry fly and upstream nymph only. Catch and release on two miles.

Wilton Fly Fishing Club
Contact: Mr A Simmons or Hon Sec, Keepers Cottage, Manor Farm Lane, Great Wishford, SP2 0PG, 01722 790231, Mobile: 07866 343593, Water: Over 6 miles of chalkstream on the river Wylye (including carriers). Species: Wild Brown Trout, fish of 2-3lb caught every season. Past record 7lb 2oz. Large head of Grayling to over 2lb 12oz. Permits: Season membership only via Secretary: Jeremy Waters, "Farleys Cottage", 25 Stockton, Warminster, Wiltshire. BA12 0SQ. jeremyg.waters@virgin. net Tel: (01985) 850411. Charges: Prices on application to secretary. Season: Trout 16th April to 15th October. Grayling 16th June to 14th March. Methods: Trout: Dry fly and upstream nymph only. Grayling: Dry fly and upstream nymph only in Trout season. Trotting also allowed from 15th October to 14th March. Barbless hooks preferred.

Wiltshire Stillwater Coarse

BRADFORD ON AVON
Rushy Lane Fishery
Contact: Mike or Val, South Wraxall, Bradford-on-avon, 01249 714558, *Mobile:* 07780 635333, *Water:* 5 lakes - 2 with specimen Carp to 35lb, plus mixed coarse lakes. *Species:* Carp to 35lb, Tench and Roach. *Permits:* By telephone only. *Charges:* On application. *Season:* Open all year. *Methods:* Dawn to dusk, no night fishing, no nets on specimen ponds, no boilies, barbless hooks only.

CALNE
Blackland Lakes
Contact: J.or B. Walden, Blackland Lakes Holiday & Leisure Centre, Stockley Lane, Calne, SN11 0NQ, 01249 813672, *Water:* One 1 acre, One 0.75 acre. *Species:* Carp to 33lb, Tench to 5lb, Roach to 4lb, Bream to 8lb, Perch to 4lb. *Permits:* Day tickets. *Charges:* 1 rod £9, extra rods £1, junior £5, 14 - 18yrs £6, extra rod £1. Night fishing 7pm - 9am £15 adult, £10 others. Juniors must be accompanied by an adult. *Season:* Open all year. *Methods:* Barbless hooks, no ground bait, no large fish or Bream in keepnets.

Bowood Lake
Contact: Estate Office, Bowood, Calne, SN11 0LZ, 01249 812102, *Water:* 6 acre lake. *Species:* Coarse. *Permits:* Available from the estate office. Season permits only - waiting list. *Charges:* Season only. £125 + VAT. Junior members £62.50 + VAT (under 16yrs) *Season:* June 2005 - March 2006. Dawn to dusk.

CHIPPENHAM
Chippenham Angling Club (Coarse Lake)
Contact: Mr Duffield, 95 Malmesbury Road, Chippenham, SN15 1PY, 01249 655575, *Water:* See entry under Avon. Carp Lake at Corsham. *Permits:* Members only, no day tickets

Ivy House Lakes & Fisheries
Contact: Jo, Ivyhouse Lakes, Grittenham, Chippenham, SN15 4JU, 01666 510368, *Mobile:* 07748 144778, *Water:* 1 Acre & 6 Acre lakes. *Species:* Carp, Bream, Roach, Tench, Chub, Perch. *Permits:* On the bank day tickets, no night fishing. *Charges:* Day tickets £5 per day (1 rod). £3 Ladies O.A.Ps etc. Match booking £5. *Season:* All year. *Methods:* Boilies & tiger nuts banned, ground bait in moderation. No fixed feeders.

Silverlands Lake
Contact: Mr & Mrs King, Wick Farm, Lacock, Chippenham, SN15 2LU, 01249 730244, *Mobile:* 07720 509377, *Water:* One spring fed 2.5 acre lake. *Species:* Carp, Tench, Bream, Pike. *Permits:* Only from the fishery. *Charges:* Day/Night tickets £5, Season tickets 12 months - £100 Adult, £65 1/2 year. £8 - 24 hour ticket. *Season:* Open all year. *Methods:* No nuts, dogs to be kept on a lead at all times.

Wyatts Lake
Contact: L. Beale, Wyatts Lake Farm, Westbrook, Bromham, Nr Chippenham, SN15 2EB, 01380 859651, *Water:* 2 acre lake

approx. *Species:* Mirror and Common Carp to 20lb. *Permits:* On site. *Charges:* £5 per person (unlimited rods). *Season:* Open all year 24 hours a day. Night fishing available. *Methods:* Good fishing practices required and expected.

DEVIZES
Devizes A.A. (Coarse Lake)
Contact: T.W. Fell, 21 Cornwall Crescent, Devizes, SN10 5HG, 01380 725189, *Water:* New 6.5 acre lake. Crookwood Lake well stocked. *Permits:* Angling Centre, Snuff St., Devizes, Wiltshire. Tel: 01380 722350. Local tackle shops in Devizes, Melksham, Trowbridge, Chippenham, Calne, Swindon. Wiltshire Angling: 01225-763835. *Charges:* Please phone for details. *Methods:* Anglers must be in possession of current Environment Agency rod licence.

Lakeside Rendezvous
Contact: Phil & Sarah Gleed, Devizes Road, Rowde, Nr. Devizes, SN10 2LX, 01380 725447, *Water:* 2 acre lake. *Species:* Carp - 29lb 4oz, Bream, Roach, Perch, Rudd, Tench. *Charges:* Day tickets not available individually. Hire of whole lake is possible and by prior arrangement, can fit up to 20 anglers - £90 per day. *Season:* No closed season. *Methods:* Barbless hooks, no nuts. Keepnets permitted in competition only. All nets etc. must be dipped.

MELKSHAM
Burbrooks Reservoir
Contact: A.J. Mortimer, 3 Talbot Close, Melksham, SN12 7JU, 01225 705062, *Mobile:* 07946 400707, *Water:* 0.75 acre Lake between Melksham & Calne, and Devizes and Chippenham in the village of Bromham (New Road). *Species:* Mirror, Common & Crucian Carp, Bream, Tench, Roach, Perch, Gudgeon, Chub. *Permits:* Please contact Melksham Angling Centre, Melksham House, Melksham: 01225 793546, or the Londis Shop in Bromham Village: 01380 850337. Calne TK Tackle: 01249 812003. Robs Tackle, Chippenham: 01249 659210. Wilts Angling, Trowbridge: 01225 763835. West Tackle, Trowbridge: 01225 755472. Spar Shop, Bath Road, Devizes: 01380 724483. *Charges:* £5 Adults. £3 Juniors and OAPs. *Season:* Open all year dawn to dusk. *Methods:* No night fishing, only one rod per person, no hooks above size 8.

Leach Pool
Contact: Leach Pool Farm, Norrington Lane, Boughton Giford, SN12 8LR, 01225 703615, *Mobile:* 07970 186589, *Water:* 1.25 acres. *Species:* Mirror and Common Carp (4 - 18lb). Tench. *Permits:* On site. *Charges:* £4.50 per rod. *Season:* Open all year dawn to dusk. *Methods:* Night fishing by arrangement only. No keepnets.

MERE
Gillingham & District A A (Turners Paddock)
Contact: Simon Hebditch (Hon. Secretary), 8 Maple Way, Gillingham, SP8 4RR, 01747 821218, *Mobile:* 07990 690613, *Water:* Turners Paddock at Stourhead Nr Mere (see also entry under river fishing Stour). *Species:* Tench 6lb, Bream 7lb, Carp 15lb, Roach 2lb, Rudd 2lb, Hybrids, Perch, Eels 6lb. *Permits:* Mr P Stone (Treasurer) The Timepiece, Newbury, Gillingham, Dorset, SP8 4HZ. Tel: 01747 823739. Mr J Candy, Todber Manor Fisheries Shop, Tel: 01258 820384. Mere Post Office, High Street,

WILTSHIRE

STILLWATER COARSE

WALDENS FARM FISHERY

Five lakes offering a variety of quality Coarse Fishing. Stocked with Pike, Perch, Golden Rudd, Carp, Roach, Barbel, Bream, Orfe, Crucians, Tench & Golden Tench

Plus purpose built Match Lake for Private and Club Hire

Contact: David & Jackie Wateridge
Telephone: 01722 710480
Mobile: 07766 451173

THE NFF
Walden GROUP

Walden Estate,
West Grimstead,
Salisbury,
Wiltshire SP5 3RJ

WITHERINGTON FARM FISHING

COARSE FISHING LAKES

Barn Moor & Selwood Lakes 1 & 2
2.5 acres. Both stocked with Tench, Bream, Chub, Roach, Golden Rudd, Perch, Common & Mirror Carp - CARP to 27lb in Lake 1

Cottage Lake 3
Bream to 7lb, Roach to 2.5lb, Tench to 3lb Carp to 16lb, small Crucians, Rudd & Dace - IDEAL FOR POLE & WAGGLER

MATCH LAKE
93 pegs designed for matchmen. 13 metres from bank to bank
Available for day ticket use

SITE FACILITIES INCLUDE: flush toilet, hot & cold snacks, drinks, bait and our NEW on-site Tackle Shop

Tackle Shop - TEL: 01722 710088

Toilet facilities for the disabled.
Most swims accessible to wheelchairs
COMFORTABLE FARMHOUSE BED & BREAKFAST
FREE FISHING FOR RESIDENTS
CARAVANS WELCOME
Please phone for more details

New Cottage, Witherington Farm, Downton, Salisbury SP5 3QX.   TEL: 01722 710021

Mere, Wiltshire. *Charges:* £5 day ticket, £25 season ticket. £12 juniors and concessions. (probable charges for 2005). *Season:* June 16th to March 14th. *Methods:* No fish in keepnets for more than 6 hours. Leave no litter. Feeder best for Bream & Tench. Waggler in shallow water. Pole off the dam wall.

SALISBURY

Harnham Kingfishers
Contact: John Slader, 46 Highlands Way, Whiteparish, Nr Salisbury, SP5 2SZ, 01794 884736, *Water:* Open to youngsters from 10 - 16. Regular meetings covering all elements of coarse fishing, including theory and practical. Fishing locally at Witherington Farm Fishery, with matches and competitions. *Charges:* Nominal joining fee.

Langford Lakes (Brockbank Lake)
Contact: Wiltshire Wildlife Trust Fishery, Duck Street, Steeple Langford, Salisbury, SP3 4NH, 01722 792011, *Water:* Brockbank lake 10 acres. *Species:* Roach, Bream, Tench, Common Carp, Perch and Pike. *Permits:* Club membership, on application in advance. *Charges:* Full details on application. *Season:* Closed season 16th March - 15th June. *Methods:* No night fishing.

Longhouse Fishery
Teffont, Nr. Salisbury, SP3 5RS, 01722 716782, *Water:* 4 lakes - Wood lake approx 1 acre plus 3 smaller lakes. *Species:* Common, Mirror, Ghost, Koi, Crucian Carp (to double figures), Roach, Rudd (2.6lb), Perch (3.9lb), Tench (3lb), Bream (3lb). *Permits:* Lakeside only. *Charges:* £5 per day, £3 per 1/2 day. *Season:* All year, only 10 days closed for pheasant shoot (October - January). *Methods:* Only bans are no particles (pulses) other than hemp or corn. No night fishing, no boilies, barbless hooks only. No large Carp in keepnets. Children under 16, must be accompanied by an adult.

Salisbury & District Angling Club (Coarse Lakes)
Contact: Rick Polden - Secretary, 29a Castle Street, Salisbury, SP1 1TT, 01722 321164, *Water:* Peters Finger Lakes and Steeple Langford. See entry under Avon Hampshire. *Species:* Carp, Tench, Bream. *Charges:* £62 per season. Concessions for Senior Citizens & Juniors. *Season:* 1st June - 31st March.

Tisbury Angling Club (Coarse Lakes)
Contact: Mr E.J.Stevens, Knapp Cottage, Fovant, Nr. Salisbury, SP3 5JW, 01722 714245, *Water:* See also entry under Nadder (3 mile stretch). Old Wardour Lake (3.5 acre), 2 miles south of Tisbury and Dinton Lake (2.5 acre), 2 miles north of Tisbury. *Species:* Roach, Chub, Dace, Bream, Perch, Crucian Carp, Carp. *Permits:* £5 p/day guest tickets. *Charges:* Adult £25 p/season, OAP £12.50, Juniors £7.50. *Season:* 16th June - 14th March.

Waldens Farm Fishery
Contact: David & Jackie Wateridge, Waldens Farm, Walden Estate, West Grimstead, Salisbury, SP5 3RJ, 01722 710480, *Mobile:* 07766 451173, *Water:* 5 lakes for approx 7.5 acres. *Species:* All coarse fish. Specimen Pike Lake. Specimen Carp Lake. 27 peg match Lake for club or private hire. *Permits:* From the bank. *Charges:* Day (dawn to dusk) tickets Adult £6, Junior - O.A.P. £4, Evenings 5 p.m. onwards £4, Match peg fees £4. Night fishing by appointment only. *Season:* Open full 12 months. *Methods:* Barbless hooks, net dips to be used, limited groundbait, no boilies, nuts or cereals. Keepnets allowed.

Witherington Farm Fishing
Contact: Tony or Caroline Beeney, New Cottage, Witherington Farm, Downton, Salisbury, SP5 3QX, 01722 710088, *Water:* 3

192

WILTSHIRE

STILLWATER COARSE

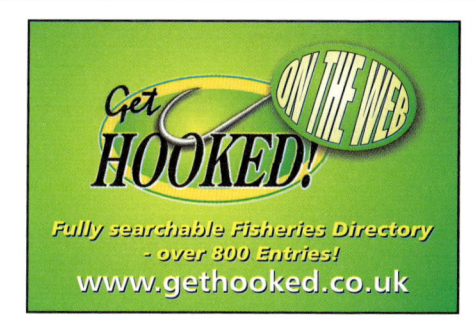

Get HOOKED! ON THE WEB
Fully searchable Fisheries Directory - over 800 Entries!
www.gethooked.co.uk

Rood Ashton Lake
A beautiful seven acre lake well stocked with quality Carp & Tench
Day tickets £5 6am-6pm. OAP's juniors £4
ENQUIRIES WELCOME FOR MATCH BOOKINGS
Home Farm, Rood Ashton, Trowbridge, Wiltshire. Tel: 01380 870272

Well stocked lakes. Plus 93 peg match lake. Toilet facilities for disabled. Most swims accessible to wheelchairs. *Species:* Carp - 27lb, Tench - 7lb, Roach - 2.5lb, Bream - 6lb, Rudd - 0.5lb, Chub - 3lb, Perch - 3lb. *Permits:* From on-site Tackle shop. *Charges:* Full day £6, Half day £4, Full day Junior under 16 / Disabled / O.A.P. £4. *Season:* All year 6.30am - Dusk. *Methods:* No boilies, barbless hooks, all nets to be dipped, no night fishing, keepnets only permitted on Match lake. No cat meat, braided hook lengths, fixed rigs.

Family day out at LONGLEAT
Warminster, Wiltshire
Set in 500 acres of parkland, 3 lakes containing carp, roach, bream, tench, perch & rudd. Tickets from the bank. Adult £7; Junior/OAP £4.00. 24hr/Night Ticket £15.00
From Warminster take A362 towards Frome, follow signs to Longleat. Further information from the bailiff, Nick Robbins on (01985) 844496
www.longleat.co.uk

SWINDON
Mouldon Hill Angling Club
Contact: Kevin Maddison, 2 Vasterne Close, Purton Village, Swindon, SN5 4EY, 01793 778272, *Mobile:* 07776 090255, *Water:* 4.5 acre lake, 3 islands, 30ft from river Ray. *Species:* Tench 3 - 6lb, Roach upto 1lb, Perch upto 2lb, Crucian Carp upto 4lb, Bream 1 - 4lb, Rudd upto 1lb, Chub upto 4lb, Dace upto 1lb and Gudgeon. *Permits:* Day tickets: Junior £1, Concessionary/OAP £2, Senior £4. *Charges:* Full membership: Junior £3, Senior £10 plus a one off joining fee of £5, providing membership is continious from season to season. *Season:* Dawn to dusk, all year, no night fishing and no close season.

BROKERSWOOD COUNTRY PARK
WELL STOCKED 5 ACRE CARP LAKE
80 ACRE COUNTRY PARK, PICNIC & BBQ SITES
Excellent Touring and Camping Facilities (dogs welcome)
Brokerswood, Westbury, Wilts
Tel: 01373 822238
Email: woodland.park@virgin.net www.brokerswood.co.uk

TROWBRIDGE
Rood Ashton Lake
Contact: Marlene Pike, Home Farm, Rood Ashton, Trowbridge, BA14 6BG, 01380 870272, *Water:* 7 acre lake available for matches - please enquire for details. *Species:* Carp, Tench, Roach. *Permits:* Home Farm and Lake View. *Charges:* 6am - 6pm £5, O.A.P.'s / Juniors £4. 6pm - 11am £4, O.A.P.'s / Juniors £3. Please enquire for match bookings. *Season:* Open all year. *Methods:* No keepnets (only competitions). No tin cans or boilies, Barbless hooks only. No nuts. No night fishing.

Tucking Mill
Contact: Wessex Water, 0845 600 4 600, *Water:* Free coarse fishing for disabled anglers from 16th June 2005 - 14th March 2006. *Species:* Roach, Chub, Tench and Large Carp. *Permits:* The site is regularly used by disabled angling clubs including Kingswood Disabled Angling Club. For more information please contact the club secretary: Trebor, 22 Newland Rd, Withywood, Bristol. BS13 9ED. Tel: 0117 9075 083 or The Westcountry Disabled Angling Association - Carey Sutton on 01275 830541. *Charges:* Each disabled angler may bring along an able bodied assistant, who may also fish, but has to use the same ticket. *Season:* 8am to sunset throughout the year except in the close season. *Methods:* No keepnets, barbless hooks.

WARMINSTER
Longleat Lakes & Shearwater
Contact: Nick Robbins, Longleat Estate Office, Longleat, Warminster, BA12 7NW, 01985 844496, *Mobile:* 07889 625999, *Water:* Longleat 3 Lakes, Top lake Carp up to 32lb, Shearwater 37 acres, Carp up to 25lb. Longleat, 20 Carp over 20lb. *Species:* Carp, Roach, Bream, Tench, Perch, Rudd. *Permits:* From bailiff on the bank. *Charges:* Adult £7, Junior/OAP £4. All 24hr/night tickets £15. *Methods:* No keepnets or carp sacks, no boilies except Longleat. No nuts, peas, beans on all lakes, no bolt rigs. Barbless hooks only.

Warminster & District Angling Club
Contact: c/o Steves Tackle, 3 Station Road, Warminster, 01985 214934, *Water:* Berkley Lake - 6 acres and Southleigh Lake at Crockerton - 2 acres. *Species:* Well stocked with all coarse fish. *Permits:* Club membership only. Details from Steves Tackle.

WILTSHIRE

Wiltshire Stillwater Trout

CALNE
Calstone Fishery
Contact: Estate Office, Bowood, Calne, SN11 0LZ, 01249 812102, *Water:* 0.75 acre reservoir. *Species:* Trout (Brown & Rainbow). *Charges:* Season only, approx £200 + VAT per rod. *Season:* 1st April 2005 - 31st October 2005, Dawn to Dusk. *Methods:* Weekly bag limits - 2 brace. All brown returned. No catch & return of Rainbow after 15th September. First 2 Rainbow must be taken on each visit.

CHIPPENHAM
Pheasant Fly Fishers
Contact: Ian MacKay, 82 Meadow Park, Bathford, Bristol, BA1 7PY, 01225 858149, *Water:* None - A fly fishing club where members fish local waters and go on organised trips further afield. *Permits:* Please contact us on the number above or phone Ricky Baptista on 01225 719175 (r2.b2@virgin.net) for more details. Anglers are welcome to attend one of our regular meetings at the Pheasant Inn, Bath Road, Chippenham at 8pm on the first Tuesday of each month. *Charges:* Club membership fees £25. *Season:* Fly fishing trips are organised throughout the year.

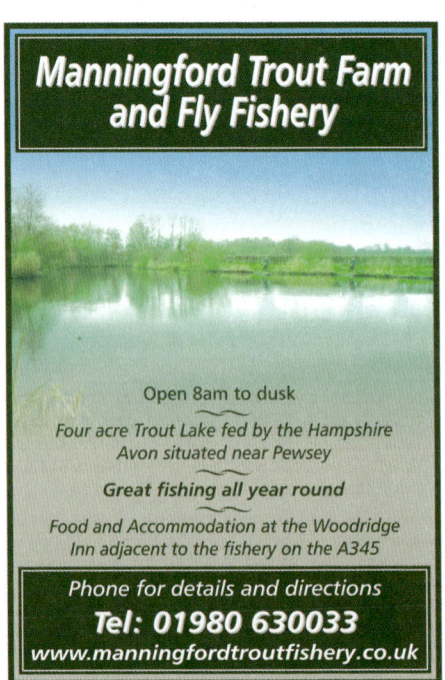

WESTBURY
Brokerswood Country Park
Contact: Mrs S.H.Capon, Brokerswood, Westbury, BA13 4EH, 01373 822238, *Water:* 5 Acre lake within 80 acre country park. *Species:* Carp, Roach, Tench, Perch, Dace. *Charges:* Adults £5, Children and Senior Citizens £4. *Season:* Closed Season 1st - 31st May. Day Visitors - From 10am to Dusk and Residents on site - 8am to Dusk. *Methods:* Barbless hooks, no boilies, no keepnets.

Clivey Ponds
Contact: Mr Mike Mortimer, Clivey Fishery, Dilton Marsh, Westbury, BA13 4BA, 01373 858311, *Mobile:* 07815 937816, *Water:* 1 acre lake. *Species:* Roach, Rudd, Bream to 2lb, Perch, Carp to 12lb, Crucians, Tench to 3lb and Gudgeon. *Permits:* On the bank or from Haines Angling Centre, 47 Vallis Way, Frome Tel: 01373 466406. *Charges:* £3.50 Day Ticket. Juniors OAPs etc. £2.50. *Season:* All year. *Methods:* Barbless Hooks only. No Groundbait.

Cuckoo's Rest Fishing Lakes
Contact: Barry & Eileen Flack, Fairwood Road, Dilton Marsh, Westbury, BA13 4EL, 01373 826792, *Water:* 1 x 4 acre lake & 1 x 2 acre lake. *Species:* Carp 23lbs, Perch 2lbs 14oz, Rudd 2lbs, Bream 2 - 4lbs, Tench 3lbs, Roach 2 - 3lbs, Chubb 2 - 3lbs, Pike 10lb. *Charges:* £4.50 p/day, £3.50 Juniors / OAP / Disabled. *Season:* All year Dawn to Dusk. *Methods:* Barbless hooks.

Eden Vale A.A.
Contact: A.E.D. Lewis, Secretary, Station Road, Westbury, 01373 465491, *Water:* 5.25 acre lake. *Species:* Carp (Common to 15lb, Mirror to 10lb), Bream to 3lb, Roach to 1.5lb, Perch to 1lb, Rudd to 0.75lb, possible Pike to 15lb. *Permits:* Railway Inn opposite lake (max 8/day), available from July 1st, Mon.-Fri. only. *Charges:* Day: £5 adult - £4 junior. Members (restricted to 15 mile radius of Westbury) at present £30, may increase in 2005. New Members £10 joining fee. Applications to Sec. with S.A.E., must be sponsored by two existing members. *Season:* Members only May 1st - July 1st, day tickets July 1st - March 15th. *Methods:* No fixed rigs, no keepnets before June 16th, no Carp or Tench in keepnets.

WILTSHIRE

DEVIZES
Mill Farm Trout Lakes
Contact: Bill Coleman, Mill Farm Trout Lakes, Worton, Devizes, SN10 5UW, 01380 813138, *Mobile:* 07761 181369, *Water:* 2 Waters of 3.5 acres each. *Species:* Rainbow Trout. All triploids from 2lb to double figures. *Permits:* Great Cheverell Post Office. One mile from fishery and open on Sunday mornings. *Charges:* 5 Fish £28, 4 Fish £25, 3 Fish £20, 2 Fish £15, 1 Fish (2hrs before dusk only) £8. *Season:* All year, 7.30am to dusk. December and January 8am to dusk. Closed every Monday except Bank Holidays. *Methods:* Fly fishing only.

MALMESBURY
The Lower Moor Fishery
Contact: Geoff & Anne Raines, Lower Moor Farm, Oaksey, Malmesbury, SN16 9TW, 01666 860232, *Mobile:* 07989 303768, *Water:* 34 acre Mallard lake. *Species:* Rainbow 14lb 5oz & Brown Trout 9lb 3oz. *Permits:* From office adjacent to car park. *Charges:* 4 Fish ticket £23, 2 Fish ticket £15, Junior 2 Fish ticket £12. *Season:* March 19th - Jan 1st 2006, 8am to dusk. *Methods:* Mallard lake - any type of fly fishing.

PEWSEY
Manningford Trout Farm & Fishery
Contact: Peter Cossburn, Manningford Bohune, By Pewsey, SN9 6JR, 01980 630033, *Water:* 4.5 acre lake fed by the Hampshire Avon. *Species:* Rainbow Trout to 20lb. Brown Trout to 10lb. *Permits:* From the fishery. *Charges:* Details from the fishery. 4 fish, 2 fish and junior tickets available. *Season:* Open all year from 8am to dusk. *Methods:* Fly fishing only.

SALISBURY
Avon Springs Fishing Lake (Stillwater)
Contact: BJ Bawden, Recreation Road, Durrington, Salisbury, SP4 8HH, 01980 653557, *Mobile:* 07774 801401, *Water:* One 4 acre lake, One 3 acre lake. One mile of upper Avon chalk stream left hand bank, see Wiltshire, river fishing. *Species:* Brown Trout 17lb 9oz, Rainbow Trout 15lb 4oz (2002). *Permits:* EA fishing licences available on site. *Charges:* £38 per day, £24 junior. Half day £30, junior £20, Eve £20. Pensioners day ticket £33 (Monday only). River and Lake ticket £50. *Season:* Open all year 8.30am to 8pm. *Methods:* Fly only no lures.

Chalke Valley Fly Fishery
Contact: Norman Barter, Vella House, Bishopstone, Salisbury, SP5 4AA, 01722 780471, *Mobile:* 07778 769373, *Water:* 2 lakes. 'Home' lake 1 acre and 'Marsh' lake 2/3 acre. Both spring fed. Maximum 4 anglers on each lake. *Species:* All Brown Trout Triploids, "Catch and Release". *Charges:* Booking requested. Wheelchair access for fishing. 8am - 12 noon £20, 12 - 4pm £15, 4pm - Dusk £25 *Season:* Open 15th April through to 16th October - 8am till Dusk. *Methods:* Dry fly with barbless hooks.

AVON SPRINGS FISHING LAKES
Superb Fishing for Brown and Rainbow Trout on Two lakes (4 acres & 3 acres)
PLUS one mile of upper Chalkstream Avon
Best Fish 2001 - Rainbow 15lb 4oz, Brown 17lb 9oz
EA Licences on site - Open all Year
Corporate Functions catered for
Recreation Road, Durrington, Salisbury, Wiltshire SP4 8HH
Tel: 01980 653557. Fax: 01980 655 267
Mobile 07774 801401. www.fishingfly.co.uk

Lakeside Rendezvous
A 6.5 acre site set In the heart of Wiltshire with our own spring fed lake offering Carp to 30lb along with Bream, Tench, Roach and Perch.

Superb and exclusive lakeside lodge, fully equipped and offering total privacy for your holiday or short break with many attractions just a short distance away.

Rowde, Nr. Devizes, Wiltshire
Tel: 01380 725447   www.lakesiderendezvous.co.uk

GREEN HILL FARM CAMPING & CARAVAN PARK
Just a stone's throw from the New Forest
OPEN ALL YEAR

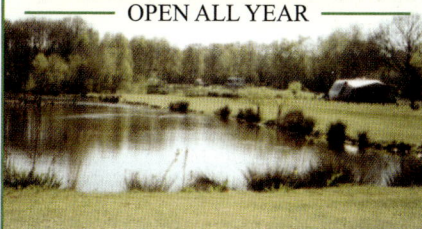

Prices from £10 per unit per night for 2 occupants.
Extra persons are £4 per person per night
This includes electricity on the main site, showers and hot and cold water. Fishing lakes are available both for caravanners and tent campers on the purchase of the appropriate docket

NEW ROAD LANDFORD, NR SALISBURY
WILTSHIRE SP5 2AZ
Tel: 01794 324117 or 02380 811506
or 07889 003902

---

www.gethooked.co.uk
Check out our Web Site!
Get HOOKED! ON THE WEB

STILLWATER TROUT

GLOUCESTERSHIRE

Gloucestershire River Fishing

CAM
Gloucestershire Disabled Angling Club
Contact: Wally Dewsnip, 56 Lower Meadow, Quedgeley, Gloucester, GL2 4YY, 01452 724366, *Water:* G.D.A.C. have 38 members of which 75% are disabled. The club fish waters on the river Cam and share Paulton lakes with the Newent Angling Club. We are taking part in the canal users festival at the Saul Junction on July 4th, 5th, 6th. *Species:* Chub, Bream, Roach, Perch. *Permits:* We are holding an open match on Lemmington lakes, contact the Secretary for more details on 01452 501465. *Charges:* Membership £10 per annum plus £5 per year lake fee. We run a junior section which is open for membership at present time. *Season:* 15th March - 16th June closed.

LITTLE AVON
Berkeley Estate Fishing Syndicate
Contact: T. Staniforth, 68 Firgrove, Chipping Sodbury, BS37 7AG, 01454 881719, *Water:* 6.5 miles of Coarse and Game fishing Little Avon from Berkeley Castle to Damery-Tortworth. *Species:* Chub, Dace, Roach, Bream, Perch, Brown Trout, Rainbow Trout and Grayling. *Permits:* From above. *Charges:* Annual membership £35. Guests may accompany members @ £5 per day. *Season:* Statutory. *Methods:* Trout season fly only. From June 16 any method. No spinning.

Charfield Angling Association
Contact: Mr Mark Lewis, Langford Mill House, Charfield Road, Kingswood, Wotton-Under-Edge, GL12 8RL, 01453 843130, *Mobile:* 07787 573468, *Water:* Approx. 3 miles of Little Avon and Ozleworth Brook. *Species:* Brown Trout, Rainbow Trout, Roach, Grayling and Chub. *Permits:* As above. *Charges:* £30 per season seniors. £15 OAPs, £7.50 juniors. *Season:* Severn Trent byelaws apply. *Methods:* Severn Trent byelaws apply.

WYE
Rotherwas Fishery
Contact: John Tipper - Frank Morris, 14 Thoresby Ave, Tuffley, Gloucester, GL4 0TE, 01452 505313, *Water:* 1 mile on the river Wye. Barbel 7lb plus, Pike to 27lb, Grayling 1lb plus. Good Dace and Roach. Also 2 x 4 acre lakes. See entry under Stillwater Coarse, Gloucester. *Species:* Carp: to 30lb. Coarse: Carp to 20lb, Bream 4lb, Perch 3lb, Tench 5lb, Roach/Rudd 2.75lb. *Permits:* Only from above. *Charges:* Day ticket £3.50. Junior £2. Season £20. Salmon Day £15. *Season:* 16th June - 30th April. *Methods:* Common sense please. Take all litter home, shut all gates and park sensibly. Please check other anglers permits. Two bailiffs patrol this beat.

Stillwater Coarse

CHIPPING SODBURY
Bathampton Angling Association (Coarse Lakes)
Contact: Dave Crookes, 25 Otago Terrace, Larkhall, Bath, BA1 6SX, 01225 427164, *Water:* Two lakes at Lydes Farm / Players Golf Club, Codrington. *Species:* Roach to 1.75lbs, Rudd to 2lb, Tench to 6.5lbs. Carp to 20lb plus, Crucian Carp, Bream to 7.5lb. *Permits:* Local fishing tackle shops (members only). *Charges:* Adults £25, combined lady and gent £35, juniors £8, O.A.P £7. Registered disabled £7, Under 12's free. To year end 31/12/05. Additional special day permit at £2 must be obtained before fishing. *Season:* Open from 8am all year round. Closing times vary according to time of year. *Methods:* Special rules apply - available from secretary and printed on permit.

CIRENCESTER
Swindon Isis Angling Club Lake No1
Contact: Peter Gilbert, 31 Havelock St, Swindon, SN1 1SD, 01793 535396, *Water:* 6 acre mature gravel pit at Cotswold Water Park (Water Park Lake 19), South Cerney, Cirencester. *Species:* Tench 9lb, lake with Carp to 30lb, Rudd to 2lb12oz, odd big Bream, usual Roach, Perch & good Pike. *Permits:* Tackle shops in Swindon, Cirencester, Chippenham and Calne. *Charges:* Club Permits: Senior £34.50. OAP and disabled £12. Juniors £8. The club permit contains two free day tickets and more day tickets can be obtained for £5 each. Year starts 1 April. *Season:* Open all year round. Club cards start 1st April. *Methods:* No bans.

FAIRFORD
Milestone Fisheries (Coarse)
Contact: Andy King, London Road, Fairford, GL7 4DS, 01285 713908, *Water:* 3.5 acre specimen Carp lake. 56 acre Pike lake. *Species:* Well stocked with Carp 40lb, Tench 9.5lb, Bream 15lb, Roach 3.5lb, Rudd, Perch 4.5lb. Separate 56 acre Pike lake 38lb. *Permits:* Day tickets available from fishery office - above address. *Charges:* £10 per day, £15 for 24hr (inc night). *Season:* Open Saturday and Sunday only. No closed season. Night fishing by arrangement. Pike lake open all year. *Methods:* No keepnets, no dogs, barbless hooks only. Pike lake - Barbless & semi - barbless hooks, minimum of 12lb b.s. line. Traces min 18lbs, 36 inch soft mesh landing net, unhooking mat, strong wire cutters.

GLOUCESTER
Huntley Carp Pools
Contact: John Tipper - Frank Morris, 14 Thoresby Ave, Tuffley, Gloucester, GL4 0TE, 01452 505313, *Water:* 2 x 4 acre lakes. 1 with Carp to 30lb. 1 with general fish, Carp, Tench, Perch, Bream, Roach, Rudd, Crucian. Also 1 mile stretch of river Wye. See entry under Gloucestershire river fishing. *Species:* Carp: to 30lb. Coarse: Carp to 20lb, Bream 4lb, Perch 3lb, Tench 5lb, Roach/Rudd 2.75lb. *Permits:* Only from above. *Charges:* To be advised. *Season:* 16th June - 30th April. *Methods:* No keepnets, barbless hooks.

Lemington Lakes
Contact: Debbie, Todenham Road, Moreton-in-Marsh, GL56

GLOUCESTERSHIRE

9NP, 01608 650872, *Water:* 4.5 acre lake, 2.5 acre lake, 2 acre lake, 1.25 acre lake, 0.75 acre lake. 5 ponds varying sizes all with coarse fish. *Species:* Each lake caters for different types of fishing with fish up to specimen sizes. *Permits:* As above. *Charges:* £7 Max two rods - specimen lake. £6 Max two rods. £4 Children up to 14th Birthday. Night fishing must be booked. *Season:* 7am - Dark (all year), match bookings taken. *Methods:* Barbless hooks only. Keep nets allowed on certain lakes.

WOTTON-UNDER-EDGE
Lower Killcott Farm Fishing
Contact: Mr E Thompson, Lower Kilcott Farm, Nr Hillesley, Wotton-Under-Edge, GL12 7RL, 01454 238276, *Mobile:* 078161 48038, *Water:* 1 acre lake. *Species:* Carp to 20lb, Roach, Rudd *Charges:* £5 day, £3 half day. *Season:* Open all year. *Methods:* Barbless hooks only, no keepnets or boilies.

Stillwater Trout

DURSLEY
Great Burrows Trout Fishery
Contact: Vernon Baxter (Manager), Nibley Green, North Nibley, Nr Dursley, GL11 6EB, 01453 542343, *Mobile:* 07754 502134, *Water:* Two acre lake. *Species:* Brown Trout, Rainbow Trout (triploid) stocked from 2lb to 5lb. *Permits:* From V. Baxter on site. *Charges:* Day tickets: 2 fish - £14. 3 fish £16. 4 fish £20. 5 fish £24. 6 fish £30. *Season:* Open all year except Christmas day. Fishing from 8am to one hour after sunset. *Methods:* Fly only. No lures. Barbless hooks only. Max hook size 12 longshank. No static fishing. No catch and release except for Brown Trout. Breeding fish to be returned if caught. No wading, fishing from platforms. Knotless landing nets only. E.A. Licence required. Tuition and equipment available.

FAIRFORD
Milestone Fisheries (Trout Lakes)
Contact: Andy King, Milestone Fisheries, London Road, Fairford, GL7 4DS, 01285 713908, *Water:* 10 acre lake and 2 acre lake. Used for Carp fishing during summer months only. *Species:* 10 acre lake: Brown trout, Rainbow trout 2lb - 20lb. 2 acre lake: Rainbow trout 1lb - 1.25lb (bank fishing only). Also Blue/Golden Trout. *Permits:* Day tickets & Season tickets plus a limited number catch and release. *Charges:* £15 upwards. *Season:* Open Saturday and Sunday only. Open 1st Oct - May 27th. Closed June, July, August. *Methods:* Catch & take or catch & release on ten acre lake only (Barbless hooks on catch & release). Fly fishing only.

GLOUCESTER
The Cotswolds Fishery
Witcombe farm, Great Witcombe, GL3 4TR, 01452 864413, *Water:* 3 reservoirs - 15 acres, 5 acres and 2 plus acres. *Species:* Rainbow Trout max weight 8lbs. *Permits:* Witcombe Farm Estate, Great Witcombe, Gloucester GL3 4TR. *Charges:* Seasonal permits available, various prices on application. Day visitor tickets - Full day £35 (6 fish), Half day (6 hrs) £20 (3 fish), Evening £15 (2 fish). Boats £10 Full day, £5 Half day, £3

Evening. Novice 6 hrs £20 (bag limit - 3 fish), pay £6 per fish taken. *Season:* 6th March - 18th October, from 8am to Dusk. *Methods:* Normal Game fishing for Trout, knotless nets. No catch and release.

LECHLADE
Lechlade & Bushyleaze Trout Fisheries
Contact: Tim Small, Lechlade & Bushyleaze Trout Fisheries, Lechlade, GL7 3QQ, 01367 253266, *Water:* Lechlade - 8 acres. Bushyleaze - 20 acres. *Species:* Lechlade - Rainbows to 27lb, Browns to 18lb. Bushyleaze - Rainbows to 17lb, Browns to 9lb. *Charges:* Lechlade: £47.50 full day, 4 fish, £32.50 half day, 2 fish. £25 evening, 1 fish. Bushyleaze: £32.50 full day, 6 fish. £27.50 full day, 4 fish. £25 half day, 3 fish. £20 evening, 2 fish. Season tickets available for both lakes. Discounted day tickets for juniors. *Season:* Open all year. *Methods:* Fly only. Boat hire and float tube hire.

Sea Fishing

CHELTENHAM
Bass Anglers Sportfishing Society
Contact: NFSA Head Office: 01364 644643,

STROUD
South & South West S.A.
Contact: NFSA Head Office: 01364 644643,

TEWKESBURY
Inlanders S.A.C.
Contact: Mike Ellard, 24 Grayston Close, Tewkesbury, GL20 8AY, 01684 292860, *Mobile:* 07952 071947, *Water:* Fishing from boat/shore, covering the westcountry with trips to Whitby and other areas. New members, adult and juniors, welcome.

WITHINGTON
Royal Air Force Sea Angling Association
Contact: NFSA Head Office: 01364 644643,

THE GET HOOKED GUIDE

Sexy Trout!

Dr. Stewart Owen

You may hear anglers speak of triploid fish, especially at trout fisheries. Triploids are in fact sterile fish, but why do we need them and where do they come from? Read on and fish biologist Dr Stewart Owen will answer these questions and give an insight into a fascinating aspect of fisheries management.

Why do we need sterile fish?

When there is a risk of introducing a new species to a fishery or catchment area, fisheries officers and managers apply the precautionary principle. There must be the 'least risk' of introduced fish affecting those already present. Where a species is non-native such as rainbow trout, fisheries managers do their utmost to prevent a viable population establishing and so reduce the theoretical risk to the natural populations of other species already present. In some cases such as with our native brown trout, the genetic diversity between river systems has recently been realised. Stocking fish of one particular blood-line in a river system containing fish of a different genetic history is now increasingly restricted. To allow some fisheries to function it is necessary to stock with either fish from a particular compatible source (such as those spawned from resident fish) or stock with sterile fish.

In the UK climate rainbow trout spawn in late winter (Jan-March) and as used to be the normal situation before fish were sterilised, the female fish swell with eggs during this period. A female invests all of her energy into producing the best eggs she can. This means that she mobilises her own muscle protein and fat from her body and sends this energy to the eggs. When you catch a fish 'in egg' her flesh quality will be poor compared to when she is not producing eggs. If a triploid fish is not able to produce eggs, then the benefit for the angler is that the flesh quality remains throughout the year.

How do fish become sterile?

There are several methods used to sterilise fish. If the fish already exist then they can be prevented from maturing using chemicals or hormonal treatments. This is effective, but very expensive and time consuming. But a method is commonly used to produce fish that are sterile from birth. This is called triploidy.

Like us, fish are made up from genetic information gained from both parents. Half of the genes come from the father, and half from the mother. Genes are the instructions to a cell of how to build proteins. They are stored in long strings of DNA that are tightly coiled into units called chromosomes. Different species have a different number of chromosomes containing different numbers of genes. A single set of genes from a parent is called a haploid set. At fertilisation, the egg and sperm come together and pair their haploid sets so the resultant baby has two complementary sets of genetic information and is referred to as being Diploid. That is it has two haploid sets. A diploid fish goes on to develop into a normal fish and will mature and reproduce when the time is right.

If the egg is physically shocked shortly after fertilisation occurs, then it is possible to produce a fish with three sets of chromosomes, a triploid fish. The egg does not in fact manufacture an extra set for itself. The extra genetic information actually comes from the female parent and is present before fertilisation. Under normal unshocked fertilisation this information is lost from the egg as it is fertilised. But a shock, such as an increase in temperature, physical shaking or an increase in environmental pressure prevents this information leaving the fertilised cell. There is no genetic modification. Genes have not been changed or manufactured. The number of chromosomes are increased because a set are not lost on fertilisation. The fertilised egg is left with three copies of genetic information rather than two. Two from the mother, and one from the father. Triploid fish grow and develop as normal. After all they have the same information within them as diploid fish. But when it comes to producing eggs for themselves, the three sets of information do not divide conveniently and so no viable eggs are produced by hen fish. Triploid males do not produce viable sperm.

This is actually a simplified account of the process. Many fish naturally have many sets of identical chromosomes. Some species are naturally tetraploid (four sets), hexaploid (six) or even heptaploid (seven). The term given to more than diploid is polyploid. Wild trout are not in fact diploid to start with. Native wild trout swimming in the rivers of Britain are polyploid naturally. So as a trout embryo is made triploid, the fish could actually contain 18 sets of genetic information.

How do fish farmers produce triploids?

To make fish triploid the newly fertilised eggs are physically shocked. In practice this means the eggs are placed in a special pressure vessel and subjected to a very high pressure. The timing after fertilisation and the actual pressure are critical to the process. If the farmer times this wrong then mistakes can be made. The balance is a fine one. Too little and it does not cause triploidy whilst too much pressure kills the eggs. It is difficult to judge the success until the fish can be sampled and examined under the microscope, or mature as adults. The triploid eggs go on to hatch and grow normally into adult fish. However it must be remembered that the process is a biological one and as such triploidisation is rarely 100% effective. Some fish of each batch seem to escape the process and mature as normal fish. We expect our suppliers to provide fry that are normally much better than 90% triploid. That is we generally expect that one fish in ten from a batch of triploids will develop eggs in maturity. It is therefore important that the farmer grades the fish to remove any hen fish before these fish are stocked into critical waters. This is a point often overlooked and a batch of triploids may still contain a small number of fertile fish.

Where do our fish actually come from?

In order to supply trout all year round for the UK markets, eggs are sourced from around the world as different geographic regions provide spawning at different times of the year. Of course some producers spawn fish artificially all year around, but UK fish are typically British, Danish and South African in origin. Eggs also come from America, Canada, Iceland, Faeroes, France, Chile and Australia. This is a tightly regulated industry with government ministry regulation and inspection that insures full trace-ability with veterinary health checks. Once the eggs have passed through the hatcheries they are 'grown-on' at one of the many restocking farms throughout the UK from where they are traded until they reach the anglers hook.

Anglers are managers of the aquatic environment

- First to flag up problems.
- Act on environmental concerns through membership with national and local associations
- Fund fisheries management through club working parties and payment of licence and angling fees

Importance of flies to the environment and anglers

Fly and invertebrate life is a natural barometer to the health of the aquatic environment

Flies/invertebrates are main prey for many fish.

Game anglers manage the environment upon which flies and invertebrates depend, and then tie imitations to lure fish to the rod

Anglers' Interest in Fly Life

In other words, aquatic flies are an integral part of the aquatic environment. The sport of angling depends on aquatic flies, whether in river or stillwater.

Contributed by the Salmon & Trout Association – Fighting for the Future of Game Angling.

To learn more about flylife and how to help visit www.salmon-trout.org or call the S&TA at 0207 283 5838.

SERVICES & SUPPLIERS

Blakewell
Water Gardens & Trout Fishing

QUALITY TROUT, CARP AND OTHER COARSE FISH SUPPLIED

Pond and Lake Design and Construction

Muddiford, Barnstaple, N. Devon. EX31 4ET.
Tel: 01271 344533 Fax: 01271 374267
Email: mail@blakewell.co.uk www.blakewell.co.uk

STAFFORD MOOR Fishery

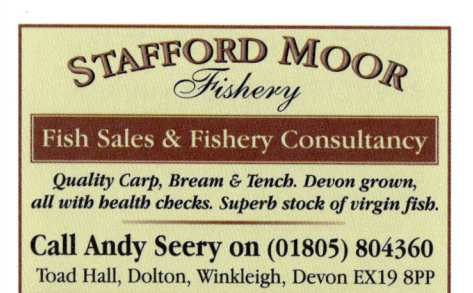

Fish Sales & Fishery Consultancy

Quality Carp, Bream & Tench. Devon grown, all with health checks. Superb stock of virgin fish.

Call Andy Seery on (01805) 804360
Toad Hall, Dolton, Winkleigh, Devon EX19 8PP

www.staffordmoor.co.uk

Nice Rainbow on a summer evening from a Cornish stillwater. Pic - the Editor

---

MARTIN COCKS
ANGLING SUPPLIES

- BOSS Tackle Developments
- Richworth
- DRAGON BAITS LTD — FARMED RAGWORM / LUGWORM
- KRYSTON ADVANCED ANGLING LTD.
- MARCEL VAN DEN EYNDE — LOKAAS AMORCE GROUNDBAIT PASTURA — 3 X WORLD CHAMPION
- SOLAR TACKLE
- ANCHOR
- mainline
- GARDNER

Supplier of the 'Get Hooked Guide'

Maggot / Dendraboena worms also available

TRADE ENQUIRIES ONLY
2 Higher Marsh Row, Exminster, Exeter EX6 8EB

Tel: 01392 832 084   Mobile: 07971 624 740

SERVICES & SUPPLIERS

Ghost Carp from Clawford.

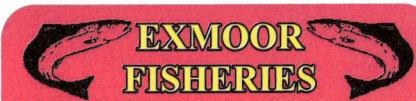

EXMOOR FISHERIES

Suppliers of Top Quality Rainbow Trout of all sizes

Ring Dave Fuller for a Quote
Hartford, Brompton Regis, Somerset TA22 9NS
Email: exmoorfisheries@eclipse.co.uk
Tel: 01398 371447 Fax: 01398 371446

Diamond Design

guides <
newsletters <
logos <
brochures <
web sites <
advertising <
mailings <
distribution <
complete print management service <

From design to production

TEL: 01271 860183
Email: info@diamondpublications.co.uk
www.diamondpublications.co.uk

SKRETTING

CREATING THE **FINEST FEED**

www.skretting.co.uk
a nutreco company

201

THE GET HOOKED GUIDE

Check out our Web Site!

Get HOOKED! ON THE WEB

Search online with the most comprehensive guide to fishing in the South West of England

Fully searchable Fisheries Directory - over 800 Entries!

Where to Stay and Featured Fisheries Sections plus details of over 150 Tackle Shops

For more Information and Advertising Rates

PHONE 01271 860183
or Email info@gethooked.co.uk

www.gethooked.co.uk

GAME

Amherst Lodge	125
Angling 2000	51
Arundell Arms Hotel	68
Avon Dam	50
Avon Springs Fishing Lakes	195
Bacon's Tackle Box	155
Bake Lakes	40
Bellbrook Valley Trout Fishery	101
Blagdon	167
Blakewell Fishery	94
Bridge House Hotel	64
Bristol Water	167
Bristol, Bath & Wilts Amalgamated Angler	149
Bryan Martin	179
Buckfastleigh River Fishing	49
Bulldog Fish Farm	95
Burrator	50
Burton Springs Fishery	167
Cameley Trout Lakes	168
Chew Valley	167
Christchurch Angling Club	118
Clatworthy	170
Clinton Arms	109
Colin Nice	179
Colliford	50
Combe Sydenham Fishery	169
Crowdy	50
David Pilkington	178
Dever Springs	138
Devon, Wiltshire & UK Fly Fishing School	179
Drift Reservoir	40
Environment Agency - Crayfish	22
Environment Agency - Rod Licence	23
Exe Valley Fishery	169
Fenwick Trout	39
Fernworthy	50
Flowers Farm Lakes	125
Fly Fishing in Somerset	146
Fox & Hounds Country Hotel	70
Gary & Annie Champion	178
Get Hooked On The Web	202
Goodiford Mill Fishery	78
Half Moon Hotel	72
Hawkridge	170
Haycorn Cottage	46
Hayrish Farm	108
Helemoor Fishery & Camping	98
Highampton Lakes	96
Hollies Trout Farm	97
Homeleigh Angling and Garden Centre	Inside back
Kennick	50
Kingfisher	73
Lance Nicholson	146
Lechlade & Bushyleaze Trout Fisheries	180
Litton	167
Lower Bruckland Trout Fishery	94
Malston Mill Farm	108
Manningford Trout Fishery	194
Meldon	50
Mike Gleave	180
Nick Hart Fly Fishing	102 & 178
Orvis Co. Inc.	65
Pollution Hotline	151
REFFIS	180
Richard Slocock	180
Ringwood & District Anglers Association	135
Ringwood Tackle	137
Rising Sun Inn	70
River Basin Management	21
Roadford	50
Robert Jones Fly Fishing	71 and 178
Rockbourne Trout Fisheries Ltd.	137
Roger Cannock	178
Roy Buckingham	178
Roy Buckland	180
Sally Pizii	180
Siblyback	50
Simon Cooper	180
Skretting	201
Snowbee (U.K.) Ltd.	99
South West Lakes Trust	50
Southwood Fishery	95
Stithians	50
Sutton Bingham	170
Tavistock Trout Fishery	100
The Barrows	167
The Total Fly Fishing Co. David Griffiths	180
Tightline Tours	33
Tom Hill	180
Topp Tackle	169
Tree Meadow Trout Fishery & Tackle	Back cover
Upavon Farm Fishing	187
Valley Springs	84
Venford	50
Watersmeet & Glenthorne Fisheries	66
Wessex Fly Fishing School	180
Wessex Water	170

ADVERTISERS INDEX

Westcountry Rivers Trust 21
Wild Trout Trust..61
Wimbleball 50
Wiscombe Park Fishery 98
Wistlandpound 50

COARSE

Airsprung Angling Association......................188
Alcove Angling Club 156
Ammo Blast Frozen Baits 42
Angling 2000 51
Argal 48
Avallon Lodges 46
Avalon Fisheries 160
Bacon's Tackle Box 155
Badham Farm Holidays 32
Bake Lakes 40
Bickerton Farm Fishery 83
Blashford Lakes 118
Borlasevath 34
Boscathnoe 48
Bridgwater Angling Association 147
Bristol, Bath & Wilts Amalgamated Angler....149
Brokerswood Country Park 193
Bullock Farm Lakes 173
Burton Springs Fishery 167
Bush Lakes 35
Bussow 48
Christchurch Angling Club 118
Clawford Vineyard .... Inside front cover
Cofton Country Holiday Park 79
Coombe Water Fisheries 83
Coombelands Coarse Fishery 78
Crafthole 48
Cranford Inn & Holiday Cottages 91
Creedy Lakes 76
Darracott 48
Darts Farm..80
Diamond Farm Caravan & Camping Park 173
Durleigh Reservoir.......................................170
East Moore Farm Fishery 92
Edney's Fisheries 160
Emborough Ponds 165
Emerald Pool Fisheries 161
Environment Agency - Crayfish 22
Environment Agency - Rod Licence 23
Exeter & District Angling Association 80
Exmouth Tackle & Sports 82

Fentrigan Manor Farm 47
Fly Fishing in Somerset 146
Follyfoot Farm 164
Franks Fishing & Pet Supplies........................77
Get Hooked On The Web 202
Glenleigh Farm Fishery 36
Godney Moor Ponds 163
Gold Oak Farm 122
Goodiford Mill Fishery 78
Green Hill Farm 195
HBS Fisheries 164
Helemoor Fishery & Camping 98
Highampton Lakes 96
Hollies Trout Farm 97
Homeleigh Angling and Garden Centre....... IBC
Jennetts..48
Kingfisher 73
Kingslake Fishing Holidays 107
Laburnum House 173
Lakeside Rendezvous 195
Lands End Farm Fishery 164
Little Allers 89
Little Comfort Farm 73
Longleat Estate 193
Lower Hollacombe Fishery 76
Lower Slade 48
Luccombes Coarse Fishery 81
Malston Mill Farm 108
Manadon Angling Supplies 88
Mangerton Valley Coarse Fishing 121
Meadowside Fishery 36
Melbury 48
Millbrook 38
Millhayes Fishery 79
Minnows Touring Caravan Park.....................91
Newberry Farm 76
Northam Farm Touring Caravan Park 159
Oaktree Carp Farm & Fishery 89
Old Mill 48
Penpol Farm Coarse Fishery 35
Plantations Leisure Ltd 162
Pollution Hotline 151
Porth 48
Retallack Waters 37
Richworth Bait 165
Ringwood & District Anglers Association 135
Ringwood Tackle..137
River Basin Management..............................21
Roger Cannock 178
Rood Ashton Lake......................................193

204

ADVERTISERS INDEX

Royalty Fishery 118
Salmonhutch Fishery 77
Shearwater 193
Silverlands Lake 194
South View Farm Fishery 81
South West Lakes Angling Association 90
South West Lakes Trust 48
Spires Lakes 86
Squabmoor 48
Stafford Moor Country Park 92
Street Angling Centre 163
Sunridge Fishery 109
Tan House Farm Lake 173
Thatchers Pet & Tackle 165
The Sedges 156
Thorney Lakes 163
Throop Fisheries 135
Tightline Tours 33
Topp Tackle 169
Tottiford 48
Town Parks Coarse Fishing Centre 87
Trenchford 48
Trencreek Farm Holiday Park 46
Trevella Park 47
Tucking Mill 170
Upham Farm Carp Ponds 81
Upper Tamar 48
Upton Lakes 107
Valley Springs 84
Viaduct Fishery 163
Waldens Farm Fishery 192
Warren Farm Holiday Centre 159
Week Farm 86
Wessex Water 170
West Pitt Farm Fishery 90
Westcountry Rivers Trust 21
Weymouth Angling Centre 127
White Acres Country Park 46
Wiscombe Park Fishery 98
Witherington Farm Lakes 192
Wood Farm Caravan Park 128
Wooda Farm Park 45
Woolsbridge Manor Farm Caravan Site 128

SEA

Ammo Blast Frozen Baits 42
Bacon's Tackle Box 155
Christchurch Angling Club 118
Colin Nice 179
Diamond Farm Caravan & Camping Park 173
Exmouth Tackle & Sports 82
Get Hooked On The Web 202
Homeleigh Angling and Garden Centre ... Inside back
Kingfisher 73
Lower Bruckland Trout Fishery 94
Manadon Angling Supplies 88
Mevagissey Shark & Angling Centre 43
Nick Hart Fly Fishing .... 102 & 178
Padstow Angling Centre 43
Phil & Jo Hyde 179
Quay Stores 106
Roger Cannock 178
Swanage Angling Centre 127
Tightline Tours 33
TW Tackle Direct 104
Variety Sports 104
Weymouth Angling Centre 127

TACKLE

Amherst Lodge 125
Anglers Heaven 74
Atlantic Angling Centre 33
Avon Angling Centre -Bristol 157
Avon Angling Centre -Ringwood 137
Bacon's Tackle Box 155
Bake Lakes 40
Bill Pugh Pets & Fishing 158
Blakewell Fishery 94
Bristol Angling Centre 168
Bristol Water 167
Brixham Bait & Tackle 93
Cadbury Garden & Leisure 166
Camel Valley Sport Fishing 41
Clive's Tackle & Bait 88
Cofton Country Holiday Park 79
Colin's 171
Exe Valley Angling 124
Exe Valley Fishery 169
Exeter Angling Centre .... Inside front cover
Exmouth Tackle & Sports 82

205

ADVERTISERS INDEX

Fly Fishing in Somerset 146
Franks Fishing & Pet Supplies................77
G Thomas & Co Ltd 85
Get Hooked On The Web 202
Goodiford Mill Fishery 78
Half Moon Hotel 72
Hollies Trout Farm 97
Homeleigh Angling and Garden Centre... Inside back
John Eadies 188
Kingfisher 73
Lance Nicholson 146
Lower Bruckland Trout Fishery 94
Manadon Angling Supplies 88
Martin Cocks 200
Mevagissey Shark & Angling Centre 43
Nick Hart Fly Fishing .... 102 & 178
Orvis Co. Inc. 65
Padstow Angling Centre 43
Quay Stores 106
Retallack Waters 37
Richworth Bait 165
Ringwood Tackle 137
Rockbourne Trout Fisheries Ltd. 137
Scott Tackle 157
Snowbee (U.K.) Ltd. 99
Stafford Moor Country Park 92
Street Angling Centre..........................163
Swanage Angling Centre 127
Tackle Trader..84
Tavistock Trout Fishery 100
Thatchers Pet & Tackle 165
The Fishing Box 87
Top Floor Tackle 123
Topp Tackle..169
Town Parks Coarse Fishing Centre 87
Tree Meadow Trout Fishery & Tackle.......Back cover
Trencreek Farm Holiday Park 46
TW Tackle Direct 104
Valley Springs 84
Variety Sports 104
Viaduct Fishery 163
Waldens Farm Fishery 192
Wessex Angling Centre 123
Wessex Fly Fishing School 180
West Bay Water Sports 124
Weston Angling Centre 165
Westsports Country Store 75
Weymouth Angling Centre 127
White Acres Country Park.....................46
Witherington Farm Lakes 192

SERVICES

Ammo Blast Frozen Baits 42
Blakewell Fishery 94
Bulldog Fish Farm 95
Diamond Designs................................201
Exmoor Fisheries 201
G Thomas & Co Ltd 85
Get Hooked On The Web 202
Manadon Angling Supplies 88
Manningford Trout Fishery 194
Martin Cocks 200
Padstow Angling Centre 43
Pollution Hotline 151
Richworth Bait 165
River Basin Management......................21
Skretting 201
Stafford Moor Country Park 92
Waldens Farm Fishery 192
Westcountry Rivers Trust 21
Westsports Country Store 75
Witherington Farm Lakes 192

HOTELS

Arundell Arms Hotel 68
Bridge House Hotel 64
Clawford Vineyard .... Inside front cover
Fly Fishing in Somerset 146
Fox & Hounds Country Hotel 70
Get Hooked On The Web 202
Half Moon Hotel 72
Laburnum House 173
Rising Sun Inn 70
Robert Jones Fly Fishing .... 71 and 178

SELF CATERING

Amherst Lodge 125
Avallon Lodges 46
Badham Farm Holidays 32
Bellbrook Valley Trout Fishery 101
Borlasevath..34
Brokerswood Country Park 193
Bullock Farm Lakes 173
Clawford Vineyard .... Inside front cover
Cofton Country Holiday Park 79

ADVERTISERS INDEX

Coombe Water Fisheries	83
Cranford Inn & Holiday Cottages	91
Creedy Lakes	76
Diamond Farm Caravan & Camping Park	173
Emerald Pool Fisheries	161
Fentrigan Manor Farm	47
Fly Fishing in Somerset	146
Get Hooked On The Web	202
Glenleigh Farm Fishery	36
Goodiford Mill Fishery	78
Haycorn Cottage	46
Hayrish Farm	108
Hollies Trout Farm	97
Kingslake Fishing Holidays	107
Lakeside Rendezvous	195
Little Comfort Farm	73
Malston Mill Farm	108
Millbrook	38
Millhayes Fishery	79
Myrtle Cottage	109
Oaktree Carp Farm & Fishery	89
Penpol Farm Coarse Fishery	35
Plantations Leisure Ltd	162
Silverlands Lake	194
Stafford Moor Country Park	92
Sunridge Fishery	109
Tan House Farm Lake	173
Tavistock Trout Fishery	100
Tightline Tours	33
Town Parks Coarse Fishing Centre	87
Tree Meadow Trout Fishery & Tackle	Back cover
Trencreek Farm Holiday Park	46
Trevella Park	47
Upton Lakes	107
Valley Springs	84
Week Farm	86
Wessex Fly Fishing School	180
West Pitt Farm Fishery	90
White Acres Country Park	46
Wood Farm Caravan Park	128
Wooda Farm Park	45

CAMPING

Brokerswood Country Park	193
Cofton Country Holiday Park	79
Diamond Farm Caravan & Camping Park	173
East Moore Farm Fishery	92
Edney's Fisheries	160
Fenwick Trout	39
Fly Fishing in Somerset	146
Get Hooked On The Web	202
Green Hill Farm	195
Helemoor Fishery & Camping	98
Kingslake Fishing Holidays	107
Minnows Touring Caravan Park	91
Newberry Farm	76
Northam Farm Touring Caravan Park	159
Oaktree Carp Farm & Fishery	89
Plantations Leisure Ltd	162
Retallack Waters	37
Salmonhutch Fishery	77
Silverlands Lake	194
Tan House Farm Lake	173
Thorney Lakes	163
Town Parks Coarse Fishing Centre	87
Trencreek Farm Holiday Park	46
Trevella Park	47
Upton Lakes	107
Warren Farm Holiday Centre	159
Week Farm	86
White Acres Country Park	46
Witherington Farm Lakes	192
Wood Farm Caravan Park	128
Wooda Farm Park	45
Woolsbridge Manor Farm Caravan Site	128

CARAVANS

Brokerswood Country Park	193
Cofton Country Holiday Park	79
Diamond Farm Caravan & Camping Park	173
East Moore Farm Fishery	92
Edney's Fisheries	160
Fenwick Trout	39
Fly Fishing in Somerset	146
Get Hooked On The Web	202
Green Hill Farm	195
Kingslake Fishing Holidays	107
Lower Hollacombe Fishery	76
Minnows Touring Caravan Park	91
Newberry Farm	76
Northam Farm Touring Caravan Park	159
Oaktree Carp Farm & Fishery	89
Plantations Leisure Ltd	162
Salmonhutch Fishery	77
Silverlands Lake	194
Tan House Farm Lake	173

ADVERTISERS INDEX

The Sedges 156	Blakewell Fishery 94
Thorney Lakes 163	Bristol Water 167
Town Parks Coarse Fishing Centre 87	Bryan Martin 179
Trencreek Farm Holiday Park 46	Bullock Farm Lakes 173
Trevella Park 47	Camel Valley Sport Fishing 41
Upham Farm Carp Ponds 81	Christchurch Angling Club 118
Upton Lakes 107	Colin Nice 179
Warren Farm Holiday Centre 159	David Pilkington 178
White Acres Country Park 46	Devon, Wiltshire & UK Fly Fishing School 179
Witherington Farm Lakes 192	Edney's Fisheries 160
Wood Farm Caravan Park 128	Fly Fishing in Somerset 146
Wooda Farm Park 45	Follyfoot Farm 164
Woolsbridge Manor Farm Caravan Site 128	Fox & Hounds Country Hotel 70
	Gary & Annie Champion 178
	Goodiford Mill Fishery 78

B & B

	Half Moon Hotel 72
	Jim Williams 180
Bellbrook Valley Trout Fishery 101	John Dawson 179
Bridge House Hotel 64	Kingfisher 73
Clawford Vineyard .... Inside front cover	Lechlade & Bushyleaze Trout Fisheries 180
Clinton Arms 109	Lower Bruckland Trout Fishery 94
Coombe Water Fisheries 83	Mike Gleave 180
Fly Fishing in Somerset 146	Nick Hart Fly Fishing .... 102 & 178
Get Hooked On The Web 202	Pete Tyjas 179
Gold Oak Farm 122	Phil & Jo Hyde 179
Half Moon Hotel 72	REFFIS 180
Hollies Trout Farm 97	Richard Slocock 180
Lower Bruckland Trout Fishery 94	Ringwood & District Anglers Association 135
Mangerton Valley Coarse Fishing 121	River Basin Management 21
Manningford Trout Fishery 194	Robert Jones Fly Fishing .... 71 and 178
Millhayes Fishery 79	Rockbourne Trout Fisheries Ltd. 137
Oaktree Carp Farm & Fishery 89	Roger Cannock 178
Penpol Farm Coarse Fishery 35	Roy Buckingham 178
Rising Sun Inn 70	Roy Buckland 180
Rood Ashton Lake 193	Sally Pizii 180
Tightline Tours 33	Simon Cooper 180
Town Parks Coarse Fishing Centre 87	Simon Ward 180
Upavon Farm Fishing 187	South West Lakes Trust 50
Valley Springs 84	South West Lakes Trust 48
Week Farm 86	Stafford Moor Country Park 92
Wessex Fly Fishing School 180	The Total Fly Fishing Co. David Griffiths 180
Witherington Farm Lakes 192	Tightline Tours 33
	Tom Hill 180
	Tony King 180

TUITION

	Town Parks Coarse Fishing Centre 87
	Tree Meadow Trout Fishery & Tackle .... Back cover
Amherst Lodge 125	Valley Springs 84
Arundell Arms Hotel 68	Waldens Farm Fishery 192
Bake Lakes 40	Wessex Fly Fishing School 180
Bellbrook Valley Trout Fishery 101	Wessex Water 170